Database Application Programming with Linux

Brian Jepson

Joan Peckham

Ram Sadasiv

Wiley Computer Publishing

John Wiley & Sons, Inc.

NEW YORK · CHICHESTER · WEINHEIM · BRISBANE · SINGAPORE · TORONTO

Publisher: Robert Ipsen
Editor: Cary Sullivan
Assistant Editor: Christina Berry
Managing Editor: Marnie Wielage
Associate New Media Editor: Brian Snapp
Text Design & Composition: Benchmark Productions, Inc.

Designations used by companies to distinguish their products are often claimed as trademarks. In all instances where John Wiley & Sons, Inc., is aware of a claim, the product names appear in initial capital or ALL CAPITAL LETTERS. Readers, however, should contact the appropriate companies for more complete information regarding trademarks and registration.

This book is printed on acid-free paper. ♾

Published by John Wiley & Sons, Inc.

Published simultaneously in Canada.

This publication is designed to provide accurate and authoritative information in regard to the subject matter covered. It is sold with the understanding that the publisher is not engaged in professional services. If professional advice or other expert assistance is required, the services of a competent professional person should be sought.

Library of Congress Cataloging-in-Publication Data:

Jepson, Brian, 1967–
    Database application programming with Linux / Brian Jepson, Joan Peckham.
      p. cm
    ISBN 0-471-35549-6 (pbk. : alk. paper)
    1. Database design. 2. Linux. I. Peckham, Joan, 1948– . II. Title.
    QA76.9.D26J48 2000
    005.75'8--dc21   00-036662

Printed in the United States of America.

10 9 8 7 6 5 4 3 2 1

For Josh Marketos,
friend, mentor, and ultimate propagandist.

CONTENTS

Welcome to the first edition of *Database Application Programming with Linux*. This book is, for the most part, about building desktop database applications for Linux, although the way we address that topic will open your mind to a lot of other great stuff. If you opened this book hoping to learn how to build an application that uses a relational database to store data, and a graphical front-end to interact with users, you came to the right place!

There is one thing we should make perfectly clear: this book does not talk about how to develop Web database applications. There are many fine books on this topic (Brian has even written a couple of them), and perhaps we will address it in a future edition of this book. However, with the growth of desktop application environments such as KDE and GNOME, we felt challenged to produce a book with a desktop focus. It wouldn't be fair to say that this book is only about plugging databases into a pretty user interface. In fact, it's much more than that. In this book, we're going to look at a lot of things that will help you build better applications, and you'll be able to apply many of these things to other programming endeavors. Here's a list of some of the topics we discuss:

Database systems. In this book, we look at five popular database systems for Linux: PostgreSQL, MySQL, Mini SQL, Sybase, and Oracle. Wherever possible (and incompatibilities permitting), we have developed example code that works with as many of these databases as possible. Differences that were known to us during writing and testing are documented where appropriate, and Chapter 9, "Databases," takes a close look at these databases. Two areas we focus on in particular are how you can get up and running with the database system of your choice, and how each database server deals with specific database development issues. We also take a good look at the different data types and date formats, two things that are confusing when developing cross-database applications.

If your favorite database system is not covered in this book, we apologize, but we had a limited amount of time to produce this book, and we chose these database systems so we could best leverage the experience of the authors. If you are interested in other database systems for Linux, see Christopher Browne's resource on this topic at www.ntlug.org/~cbbrowne/rdbms.html.

Conceptual Modeling. In this book, we spend as much time talking about what you must do to prepare for programming as we do about programming itself (I think I heard a groan from the back of the room). Don't fear—

even the chapters about analysis and design are peppered lightly with some concrete examples, and we think you'll find it useful. We won't mind if you skip ahead to the implementation-oriented stuff, which begins in Chapter 9. We're hoping that if you do that, you'll eventually come back to the earlier stuff.

UML and Patterns. Perhaps these are two buzzwords you've heard a lot, or perhaps these are two things with which you are familiar. For those who don't know, UML and Patterns are modeling aids that are used by programmers and designers to better communicate with others. UML is a notation that documents a number of things, including the mental model you have of a system that you're going to build, the classes that make up a system, and how these classes are related. Patterns are a way of expressing *solutions to problems in a context*. When you are looking at a problem that needs to be solved, you can apply one or more Patterns to reach a solution. This makes it easy for you to find a solution, gives you confidence that you are doing something tried and true, and makes it easier for other people to understand your design. Chapter 7, "Object-Oriented Analysis," and Chapter 8, "Object-Oriented Design," talk about how you can apply UML and Patterns to analyze and design your project.

SQL. Chapter 2, "Database Design," specifically addresses SQL, the programming language used by all five database servers we discuss in this book. Before we dive into the SQL, though, we take a good look at how to design a database in the context of a problem that needs to be solved. We look at a particular set of requirements, plan a database for a system, and refine it until it's designed well enough to work well with an SQL database system. Then, we show you how to create the tables that make up the database, and how to work with them in SQL. Appendix A, "SQL Reference," will help you find your way around the language. Chapter 9 treats many database issues, including several special topics in SQL.

Programming languages. Chapters 11, 12, and 13 cover Java, Perl, and C, respectively. In all three chapters, we look at how you can develop graphical applications in these languages that talk to an SQL database back-end. Chapter 13 looks at C programming in the context of GNOME, an exciting desktop application framework for Linux and other operating systems.

Who Can Use This Book

Before we wrote this book, we decided to keep one user in particular in mind: someone who has been using the Linux system for a little while, and who may have learned a bit of programming. This is not to say that expert users or complete novices should be afraid; in fact, we felt that by targeting the inexperienced programmer, we would diminish barriers to entry as much as possible. Also, by concentrating on delivering a lot of information in this book, we felt there would be plenty of interest for even the most experienced programmers.

How to Use This Book

For the total Linux newbie, we suggest that you take the time to get comfortable with Linux, and get to know your way around the Linux shell (bash, the Bourne Again Shell) before you try to tackle this book. It's best if you've had some experience doing light programming in a language such as Perl, Tcl, or Python, and that you understand the basics of programming (functions, variables, and data structures such as arrays, linked lists, and hashtables, for example).

For the expert developer, there are certainly parts of the book that you can skip, if you feel like it. We think that the chapters are set up in a way that you can simply read the first few paragraphs of each chapter to decide whether the chapter will be helpful.

For the rest of you (and total newbies after you've learned the basics), we'd like you to try going through the book from start to finish. The first thing you'll see is Chapter 1, "Requirements," which talks about software development from a very traditional perspective. Although we use this approach as the basis of the next three chapters (Chapter 2, "Database Design"; Chapter 3, "User Interface Design"; and Chapter 4, "Construction"), we take a fresh look at the issue in the chapters that follow. Chapter 5, "Object-Oriented Programming," is a quick introduction to object-oriented programming, and in Chapter 6, "Software Engineering," we look at software engineering from an open source perspective. Finally, we wrap up the Part One of the book by looking at how you can use UML and Patterns to design a system. Then, it's on to Part Two.

Part Two of the book looks at implementation issues. Chapter 9 looks at what you need to get up and running with any of the five database servers we talk about in this book. Chapter 10, "Linux Development Tools Catalogue," takes a quick look at various tools that will help you develop Linux database applications; everything from graphical query tools to environments that are similar to 4GL tools like Access. From there on, the next chapters look at programming database applications in Java, Perl, and in C under the GNOME framework. After that, we wrap up the book with chapters on distributed components and CORBA.

What's on the Web Site?

The companion Web site that accompanies this book can be found at www.wiley.com/compbooks/jepson. At this site you can find the source code to the example programs, links to resources that relate to this book, and any corrections to errors we find in the book or example programs. You can also use the Web site to get in touch with the authors.

From the Authors

The authors of this book would like to thank:

Monty, the MySQL Manager, for his helpful scrutiny of many chapters; Scott Spiegler, for helpful comments on some of the material in this book; Angela Smith, Christina Berry, Cary Sullivan, Marnie Wielage, and Bob Ipsen from Wiley, for their patience and guidance; Ty Akadiri, friend and coworker at quantumStream, for his expert advice on the book and insights into what Ahab was *really* thinking as he brandished that harpoon; Rodrigo Moya, Michael Lausch, Stephan Heinze, Leif Wickland, and other members of the gnome-db mailing list, for guidance on the GNOME-specific portions of this book; Elliot Lee, Duncan Grisby, and other members of the ORBit mailing list for helpful suggestions on the CORBA chapter examples.

Joan and Brian would like to thank:

Our family and friends for their emotional support during this time; Seiji and Yeuhi for their support and patience with distracted parental units; Oscar and Lotus for reminding us when their food bowls needed filling, thus providing a chance to step away from the keyboard for a few minutes.

Ram would like to thank:

My wife, Laura; my parents, Eileen and Sadasiv; Shonal; Srinivas; Mohan, who had to actually use some of these ideas; and all of the folks at quantum-Stream.

## PART ONE

Technique

## CHAPTER 1

Requirements

"Building a 4-foot tower requires a steady hand, a level surface, and 10 undamaged beer cans. Building a tower 100 times that size doesn't merely require 100 times as many beer cans. It requires a different kind of planning and construction altogether."

Steve McConnell, *Code Complete*

Recognizing the potential irony of having a reference to a Microsoft book in the first sentence of a book about Linux, we added three extra sentences much as you would pad a data structure with extra bytes in hopes of aligning it optimally in memory. But, there's nothing we can do about that quote up there. It's from the same book, and we like that quote, so there it stays!

In *Code Complete* (Microsoft Press, 1993), Steve McConnell suggests that building a physical structure is an appropriate metaphor for software construction. Building a medium-sized software system is very close in complexity and cost to building a single-family house. Building a large software system parallels the complexity and cost of a large office building.

As with constructing a physical structure, the cost of fixing mistakes goes up the longer the mistake goes undetected. If you realize you need to make a fundamental change to the foundation of a house just as the shingles are going on, the cost can be prohibitive. It's the same for software development: The earlier a defect is introduced, the more expensive it is to fix as time goes on. For example, an error in the requirements analysis may cost a negligible amount with respect to the overall cost of the project if it is detected while you are validating the requirements. It will cost significantly more if it is detected while you are implementing the software. For this reason, it's important to get the requirements right. Before you build a system, make sure you are solving the right problem.

In this chapter, we'll look at some approaches to the traditional problems of system design. However, in Chapter 6, "Software Engineering," we'll take a fresh look at these problems in the context of open source development processes.

Toward a System Design

To build a system, you need a good blueprint. The first step in developing this blueprint is to state the problem that the system will solve. From there, you can develop a requirements document that states what the functionality of the system will be. You can then design the system, starting with its architecture, and move on to the design of its individual components.

The Problem Definition

The problem definition states the problem that needs to be solved. When I wrote that last sentence, I was tempted to say "the problem that the system will solve," but even that supposes too much. As a general guideline, the problem definition should state the problem without specifying a solution, including whether a system will be developed to solve the problem. This leaves room for other solutions to problems, such as modifications to existing business processes. Like other stages of the requirements process, the problem definition should be developed by the users, system designers, and developers working together.

Let's take a look at a problem definition that violates this guideline:

We need a system to capture the amount of time an employee spends working on a given task and store that information in a database so we can query it later.

This problem definition skips over the problem itself and jumps right to the solution. It would be better to say:

Our present method of tracking the amount of time an employee works on a given task is inefficient. This method uses a spreadsheet for each employee to track information. It is error-prone, difficult to extract information from, and difficult to consolidate. Consolidating spreadsheets from multiple employees is the most time-consuming and error-prone part of this process.

Given a statement of the problem, you can move on to analyzing the problem and coming up with a requirements specification.

Requirements Analysis

The process of analyzing requirements begins with an analysis of the problem definition, and goes on to define and specify the requirements. The requirements analysis is a process that brings you and the user community together to discuss *what must be done*. The problem definition is your first clue. At the end of the process, you'll have a document that states what the user needs and what the user will get.

Working with People

To do a thorough job of requirements analysis, you'll need to spend time with your user community, their managers, and other people affected by the system (such as the developers of systems that your system needs to exchange data with). All of these people are collectively referred to as *stakeholders*. To gather information for requirements analysis, you'll need to interview the stakeholders, converse with them to clarify ambiguities, and, ultimately, obtain their approval on the completed requirements document. This approval is colloquially called "buy-in," and reinforces the notion that the stakeholders have something invested in the success of the project.

In *Software Engineering* (Addison-Wesley, 1995), Ian Sommerville discusses several issues to keep in mind when you interact with stakeholders:

Differing terminology. Some stakeholders, such as end users, cannot articulate their needs in technical terms. Instead, they will articulate their needs using terms and concepts they are familiar with. These terms and concepts may not be familiar to you, the software engineer. You'll need to become familiar with the concepts and terminology of the problem's domain. If possible, ride shotgun with users and learn their business.

Misunderstanding of scope and scale. Stakeholders who are not versed in software engineering have no idea of the costs and complexity involved with software development. You should use metaphors (such as the one discussed at the beginning of this chapter) to explain how complicated software development is. Explain that it's easy to verify when something like a Web page is finished by inspection (and the fact that the Web browser doesn't generate an error when you load the document). You can't do this with software. In practice, you can't verify the correctness of software with 100-percent confidence.

Conflicting requirements. Different stakeholders may have requirements that conflict with others. This is especially likely if the group of stakeholders is made up of members from different communities and corporate cultures. Citing the requirements in a document that is readable by both you and the stakeholders helps everyone to come to a consensus on the end product. It also becomes the basis of a contract between the developers and the stakeholders.

External influences. Remember that political, business, and economic factors have an influence on the process. A high-level agenda may influence the way in which users deal with the requirements process. High-level organizational changes can result in a project being canceled. If business practices change, the requirements may also change.

The Analysis Process

Sommerville describes six activities that make up the requirements analysis process. These activities do not always happen in sequence. In other words, as you complete one activity, you may learn something that changes your understanding of an activity you've already completed. This iterative process is one of continual refinement. The following are some important steps in the analysis process:

Domain understanding. The domain is the area or realm that the problem affects. Before you analyze the problem and the requirements, you need to become an expert in the domain. For example, in investment banking, programmers often spend time on a trading desk to learn about the business. Some of them master the business so well, they become traders or analysts themselves. Many good software engineers have been lost this way!

Requirements collection. Don't wait until you've mastered the users' business to start learning about what they want. Interview the stakeholders to learn what kind of system they need. Write everything down. As you do this, you'll also develop a better understanding of the problem domain.

Classification. After you collect requirements, you'll no doubt be left with a random collection of notes written on cocktail napkins, index cards, and the back of your hand. Classification takes these random items and structures them by grouping similar or related items into the same general classifications. For example, you might classify all the attributes of a consultant (such as name, address, phone number) into data-related requirements, and all the activities (such as "set the consultant's rate," or "assign the consultant to a project") directly into functional requirements.

Conflict resolution. If the problem involves different stakeholders, you may be left with some conflicting requirements. You'll need to find these conflicts and resolve them. This process can be politically tricky. For example, in some cases, this conflict resolution can reanimate rivalries within the organization that had long slumbered.

Conflict resolution may also emphasize gaps in the knowledge of Pointy-Haired Bosses (of Dilbert fame: also known as PHBs). It's not always easy telling someone who signs the paychecks that he or she is wrong, but in many cases, the people in the trenches know better than the higher-ups.

If you want to master the fine art of dealing with such situations, you might look at books on topics such as conflict management, interpersonal conflict, problem employees, or business communication.

Prioritization. Users may ask for the world. While you can't give it all to them, you can ask them to prioritize their needs. This lets you determine what is most important, and sets the stage for creating incremental deliverables later on in the process.

Validation. By now, you have a set of raw requirements. Next, you need to review the raw requirements to determine whether you have everything the stakeholders think they want. This won't be the last time you'll validate the requirements, but it's good to validate them before you move toward the final requirements document.

Assuming that we've been through this process with the problem definition that appears at the beginning of this chapter, the raw requirements might look like:

Timesheet System Requirements

A system is needed that automates the capture and reporting on the number of hours a consultant works on a project. Our company provides consulting services, and we need to track how the consultants spend their time, and use this information to invoice the customers.

Each consultant may be assigned to one or more projects. The rate for that consultant is determined on a per-project basis. A project is associated with a single customer, who is responsible for paying us the consultant's rate.

Each project is broken down into tasks that have a fixed start and end date. When a consultant submits the number of hours she worked on a given day, those hours must be associated with a particular task.

The system should track the following information about a consultant:

First name.
Last name.
Address.
Home phone number.
Projects the consultant is assigned to.
The rate at which the consultant is billed to each project.

The Staff Coordinator is responsible for assigning consultants to projects and setting their rates.

The system should track the following information about a project:

Customer name.
Customer address.

Manager in charge of the project.
Manager's phone number.
Manager's fax number.
Project name.
Project start date.
Project end date.

The Staff Coordinator is responsible for adding customers and projects to the system.

The system should track the following information about a task:

Start date.
End date.
Company name.
Project name.
Task code.

The Clerk is responsible for maintaining a list of tasks.

The task must also contain a list of days and hours (a timesheet). Each timesheet must contain:

The consultant's name.
The week-ending date (the Saturday at the end of the week).

Each timesheet entry must contain:.

Day of week.
Task code.
Total hours.

How a consultant is to submit a timesheet. By 9:00 A.M. every Thursday, the consultant should submit a timesheet for the preceding week. (This form is shown in Figure 1.1.)

How the Clerk is to enter a timesheet into the system. When all the timesheets have been collected, the Clerk will enter in each consultant's timesheet information. They need to give the system all the information that is on the timesheet.

Consultant Name: _____

Week Ending Date: _____

Sunday		Monday		Tuesday		Wednesday		Thursday		Friday		Saturday	
Task	Hours	Task	Hours	Task	Hours	Task	Hours	Task	Hours	Task	Hours	Task	Hours

Figure 1.1 The consultant's timesheet form.

How the Staff Coordinator gets the timesheet figures. The system should gener-ate a Weekly Summary Report that lists each customer name. For each customer name, the report should state the total number of hours for all consultants, and the total amount to bill the customer. Within each customer, the report must show each project, the total number of hours for all consultants who billed to that proj-ect, and the total amount to bill for that project. Within each project, the report must show the name and rate of each consultant who worked on the project, the name of the task he or she worked on, and the total amount of hours and dollar amount billed for that task. An example of the report is shown in Figure 1.2.

Weekly Summary Report

```
Week Ending: October 27, 2001
Customer: Consolidated Consolidation
Total Hours:   33.50
Total Cost: $3837.50

  Project: The Big Secret
  Total Hours:   27.50
  Total Cost: $3087.50
  Consultant      Rate       Task              Hours    Cost
  Joe Frobnitz    $125.00    Process Analysis  12.00    $1500.00
  Joe Frobnitz    $125.00    Lecture            8.50    $1062.50
  Oscar Frodus     $75.00    Scrubbing          7.00    $ 525.00

  Project: No Squeaky Cheese
  Consultant      Rate       Task              Hours    Cost
  Total Hours:    6.00
  Total Cost: $ 750.00
  Joe Frobnitz    $125.00    Taunting           6.00    $ 750.00
```

Figure 1.2 Weekly summary report.

A Viewpoint Model for Analysis

Once you have the raw requirements written down and validated, you can make them easier to understand and absorb by using several representational models. For example, Sommerville suggests a *viewpoint model*. Used in conjunction with the raw requirements, viewpoint model diagrams can provide a great deal of insight about a system, and serve as the basis for the requirements document, system architecture, and detailed system design.

The viewpoint analysis takes a look at the requirements from the viewpoint of different users. Figure 1.3 shows a possible viewpoint hierarchy for the timesheet requirements.

Sommerville places the viewpoint model within a larger requirements analysis framework, which is worth investigating for further research on requirements analysis. For the purposes of the analysis in this chapter, the viewpoint hierarchy suffices to provide a visual representation of the requirements. This technique can also be used as inspiration for user scenarios (as described in Chapter 3, "User Interface Design") or use cases (see Chapter 7, "Object-Oriented Analysis") to arrive at a better understanding of the requirements.

The Formal Requirements Document

Sommerville points out three major problems with requirements that are specified in natural language. First, natural language is ambiguous. Anyone who has read a document in legalese knows the extremes to which we must go to make natural language precise. Second, a free-flowing natural language description can fail to distinguish between important categories of information (such as functional versus nonfunctional requirements, described in the next paragraph). Finally, requirements that are expressed using informal nat-

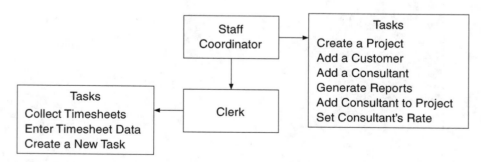

Figure 1.3 Viewpoint hierarchy for the timesheet system requirements.

ural language may amalgamate requirements (that is, they may express multiple requirements as a single requirement).

To avoid these problems, we need to put the raw requirements into a more formal statement. The level of formality will depend on the complexity of your project and your own style. Aside from the format presented here, Sommerville discusses alternative formats, including Program Design Language (PDL), a structured pseudocode notation used to design programs. We discuss PDL in Chapter 4, "Construction."

The raw requirements we have discussed so far include only *functional requirements*, which are the requirements directly related to the purpose of the system. Another class of requirements is *nonfunctional requirements*. These are usually constraints, such as choice of operating system, development language, response time, and so forth.

In the formalized requirement that follows, I have used three guidelines, inspired by Sommerville:

Each requirement should express only one system task. Do not express multiple requirements as a single requirement.

Use a stylized notation. For example, the key points of a requirement are shown in bold, and a numbered outline system is used to group related requirements.

Justify each requirement. Notice that each requirement is accompanied by a rationale.

Here are the requirements for the timesheet system:

Timesheet System Requirements

1.1 Overview of Business Needs

A system is needed that automates the capture and reporting on the number of hours a consultant works on a project. Our company provides consulting services, and we need to track how the consultants spend their time, and use this information to invoice the customers.

1.1.1 The Consultant

A consultant is an employee of the company who is hired out to various customers. Each consultant may be assigned to one or more projects. The rate for that consultant is determined on a per-project basis. A project is associated with a single customer, who is responsible for paying us the consultant's rate.

1.1.2 The Project

Each project is broken down into tasks that have a fixed start and end date. When a consultant submits the number of hours she worked on a given day, those hours must be associated with a particular task.

2.1 Data Entities

The system should track certain entities, such as consultants and customers. Each entity has a number of attributes.

2.1.1 The Consultant

The system should store the following information about a consultant:

First name.
Last name.
Address.
Home phone number.
Projects the consultant is assigned to.
The rate at which the consultant is billed to each project.

2.1.2 The Project

The system should store the following information about a project:

Customer name.
Manager in charge of the project.
Manager's phone number.
Manager's fax number.
Project name.
Project start date.
Project end date.

2.1.3 The Customer

The system should store the following information about a Customer:

Customer name.
Customer address.

2.1.4 The Task

The system should store the following information about a task:

Start date.

End date.
Company name.
Project name.
Task code.

2.1.5 The Timesheet

The task must also contain a list of days and hours (a timesheet). Each timesheet must contain:

The consultant's name.
The week-ending date (the Saturday at the end of the week).

2.1.5.1 The Timesheet Entry

Each timesheet entry (a line item on the time sheet that corresponds to work done on a task for a given day) must contain:

Day of week.
Task code.
Total hours.

3.1 Data Entry Requirements

The system shall provide various forms to support entering data into the system.

3.1.1 Consultant-Related Data Entry

The system shall provide a Consultant Maintenance form, which must support the following operations:

3.1.1.1 Add a Consultant

The Consultant Maintenance form must allow the user to add a consultant to the system. To add a consultant, the user must supply the Consultant's first name, last name, address, and home phone number.

Rationale: As new consultants join our company, we need to add them to the system.

3.1.1.2 Delete a Consultant

The Consultant Maintenance form must allow the user to delete a consultant from the system.

Rationale: As consultants leave our company, we need to delete them from the system.

3.1.1.3 Assign a Consultant to a Project

The Consultant Maintenance form must allow the user to assign a consultant to a customer's project.

Rationale: Our principal source of income is derived from hiring consultants out to customers.

3.1.1.4 Set the Consultant's Rate for a Project

The Consultant Maintenance form must allow the user to set the consultant's rate for a project.

Rationale: The rate for a consultant is negotiated on a per-project basis.

3.1.2 Customer-Related Data Entry

The system shall provide a Customer Maintenance form, which must support the following operations:

3.1.2.1 Add a Customer

The Customer Maintenance form must allow the user to add a customer to the system. To add a customer, the user must supply the customer name and address.

Rationale: As we start doing business with new customers, we need to add them to the system.

3.1.2.2 Delete a Customer

The Customer Maintenance form must allow the user to delete a customer from the system.

Rationale: As we conclude our business with certain customers, we need to delete them from the system.

3.1.3 Timesheet-Related Data Entry

The system must provide a Timesheet Maintenance form, which must support the following operations:

3.1.3.1 Input Timesheet Information

The Timesheet Maintenance form must allow the user to add a timesheet to the system. To add a timesheet, the user must supply the consultant name, and the week-ending date.

Rationale: Each timesheet is handled on a weekly basis.

3.1.3.2 Input Hourly Detail

Once a user has added the consultant and week-ending date to a timesheet, the user must add the hourly detail. The hourly detail consists of the day of week (Sunday, Monday, Tuesday, Wednesday, Thursday, Friday, or Saturday), the number of hours, and the task that the hours pertain to.

Rationale: In order to manage the efficiency of our consultants, we need to track their time usage at the task level.

3.1.3.3 Create New Task

If the user tries to enter hourly detail for a task that does not exist already, the Timesheet Maintenance form must allow that user to add the task to the system.

Rationale: All billable hours must be associated with a particular task.

3.2 Reporting Requirements

This section describes each report that the system must produce.

3.2.1 Weekly Summary Report

The system should generate a Weekly Summary Report, which has three levels of detail. Figure 1.2 shows an example of this report.

Rationale: This information is needed by the Staff Coordinator to perform her duties.

3.2.1.1 Weekly Summary Report: Customer Detail

For each customer name, the report should state the total number of hours for all consultants, and the total amount to bill the customer.

Rationale: The Staff Coordinator needs this information to produce an invoice for the customer.

3.2.1.2 Weekly Summary Report: Project Detail

For each customer, the report must show each project, the total number of hours for all consultants who billed to that project, and the total dollar amount to bill for that project.

Rationale: This gives the Staff Coordinator the ability to quickly access the cost to the customer of an individual project.

3.2.1.3 Weekly Summary Report: Consultant Detail

Within each project, the report must show the name and rate of each consultant who worked on the project, the name of the task he or she worked on, and the total amount of hours and dollar amount billed for that task.

Rationale: This provides the level of detail needed to track the utilization and efficiency of a consultant.

4.1 Nonfunctional Requirements

A number of nonfunctional requirements have been specified.

4.1.1 Hardware

This system must be deployed on SPARC, Alpha, and Intel hardware.

Rationale: We have a large investment in older models of these machines, and we have no budget to replace them immediately.

4.1.2 Operating System

This system must be portable to Linux, OpenBSD, or NetBSD.

Rationale: We found that any of these operating systems offer the optimal solution for keeping our hardware running with a modern, efficient operating system. They provide support for older models that the hardware vendors' operating systems either do not support, or on which the hardware vendors' operating systems perform poorly.

4.1.3 Memory

Each component of this system should require no more than 4 to 8 megabytes of physical and virtual memory.

Rationale: All of our machines have a minimum of 48 megabytes of memory, but our users may want to run other applications at the same time, such as Netscape or a word processor.

5.1 Forms

This section describes paper forms that act as input for the data entry process.

5.1.1 The Timesheet Form

The Consultant must submit a timesheet form on a weekly basis. (This form is shown in Figure 1.1.)

Using a Prototype to Validate Requirements

Once you have established the formal requirements, you need to validate them. One of the best methods for validating requirements is to build a prototype. This prototype should not be confused with a prototype of the user interface, which is discussed in detail in Chapter 3.

As difficult as it may be to let something go, in most cases, you should throw away (or archive) your prototype and implement the system almost from scratch. You don't have to throw away everything. If you have followed a modular approach in building the prototype, you can reuse some of the modules and/or objects you built while you developed the prototype. Take care when invoking this privilege, however. If you know that you might want to reuse a module, build it as though you were building it for a production system, not for a prototype. It may slow things down in the short term, but in the long run, you will save time.

Sommerville warns against building a general-purpose prototype. A prototype should have one purpose, such as one of the following: prototyping the user interface, validating the requirements, or demonstrating the feasibility of the project. If you are (and you should be) using the prototype to verify the requirements, make sure this is the only thing you use the prototype for. A prototype that is put together to validate the requirements may not make the best user interface prototype.

What to build the prototype with. Fortunately, Linux users have at their disposal many wonderful tools for developing prototypes. Any of the most popular scripting languages, such as Perl, Python, or Tcl, support a variety of user interfaces. These scripting languages can be used to quickly develop a prototype complete with a user interface and database connectivity (and any of these languages is fine for building the final product, as well).

How much design? How much design needs to go into the prototype? To a large extent, you should use this book to familiarize yourself with the techniques for building an application. Then, as you are building a prototype, you can select the techniques that you feel are appropriate for the level of detail your prototype will capture. Many prototypes focus on areas of uncertainty in the requirements: If the area of uncertainty is in something that greatly affects the database design, you may want to put more effort into the prototype's database design.

The Volatility of Requirements

There is no such thing as a stable set of requirements. All you can hope for is a snapshot in time of what the stakeholders need. As time goes on, the requirements will change. In fact, it is likely that they will change as you design and develop the system. With this in mind, you need a firm change control procedure in place. The stakeholders must understand that a change in the requirements can have one of two outcomes.

- The change will be incorporated in the system you are writing, in which case it will involve additional expense as you adjust the schedule.
- The change can be incorporated in a future release of the system.

One key to successfully building a system is successfully managing changes in the requirements. McConnell suggests some strategies for managing changes that can help you as you develop the software (however, see Chapter 6's section titled *The Cathedral and the Bazaar*, which refers to and is titled after Eric S. Raymond's essay of the same name, for a different perspective on this problem):

Create a formal procedure for requesting changes. This will help you manage the inevitable flood of requests and keep them from overwhelming you.

Establish a change-control board. The change-control board is a committee or group that is responsible for deciding what changes are allowed to be made.

Deal with changes in batches. All of us have given in to the urge to implement a change that *seems* easy to implement. If you implement every change this way, some good changes might fall through the cracks if they occur to you too late in development. Dealing with them in batches also gives small changes greater visibility in the overall schedule.

Estimate the cost of every change. Because of the inherent complexity in software development, even the simplest change can have large effects on other parts of the system. Before you agree to a change, make sure you know what it will cost.

Major change requests indicate something is wrong. If you're getting major change requests during development, you should strongly consider applying the brakes on the development process and going back to the requirements stage. Perhaps you had been prototyping to validate the requirements without knowing it!

The System Architecture

Before you can proceed to a detailed design of the system, you need to sort out the system's architecture. The architecture is a high-level model of the system that clearly depicts its subsystems and the connections among them.

System Structuring

When you break the system down into its structure, you need to divide it into subsystems, smaller systems that function independently of other subsystems. The requirements document shown earlier in this chapter hints at a system made up of three independent smaller systems: a Consultant Maintenance subsystem, a Company Maintenance subsystem, and a Timesheet Maintenance subsystem.

The fact that these subsystems exchange data does not make them dependent upon each other. Instead, we look to one of the models that Sommerville discusses, the *repository model*. In one type of the repository model, each subsystem exchanges data with the others through a shared database. Since this is a book about building database applications, we are going to use this model for every example in this book. Figure 1.4 shows a possible structure for this system.

Some features of the repository model include:

Agreement. Each subsystem must agree on the structure of the shared database. Since this book approaches database design from a system level (rather than on a subsystem-by-subsystem basis), this is not a problem. Chapter 2, "SQL and Relational Database Design," discusses how you can take the system requirements and develop a database design.

Centralization. The database administrator can maintain central control over access control, security, backups, and other issues.

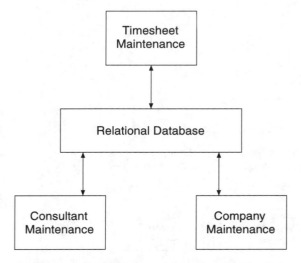

Figure 1.4 Repository model for the timesheet system.

Extensibility. Since there is an agreed-upon database structure, new tools can be easily integrated into the system.

Control Modeling

The next step is to model how control will flow within and between the subsystems. One of the models that Sommerville discusses is the *event-based control model*. In this model, there is no central system that governs the flow of control. Instead, events that originate *outside of the system control* determine which subsystems are activated and how control flows between subsystems. Such events can come from other systems or from the system's user interface.

Since this book is concerned with GUI-enabled desktop database applications, as opposed to batch-oriented systems, the event-based model fits our example rather well.

However, if we assume the existence of a single application entry point, we need to include that entry point (the Main Screen in Figure 1.5) in our control model. So, our model derives a bit from a *centralized control model* (also discussed by Sommerville), as well as an event-based control model. In the centralized model, a single subsystem takes responsibility for the initial control of the other subsystems. Figure 1.5 shows a control model for the timesheet system.

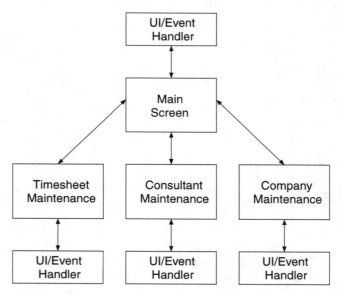

Figure 1.5 Control model for the timesheet system.

Rather than being completely controlled by a subsystem that has central control, many parts of it will be controlled by responding to external events: a user starting the application, clicking the mouse, or typing some text.

Modular Decomposition

Once you have completed the previous steps, you can move on to breaking the system into smaller pieces. One of the biggest problems with large software projects is that it is not possible for any one person to comprehend the system as a whole. When you break the system down into smaller pieces, you create manageable components that can be understood by one person. In Chapter 8, "Object-Oriented Design," we look at techniques for designing systems that are made of manageable components.

System Design

There are three activities involved in designing the types of applications we are covering in this book: database design, user interface design, and module or object design. Once these activities are completed, developing the system becomes quite manageable. Although this book presents them in a specific order, don't look at these activities as something that must be performed one at a time, in sequence to completion. It's much more iterative than that. In fact, you may complete your database and user interface designs, and when you move on to object design, you may learn something that sends you back to user interface design. The reality is that these activities feed into one another.

Database design. This activity models the system data in a manner than can be easily processed by a relational database system. Unfortunately, the output of this process is not always something that is intuitive to humans. Instead, the output of the database design process ensures that the database is correct, consistent, and efficient. The burden falls on the user interface design to present a pretty face. Database design is covered in detail in Chapter 2.

User interface design. This activity models the system's data and behavior in a visual manner. User interface design involves many factors that affect human cognition, such as memory (human, not computer memory) issues, spatial organization, and aesthetics. User interface design is discussed in Chapter 3.

Module or object design. Object-oriented analysis and design models the system's data and behavior in a way that is close to how humans think of real-world objects. Modular design isolates related processes and data in a way that maximizes code reuse. Chapter 4, "Construction," discusses modularity, and object-oriented concepts are introduced in Chapter 5, "Object-Oriented Programming." Chapters 7 and 8 discuss object-oriented analysis and design.

Summary

Before you start building software, it's important to make sure you are solving the right problem. To this end, there are four areas you need to pay special attention to:

The problem definition. This answers the question, "why am I building this system?" It's the most important thing to get right. If you don't get the problem definition right, you run the risk of solving the wrong problem.

Requirements analysis. In order to build up a document that serves as a roadmap for the system, you need to analyze the problem. To do this, you will need to become involved with the stakeholders, understand their business needs, and pay attention to many details.

The formal requirements document. Using a formalized, organized approach, you can build a document that unambiguously specifies what it is you are to build. As you build the system, you will need to exert some control over the changes that will be made to the requirements.

The prototype. Once you have developed this document, you may need to validate the requirements with a prototype.

System architecture and design. Before you can proceed to the design of the system objects, the database, and the user interface, you must determine the architecture of your system. This encompasses three stages: system structuring, control modeling, and modular decomposition. The concepts discussed in Chapters 4, 5, 7, and 8 can be applied to modular design.

This chapter offers the image of building a physical structure as a metaphor for constructing a software system. It's important to keep in mind that one metaphor does not fit all cases. In practice, the building metaphor is most appropriate to the specification and design stage of a software project. Where it still fits in other stages, we'll build on this metaphor. However, in Chapter 6, "Software Engineering," we'll take a look at some of the advantages that the open source approach can offer over (or in combination with) the approaches discussed in this chapter.

## CHAPTER 2

Database Design

Database systems use tables to store information about real-world objects or concepts (entities). A table is a container for data. For example, a table of invoices is analogous to a file cabinet full of invoices. The advantage of the database table is ease of searching. You can easily search the table for all invoices from a given date or for a particular customer. With the file cabinet, this is not so easy.

In a relational database system, relationships between tables mirror the relationships between entities you are trying to model. Flat-file database systems organize information into tables, much as relational database systems do. However, flat-file systems do not provide facilities for creating and managing relationships between tables. In a relational database system, the relationships between tables help you model the real-world behavior of entities in your database.

A table is essentially a grid of rows and columns. Each row represents a particular instance of an entity (such as a person, place, or thing). For example, if you have a table called Person, then each row contained in that table corresponds to a particular person. Table 2.1 illustrates this.

It may be helpful to think of a relational database system in object-oriented terms. If you think of each row as an *instance*, then you can think of each column as an *attribute* (or property). For example, a person might have a certain address, telephone number, or seating preference at major sporting events. If you locate an intersection of a row and column, you also identify a single value, such as Brian Jepson's telephone number.

Table 2.1 A Simple Table

NAME	ADDRESS	PHONE
Brian Jepson	100 Carrot Dr.	555-1000
Jack Sprat	55 Salt Pork Way	555-1001
Mothra Goose	10 Storyville Ln.	555-1002

For most database management systems, any parallels between the database and objects end here: Purely relational database management systems are not object oriented. All but two of the database systems we cover in this book are purely relational. The exceptions are PostgreSQL and Oracle, which have object-relational features (however, this book does not cover those features).

Hitting the Ground Running

In this chapter, we'll look at databases from a conceptual and design viewpoint. If you do not currently have a database system installed, and would like to use one to work through the SQL examples later in this chapter, you should visit Chapter 9, "Databases," and get set up with a database before you read this chapter.

Designing a Database

In order to get the most performance and flexibility out of a database, you should follow an established set of database design guidelines. These design guidelines result in database systems that scale well and can handle everything from the simplest to the most exotic queries.

In typical database systems, you will only be concerned with the logical structure of the database: the tables, their columns, indexes, and the relationships between tables. The physical structure of the database is handled by the database management system (DBMS), and includes how and where the tables are stored on disk, the algorithms used to index tables, and other facets of database management you won't have to worry about.

Let's look at the steps involved in designing a simple database. You can follow these steps in designing your own databases.

Identify the Entities You Want to Represent

The first step in designing a database is to make sure you know what entities you want the database to represent. For example, if you are designing a database for a public library, two of the entities your database will represent are books and patrons.

It is also helpful if you have some ideas about how the entities interact with one another. If patrons can take out several books at a time, your logical database design will be different than it would if patrons are allowed to take out only one book.

In the case of a public library, it seems to make sense to take for granted that patrons can take out more than one book. However, it is a good habit to explicitly specify these sorts of constraints before you design a database. Something that is obvious to one person may not be obvious to another, and you will avoid much misunderstanding if you spell out all the issues in advance.

This stage of database design is dependent on requirements analysis and definition, which is covered in detail in Chapter 1, "Requirements." Let's examine the database requirements for a public library database. As we do this, let's make sure the following questions are answered:

What are the concepts and/or real-world objects you are trying to model? You can answer this question by reading the requirements and looking for nouns (persons, places, and things) that the requirements seem to focus on. For example, patrons and books are obvious concepts at first glance. The section titled *Identify Concepts* in Chapter 7, "Object-Oriented Analysis," describes a more rigorous approach to answering this question.

How is each relationship qualified? For example, there is certainly a relationship between patrons and books. What phrase best describes that relationship? For another approach to answering this question, see the *Discover and Diagram Associations* section in Chapter 7.

What constraints exist? For example, is there a stated limit on the number of books a patron can check out? Under what circumstances would a patron be prohibited from borrowing a book?

Use the Requirements

Like other aspects of system requirements, the database design is subject to change over the life of your software. You will come up with an initial requirements definition that will be subtly modified as you grow closer to an initial release of the software. Even after the software is released, future versions will be introduced by changes in the requirements, which necessitate changes in the structure of the application or underlying database.

Bearing all this in mind, and imagining a perfect world where requirements are complete and correct the first time, here are the requirements for a public library's database system. These requirements follow the format shown in Chapter 1, but describe the requirements with less detail than the example requirements in that chapter.

1.1 Overview of Business Needs

The principal activity of the library is to loan books to patrons. To support this, we need to track overdue books, handle fines, and support other related activities. The volume of loans exceeds the library's ability to process this by hand, so a system is needed that automates the process.

1.1.1 The Book

The term *book* is used to refer to any material the library loans to a patron. While it is usually a book, it may also be a periodical, audio recording, videotape, or other material.

1.1.2 The Patron

A patron is someone who uses the library. She may borrow any number of books, but the books must be returned by a specific date.

2.1 Data Entities

The system should represent certain entities. Each entity has a number of attributes.

2.1.1 The Book

The system should store the following information about a book:

title.
ISBN number.
volume letter or number (optional).
edition number.
author.
publisher code.
publisher name.
binding type (hardcover, paperback, or bound at the library).
publication date.
city of publication.

2.1.2 The Patron

The system should store the following information about a patron:

first name.
last name.
middle initial.
home address.
phone number.

3.1 Functional Requirements

The system shall support the following functionality:

3.1.1 Borrow a Book

A patron may borrow as many books as she wants.

Rationale: The purpose of the library is to make certain materials available for loan.

3.1.1.1 Overdue Books

The patron may not borrow any books if she has one or more overdue books.

Rationale: To deter patrons from keeping a book longer than the loan period.

3.1.1.2 Duration of Loan

The patron may check out a book for a period of time, which defaults to two weeks. The system should track the date the book was checked out and the date it is due.

Rationale: Enforcing a loan period ensures that all patrons have a fair chance to borrow a book.

3.1.2 Return a Book

The system should track the date a book was returned.

Rationale: This can be used later to resolve disputes about whether a book was returned or when it was returned.

3.1.2.1 Calculate Fines

When an overdue book is returned, the system should calculate the total fines due.

Rationale: The fines are used to deter patrons from keeping a book longer than the loan period.

3.1.3 Pay Fines

The patron may pay fines at any time. The amount that she pays is deducted from the amount owed.

Rationale: Patrons must pay their fines.

3.1.4 Place a Hold on a Book

If another patron wants the book while it is checked out, a "hold" is issued on the book, and the patron who checked it out is notified that someone else is waiting for it.

Rationale: There is a chance that the current borrower is finished with the book, and if she knows that someone else is waiting for it, she might return it sooner than the due date.

3.2 Reporting Requirements

The system should support the following reporting functions:

3.2.1 Report of Checked-Out Books

The system should list all books that are currently checked out, and by whom.

Rationale: We will use this report on a weekly basis to get a feel for what books are currently popular. This information will guide future book acquisitions.

3.2.2 Report of Overdue Books

The system should generate a separate report of overdue books for each patron who has overdue books. The report should calculate and include the outstanding fines as of the printing date.

Rationale: This report will be used to mail a reminder to patrons who have overdue books.

3.2.3 Historical Report

The system should generate a report of all books that have been checked out and by whom.

Rationale: We'd like to be able to know how popular a book is and suggest books to patrons based on books they have checked out in the past. This will also be used to guide future book acquisitions.

3.2.3.1 Borrowing History Toggle

We'd like the ability to turn historical tracking on and off for a patron. If a patron does not want her borrowing history tracked, we want to automatically purge a borrowing record for that patron as soon as the book is returned.

Rationale: Some customers may have privacy concerns about the tracking.

These requirements are somewhat less complete than you might encounter with a real-world system (for example, they do not specify any nonfunctional requirements), but they are sufficient for the simple database in this chapter. Although you go into the design process with the assumption that the requirements are complete, the requirements do not account for the needs of the database. As a result, the database design process has the freedom to alter relationships, create new entities, and move attributes around.

You'll see that the design process raises questions that clarify the requirements. By the time you finish the design process, you will have asked the users some more questions, and you will have a more complete specification.

Identify Likely Entities

Since we're in the design stage, we're going to use design jargon, and avoid implementation-oriented words such as *table* and *column*. For now, we'll stick with *entity* and *attribute*. In the end, though, our entities will become tables and our attributes will become columns through the use of the Data Definition Language (DDL), a set of instructions written in SQL that create the tables we will have designed (SQL stands for Structured Query Language, which is a programming language for working with databases). For the most part, DDL consists of CREATE TABLE statements, as we'll see later in the chapter.

The requirements we've got suggest that we should start out with two entities: books and patrons. While it is not implicitly stated, there is another entity, the *borrows* relationship, which links books up with patrons and has some attributes of its own (when the book was borrowed, when it is due, and whether there is a hold on the book).

We'll use a *data structure diagram* to illustrate each entity, its attributes, and the way the entities are related. This introduces something new: You know that a database is a collection of related tables (or *entities*, as we call them when we are designing the database), but so far, nothing has been revealed that would indicate how they are related.

Keys

You relate two entities together by linking a *key* from one entity to a key on the other entity. There are two types of keys. The first, a *primary* key, is one or more attributes that identify one and only one instance of an entity.

For example, suppose that the Patron entity has an attribute called Patron ID, and that the Book entity has an attribute called Book ID. In the case of the Patron, the ID could be a number stamped on the patron's library card. In the case of the Book, the ID could be its ISBN number. Although these IDs are attributes, they are also primary keys. What matters is that *a primary key identifies one and only one instance of an entity*. The primary key is sometimes said to *uniquely identify* an instance of the entity. No two instances should have the same primary key value. If this holds true for the Patron ID and Book ID, then these attributes are suitable primary key values.

The second type of key is a *foreign* key. This is one or more attributes in an entity that point to the primary key of another entity. For example, suppose that you want to keep track of the patrons' favorite books. One way to do this is to add an attribute to the Patron entity called Favorite Book ID. This column would contain the ID of a patron's favorite book, and as such, is a foreign key into the Book entity.

You'll notice that the IDs aren't explicitly specified in the requirements definition. This is very common, since phrases like "primary keys identify one and only one instance" rarely enter the heads of the user community! It is safe to say that for any entity, you will always need a key. Some entities have obvious keys, like a book's ISBN number. For other entities, it may not be so obvious where to find a key. In some cases, the keys will have to be completely artificial. This is generally handled by using a counter to generate sequential values each time a row is added to a table: the first instance of an entity gets ID one, the second instance gets ID two, and so forth. For details on creating sequential key values, see the section titled *Generating Unique Values* in Chapter 9, "Databases."

Relating Entities

Once you have established the keys for your entities, you can think about how the entities are related. The relationship between Patron and Book seems simple at first: One Patron "borrows" many books. Can one book be borrowed by many patrons? Although only one patron may borrow a particular book at a time, many patrons can borrow the same book over time.

So, there will be a many-to-many relationship between books and patrons: One patron may take out many books, and many different patrons can take the same book out over time.

However, no two patrons may take out the same book at the same time. This may be obvious to a human, but not so obvious to a computer system. As a result, it is a constraint that must be noted. Using the paper and pencil techniques outlined in this chapter, such constraints cannot be handled at the design level, but will have to be handled somewhere, perhaps programmatically. Some Computer Aided Software Engineering (CASE) tools allow you to specify this sort of constraint at design time.

In this chapter, we'll use an Entity:Attribute notation to talk about specific attributes. The : tells you that the attribute belongs to the entity. So, Book:ISBN refers to the ISBN attribute of the Book entity.

A many-to-many relationship is modeled by creating an entity between two entities. In this case, we're creating the Borrows entity between Patron and Book. The Borrows entity has the following attributes:

ISBN. The book that is checked out, a foreign key reference to Book:ISBN.

Patron ID. The patron who borrowed the book, a foreign key reference to Patron:Patron ID.

Borrowed Date. The date on which the book was borrowed.

Due Date. The date on which the book must be returned.

Return Date. The date on which the book was returned.

Hold Requested. Whether a hold is requested on the book.

Requestor ID. The patron who placed the hold, a foreign key reference to Patron:Patron ID.

Because a patron may borrow a book more than once, ISBN and Patron ID are not sufficient to uniquely identify a borrowed book. For example, if a patron borrows Philip K. Dick's *Divine Invasion* on August 15, 1989, and then again on February 17, 1999, we have no way of differentiating between the two loan periods. So, we need to use ISBN, Patron ID, and Borrowed Date as a primary key to uniquely identify the loan of a particular book.

Figure 2.1 shows the data structure diagram for the current data model. The boxes list all of the attributes for a given entity, and the arrows connect attributes that are related (such as Book:Patron ID to Patron:Patron ID). Although the *Patron:Purge History?* attribute was not explicitly listed in the requirements, it is needed to satisfy requirement 3.2.3.1. The collection of tables that make up the database that models a specific problem domain is called a *schema*.

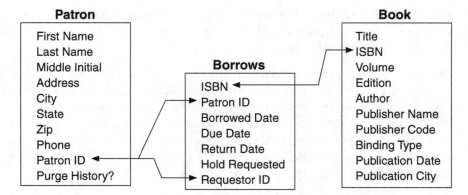

Figure 2.1 Our first try at a data structure diagram for the Library database.

We built up our schema by following a simple series of steps:

1. Identify obvious entities in your data model requirements.
2. If an entity does not have an obvious primary key (such as Book:ISBN), add an artificial primary key (such as Patron:Patron ID).
3. Determine the relationships between entities.

Normalization

At this point, we are far from done. There are a number of nonobvious problems with the database that can be solved by following a process known as *normalization*. Normalization is a process that changes your database structure to match one or more of the *normal forms*. The normal forms are established data design standards that let you develop databases that scale well (even when your tables have lots of rows), and can be queried in a flexible manner.

First Normal Form

The first normal form (1NF) seeks to *eliminate repeating attributes* from entities. A repeating attribute is an attribute that has multiple values for a given instance. Although it's not obvious from looking at the data structure, if you think about books and authors for a moment, you'll realize that one book can have several authors. If we were to accommodate multiple authors with our current data model, we'd have to allow for repeating values: some books would have one, two, or more authors as shown in Figure 2.2.

Repeating attributes can be problematic in a number of ways:

They can result in wasted storage. If you allow an entity to contain repeating attributes, you need to include attributes for each value (Author One, Author Two, Author Three, and so forth). Most books will probably have one author. For those, the Author Two and Author Three attributes will remain empty, which is a waste of space.

Using repeating attributes requires you to live with arbitrary constraints. If you design the database to handle up to three authors per book, you will need to modify the structure of your database when you come across a book with four or more authors.

If you use repeating attributes, you will find that it is more difficult to formulate queries on your database. This is because SQL was designed with the same considerations that went into the design of the normal forms.

How do we resolve this problem? The first step is to create a new entity to represent the repeating values. In this case, the entity would be an author, so it makes sense to add an Author entity. The Author entity will have the following attributes: First Name, Last Name, and Author ID.

Because one author can write many books and one book can have many authors, we'll use a many-to-many relationship. In order to represent this relationship, we need to create a new entity, which, like the other entities, will become a table when we write the DDL. We'll call this new entity "Author Of" to signify that a particular Author entity is the author of a given Book entity. The Author Of entity has the following attributes: Author ID and ISBN. Together, these values form a *compound primary key* (two or more attributes that identify a unique instance of the Author Of entity). Because an author can write a book only once (for the purposes of this example, we are discounting multiple revisions of the same book), an instance of the Author Of entity is *uniquely identified* by a combination of ISBN and Author ID.

Figure 2.3 shows the current database design in 1NF.

Title	Author(s)		
Linux Database Programming	Peckham, J.	Jepson, B.	Sadasiv, R.
Programming Web Graphics	Wallace, S.		
The Book Never Written	Marketos, J.	Jepson, B.	

Figure 2.2 The Book entity sporting repeating values for authors.

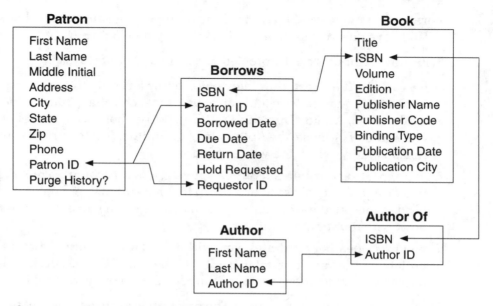

Figure 2.3 The current database design in 1NF.

Summary of moving a database to 1NF:

1. Identify repeating attributes.
2. Create another entity to represent repeating attributes as rows.
3. If there is a one-to-many relationship between the original entity and the new entity, add a foreign key to the new entity that points to the original entity. If, for example, some strange rule stated that an author could only write one book in his or her lifetime, we would have added an ISBN number to the Author entity to indicate which book an author wrote. Instead, we have a many-to-many relationship.
4. If there is a many-to-many relationship between the original entity and the new entity, create a new entity, such as "Author Of," to link the two entities.

Second Normal Form

The second normal form (2NF) requires that every attribute must depend on the entire primary key. This only pertains to entities with compound primary keys (primary keys made up of more than one attribute), such as the Author Of or Borrows entity. Although both of these entities represent relationships,

2NF is not limited to entities that represent relationships. Any entity that has a compound primary key should go through this process.

To determine whether the database is in 2NF, we need to examine each attribute in the Author Of and Borrows entities and consider whether that attribute is dependent on the entire primary key, or just one part of the primary key.

What does it mean to be dependent on the entire primary key? Consider Borrows:Due Date and Borrows:Return Date. The attributes Patron ID, ISBN, and Borrowed Date uniquely identify a particular loan, and the Due Date and Return Date attributes answer the questions "When was a particular loan due, and when was the loaned material returned?" Consequently, we say that these two attributes are dependent on the entire compound primary key (the combination of Patron ID, ISBN, and Borrowed Date).

What does it mean to be dependent on *part* of the compound primary key? Consider Borrows:Hold Requested and Borrows:Requestor ID (remember, Requestor ID is another patron, not the patron who the loan is made to, but someone else who wants the book). Are these attributes related to a particular loan, to the patron that borrowed a book, or just to a book? One way to phrase this question so that a user could answer it is, "Can a patron put a hold on a book even if it's not currently lent to someone?" Let's suppose that the answer to this is yes—perhaps the library allows patrons to hold a book by telephoning the library or using the Internet. This would allow a patron to hold a book between the time she realizes she needs it and the time she can get to the library to actually check it out.

So, the attributes Hold Requested and Requestor ID are only dependent on one part of the compound primary key: the ISBN, which corresponds to the Book entity. Further investigation (conversations with the imaginary librarians) reveals that only one person can have a hold on a book at a time, and the library does not want to track a book's hold history. If we needed to issue multiple holds, or track the hold history, then the hold information might go into a new entity. Since this is not the case, it makes perfect sense to move these attributes into the Book entity.

We still have one other entity to consider, Author Of. Fortunately, the only attributes in the Author Of entity are those that make up the primary key, so there is no need to make any changes to this entity. Figure 2.4 shows the database in 2NF.

To move a database to 2NF:

1. Identify any attributes that are not dependent on all the attributes that make up a compound primary key.

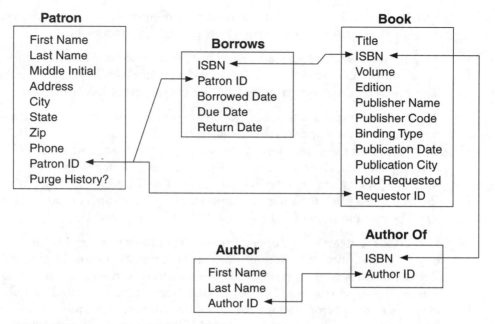

Figure 2.4 The database design in 2NF.

2. If you have found attributes that are only dependent on one part of the primary key, consider where you might put those attributes. If the primary key is made up of foreign keys that refer to other tables (such as Patron and Book), it is likely that you'll be able to move the offending attribute(s) to one of those tables.

Third Normal Form

The third normal form (3NF) is similar to 2NF, but extends to all primary keys, including compound and simple primary keys (where only one attribute makes up the primary key). 3NF asks you to look at every attribute that is not part of the primary key (these are called nonkey attributes), and attempt to eliminate any nonkey attributes that are dependent on another nonkey attribute. In other words, if the attribute isn't part of the primary key, and it's dependent on something other than the primary key, it should be eliminated.

For example, consider Book:Publisher Name. What is this nonkey attribute dependent on? This is a little tricky, because the publisher code, an international code that identifies a publisher, is embedded in the ISBN number. So, the Publisher Name is really dependent on the Publisher Code. At this point, the table is a little bit of a mess. We have to deal with this mess before we can decide what Publisher Name is dependent on.

Here are some possible solutions to clean it up:

- Represent the publisher code as an attribute in the Book entity.
- Split the ISBN into two attributes, Publisher Code and Book Code. Then, you can regenerate the ISBN by concatenating the two.

The first choice is by far the cleanest alternative. While it introduces redundant information into the Book entity, it is a reasonable trade-off to make. On the other hand, since ISBN is always referred to as a whole, breaking it into two is an artificial step that will increase the complexity of the system without sufficient advantage.

So, let's add the Publisher Code attribute to the Book entity. This puts the analysis of Publisher Name into a new context: Publisher Name is not dependent on an attribute that is part of the primary key; instead, it is dependent on a nonkey attribute, the Publisher Code. To resolve this, you should use Publisher Code as a primary key for a new Publisher entity, and link that entity to the Book entity using a foreign key. The Publisher entity now contains the Publisher Code and Publisher Name attributes.

Why take this step? If you allow the publisher name to be stored with every book, you can run into some problems when the table is actually implemented. For example, how many permutations of a publisher's name are there? Consider the publisher of this book: "Wiley Computer Publishing," "John Wiley Computer Publishing," "John Wiley and Sons Computer Publishing," names a few possibilities, not taking into account the possibility that there may be misspellings of the name! These sorts of inconsistencies can lead to complicated data retrieval problems in the long run. Moving the publisher name into its own table eliminates these kinds of problems.

What about Publication City? You might be tempted to think that this is a function of who the publisher is, but that's not necessarily the case. A publisher may publish different books in different cities, and in fact, a single book may be published in different cities simultaneously. In the interests of keeping the database design simple, we'll only list one city per book. A real-world system would probably need a City entity and a Published In entity to model the relationship between books and cities.

Figure 2.5 shows the new database design, with the Book entity linked to Publisher on a foreign key.

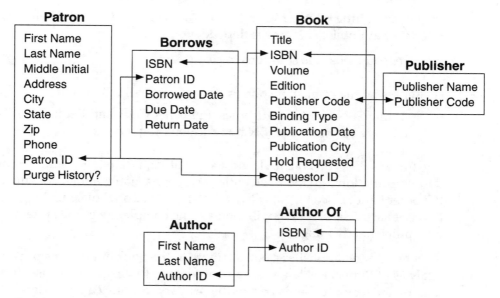

Figure 2.5 The database design in 3NF.

In this case, we identified an attribute that belongs to another entity that we hadn't created yet. It's entirely possible that you could identify attributes that belong to an entity that you've already created. In that case, you would move them from the original entity to the appropriate entity.

To move a database design to 3NF:

1. Identify any attributes that are not dependent on the primary key.
2. If you have found attributes, such as Publisher Name, that are dependent on a nonkey attribute, consider where you might put those attributes. If an appropriate entity already exists, move the attribute(s) to that entity. In some cases, as with the Publisher entity, you may need to create a new entity.
3. If you have to create a new entity, make sure you come up with a way (one-to-one, one-to-many, many-to-many) to represent that relationship. In the example database, we used a foreign key in the Book entity to model a one-to-many relationship (one publisher may publish many books).

Building a Data Dictionary

Before you create the tables, you must create a data dictionary for the database. The data dictionary is a written reference about each entity and attribute. At this stage, you'll need to make decisions about what data type to use for each attribute when you create tables. A list of some common SQL data types is included in Table 2.2. You can specify the length of some types, and common minimum and maximum sizes for these types are shown as a range in parentheses after the name. Different database engines have different ranges, and this table just shows some commonly found examples.

Data Type Sizes

Some data types, such as CHAR, can take on different sizes depending on how you declare a column. For example, when you declare a column as CHAR(50), 50 bytes of space are allocated for that column. This means that every row in the table will reserve 50 bytes of space for that column, even if the column is blank or if the data in it only fills it partially with a value that is less than 50 bytes in length, such as "Hello."

Some data types, such as DECIMAL, can take on different sizes and precisions. For example, a column declared as DECIMAL(10, 2) under Sybase or Oracle can have 10 digits, two of which appear to the right of the decimal point. Actually, some database servers interpret this differently: Early versions of MySQL count the decimal point as a digit, so you really get seven digits to the left of the decimal point. For the record, Mini SQL does not support the DECIMAL data type (but it supports the REAL data type, which defaults to a certain width and precision: It does not take a width and precision as an argument). For a list of databases supported by various database servers, see Table 9.7, the *Data Type Cross-Reference Table* in Chapter 9.

NULL (The Sound of No Hands Clapping)

There will be times when you don't know a value, but you need to add some data to your database. Suppose you know a patron's name, but not the patron's middle initial? It's not appropriate to leave the patron's middle initial blank, because there is no way to tell if that means the patron doesn't have a middle initial or if the patron's middle initial is unknown.

SQL supports a special state called NULL for these sorts of situations. When you don't know the value for a column, you can set it to NULL. Some columns can never be NULL, though, such as primary or foreign keys, or data that is too important to leave incomplete. For example, while it would be acceptable to let the volume of a book remain unknown, you would have trouble if the ISBN or publisher_code were NULL: When you try to examine a set of tables like book and publisher, books without publishers may mysteriously "drop out" of sight when you issue certain queries. See the section titled *Joins* later in this chapter for details.

Table 2.2   Some (Not All) SQL Data Types

NAME	PURPOSE
CHAR(1-255)	Short text data, such as names, phone numbers, mixed numeric and text identifiers.
INTEGER	Numeric integer data such as quantity, numeric identifiers, and yearly salary. Often abbreviated INT.
REAL	Floating point data such as hourly wage, price per pound, and velocity. Synonyms include FLOAT, DOUBLE, and DECIMAL.
DATE	Date value, such as August 1, 1999.
TIME	Time value, such as 10:10 A.M.
DATETIME	Combined date and time value, such as 10:10 A.M. on August 1, 1999.
BIT	True or false value that indicates one of two states, such as on/off, active/inactive, and wet/dry.
MONEY	Currency value, such as $100.95.

Bit or Not?

Some database servers do not support a bit data type. On those servers, some developers choose to use the smallest numeric data type, such as INTEGER or SMALLINT, and store a 0 or 1 on the column. The reason they choose the smallest data type is that you only need one bit to store a true or false value (real bit columns are, as the name suggests, only one-bit wide). It's a good idea to save space where you can because wasted space in one column is amplified when there are many rows in a table.

Because this book is targeted at users of a few different database servers, and since not every one of these servers supports a bit type, we'll use INTEGER fields in this way. Also, some servers, such as PostgreSQL, support BOOLEAN instead of BIT.

Let's take a look at each entity, and build a data dictionary as we go. Notice that the names of things are changing somewhat as we go: In order to follow convention, the table column names will be in lowercase, and they won't have any spaces in the name. Most database systems will not allow you to use column names (or table names, for that matter) that have spaces.

Patron

The Patron entity has the following attributes: First Name, Last Name, Middle Initial, Address, City, State, Zip, Phone, Patron ID, and Purge History?.

You can use a CHAR data type for most of these columns. Note that with Phone, we're stripping out the nondigit characters when we store it (see Table 2.3). Because U.S. telephone numbers follow a predictable format, it's easy to reformat this number for display when necessary, while storing it with the minimal amount of space.

What about Zip? At first guess, it might make sense to store it as an integer. However, in Rhode Island, where many zip codes start with a zero, you'd run into trouble: A zip code like 02881 would be stored as 2881, since the leading zero would automatically be truncated. Also, zip+4 codes have a hyphen and four extra digits. Better to use CHAR(11) for those. That leaves Patron ID, which will be stored as an INTEGER, and Purge History?, which will be stored as an INTEGER, for reasons explained in the sidebar titled *Bit or Not?*. Table 2.3 shows the data dictionary entry for Patron.

Book

The Book entity has the following attributes: Title, ISBN, Volume, Edition, Publisher Code, Binding Type, Publication Date, Publication City, Hold Requested, and Requestor ID. For Title, Volume, and Publication City, you should definitely use the CHAR data type. The Edition will be an INTEGER. The ISBN code is numeric, but it contains hyphens. Unlike the Patron:Phone, it's not obvious where the nondigit characters go (with a phone number, there are exactly three digits in the area code, three in the exchange, and four in the rest of the number), so it makes sense to use a CHAR type. We don't

Table 2.3   Patron

COLUMN	TYPE	DESCRIPTION
first_name	CHAR(25)	The Patron's first name.
last_name	CHAR(25)	The Patron's last name.
middle_initial	CHAR(1)	The Patron's middle initial.
address	CHAR(25)	Street address.
city	CHAR(25)	The city name.
state	CHAR(2)	Two-letter USA state code.
zip	CHAR(11)	Zip+4 code.
phone	CHAR(10)	Phone number, stripped of the nondigit characters. So, a number such as (999) 999-9999, would be stored as 9999999999.
patron_id	INTEGER	Primary Key. Unique ID for each patron.
purge_history	INTEGER	If the patron wants his or her borrowing history purged, this is set to 1 (otherwise, 0).

know for sure whether Publisher Code can contain leading zeros or other nondigit characters, so it's safest to use CHAR for Publisher Code as well.

Binding Type is a little tricky. There are only three binding types we know of right now: hardcover, paperback, and custom-bound at the library (sometimes they repair broken books). One solution (the solution we chose) would be to use a three-letter mnemonic code for this field. The user doesn't have to remember this code, though. For example, on a data entry form, you could still use a pull-down menu that is labeled with the selections "hardcover," "paperback," and "custom," but which ends up populating the database with the correct mnemonic value. If you are using a database, such as PostgreSQL, that supports enumerated data types, you could use that feature here.

Although the publication_date column's name suggests that we use a DATE data type, we're only interested in the year of publication, so we'll use an INTEGER type for that (and change the name of the column to publication_year to avoid confusion).

Finally, the Hold Requested column will be INTEGER (by the logic discussed in the *Bit or Not?* sidebar), and the Requestor ID column will be NUMERIC, the same as Patron:Patron ID. Table 2.4 shows the data dictionary entry for Book.

Borrows

The Borrows entity is relatively straightforward. Its composite primary key is a combination of ISBN and Patron ID: Each of these columns will be the same

Table 2.4   Book

COLUMN	TYPE	DESCRIPTION
title	CHAR(50)	The title of the book.
isbn	CHAR(25)	Primary key. The International Standard Book Number.
volume	CHAR(10)	The volume number or letter of the book.
edition	INTEGER	The edition number of the book.
publisher_code	CHAR(25)	The publisher code.
binding_type	CHAR(3)	One of HRD, PAP, or CUS.
publication_year	INTEGER	The year when the book was printed.
publication_city	CHAR(25)	The city where the book was printed.
hold_requested	INTEGER	If someone has put a hold on the book, this is 1 (otherwise, 0).
requestor_id	INTEGER	The ID of the patron who put the hold on the book. A foreign key into Patron.

Table 2.5   Borrows

COLUMN	TYPE	DESCRIPTION
patron_id	INTEGER	One part of the primary key. This is a foreign key into Patron.
isbn	CHAR(25)	One part of the primary key. This is a foreign key into Book.
borrowed_date	DATE	One part of the primary key. The date the book was borrowed.
due_date	DATE	The date on which the book must be returned.
return_date	DATE	The date on which the book was returned.

as the type of the corresponding columns in the Book and Patron tables. The remaining columns, Borrowed Date, Due Date, and Return Date will be of type DATE. Table 2.5 shows the data dictionary entry for Borrows.

Author, Author_Of, and Publisher

The remaining three tables are simple and straightforward. The author's first and last names are type CHAR, and the author ID is INTEGER. The publisher's name and code is CHAR. Tables 2.6, 2.7, and 2.8 show the data dictionary entries for these tables.

Table 2.6   Author

COLUMN	TYPE	DESCRIPTION
first_name	CHAR(25)	The author's first name.
last_name	CHAR(25)	The author's last name.
author_id	INTEGER	Primary key. The ID of the author.

Table 2.7   Author_Of

COLUMN	TYPE	DESCRIPTION
isbn	CHAR(25)	Foreign key into Book.
author_id	INTEGER	Primary key. The ID of the author.

Table 2.8   Publisher

COLUMN	TYPE	DESCRIPTION
publisher_name	CHAR(25)	The publisher's name.
publisher_code	CHAR(25)	Primary key. The code of the publisher.

Leftovers

There will certainly be some leftovers that can't be handled by the database system. Suppose that a patron may not have more than 10 books checked out at any time. While high-end database systems like Sybase, Oracle, and PostgreSQL can handle these sorts of constraints (see the sections titled *Invalid Values* and *Triggers* in Chapter 9), lightweight SQL engines like Mini SQL cannot. Leftovers such as these will have to be handled by your application. Be sure that the leftovers are documented and communicated to whoever is working on the front-end of the application lest they fall through the cracks.

Digging Deeper

We did not model everything that the library system would need, such as tracking the amount of fines owed. Because this chapter focused primarily on applying the normal forms, we did not pay as much attention to capturing the entities that need to be modeled. Instead, we started out with two simple entities (Patron and Book) and started from there. Chapter 3, "User Interface Design," offers some simple techniques for finding entities that need to be modeled. Chapter 7 provides a survey of a more rigorous technique that can be used to discover what entities or objects are lurking in your requirements. In fact, you can perform the steps in Chapter 7 to create a conceptual model before you do your database design, and normalize the conceptual model into a database design.

SQL

Structured Query Language (SQL) is a programming language that you can use to manipulate information contained in a relational database. Use SQL to create tables, modify data, and issue queries.

Each database system uses a slightly different SQL syntax. We'll try to stick to examples that use a common subset of SQL; however, where there are differences, we will note them. Each database management system uses a different method of sending SQL statements to the database server.

If you want to try out these commands as you read through the chapter, you should see the *SQL Monitors* section in Chapter 9 to learn how to issue SQL statements to the database you are using. See the *What's on the Web Site?* section in the introduction for the location of example programs, including the SQL examples in this chapter. Before you can execute SQL statements, you will need to install a database server, have a database that you can create tables in, and be able to use an SQL monitor program to issue queries. See the particular subsection (*PostgreSQL, Mini SQL, MySQL, Oracle,* or *Sybase Adaptive Server Enterprise*) under *Getting Started with an RDBMS* in Chapter 9 that corresponds to the database server you are planning to use.

Creating Tables

To create a table, use the CREATE TABLE statement, which is a straightforward translation of the information we put into the data dictionary in the previous section. Before you construct a CREATE TABLE statement on your own, check Table 9.7, the *Data Type Cross-Reference Table* in Chapter 9 that shows the data types supported by each of the database servers we used in writing this book (Oracle, Sybase, Mini SQL, MySQL, and PostgreSQL). Although there is a common SQL dialect that all these database servers speak, there are some differences, especially in terms of which data types the server supports.

Identifiers

An identifier is the name of something, like a table, column, or variable. Identifiers should not be confused with literal values, such as the integer value 100 or the string value "This string has 29 characters". While you can generally use any character on the keyboard in a literal string, there is a limited set of characters that you can use in an identifier.

All the database servers we tested allow you to use identifiers that start with an alphabetic character (a–z and A–Z) that is followed by one or more alphanumeric characters (a–z, A–Z, 0–9, and _, the underscore character). Examples of valid identifiers include A, A1, Author, Author_Number. Invalid identifiers include 100, 10Author, and Author#.

The CREATE TABLE statement looks like this:

```
CREATE TABLE <table name> (<column declaration list>)
```

where <table name> is any valid identifier that your database server supports, and <column declaration list> is a comma-delimited set of column declarations of the form:

```
<column name> <type> [ ( <optional-size> [, <optional-precision> ]) ]
```

Such as:

```
first_name CHAR(25)
customer_id INT
unit_price NUMERIC(10, 2)
```

To put together a CREATE TABLE statement, you must consult your data dictionary to find out what columns and data types appear in each table. You then need to consult Table 9.7, the *Data Type Cross-Reference Table* in Chapter 9 to determine which data type your database system supports. For the Patron entity, we can construct a CREATE TABLE statement that works for all of the database servers (with a minor exception as described in the sidebar *NULL or NOT NULL?*) we are treating in this book:

```
CREATE TABLE patron
     (first_name      CHAR(25) NOT NULL,
      last_name       CHAR(25) NOT NULL,
      middle_initial  CHAR(1),
      address         CHAR(25),
      city            CHAR(25),
      state           CHAR(2),
      zip             CHAR(11),
      phone           CHAR(10),
      patron_id       INTEGER  NOT NULL,
      purge_history   INTEGER)
```

The next table we're going to create is book. Here is the CREATE TABLE statement for the book table:

```
CREATE TABLE book
     (title             CHAR(50) NOT NULL,
      isbn              CHAR(25) NOT NULL,
      volume            CHAR(10),
      edition           INTEGER,
      publisher_code    CHAR(25),
      binding_type      CHAR(3),
      publication_year  INTEGER,
      publication_city  CHAR(25),
      hold_requested    INTEGER,
      requestor_id      INTEGER)
```

The remaining tables are now straightforward translations of the data dictionary we created earlier, with the exception of the data type for the borrowed_date, due_date, and return_date columns. Aside from Sybase, all the database systems covered in this book support the DATE data type. That's not a big problem, though. For Sybase, you can either change the CREATE

NULL or NOT NULL?

Unlike the other database systems we're covering in this book, Sybase assumes that all columns will not accept NULLs unless declared otherwise. As a result, you must change these CREATE TABLE statements to declare the columns NULL (except for the ones that say NOT NULL, of course), which tells Sybase that it's okay for these columns to have NULL values in them. Using Sybase, the patron table should be created with:

```
CREATE TABLE patron
    (first_name     CHAR(25) NOT NULL,
     last_name      CHAR(25) NOT NULL,
     middle_initial CHAR(1)  NULL,
     address        CHAR(25) NULL,
     city           CHAR(25) NULL,
     state          CHAR(2)  NULL,
     zip            CHAR(11) NULL,
     phone          CHAR(10) NULL,
     patron_id      INTEGER  NOT NULL,
     purge_history  INTEGER  NULL)
```

Some databases, such as PostgreSQL and Mini SQL, do not support the NULL constraint (it is assumed unless NOT NULL is specified), so we will not use the syntax shown above universally. However, if you are using Sybase, you must change the definitions of the other tables in this manner.

TABLE statement to use the correct data type (DATETIME), or create a new DATE data type with this command:

```
sp_addtype DATE, DATETIME, NULL
```

(Make sure you issue this command in each Sybase database you want to use this data type in. For more details on Sybase databases, see the *Sybase Adaptive Server Enterprise* section in Chapter 9.)

This solution does not make our cross-platform issues disappear, because each database server may require that date literals be stated in a slightly different date format. The various date formats are shown in Table 9.8, *A Sampling of Date Formats*, in Chapter 9.

```
CREATE TABLE borrows
    (patron_id       INTEGER  NOT NULL,
     isbn            CHAR(25) NOT NULL,
     borrowed_date   DATE     NOT NULL,
```

```
       due_date                DATE      NOT NULL,
       return_date             DATE)

CREATE TABLE author
   (first_name                 CHAR(25) NOT NULL,
    last_name                  CHAR(25) NOT NULL,
    author_id                  INTEGER  NOT NULL)

CREATE TABLE author_of
   (isbn                       CHAR(25) NOT NULL,
    author_id                  INTEGER  NOT NULL)

CREATE TABLE publisher
   (publisher_name             CHAR(25) NOT NULL,
    publisher_code             CHAR(25) NOT NULL)
```

Putting Data into the Database

Once you have created the tables, you will need to put some data into those tables. Use the INSERT statement to add new rows to the table. The INSERT statement creates a new row in the table, and fills one or more of the new row's columns with data. Choose which columns to fill with data by including a list of columns and values.

The INSERT statement consists of the keywords INSERT INTO, followed by the table name. After the table name, the columns appear in a parenthesized list, and the values to insert appear in a second parenthesized list preceded by the VALUES keyword. One general form of the INSERT statement looks like:

```
INSERT INTO <table name>
    ( <column-list> )
    VALUES ( <value-list> )
```

If your CREATE TABLE statement declared a column NOT NULL, you must specify that column in the INSERT statement. For example, you could add a row to the patron table with the following command:

```
INSERT INTO patron
    (first_name, last_name, patron_id)
    VALUES ('Brian', 'Jepson', 100)
```

However, the following command would fail, because you did not specify the first_name column, and the database assumes that you want to insert a NULL for the first_name column (as well as all the other columns you didn't specify; if those columns were created as NOT NULL, the database will generate errors when you try to insert a NULL):

```
INSERT INTO patron
    (last_name, patron_id)
    VALUES ('Jepson', 100)
```

NOTE

If you do not include a column in an INSERT statement, the database will insert a NULL value for that column when it creates the new row. If you have specified a default value for that column in the CREATE TABLE statement, it will use that value instead of NULL. For example: _CREATE TABLE employee (salary INT DEFAULT 60000)_. Similarly, some database servers support auto-increment columns, which are assigned successive values each time you insert a new row (see the section titled _Generating Unique Values_ in Chapter 9).

If your INSERT statement specifies values for all columns in the table, you don't need the <column-list>. For example, this INSERT statement inserts a row into the patron table:

```
INSERT INTO patron
VALUES ('Brian', 'Jepson', 'C', NULL, 'Kingston', 'RI',
'02881', NULL, 100, 0)
```

WARNING

Although you _can_ omit the names of the columns, that doesn't mean you _should_. When you take out the column names, you make your code hard to read. Also, if you add columns to the table in the future (see the section titled _ALTER TABLE (Changing the Structure of a Table)_ in Appendix A), your old INSERT statements won't work because an INSERT without column names must have values for all the columns in the table.

To add data to the database, you must issue a series of INSERT statements. The following statements add four authors to the author table:

```
INSERT INTO author
    (first_name, last_name, author_id)
    VALUES ('Antonin', 'Artaud', 100)

INSERT INTO author
    (first_name, last_name, author_id)
    VALUES ('Philip K.', 'Dick', 110)

INSERT INTO author
    (first_name, last_name, author_id)
    VALUES ('Brian', 'Jepson', 120)

INSERT INTO author
    (first_name, last_name, author_id)
```

```
VALUES ('David', 'Hughes', 130)
```

These INSERT statements add three publishers to the publisher table:

```
INSERT INTO publisher
    (publisher_name, publisher_code)
    VALUES ('Grove', '0-802')

INSERT INTO publisher
    (publisher_name, publisher_code)
    VALUES ('Vintage Books', '0-679')

INSERT INTO publisher
    (publisher_name, publisher_code)
    VALUES ('Wiley Computer Publishing', '0-471')
```

To add some books, you must first INSERT some rows into the book table, and then INSERT rows into the author_of table to associate each book with an author. Notice that the books have publisher_code columns that link a book to a row in the publisher table.

```
INSERT INTO book
(title, isbn, volume, edition, publisher_code, binding_type,
publication_year, publication_city, hold_requested, requestor_id)
VALUES ('The Theater and its Double', '0802150306', NULL, NULL,
'0-802', 'CUS', 1958, 'New York', NULL, NULL)

INSERT INTO book
(title, isbn, volume, edition, publisher_code, binding_type,
publication_year, publication_city, hold_requested, requestor_id)
VALUES ('Now Wait for Last Year', '0-679-74220-4', NULL, NULL,
'0-679', 'PAP', 1966, 'New York', NULL, NULL)

INSERT INTO book
(title, isbn, volume, edition, publisher_code, binding_type,
publication_year, publication_city, hold_requested, requestor_id)
VALUES ('The Game Players of Titan', '0-679-74065-1', NULL, NULL,
'0-679', 'PAP', 1963, 'New York', NULL, NULL)

INSERT INTO book
(title, isbn, volume, edition, publisher_code, binding_type,
publication_year, publication_city, hold_requested, requestor_id)
VALUES ('The Official Guide to Mini SQL 2.0', '0-471-24535-6', NULL,
NULL, '0-471', 'PAP', 1998, NULL, NULL, NULL)
```

The remaining statements associate each book with one or more authors. By themselves, these statements aren't very readable. However, if you view them as a cross-reference between the author and book table, they make more sense. For example, the first INSERT creates an association between the book having the isbn column equal to 0802150306 and the author row having the author_id equal to 100. In plain English, this tells us that Antonin Artaud is the author of *The Theater and Its Double*.

```
INSERT INTO author_of
(isbn, author_id)
VALUES ('0802150306', 100)

INSERT INTO author_of
(isbn, author_id)
VALUES ('0-679-74220-4', 110)

INSERT INTO author_of
(isbn, author_id)
VALUES ('0-679-74065-1', 110)

INSERT INTO author_of
(isbn, author_id)
VALUES ('0-471-24535-6', 120)

INSERT INTO author_of
(isbn, author_id)
VALUES ('0-471-24535-6', 130)
```

Getting Data out of the Database

Use the SELECT statement to pull rows and columns out of the database. In a monitor program such as msql, psql, or isql, the results of a SELECT statement appear in a tabular format, as shown here:

```
publisher_name           |title
-------------------------+-----------------------------------
Wiley Computer Publishing|The Official Guide to Mini SQL 2.0
Vintage Books            |Now Wait for Last Year
Vintage Books            |The Game Players of Titan
Grove                    |The Theater and its Double
(4 rows)
```

For more details on these monitor programs, see the *SQL Monitors* section in Chapter 9.

The most basic form of the SELECT statement gets all the rows and columns from a table:

```
SELECT <column-list>
    FROM <table>
```

The <column-list> can be a comma-delimited list of column names, or the character * to denote all columns. Here is a SELECT statement that fetches all the authors:

```
SELECT * FROM author
```

Here is a SELECT statement that just fetches the authors' first and last names:

```
SELECT first_name, last_name FROM author
```

Using SELECT Statements in Your Applications

In a database application, the rows are usually returned as a data structure such as an array, a linked list, or an instance of an object that represents the results (as with Java, C++, Perl). In most programming environments, the data structure that contains the result set is row oriented: You step through each row in the result set and fetch the columns. Here is some pseudocode that outlines the typical steps for issuing a query and fetching the results:

```
Open a connection to the data server.
Execute the query.
If the query was successful:
    For each row in the result set:
        Fetch the row.
        Do something with the data in each column.
    Close the result set.
Close the connection to the data server.
```

Ordering Result Sets

You can control the way in which results are sorted. To sort the results of a SELECT statement, use the ORDER BY clause. Here is the general form of a SELECT statement with an ORDER BY clause:

```
SELECT <column-list>
    FROM <table>
    ORDER BY <column> [ASC | DESC] [, <column> [ASC | DESC]] ...
```

The following SELECT statement retrieves all authors, and sorts them by their last name:

```
SELECT last_name, first_name FROM author ORDER BY last_name
```

Use DESC to sort in descending order:

```
SELECT last_name, first_name FROM author ORDER BY last_name DESC
```

This SELECT statement retrieves all book titles, binding types, and publication year, sorted by binding type first and then by publication year:

```
SELECT binding_type, publication_year, title
    FROM book
    ORDER BY binding_type, publication_year
```

The performance of sort operations may be improved by adding an index on the column(s) you want to sort by (see the upcoming section, *Indexes*).

Filtering Result Sets

Most of the time, you don't want to retrieve the entire contents of a table. Instead, you usually need to retrieve rows that match a given criteria. In this case, you will find the WHERE clause handy. The WHERE clause allows you to specify a set of constraints on the results before they are sent back to you. The general form of an SQL statement with a WHERE clause is:

```
SELECT <column-list>
    FROM <table>
    WHERE <condition>
    [ AND|OR <condition> ]...
```

The <condition> is a logical expression, such as *author_id = 100* ("author id equal to 100") or *publication_year > 1965* ("year of publication is greater than 1965"). When you use a conditional expression in a WHERE clause, the SELECT statement only retrieves records matching that criteria.

Most conditions will be expressed with one of the operators shown in Table 2.9.

For example, here is an SQL SELECT that retrieves all books that were published after 1965:

```
SELECT title, publication_year
    FROM book
    WHERE publication_year > 1965
```

This SELECT retrieves all books that were not published in 1963:

```
SELECT title, publication_year
    FROM book
    WHERE publication_year <> 1963
```

Table 2.9 Conditional Operators

OPERATOR	SAMPLE	MEANING
=	*\<expr1\>* = *\<expr2\>*	*\<expr1\>* must be equal to *\<expr2\>*
>	*\<expr1\>* > *\<expr2\>*	*\<expr1\>* must be greater than *\<expr2\>*
<	*\<expr1\>* < *\<expr2\>*	*\<expr1\>* must be less than *\<expr2\>*
>=	*\<expr1\>* >= *\<expr2\>*	*\<expr1\>* must be greater than or equal to *\<expr2\>*
<=	*\<expr1\>* <= *\<expr2\>*	*\<expr1\>* must be less than or equal to *\<expr2\>*
<>	*\<expr1\>* <> *\<expr2\>*	*\<expr1\>* must *not* be equal to *\<expr2\>*
LIKE	*\<expr1\>* **LIKE** *\<pattern\>*	*\<expr1\>* matches pattern (% matches any string, _ matches any single character)

This SELECT statement fetches all the books published in the 1960s:

```
SELECT title, publication_year
    FROM book
    WHERE publication_year >= 1960
    AND publication_year <= 1969
```

This SELECT gets all books whose titles start with "The":

```
SELECT title
    FROM book
    WHERE title LIKE 'The%'
```

This SELECT fetches all authors whose last name matches D__k (where there are exactly two letters between D and k, such as Dick, Dark, or Dock):

```
SELECT first_name, last_name
    FROM author
    WHERE last_name LIKE 'D__k%'
```

(The extra % takes care of databases like PostgreSQL that try to match the trailing whitespace. See the section titled *Data Type Sizes*, earlier in this chapter.)

Finally, this SELECT statement retrieves all the books published by either Grove or Wiley Computer Publishing:

```
SELECT title
    FROM book
    WHERE publisher_code = '0-802'
    OR publisher_code = '0-471'
```

Joins

In the final SELECT example, you saw an example where you had to use the publisher code to filter the result set by publisher. What would you do if you wanted to see the name of the publisher in the result set? You can specify more than one table in the FROM clause and use the WHERE clause to specify how those tables are related to each other. The general form of a join looks like:

```
SELECT <column-list>
    FROM <table1>, <table2> [, <table3> ]...
    WHERE <table1>.<primary-key> = <table2>.<foreign-key>
    [ AND <table2>.<primary-key> = <table3>.<foreign-key> ]...
```

Consider the publisher table as <table1> and the book table as <table2>. The publisher table's primary key is publisher_code, and the book table's foreign key reference to publisher has the same name. Therefore, if you want to select a list of titles and publishers, you can issue this query:

```
SELECT book.title, publisher.publisher_name
    FROM publisher, book
    WHERE publisher.publisher_code = book.publisher_code
```

NOTE In this section, foreign key refers to a column that is a reference to a column in another table. Although the use of the word *key* implies that we are talking about an index, there is no rule that says the foreign key actually has to have an index. In some cases, it may be a simple column without an index. In many circumstances, though, it is generally beneficial to have an index that corresponds to the column. For details on creating indexes, see the upcoming section titled *Indexes*.

This example introduced the dot (.) operator. The dot operator lets you specify the table that contains a column, and is used here to eliminate ambiguity. Without the dot operator, the database server wouldn't know which table the publisher_code on the left came from, and which table the publisher_code on the right came from. Even though it's obvious to us, it's not obvious to the data engine. It's a good idea to use the dot when you have more than one table in a SELECT statement, since it also makes it easier for other programmers to understand how the SELECT statement works.

You can also use joins with cross-reference tables like the author_of table. Here is the general form of a SELECT statement that uses a cross-reference table to join two tables:

```
SELECT <column-list>
    FROM <table1>, <crossref> , <table2>
```

```
WHERE <table1>.<primary-key> = <crossref>.<foreign-key1>
AND <table2>.<primary-key> = <crossref>.<foreign-key2>
```

Consider author as <table1>, book as <table2>, and author_of as <crossref>. The primary key of author is author_id, and the foreign key reference from author_of to author is also named author_id. The primary key of book is isbn, and the foreign key reference from author_of to book is also named isbn. If you want a list of books and authors, here is a SELECT statement that will accomplish that:

```
SELECT author.first_name, author.last_name, book.title
    FROM author, author_of, book
    WHERE author.author_id = author_of.author_id
    AND book.isbn = author_of.isbn
```

For further information on the SELECT statement, see Appendix A.

Outer Joins

Let's suppose that we have a book in the database for which the publisher is unknown. You could insert it with this INSERT statement, which puts a NULL in the publisher_code field (both shown in bold):

```
INSERT INTO book
(title, isbn, volume, edition, publisher_code, binding_type,
publication_year, publication_city, hold_requested, requestor_id)
VALUES ('The SK Electric Posse Guide to Life', '100-100-100', NULL,
1, NULL, 'CUS', 1998, 'Kingston', NULL, NULL)
```

Next, if you try to issue this SELECT statement:

```
SELECT book.title, publisher.publisher_name
    FROM publisher, book
    WHERE publisher.publisher_code = book.publisher_code
```

the row is mysteriously absent.

```
+------------------------------------+----------------------------+
| title                              | publisher_name             |
+------------------------------------+----------------------------+
| The Theater and its Double         | Grove                      |
| The Game Players of Titan          | Vintage Books              |
| The Official Guide to Mini SQL 2.0 | Wiley Computer Publishing  |
+------------------------------------+----------------------------+
3 rows in set (0.00 sec)
```

There is a special join, an *outer* join, that can take care of this problem. What the outer join does is look at one side of the join (<table1>.<column> =

<table2>.<column>) as an outer portion. In the case of this SELECT statement, the book.publisher_code will be the outer portion. The outer portion of the join gets special treatment in that *all rows are selected* from the table in the outer portion, whether the join succeeds or not. If the join doesn't succeed, there's no way it can find a value for publisher_name, so publisher_name is set to NULL for books with no publisher code. Here are the results of the outer join:

```
+-----------------------------------+---------------------------+
| title                             | publisher_name            |
+-----------------------------------+---------------------------+
| The Theater and its Double        | Grove                     |
| The Game Players of Titan         | Vintage Books             |
| The Official Guide to Mini SQL 2.0 | Wiley Computer Publishing |
| The SK Electric Posse Guide to Life | NULL                    |
+-----------------------------------+---------------------------+
4 rows in set (0.01 sec)
```

Each database system uses a different syntax for the outer join:

MySQL. MySQL supports the SQL 92 standard LEFT OUTER JOIN syntax. In this SELECT statement, book is on the left side of the outer join, and publisher is on the right. Notice that publisher is not specified in the FROM clause and that no WHERE clause is needed, since this is all specified in the LEFT OUTER JOIN clause:

```
SELECT book.title, publisher.publisher_name
    FROM book
    LEFT OUTER JOIN publisher
    ON book.publisher_code = publisher.publisher_code
```

Sybase. To construct an outer join under Sybase, add an asterisk (*) to the left or right of the equal sign in the join. To make the leftmost term the outer component, the asterisk should point to the leftmost term, as in *=. To make the rightmost term the outer component, the asterisk should point to the rightmost term, as in =*. Here is a left outer join in Sybase that preserves all the data in the book table, even if the publisher_code is NULL:

```
SELECT book.title, publisher.publisher_name
    FROM book, publisher
    WHERE book.publisher_code *= publisher.publisher_code
```

Oracle. Oracle does things slightly differently. Instead of marking the outer component, you mark the inner component. Further, the marking appears to the right of the component as a (+), as shown here:

```
SELECT book.title, publisher.publisher_name
    FROM book, publisher
    WHERE book.publisher_code = publisher.publisher_code (+)
```

PostgreSQL. PostgreSQL can accomplish this same task using the UNION keyword. UNION joins together two queries into a single result set. The first query finds all the books that have publishers, and the second finds all books that have the publisher_code column set to NULL. This has the same effect as an outer join:

```
SELECT book.title, publisher.publisher_name
    FROM publisher, book
    WHERE publisher.publisher_code = book.publisher_code
    UNION SELECT title, NULL
        FROM book
        WHERE publisher_code IS NULL
```

Mini SQL. Mini SQL does not support outer joins or unions.

Updating Data in the Database

You can modify existing rows using the UPDATE statement. The UPDATE statement should be qualified with a WHERE clause, or the update is applied to *every row in the table*. The general form of the UPDATE statement is:

```
UPDATE <table>
    SET <column> = <value> [, <column> = <value>] ...
    WHERE <condition>
    [ AND|OR <condition> ]...
```

For example, to change Brian Jepson's first name, either of these two UPDATE statements would do the job (although the second is preferred, since it uses a primary key to locate the row, and primary keys do no change as long as the row exists):

```
UPDATE author
    SET first_name = 'Buh-Rian'
    WHERE first_name = 'Brian'
      AND last_name  = 'Jepson'

UPDATE author
    SET first_name = 'Buh-Rian'
    WHERE author_id = 120
```

Deleting Data from the Database

You can delete rows using the DELETE statement. The DELETE statement also uses a WHERE clause to specify which rows to delete. If you don't include a WHERE clause, *every row in the table* is deleted!

The general form of the DELETE statement is:

```
DELETE FROM <table>
    WHERE <condition>
    [ AND|OR <condition> ]...
```

For example, you could delete the book *Now Wait for Last Year* with either of the two commands (although the second is preferred, since it uses the primary key):

```
DELETE FROM book
    WHERE title = 'Now Wait for Last Year'
```

```
DELETE FROM book
    WHERE isbn = '0-679-74220-4'
```

WARNING
If you do not include a WHERE clause in the UPDATE or the DELETE statements, the changes are applied to *every* row in the specified table. It's so important, we felt it best to say it twice!

Indexes

If you create indexes on your tables, the performance of some retrieval operations can be greatly improved. In general, it makes sense to create an index for each primary key and foreign key in a table, because these are the most heavily used columns in join operations.

There is a special type of index, called a *unique* index, that enforces the uniqueness of the key. This is useful for primary keys: The very definition of primary keys requires that they are unique within the table. For example, there must only be one author with a given author id (such as 100), and no two authors may have the same author id.

NOTE
If you declare a column as PRIMARY KEY in the CREATE TABLE statement, an index will be automatically created for it.

The general form of the CREATE INDEX statement is:

```
CREATE [UNIQUE] INDEX <index-name>
    ON <table> ( <column> [, <column>]...)
```

For example, to create a UNIQUE index on patron.patron_id, issue the following CREATE INDEX statement:

```
CREATE UNIQUE INDEX ix_patron_id
    ON patron (patron_id)
```

The composite primary key of the *borrows* table is a combination of patron_id, isbn, and borrowed date (the assumption, which might not hold true in the real world, is that while a patron may take out a book more than once, she can only borrow it one time on a given day, since there is only one book). To enforce the uniqueness of that primary key, you could declare the following unique index:

```
CREATE UNIQUE INDEX ix_borrows
    ON borrows (patron_id, isbn, borrowed_date)
```

Here is an example of a nonunique index. This index exists to improve the performance of joins involving the author_of.isbn column.

```
CREATE INDEX ix_author_of_isbn
    ON author_of (isbn)
```

Summary

Relational database systems give you the ability to model real-world objects and the relationships between them. Because the most intuitive way to design tables is not always the most efficient in terms of system resources, database design is a critical activity that must be performed before you create the tables. Avoid the temptation to skip the normal forms: Although an non-normalized database system may perform acceptably well for small data sets, small increases in the size of a data set can sometimes cause huge performance hits (see the section *Analyzing Time Complexity* in Chapter 4, "Construction").

PostgreSQL, Sybase, Oracle, Mini SQL, and MySQL share many things in common, but outer joins, dates, and other implementation details may differ greatly. The section titled *Modularity* in Chapter 4 suggests some strategies for isolating these sorts of differences using modular programming techniques. Nevertheless, you should focus on achieving a mastery of SQL in general, but keep yourself educated about quirks and implementation differences.

User Interface Design

"But wait a minute, if these new devices are so wonderful, why do we need special dedicated staff members to make them work—'power users' or 'key operators'? Why do we need manuals or special instructions to use the typical business telephone? Why do so many features go unused? And why do these devices add to the stresses of life rather than reduce them?"

Donald A. Norman, *The Design of Everyday Things*

This chapter offers you exposure to the art of building user interfaces. While this chapter covers many of the issues involved with this art, it cannot claim to be a comprehensive text on the topic. Think of this chapter as a prelude to deeper involvement in user interface development.

Although this chapter is intended as an introduction, it includes a methodology for developing user interfaces. While this methodology works for simple applications, you should consult some of the resources that are mentioned in this chapter. User interface design and implementation is complicated and should, in theory, require the involvement of programmers, human factors engineers, and graphical designers. Nonetheless, this chapter should open your eyes to some of the issues, and give you a jumping-off point for further studies.

The Development Process

When a programmer develops a user interface, there is sometimes a tendency to assume that the developer knows best. This can lead the programmer to develop the user interface without involving the user. This approach ignores the word *user* in user interface.

To develop a user interface that makes life easy for users, developers, and innocent passersby, you should follow a dynamic, iterative process that involves the user as much as possible.

NOTE

When you consider software development processes, keep in mind that the process must be implemented in an iterative fashion if it is to succeed. That is, you will have to repeat parts of the processes at various times. For example, you might complete the step titled "involve the user," only to find that you need to walk through that step one more time before you can move on to the next step. It's almost definite that you will complete the entire cycle once, and return to the beginning to complete the cycle again.

The following steps summarize the example UI development process we'll use in this chapter (this process was inspired by the ideas in Theo Mandel's *The Elements of User Interface Design* [Wiley, 1997]):

1. *Consider the requirements.* Before you consider the user interface, you'll encounter the requirements for the system. Requirements are discussed in detail in Chapter 1, "Requirements." While it's possible that important user interface elements will be identified in the requirements, the user interface probably won't be completely specified. This doesn't give the programmer free license to create any user interface she wishes. Rather, it suggests that some questions need to be asked, answered, and perhaps asked again.

2. *Involve the user.* The human component of your system is the most important. Without the human, the software has no one to serve, no duties to perform. The user decides which features to use, which features are too baroque to be used (like the digital clock on most VCRs), and whether the system is used at all. The user is at the center of a system with a user interface. Because of this, the user needs to be consulted on the design of the user interface as early and often as possible.

3. *Follow established design guidelines.* Many user interface guidelines have been developed by operating system developers and vendors. The best of these guidelines take into account such issues as how people react to different types of visual stimuli, form conceptual models of systems, and react when confronted by good and bad design. Established design guidelines are what their name suggests: a collection of information that guides you in developing an interface, not rigid rules that take the creative component out of user interface design.

4. *Develop a UI prototype.* The user interface (UI) prototype is a mocked-up implementation of the system's user interface. A *mock-up* is an implementation that includes all of the visual components, and just enough code to let users move around the system. The mock-up offers none of the business logic or connection to the back-end database. It is necessarily quick and dirty. In many cases, you will find it easiest to develop prototypes in a

scripting language like Perl or Python in conjunction with a tool like Glade (see Chapter 13, "GNOME"), rather than in C, C++, or Java.

Your users should experiment with the UI prototype to determine whether and how the system integrates with their workflow. Don't give them the UI prototype and ask them to tell you how they liked it. Instead, watch your users when they use the UI prototype. Do you notice any awkward interactions? Do the users get panicked or show signs of stress?

5. *Refine the UI prototype until nearly perfect.* Modify the design of the user interface and adjust the UI prototype until you have something that the users can work with. Don't rush your users through this step just so they sign off on it quickly. Poorly designed user interfaces create a support burden, stress out the user community, and increase tension between the users and developers. Avoid the temptation of the quick sign-off!

6. *Develop the implementation.* Once you have an acceptable UI prototype, you can develop your system and its user interface. As with the UI prototype, you should involve the user with this step. There is no doubt that you will have to adjust the design somewhat during this lengthy process. As you clarify ambiguities in the system design (even if they don't affect the UI directly), you will change the specification, and this will directly or indirectly affect the design of the user interface. When this happens, update the design of the user interface and the UI prototype, and involve the users in these changes.

7. *Perform usability testing.* Even if the UI prototype and the implementation appear identical down to the smallest widget, a UI prototype feels a lot different than a system that actually does something with the data the users put into it. Once you have an implementation of the system, you will need to perform usability testing. If you identify parts of the system that slow or frustrate users, or simply don't fit into their workflow, you may need to change the implementation.

Again, keep the UI prototype up to date with the implementation, since you might need to refer to the prototype as you develop further revisions of the system.

Consider the Requirements

The requirements are the framework within which you have the freedom to design and develop a user interface that meets your users' needs. Your users' needs are different from (but not incompatible with) the system requirements in that the users need a user interface that lets them exercise all the features of the system with no stress or discomfort.

Let's consider a specification for a hypothetical system:

Contact Management System (CMS) Requirements

1.1 Overview of Business Needs

A system is needed to track customers, companies, and meetings between our representatives and customers.

1.1.1 The Customer

A customer is a current, potential, or former client.

1.1.2 The Company

A company is a business or organization that the customer is affiliated with.

1.1.3 The Meeting

The term *meeting* encompasses all types of information exchanges with a customer, including telephone calls, meetings, email, etc.

2.1 Data Entities

Each entity that the system tracks has a number of attributes.

2.1.1 The Customer

The system should store the following information about a customer:

Name.
Company name.
Email address.
Fax number.
Phone number.

2.1.2 The Company

The system should store the following information about a company:

Name.
Address.
Phone number.
Fax number.
Industry type (such as telecommunications, bioengineering, or finance).

2.1.3 Meetings

The system should store the following information about a meeting:

Date.
Time.
Type (email, phone, face-to-face).
List of attendees (customers).
Location.

3.1 Data Entry Requirements

The system shall provide various forms to support entering data into the system.

3.1.1 Customer-Related Data Entry

The system shall provide a Customer Maintenance form, which must support the following operations:

3.1.1.1 Add a Customer

The Customer Maintenance form must allow the user to add a customer to the system. To add a customer, the user must supply the customer's name, company name, email address, fax number, and phone number.

Rationale: As we do business with new customers, we need to capture and store their information.

3.1.1.2 Edit a Customer

The Customer Maintenance form must allow the user to edit the details of an existing customer. The user may modify the customer's name, company name, email address, fax number, and phone number.

Rationale: As a customer's information changes, we need to keep the system up to date.

3.1.1.3 Delete a Customer

The Customer Maintenance must allow the user to delete a customer.

Rationale: If we stop doing business with a customer, we may want to purge that customer from the system.

3.1.2 Company-Related Data Entry

The system shall provide a Company Maintenance form, which must support the following operations:

3.1.2.1 Add a Company

The Company Maintenance form must allow the user to add a company to the system. To add a company, the user must supply the company's name, address, phone number, fax number, and industry type.

Rationale: As we do business with new companies, we need to capture and store their information.

3.1.2.2 Edit a Company

The Company Maintenance form must allow the user to edit the details of an existing company. The user may modify the company's name, address, phone number, fax number, and industry type.

Rationale: As a company's information changes, we need to keep the system up to date.

3.1.2.3 Delete a Company

The Company Maintenance form must allow the user to delete a company.

Rationale: If we stop doing business with a company, we may want to purge that company from the system.

3.1.3 Meeting-Related Data Entry

The system shall provide a Meeting Maintenance form, which must support the following operations:

3.1.3.1 Add a Meeting

The Meeting Maintenance form must allow the user to add a meeting. To add a meeting, the user must supply the date and time of the meeting, type of meeting, a location (optional), and list of attendees (see 3.1.3.3 and 3.1.3.4).

Rationale: As new meetings happen, we want to track them in the system.

3.1.3.2 Edit a Meeting

The Meeting Maintenance form must allow the user to edit the details of a meeting. The user may modify the date and time of the meeting, type of meeting, location (optional), and list of attendees (see 3.1.3.3 and 3.1.3.4).

3.1.3.3 Add a Customer to a Meeting

The Meeting Maintenance form must allow the user to add a customer to a meeting.

Rationale: We need to track who attended the meeting.

3.1.3.4 Remove a Customer from a Meeting

The Meeting Maintenance form must allow the user to remove a customer from a meeting.

Rationale: If a meeting is entered into the system before it occurs, one or more customers may decide not to attend.

3.1.3.5 Delete a Meeting

The Meeting Maintenance form must allow the user to delete a meeting.

Rationale: If a meeting is canceled, or if a meeting is entered erroneously, we need to remove it from the system.

3.2 Messaging Requirements

The system should support the ability to send messages.

Rationale: We need the ability to communicate rapidly and simply with customers and companies.

3.2.1 Fax Messages

The system should let the user fax a message to specified recipients.

3.2.1.1 Fax a Message to a Customer

The system should let the user fax a brief message to a customer.

3.2.1.2 Fax a Message to a Customer List

The system should let the user fax a brief message to a list of customers associated with a meeting.

3.2.1.3 Fax a Message to a Company

The system should let the user fax a brief message to a company.

3.2.2 Email Messages

The system should let the user send an email message to specified recipients.

3.2.2.1 Email a Message to a Customer

The system should let the user email a brief message to a customer.

3.2.2.2 Email a Message to a Customer List

The system should let the user email a brief message to a list of customers associated with a meeting.

This is a simple system. Unlike a real-world system, this system doesn't have any requirements for reporting or connection to external systems.

Involve the User

> "With a mind like yours, you'll probably want the land-crab."
>
> Hunter S. Thompson, "Fear and Loathing in Las Vegas"

When you (as a user) meet a new system, you make discoveries and inferences about how that system works. As you get more familiar with the system, you build up a mental model of how that system works. Mandel describes this mental model as "an internal representation of how users understand and interact with a system."

Every user's mind is different, so every user's mental model is a little different. Throughout the development of the prototype and implementation, it's your job to discover the common elements of users' mental models.

Which comes first, the mental model of a system or the system itself? Before you develop the system, you can use a set of techniques to develop an immature mental model of the system. This immature model must be reconciled with the system requirements to produce a model that is compatible with the user's mind.

Mandel suggests using a set of techniques to discover the user's mental model, which are discussed in *Object-Oriented Interface Design: IBM Common User Access Guidelines* (QUE, 1993). The first four of these techniques should be done as early in the design and development process as possible, but should be repeated as necessary throughout the lifecycle of the software:

- Analyze the user's tasks.
- Survey and interview potential users.

- Visit the user's work sites.

- Gather input and feedback from users (not their managers—you need to hear it from the people who are doing the work!).

Mandel and IBM include a fifth technique, usability testing, but this task is performed later in the lifecycle of the software. Using the common elements you obtain by using these techniques, you must ensure that your prototype and implementation fits or complements the user's mental model.

Follow Established Design Guidelines

There are two general types of guidelines you need to consider when developing UI prototypes and UI implementations. The first type of guidelines concerns a general approach to how humans interact with computers. Mandel provides three golden rules of user interface design that should guide you as you develop your prototypes and implementations. This section summarizes these rules.

The second type of guidelines is more specific. You might have a set of guidelines that pertain to your development environment (such as KDE, GNOME, or GNUstep). You may also have a set of design guidelines that your department or company uses. These types of guidelines are often very specific and pertain to things such as required controls (for example, an Exit menu option, or OK and Cancel buttons), interoperability with other applications, and how to deal with specific situations such as whether the application can have any modal components.

You can find documentation for KDE and GNOME, including user interface guidelines, at http://developer.kde.org/documentation/standards/kde/index.html and www.gnome.org/gdp/ (but check the main sites www.kde.org and www.gnome.org for the latest information). Java's design guidelines are available in the book *Java Look and Feel Design Guidelines* by Sun Microsystems (Addison-Wesley, 1999) and online at http://java.sun.com/products/jlf/guidelines.html. Operating system vendors such as IBM, Apple, and Microsoft also publish user interface style guidelines.

Mandel's Golden Rules

Mandel suggests three golden rules of user interface design: Place users in control, reduce their memory load, and make the UI consistent.

Place Users in Control

When I walk to the University of Rhode Island campus, I almost always need to cross the quadrangle. When I do that, I see a lot of paths worn in the grass where there should be sidewalks, and I see a lot of sidewalks where there should be paths. Mandel relates the story of a designer who needed walkways through a grassy area. The designer planted grass everywhere and let people walk where they wanted. After a while, the worn paths made it clear where the walkways belonged, and the walkways were constructed. This is an excellent example of putting users in control.

Mandel outlines 10 principles that you can follow to place your users in control of the user interface:

Use modes judiciously. Anyone who has been in the same room as a novice using the vi editor is familiar with a recurring beeping sound. This sound comes when the novice gets stuck in command mode and can't figure out how to get back to input mode. The vi editor (one of the default text editors that comes with Linux and one of my editors of choice) has two modes: command and input. When you are in input mode, you can type text freely. To issue a command (such as *save file*), press Escape to switch to command mode, issue the save command (:w), and press a command key (such as i) to return to input mode. It's easy for novice users to get very confused by this operation.

For those who like it, vi's modal operation works well. However, unnecessary use of modes can take control away from the user for no good reason at all. Some modes make sense. When your application encounters an exceptional situation, for example, you might need to have a modal alert box pop up. Until the user clicks OK or Cancel, she can't do anything else with the program. Design tools need modes of operation, too. If I am using tgif (a free figure-drawing tool) to draw a rectangle, I click on the toolbar to put the program in rectangle mode. When the program is in rectangle mode, it behaves differently than if it was in text entry mode.

Allow users to use either the keyboard or mouse. Although the mouse is required for the operation of the X Window System, you should provide alternative input methods. Some users don't want to use the mouse: They may want to develop a keying rhythm that doesn't involve five-second pauses while they fumble for the mouse. Some users have disabilities that prevent them from using the mouse or make the mouse awkward to use. Every mouse-based operation in the system should have a keyboard equivalent.

Allow users to change focus. Let users switch tasks quickly without having to save or discard the changes they are working on. For example, if I am editing a customer's details and I am suddenly reminded that I promised to have all my calls updated before I go to lunch, I'd like to be able to take care of updating the calls, and after lunch, go back to where I was with the customer's details.

Display descriptive messages and text. Take care to use messages that are understandable, even to novice users, by not using a lot of jargon or technical terms. Don't write messages, particularly error messages, that blame the user for errors that occurred. Messages and text in your applications should be well-written by writers skilled in whatever language(s) your users speak and read natively.

You should consider internationalization issues when you develop text labels, messages, and error messages. Learn about the internationalization features that the development environment offers.

Provide immediate and reversible actions, and feedback. When something happens in your application, provide a visual response, such as changing the state of a visual object or putting a message in the status bar. Use progress indicators to show the progress of long tasks. Provide a status bar that shows the state of the application and displays informative messages to the user. You should provide undo and redo options for most tasks. When a task is irreversible, you should make it clear that there is no return from it.

Provide meaningful paths and exits. Your user interface should let users move through the application any way they want, and the system should use cues to make it clear what the system is currently doing, so users know where they are in the system at any given time.

Accommodate users with different skill levels. Novice users will do novice things with your application, and expert users will do expert things with it. Make sure your application supports different skill levels by making easy things easy, and difficult things doable.

Make the user interface transparent. Strive to make the users notice the user interface as little as possible. Mandel says the users should "feel like they are reaching right through the computer and directly manipulating the objects they are working with." One technique to achieve transparency is to use objects and actions to mimic the real-world objects (see also the list item *Allow users to directly manipulate interface objects*). For example, let your users print by dragging TeX, HTML, and other documents to the printer icon.

Allow users to customize the interface. KDE and GNOME can be customized in many ways: Users can control the appearance of windows, menus, and many other parts of the desktop. Make sure your application follows the user-defined customizations for the overall user interface. This ensures a consistent look and feel between applications. You can let users tweak other aspects of your application, such as the contents of menus, mapping of shortcut keys, and layout of toolbars.

Allow users to directly manipulate interface objects. Although Mandel suggests that you provide keyboard equivalents for every activity, he also reminds you to let users directly interact with objects. Let users drag addresses into an email, unused files into trash cans, and documents to printers. Use visual metaphors to simplify complex operations.

Reduce User's Memory Load

Human memory is tricky—we can store tiny bits of data in short-term memory, but we can retrieve it rapidly and reliably. We can store enormous amounts of data in long-term memory, but we *cannot* retrieve it rapidly or reliably. We often spend long periods of time trying to remember something that is in long-term memory, and sometimes we forget things. Reminders and cues can help get things out of long-term memory.

Mandel's second golden rule of user interface design asks us to do everything we can to reduce the user's memory load. Taking into account the constraints of human memory, Mandel offers the following principles to reduce memory load:

Relieve short-term memory. Don't require users to jot down notes while they are using your application. For example, don't give the user a code number and require the user to supply that code number a few screens later. Wherever possible, carry as much information through different stages of the system. When this is not possible, allow users to back up nondestructively (as a wizard, shown in Figure 3.1, does with its Next and Back buttons), or use cut and paste to move important information around.

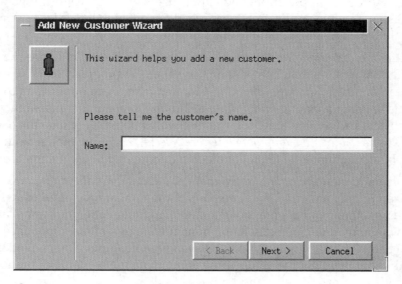

Figure 3.1 Using a wizard to add a new customer.

Rely on recognition, not recall. Don't tax your users' long-term memory by asking them to remember things like airport codes and state abbreviations. Provide pop-up and pull-down menus to select lists of data.

Provide visual cues. Use as many cues as possible to let the users know what state they are in (such as creating a new record versus editing an old record). Use elements such as status bars, scrollbars, and enabled/disabled buttons (like a bold or italic text indicator in a word processor) to let the users know what's happening. Make it possible for them to take a coffee break, come back to their computer, and know *exactly* where they left off with a glance at the screen.

Provide defaults, undo, and redo. If you let your users customize different aspects of your application, give them a way to return to the defaults. That way, if they choose an unreadable default font or wildly contrasting colors, they can return things to the way they were. Provide as many levels of undo as possible, and include a redo option that reverses the action of the undo. Undo and redo let your users make some changes, and then step back and forth through the changes they made to figure out what is going on.

Provide interface shortcuts. Provide keyboard equivalents that are consistent with other applications. For example, Ctrl+C is a common shortcut for copying, and Ctrl+V is a common shortcut for pasting. Look at other applications or a style guide for common shortcuts, and adopt them if they are standard for your application environment.

Promote an object-action syntax. Let the users select an object (such as a file or a bunch of text), and then right-click to see a list of actions that are appropriate for the object. This way, users don't need to remember what actions are applicable to a given object.

Use real-world metaphors. Users already know how to use file folders, trash cans, and recycling bins. Use visual metaphors, such as dragging a document to a folder, for common actions.

Use progressive disclosure. Don't dump all the features of your application in the users' laps. Put common tasks at their fingertips and let them look around a bit for the less common features. As they master the simple tasks, they will naturally investigate and learn more about the complex tasks if needed.

Promote visual clarity. Don't clutter up your screen. Group controls together that are conceptually related. Learn about techniques for visual organization so users can find what they need without getting a headache. Edward Tufte's *The Visual Display of Quantitative Information* (Graphics Press, 1992) and *Envisioning Information* (Graphics Press, 1990) include ideas are applicable to any graphical presentation of information.

Make the User Interface Consistent

Mandel's third golden rule outlines techniques you can use to make user interfaces consistent. Consistency reinforces learning and allows users to transfer skills between applications. Mandel lists five techniques for building consistent user interfaces:

Sustain the context of the user's tasks. Users should be able to move smoothly throughout the operation of the application. Make cues available to show where the user has been and where he is going. Don't make the user switch modes gratuitously or switch between keyboard and mouse needlessly.

Maintain consistency within and across products. Attach established meanings to common elements. An OK button, for example, should approve an action and close a dialog, and a Cancel button should cancel pending changes and close the dialog. Text you can edit (such as a text field) is usually shown in a box with a different background than the enclosing screen. Text you can't edit (such as the label for a text field) is usually shown with the same background as the enclosing screen. Follow consistent conventions within your own application and follow the standards that other programs adhere to.

Keep interaction results the same. This technique can be thought of as a supplement to maintaining consistency. Make sure that the results of common actions are the same throughout your application. If the user presses Ctrl+P in one part of the application, make sure it does the same thing (or nothing at all) in another part of the application. Users get surprised when the same action yields different results.

Provide aesthetic appeal and integrity. Use consistent design techniques throughout your application. Use a consistent set of fonts, colors, and layout styles to build your application. Don't choose design elements that are inconsistent with other applications.

Encourage exploration. Develop engaging user interfaces that encourage users to explore. This exploration is how novice users become experts. To encourage exploration, make sure the interface is friendly, enticing, and that it includes features, such as wizards, that guide the user through otherwise intimidating tasks.

Develop and Refine the UI Prototype

To develop the UI prototype, we're going to use an example design process. Since this chapter is only an introduction to user interface design, we're taking the liberty of taking shortcuts. Mandel outlines a comprehensive iterative design process that should be considered for large and complicated projects.

In a real-world system, you would analyze the requirements and generate as many user scenarios as possible through meeting with the users, gathering information, and brainstorming. The user scenarios describe hypothetical interactions a user might have with the system. The requirements shown earlier in this chapter hint at certain types of interactions, and in a real-world system, would be taken together with the user scenarios to determine the possible interactions a user could have with the system.

Some of the object-oriented analysis artifacts, such as use cases and conceptual models, may be useful as well. See Chapter 7, "Object-Oriented Analysis," for more details. In fact, if you defer user interface design until after you have done a first pass at the object-oriented design, you can reuse a lot of the analysis artifacts, such as use cases and the conceptual model, in your user interface design.

Find the Nouns and Verbs

The first step is to find all the nouns and verbs in the user scenarios and the requirements. In this example, we don't have any user scenarios, so we're using the requirements for this analysis. To build this list, you should underline all the nouns and verbs in a printout of the requirements.

Here is a list of all the verbs:

- add
- edit
- delete
- remove
- fax
- email

The two actions, fax and email, suggest that we also add two nouns: fax machine and mailer. Here is a list of all the nouns:

- customer
- meeting
- company
- customer name
- company name
- company address
- customer email address

- customer fax number
- customer phone number
- company phone number
- company fax number
- industry type
- date
- time
- meeting type
- list of attendees
- location
- message
- fax machine
- mailer

Grow a Tree

Next, sketch out an object/attribute tree that shows each noun and its contents. You'll need to examine each noun and determine if it is a standalone concept or an attribute of another concept. The *Add Attributes* section in Chapter 7 covers a more robust method for discovering and categorizing attributes. Figure 3.2 shows the tree for the Contact Management System (CMS).

Meetings are at the top of the tree. They contain date, time, type, location, and an attendee list. The attendee list, in turn, contains customers. A customer contains customer name, email address, fax number, phone number, and a company. A company, at the bottom of the tree, contains company name, address, fax number, and industry type. There are two items that hang out by themselves: fax machine and mailer.

Find Objects

When you find a top-level node or a node in the tree that contains other nodes, you have found an *object* that needs to be represented conceptually in the system. Anything else is an *attribute.* In general, objects are represented by forms and icons, and attributes are represented by controls, such as a text field, drop-down menu, or radio button. When an object contains another object (such as a customer that contains a company), you should represent that object as an attribute of the container *and* as its own object. In practice, this means you should have a drop-down menu on the customer form to

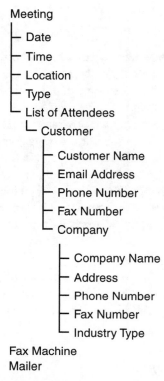

Meeting
├ Date
├ Time
├ Location
├ Type
└ List of Attendees
    └ Customer
       ├ Customer Name
       ├ Email Address
       ├ Phone Number
       ├ Fax Number
       └ Company
          ├ Company Name
          ├ Address
          ├ Phone Number
          ├ Fax Number
          └ Industry Type

Fax Machine
Mailer

Figure 3.2　Object/attribute tree for the Contact Management System.

select which company it contains, and you will have a separate form to add, edit, or delete company attributes.

Although the customer belongs to a company in one conceptual model (at best, the employer as a tribe—at worst, the employer as proprietor), the company is contained in customer because it fits with the conceptual model that the CMS uses. You often ask a person "who do you work for?" but you rarely ask a company "who works for you?" Both conceptual models are valid, but CMS is about meetings, which are about customers, who happen to have an employer as an attribute.

Design Icons for Objects

At this point, you can design (or select) icons for the objects you have identified. If you don't want to design your own, there are freely redistributable icons available on the Internet, such as the Window Manager Icons Project at http://wm-icons.sourceforge.net/, and Anthony's Icon Library at www.sct .gu.edu.au/~anthony/icons/. *The Icon Book*, by William Horton (Wiley, 1994), includes sample icons and information about designing your own icons.

Objects versus Objects

When I talk about objects in the context of user interfaces, I am talking about elements that make up the conceptual model. Essentially, objects are things the user interacts with, or something the user thinks about in terms of doing something to the object, or having the object do something.

When I talk about objects in the context of object-oriented programming, I am talking about a programming term that has much more specific meaning. See Chapter 5, "Object-Oriented Programming," for a description of objects in this context.

In the real world, there may be some overlap between user interface objects and programming objects. For example, you may have a Customer object in the user interface, and also a Customer object in your application's object model.

Figure 3.3 shows the icons I have designed for each of the container objects in the tree. To design these, I used kiconedit, an icon editor that comes with KDE. KDE is a freely redistributable desktop environment and application development toolkit for Linux.

Determine Appropriate Actions for Objects

Next, you must build a table of actions that can be done to or with each object. For example, you can *add* a new meeting, *send a fax* to a company with the fax machine, or *mail a message* to a customer.

Figure 3.4 shows each object and the various actions that can be performed with respect to that object. Now, you can begin to build some of the UI components.

Determine Forms and Menu Actions

Next, you should create forms for each item in the data entry requirements. This list may not always be complete. For example, if the database normalization process (see Chapter 2, "Database Design") creates any new entities, you might need a separate maintenance screen for them. The important thing to remember is that other stages in the design process (such as database design

Figure 3.3   Customer, Meeting, Company, Fax, and Mailer icons.

Meeting	Add Edit Delete
List of Attendees	Add Customer Remove Customer Send Email Send Fax
Customer	Add Edit Delete Send Email Send Fax
Company	Add Edit Delete Send Fax

Figure 3.4 Table of objects and actions.

and object-oriented analysis and design) may have an impact on what goes into the user interface.

Also, the forms we discover in this chapter are focused on the needs of the data. You should compare this approach with the use-case driven techniques in Chapters 7 and 8, which may provide insights toward developing a more complete user interface that takes all business processes into consideration.

Each form needs menu options to represent actions. The menu options represent the actions listed in Figure 3.4. In addition to the options in that figure, there are some implied actions that you need to account for.

NOTE

Any action involving editing a control (such as adding or editing a new record where you might need to type a customer's name or address) will need standard edit menu options such as Undo, Redo, Copy, Cut, Paste, and Select All. See your platform or desktop environment's style guidelines for how these should be implemented.

The Edit action (applicable to meeting, company, and customer) implies that you need to provide a method of locating items you want to edit. A simple but cumbersome technique is to provide first, last, next, and previous actions that navigate through the lists. You can make this a little easier to deal with by adding a control to quickly seek an item that matches a given criteria. You should add these actions to a toolbar and to the menu. (Figures 3.8 through 3.10 show the toolbar. Figure 3.6 also shows the toolbar, with the seek/search control activated.)

There are common items that should appear on each form. Table 3.1 shows a list of common actions, the menu bar item the action is assigned to, the menu name it is given, and an accelerator key that it's assigned to Figure 3.5 shows the common menu items.

The Find Record functionality should be handled by an editable drop-down menu on the toolbar. The user can click the edit region in the menu, then type

Table 3.1   Common Actions for Each Form

MENU BAR	MENU TITLE	ACTION	KEY
File	New	Add	Ctrl+N
File	Delete	Delete	Ctrl+D
File	Save	Save*	Ctrl+S
File	Revert	Discard changes you have made to a record*	Ctrl+R
Edit	Copy	Copy selected text from a field*	Ctrl+C
Edit	Cut	Cut selected text from a field*	Ctrl+X
Edit	Paste	Paste clipboard into a field*	Ctrl+V
Edit	Select All	Select all text in a field*	Ctrl+A
Edit	Undo	Undo changes to a field*	Ctrl+Z
Edit	Redo	Redo changes to a field*	Ctrl+Y
File	Exit	Exit	Ctrl+Q
Meeting, Company, or Customer menu	Next	Next Record[†]	Alt+N
Meeting, Company, or Customer menu	Previous	Previous Record[†]	Alt+P
Meeting, Company, or Customer menu	Last	Last Record[†]	Alt+L
Meeting, Company, or Customer menu	First	First Record[†]	Alt+F
Meeting, Company, or Customer menu	Find	Find Record[†]	Ctrl+F

* Implied by Edit, Add actions.
† Implied by Edit action.

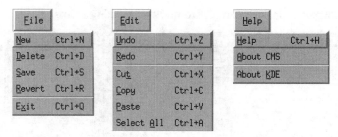

Figure 3.5   The File, Edit, and Help menus common to all forms in CMS.

in a search term or press Ctrl+F to select the control. As the user types, the control will search for matching records and limit the drop-down menu to show matching records. Figure 3.6 illustrates how this works with a company.

Next, you need to decide what special actions each form needs. Table 3.2 shows special menu actions for meeting, customer, and company. The corresponding menus are shown in Figure 3.7.

NOTE

Actions that associate two objects together, such a choosing a customer's company, or adding customers to a list of attendees, are not handled by menus. Instead, these should be handled by controls. This is because the association is an attribute of an object. For example, a list of attendees is an attribute of a meeting.

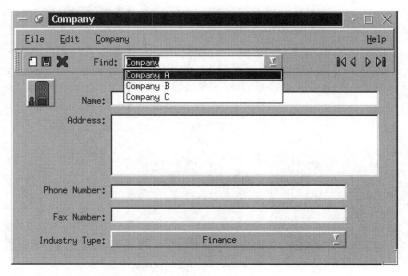

Figure 3.6   Searching for a Company.

Table 3.2   Specific Actions for Company, Customer, and Meeting Forms

FORM	ACTION	MENU BAR	MENU TITLE	KEY
Company	Send Fax*	Company	Fax Message	Alt+X
Customer	Send Email†	Customer	Send Email	Alt+S
Customer	Send Fax*	Customer	Fax Message	Alt+X
Meeting	Send Email to Attendees†	Meeting	Send Email to Attendees	Alt+S
Meeting	Send Fax to Attendees*	Meeting	Fax Message to Attendees	Alt+X

* implied by Fax Message action.
† implied by Send email Action.

In theory, the fax and email actions would bring up another form, although the corresponding forms are not shown in this chapter. To send an email message or fax, you could also drag the icons shown on the forms in Figures 3.8 through 3.10 to the desktop icons for the fax machine and mailer (see Figure 3.3).

Take Care of the Attributes

Look back at Figure 3.2 to see a list of all attributes in each object. You should go through each attribute and choose a control type for each. Table 3.3 shows one possible arrangement. You should consider the style guide for your development environment, the types of controls that are available, and your users' needs as you develop this list. Figures 3.8, 3.9, and 3.10 show all three forms with the controls from Table 3.3.

Once you have a prototype of the user interface, you need to watch the users work with it and test it. Their feedback will let you improve the user interface. Be wary of requirements changes at this stage. If the users ask for major

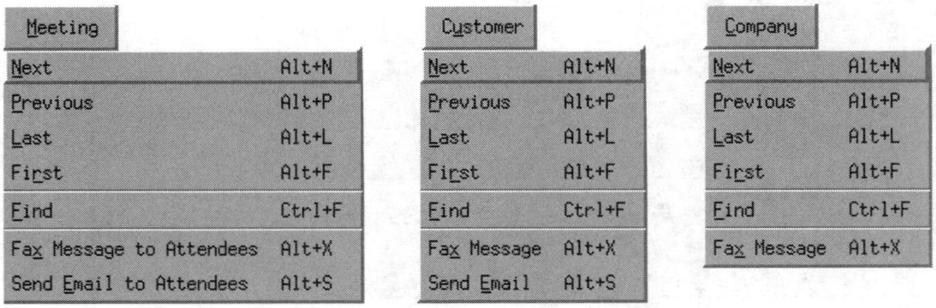

Figure 3.7   Special menus for Meeting, Customer, and Company.

Table 3.3   Attributes and Controls

FORM	ATTRIBUTE	ACTION	CONTROL TYPE	NOTES
Meeting	Date	Edit	Text Field	
Meeting	Time	Edit	Text Field	
Meeting	Location	Edit	Text Field	
Meeting	Meeting Type	Edit	Drop-Down Menu	Choices are Phone Call, Email, Face-to-Face Meeting, or Online Meeting.
Meeting	Attendees List	View	Scrolling List	
Meeting	Attendees List	Add Attendee	Push Button	Brings up a Customer chooser dialog (not pictured) with a control similar to the search widget in Figure 3.6.
Meeting	Attendees List	Delete Attendee	Push Button	
Customer	Name	Edit	Text Field	
Customer	Email Address	Edit	Text Field	
Customer	Phone Number	Edit	Text Field	
Customer	Fax Number	Edit	Text Field	
Customer	Company	Edit	Drop-Down Menu	
Company	Name	Edit	Text Field	
Company	Address	Edit	Text Area	
Company	Phone Number	Edit	Text Field	
Company	Fax Number	Edit	Text Field	
Company	Industry Type	Edit	Drop-Down Menu	Choices are in a database table.

changes in the system, you should forget about using your prototype to validate the user interface, and instead concentrate on validating the requirements. You may even need to do some major changes to the prototype to accommodate this. While this will have a noticeable impact on your schedule, it will ensure that you are delivering the right thing.

For a discussion of related issues, see the section titled *The Volatility of Requirements* in Chapter 1.

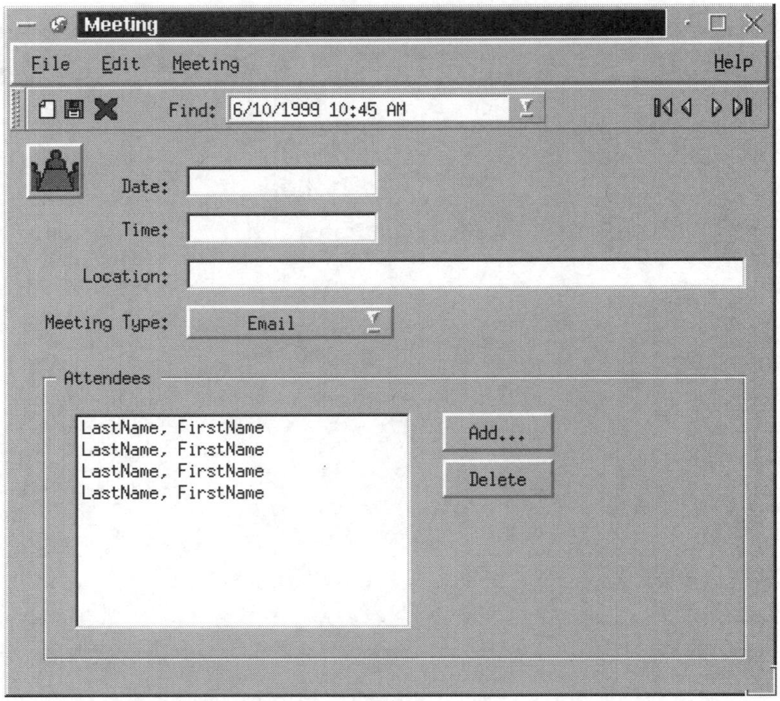

Figure 3.8   The Meeting Maintenance form.

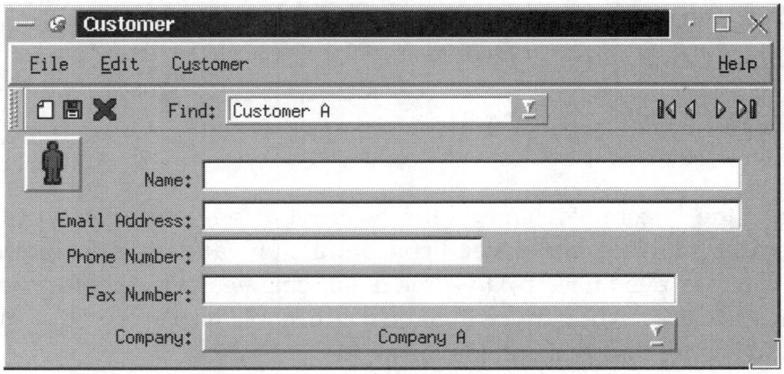

Figure 3.9   The Customer Maintenance form.

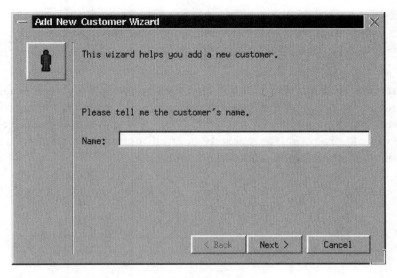

Figure 3.10   The Company Maintenance form.

Develop the Implementation

If you have developed a UI prototype before the database and object design are completed, you will need to finish those activities before you can build the implementation. Implementation draws on code construction skills, database design and implementation, the UI design, and object design and implementation. Implementation issues are discussed beginning in Chapter 9, "Databases," and continue throughout the remaining chapters.

Perform Usability Testing

Usability testing allows you to determine whether the user interface can serve the needs of the user. We don't address this topic in this book, but it is treated well in Mandel's *Elements of User Interface Design*.

Summary

Developing a user interface is a complicated process that can be made a little easier by following established guidelines and implementing proven techniques. This chapter provides both techniques and guidelines, but is far from the final word on the topic. If you are going to build a lot of user interfaces in your career, you have an interesting road ahead of you: There is a great deal of engrossing reading on the subject of human factors, design, and user interfaces.

Although the user interfaces in this chapter were originally developed using KDE and the *qtarch* tool, the concepts and ideas are transferable to other environments. Starting with Chapter 11, "Java, Swing, and JDBC," we'll build example programs for a variety of environments and pay some special attention to their strengths and peculiarities.

Construction

". . . if there's going to be a program, there has to be construction, and that makes construction a uniquely fruitful area in which to improve development practices."

Steve McConnell, *Code Complete*

C onstruction (or implementation) refers to the activities you engage in when you're writing code. All too often, programmers simply sit down at the keyboard and start writing a program. Even if the programmer doesn't have the ideas, he often types something. I heard a story of one consultant who used to type as loudly and as rapidly as possible, to create the illusion of progress. In fact, this consultant would, at times, open a text editor and type screen after screen of gibberish. But, it looked like he was working, because he was doing what people expect programmers to do: type.

In reality, programmers don't (or shouldn't) spend all of their time typing. Even if you have an army of designers to provide high-level designs, code construction is not something that should be done without deliberate thought. This chapter discusses some strategies you can use to prepare for the program, module, or routine you are constructing. These strategies can provide resourcefulness in the form of reusable code, clarity in the form of readable programs, and epiphanies in the form of well-designed routines.

Finding Reusable Code

If someone has already written it, why should you write it again? If there's one thing the free software community is famous for, it's sharing code. Free software isn't only about software packages like Linux, GIMP, or GNUstep. It's also about libraries of reusable code, like libc, GLib, and GD.

In many cases, developers work on a software package and say, "hey, someone else could use pieces of this application." Such is the case with GTK+ and GLib. These two libraries were developed for the GIMP project, but eventually developed a life of their own. Now there are many applications that use one or both of these libraries. In other cases, developers realize the need for a new library, and begin implementing it for all to use.

The Importance of Reuse

If you can find some reusable code that fits your need and integrates well into your project, you will realize two immediate benefits. First, you'll have a lot less programming to do, so you get an immediate productivity gain. Second, if the reusable code in question is a common Linux component (such as GLib, GTK+, or QT), you don't need to include that library in your distribution (since it already comes with Linux). This will decrease the overall size of your application.

Identifying Good Code

When you find a package of reusable code, how do you know if it is good or bad? If it has a version number like 0.01, you can be sure it's *not* for general use. Look at how the package is categorized. The standard Perl source code repository, CPAN (the Comprehensive Perl Archive Network), includes a coding system that identifies many aspects of the package, such as whether it is alpha quality, beta quality, released, supported by a maintainer, mailing list (or not supported at all). Other repositories may have similar coding.

The Word on the Street

What's the word on the street about the package? Search a Usenet news archive like www.deja.com for occurrences of the package name. Read what people have to say, but be sure to read the follow-up messages. All too often, a new user gets frustrated with the documentation and posts something like "The libXYZ package is terrible! I can't figure out how to use function abc!" Sometimes, these sort of complaints won't even get a follow-up (either because they are confrontational or because they don't provide enough information), so take them with a grain of salt. Look for detailed critiques of the package followed by thoughtful discussion.

If there is a newsgroup or mailing list dedicated to the package, that is a good sign that the developers take the package seriously. If the newsgroup or mailing list has been around for a long time and is fairly active, that's a sign that the package is somewhat established.

Documentation

Does the package come with documentation and example code? Is the documentation easy to read? You can look at the documentation and example code to decide whether the package will integrate well with the application you are building.

Good packages don't necessarily always come with good documentation, but good documentation is often a sign of a good package.

Comments

Take a look at the source code for the package. Are there any comments? Are major data structures and key functions documented within the code? A lack of comments (or unreadable comments) is a warning sign. Without comments, the code will be difficult to maintain, and the package's maintainers may have trouble fixing bugs that arise in the code.

Readability and Learnability

Comments are important, but so is the readability and learnability of the source code. In the best of all possible worlds, the source code will be so well structured and well written that there will be no need for comments. I don't think anyone has achieved this yet, though. See the section *Style and Technique* later in this chapter for a discussion of issues that affect how readable and learnable source code can (and should) be.

Repositories, Resources, and Libraries

Many programming languages have repositories of source code available. These repositories accept and categorize submissions of source code, and act as a clearinghouse for freely redistributable collections of code. Table 4.1 lists several of the better-known repositories.

Also, certain weblogs, such as Freshmeat (www.freshmeat.net) specialize in listing software and announcing new releases. For example, the development libraries listing at Freshmeat (www.freshmeat.net/appindex/development/libraries.html) lists hundreds of libraries.

Table 4.1 Reusable Code Resources

LANGUAGE	NAME	URL (HTTP:// UNLESS SPECIFIED)
C/Others	SNIPPETS	www.brokersys.com/snippets
C/Others	netlib	netlib.bell-labs.com/netlib/
C	Walnut Creek	ftp://ftp.cdrom.com/pub/algorithms/c
C	Lysator Academic Computer Society	www.lysator.liu.se/c/c-www.html#c
C++	Available C++ Libraries FAQ*	www.trumphurst.com/cpplibs/
Java	GNU Java Packages	www.gnu.org/software/java/java-software.html
Java	Giant Java Tree	www.gjt.org/
Objective C	comp.lang .objective-c FAQ, part 2*	ftp://ftp.ics.ele.tue.nl/pub/objc/classes
Perl	Comprehensive Perl Archive Network	www.perl.com/CPAN
Python	Contributed Modules	www.python.org/download/Contributed.html
Tcl	Tcl Resource Center	www.scriptics.com/resource/software/extensions/

* Also available as a periodic newsgroup posting

NOTE

This section includes a lot of URLs. From time to time, Web sites are reorganized and the URLs no longer point to a valid resource. If that happens, you should try the next level up in the URL and see if that works, until you work your way back to the hostname. For example, if www.somehost.com/something/interesting doesn't work, try www.somehost.com/something and look around for what you're interested in. If that doesn't work, try www.somehost.com. If you still can't find the resource, check out the companion Web site for this book at www.wiley.com/compbooks/jepson. We'll do our best to make sure this site has all the latest links.

The C Library

Some distributions of reusable code are organized into libraries, collections of routines that you can link into your own applications. The C library, or libc, is the Free Software Foundation's implementation of the standard Unix C library. This library implements system calls for basic operating system functions such as memory management, string manipulation, and file management. Every Unix and Linux system comes with a C library. The C library is a fundamental part of the operating system.

The C library's functions are documented in Chapter 3 of the system man pages and in good books on Unix C programming such as *C: A Reference Manual* by Samuel P. Harbison and Guy L. Steele (Prentice Hall, 1994), or *The Unix Programming Environment* by Brian W. Kernighan and Rob Pike (Prentice Hall, 1984).

Browsing the C Library

To see a list of all functions in the GNU C library, visit the GNU C Library online documentation at www.gnu.org/manual/glibc/libc.html and consult the section titled *Function and Macro Index*. At the time of this writing, this section could be found at www.gnu.org/manual/glibc/html_chapter/ libc_35.html.

If you're interested in a particular function, you can type *man <function name>*, as in:

```
man acos
```

This displays the man page for the *acos* function, part of which is shown here:

```
ACOS(3)              Linux Programmer's Manual          ACOS(3)

NAME
       acos - arc cosine function

SYNOPSIS
       #include <math.h>

       double acos(double x);

DESCRIPTION
       The  acos()  function calculates the arc cosine of x;
       that is the value whose cosine is x.  If x falls
       outside  the range -1 to 1, acos() fails and errno is
       set.
```

If you are interested in seeing the man pages for the system calls implemented by the kernel, try:

```
man 2 syscalls
```

In general, you should use the C library to invoke system calls, but there may be cases where you need to invoke them directly.

You can use the apropos command to look for functions on certain topics. Beware that this will show you all man pages on the subject (including utilities and libraries for other languages such as Perl). Here is an example:

```
$ apropos string
atof (3)              - convert a string to a double
atoi (3)              - convert a string to an integer
atol (3)              - convert a string to a long integer
bstring (3)           - byte string operations
bzero (3)             - write zeros to a byte string
confstr (3)           - get configuration dependent string
yes (1)               - output a string repeatedly until killed
```

Other Libraries

The libraries listed in Table 4.2 can be used directly with C or C++. If you want to use them with another language, such as Perl, Tk, or Java, you should check the home page for the library or a language-specific repository (see Table 4.1) to see if there is a wrapper for the library. A *wrapper* is a thin layer between your programming language and a library written in another language. For example, Perl users can use the GD library (which is written in C) via the GD Perl module, which is a wrapper written in a hybrid of C and Perl (GD, like other Perl modules, is available at CPAN). If you can't find a wrapper for your language, you may be able to use a tool such as SWIG (Simplified Wrapper and Interface Generator) to generate a wrapper. You can find SWIG at www.swig.org.

License Combatibility

In the brave new world of free software, there are many free software licenses from which to choose. These licenses come with a bewildering assortment of names like GPL, LGPL, QPL, NPL, the Aladdin License, the Artistic License, and public domain. Even more bewildering is the assortment of legalese and the fact that licenses seem to be more combative than compatible.

If you are building an application out of components with differing licenses, you may need to read the licenses carefully or consult your local self-proclaimed intellectual property expert to figure out, for example, whether you can release a software package under the NPL if you are using some libraries that are covered under the GPL. Many combinations are possible. In general, libraries released under the LGPL are compatible with the various

Table 4.2   Some of the Many Reusable Libraries Available

LIBRARY	DESCRIPTION	HOME PAGE
GLib	Provides C routines for working with data structures such as hashes, trees, and lists	www.gtk.org
Mesa	3-D graphics API that is very similar to OpenGL	www.mesa3d.org
ORBit	Corba implementation	www.labs.redhat.com/orbit
PAM	The Pluggable Authentication Modules library, which lets you control how applications authenticate users	www.us.kernel.org/pub/linux/libs/pam
readline	Library for providing a command-line user interface	ftp://ftp.gnu.org/gnu/readline
LessTif	Implementation of OSF/Motif GUI Toolkit	www.lesstif.org
GD	PNG manipulation library (as of this writing, it is not clear whether future versions of GD will support GIF images)	www.boutell.com/gd
ncurses	Freely redistributable clone of SVR4 curses, a library for managing an application's display on text-mode terminals	www.clark.net/pub/dickey/ncurses/ncurses.html
MyISAM	Freely redistributable library for manipulating database files at a lower level than SQL	www.mysql.com/download.html

other licenses. LGPL once stood for Library General Public License, but it now stands for Lesser General Public License, to reflect the Free Software Foundation's opinion that they would rather see developers working with the GPL and compatible licenses exclusively.

An excellent comparison of various licenses can be found in Bruce Peren's chapter (*the Open Source Definition*) from the book *Open Sources* (O'Reilly, 1999). This chapter can be found online at www.oreilly.com/catalog/opensources/book/perens.html.

Style and Technique

Many heated arguments have erupted over matters of style. There are only two sure things when it comes to these matters: There is more than one right way, and the most important thing is to be consistent.

Someone will have to read your code at some point, and there's a good chance that more hours will be spent reading, learning, maintaining, and enhancing your code than you will spend building the code. This is true of any software, even inhouse systems, but it is especially true of free software. Choose a style that makes for readable and understandable code. Apply this style in a consistent fashion, and your code will be well understood.

This section is necessarily terse, because this is not a book on programming style. Many of the issues in this section are treated well in other books. *Code Complete* by Steve McConnell (Microsoft Press, 1993) provides a thorough treatment of these and many other issues covered in this chapter.

This section is also necessarily general, because the techniques in this book apply to many languages. If you are not sure about the stylistic conventions for a language, you should check the documentation for the language to find information about stylistic conventions. This is especially important if you are writing libraries to be used by other programmers, since your adherence to convention could affect the success of your software.

Naming Conventions

Things need names. Without names, they are just things. Variables, functions, methods, classes, and tables all need names.

StudlyCaps versus studlyCaps versus all_lowercase. When you create a name made up of more than one word, you need to decide how to make it readable. For example, getemployeeid is descriptive of an action, but hardly readable. The three most common ways of dealing with this is with StudlyCaps, studlyCaps (like StudlyCaps but with the first word in lowercase), or all lowercase with underscores: GetEmployeeID, getEmployeeID, or get_employee_id. Which one of these you use depends on your personal preferences and what the conventions are for the programming language you use.

Choose names that are descriptive. The more important something is, the more descriptive its name should be. While it's okay to name a loop control variable *i* for a short loop, because it is traditional practice among programmers, a more descriptive name would be needed for a loop that exceeds 50 lines of code and refers to the loop control variable many times. In such cases, the loop control variable takes on a meaning beyond looping, and meshes more closely with the overall intent of your code.

For example, here's a small loop in Java where a short loop variable name (*i*) is acceptable:

```
for( int i = 0; i < employees.length; i++ ) {
    System.out.println( employees[i].getName() );
}
```

Here is a longer loop where a more descriptive name is called for:

```
for( int emp_index = 0;
    emp_index < employees.length;
    emp_index++)
{

    String emp_name = employees[emp_index].getName();
    int emp_salary = employees[emp_index].getSalary();

    // ... and so on ...

    int performance_factor =
        getPerformanceFactor( employees[emp_index].getID() );
    int new_salary =
        (emp_salary * performance_factor) / 10 + emp_salary;

    System.out.println(emp_name + " now earns " + new_salary);

}
```

A descriptive name should say as much about the variable, module, class, function, or method as possible. Names of functions, procedures, and methods often involve an action. In object-oriented programming, methods belong to classes, so it's clear what type of object is performing the action. Consider the following methods: employee.getSalary(), fido.chase_cat(), and physician.healThySelf().

Procedures and functions are associated with structured, rather than object-oriented, programming, so there is usually no object involved. So, you need to make the name a little longer in order to make it clear what is the source or the target of the action. Consider the following functions: attack_troll_with_sword(), getEmployeeSalary(), and debit_account().

Be wary of abbreviating names—it's often necessary to do so, but if abbreviations are not chosen carefully, your code can become confusing. McConnell suggests some simple tests, some of which are listed in Table 4.3.

Table 4.3   Suggestions for Short Names

TEST	GOOD	BAD
Did you make the abbreviation to save just one character?	June, July	Jun, Jul
Can you pronounce the name?	emp_name, cust_id, first_nm	emplnm, cstmr_id, frstnm
Did you avoid names that are easily mispronounced?	first_indvar, first_ivar, first_ind	findvar (pronounced ef-ind-var for first independent variable, mispronounced find var)
Did you use consistent abbreviations?	cust_num, emp_num, company_num, invoice_num	cust_no, emp_index, company_num, num_invoice

Name boolean variables in the affirmative. Avoid names that are stated in the negative, such as no_more_results. A program might one day ask the question !no_more_results, which you would read mentally as "not no more results." Not only is this questionable English, but it imposes an additional mental burden. Rethink your code to use a variable name such as more_results. Ideally, your boolean variables should suggest a question that you would answer with true or false. McConnell suggests putting the verb "is" in front of your boolean variables, but in some cases, other verbs such as "has" are helpful. Consider: is_done, has_more_results, and is_still_fetching.

Indentation

To tab or not to tab, is that the question? Using tabs or spaces to indent your code makes it much more readable. The drawback of tabs is that their size is dependent on your editor. If you use four-character tab stops, someone else might load your source code into an editor set for eight-character tab stops. If that happens, there is a good chance some of your source code will scroll off the right side of the screen. Many editors let you set the Tab key so it inserts spaces instead of tabs, so you can use spaces instead of tabs to control exactly how the text will be laid out.

It's a good idea to plan for 80-column screens. It's true that many programmers use an editor under the X Windows system and can size the screen to absurdly large widths. However, historical constraints on terminals have established an 80-column convention. Before you reject this notion, remember that email and Usenet postings look best under 80 columns, and this constraint is enforced by terminal-based mail and newsreaders (many of which are still very popular, like pine, elm, tin, and slrn). If you send a source code file to someone via email or post the source to a Usenet newsgroup, you stand a good chance that the text will wrap in strange ways, which could result in code that won't run.

Here is an example listing of C code that is laid out using four-character tab stops:

```
int send_confirmations( results_t result_set,
                        confirm_t confirm,
                        contact_info_t sender_info)
{

    int i;
    customer_t customer;

    if ( has_more_data(result_set) ) {

        for (i = 0; i < get_reccount(result_set); i++) {

            customer = fetch_record(result_set);

            if ( in_usa(customer) ) {

                fax_usa(customer, sender_info, confirm);

            } else {

                fax_non_us(customer, sender_info, confirm);

            }

        }
    }

}
```

And here is the same rendered with eight-character tab stops:

```
int send_confirmations( results_t result_set,
                                                confirm_t co
nfirm,
                                                contact_info
_t sender_info)
{

        int i;
```

```
        customer_t customer;

    if ( has_more_data(result_set) ) {

            for (i = 0; i < get_reccount(result_set); i+
+) {

                customer = fetch_record(result_set);

                if ( in_usa(customer) ) {

                    fax_usa(customer, sender_inf
o, confirm);

                } else {

                    fax_non_us(customer, sender_
info, confirm);

                }

            }
        }

    }
```

Assume that people reading your code will use an 80-column screen, and try to keep your code under 75 columns wide. If you use tab stops with four or fewer characters, try to keep your code under 65 columns wide. People reading your code who use eight-character tab stops (the default in many editors) will thank you for it.

Blocks and Braces

How do you like your curly braces? Do you keep them with your structured programming statements, or do they live by themselves? The Jargon file (www.tuxedo.org/jargon) lists four styles: 1TBS (One True Brace Style), Allman style, Whitesmiths style, and GNU style.

1TBS style:

```
if ($weather eq 'windy' and $season eq 'spring') {
    fly_a_kite();
}
```

Allman style:

```
if ($weather eq 'warm' and $season eq 'summer')
```

```
    {
        take_a_swim();
    }
```

Whitesmiths style:

```
    if ($weather eq 'snow' and $season eq 'winter')
            {
                go_sledding();
            }
```

GNU style:

```
    if ($weather eq 'clear' and $season eq 'fall')
      {
        look_at_foliage();
      }
```

Whatever brace style you choose, be sure you apply it consistently. Exceptions to this consistency should be consistent. For example, most of the examples in this book use 1TBS. Where the keyword and any conditional clauses take up more than one line, Allman style is often used, as shown here:

```
    if ( $humidity == 99
        and $weather eq 'hot'
        and $season eq 'summer'
        and !defined($car) )
    {
        suffer();
    }
```

Comments

Comments can be either burdensome or liberating, depending on how you approach them. If you approach commenting as something that's done just to placate people who ask you to comment your code, you probably won't bother to write comments. If you realize that writing comments can make it easier to understand your code (even as you are writing it) and easier to develop your code, you might give comments a chance. This section draws on *Code Complete* and lists a few of the commenting strategies provided in the book that will make commenting easier and more beneficial.

Use Program Design Language (PDL). PDL lets you design routines at a low level using plain English (or whatever language you are using). When you use PDL, you write out what you want the routine to do using an informal pseudocode. After that, you turn the PDL into comments, and develop the code. This low-level approach lets you document the intent of the routine. This documentation becomes a permanent part of the code: comments that you keep up to date as the code evolves. See the section *Building Routines and Modules* later in this chapter for more details.

Use comments to describe your intent. Don't write comments that simply repeat what the code does. Instead, write comments that describe the intent. Focus on the why, not the how. For example, here is a bit of Python code that documents *how* things are happening:

```
# Multiply sales by the rate, and add the result to base.
#
total = base + (sales * rate)
```

Contrast that example to this code, which documents *why* the calculation is happening, which preserves your intent:

```
# Calculate the sales commission and add it to the base
# to figure out the employee's total salary.
#
total = base + (sales * rate)
```

Avoid gratuitously complex formatting. Don't use excessively ornamental or complicated formatting, because it will be so complicated that no one will bother to update it. Consider this bizarre case:

```
##############################
# Written By: Brian Jepson
##############################
# Last Modified: June 7, 1999
##############################
#
# Function Index:
#
# +----------------+-------------------------------------+
# | Function Name  | Purpose                             |
# +----------------+-------------------------------------+
# | calc_bonus()   | Determine employee's bonus.         |
# | get_new_id()   | Gets the next sequential ID from the|
# |                | database.                           |
# | print_summary()| Prints a report of all employees'   |
# |                | sales summarized by product line.   |
#
# ... etc., etc.
```

This sort of complicated formatting will involve lots of tedious mucking about with pluses, dashes, and pipes, and probably won't be maintained.

Comment the bizarre and unusual. If you have written code that works around undocumented problems in the language, comment it (but don't forget to report the bug to the maintainer of the programming language!). If you have a good reason to deviate from programming style conventions or use an unusual algorithm, comment that as well. McConnell gives the example of using a right bitwise shift to perform division by two. Here is an example of that in Perl:

```
# Divide $num by two using a right bitwise shift.  This is
# faster than integer division in some environments.
print $num >> 1;
```

Commenting variables. You should comment variable declarations, taking care to specify whatever units are applicable.

```
my $speed = 100;       # speed in kilometers/hour
my $altitude = 30000;' # height in inches
```

Use the Revision Control System (RCS) to maintain a change log. In addition to the suggestions in *Code Complete*, we suggest that you take advantage of RCS to track information about the program and changes to it. RCS tracks and manages modifications to source code and is available in most (if not all) Linux distributions. The RCS home page is at www.cs.purdue .edu/homes/trinkle/RCS/.

RCS should be installed by default on most Linux distributions. If it's not installed on your system, check the installation media for an RCS package you can install. To get started with RCS, log on to Linux, and run the command *man rcsintro*. This brings up a man page that explains the basics of using RCS.

If you put the string *Id* in a comment, RCS expands it to include information about the program:

```
#!/usr/bin/python
#
# example5.py
#
# Calculate an employee's bonus.
#
# $Id$
#
```

Here is the expanded version, shown after the first time you check it in and out. RCS automatically inserts the new information. The new comment shows the filename, the version number, the date and time it was modified, the user who made the changes, and the state of the file:

```
#!/usr/bin/python
#
# example5.py
#
# Calculate an employee's bonus.
#
# $Id: example5.py,v 1.1 1999/06/17 15:08:42 bjepson Exp $
#
```

When you check a file into RCS, you are prompted for a description of the change, and your response is entered into the RCS system. If you include the string Log in a comment, RCS will add the description to the source code each time you check it in:

```
#!/usr/bin/python
#
# example6.py
#
# Calculate an employee's bonus.
#
# $Log$
#
```

Here is the same file, after multiple users have entered changes into the RCS system:

```
#!/usr/bin/python
#
# example6.py
#
# Calculate an employee's bonus.
#
# $Log: example6.py,v $
# Revision 1.4  1999/06/17 15:17:35  bjepson
# Removed a test inside a loop that was related to file
# locking under the old DBM-based system.  It's no longer
# needed now that we are using an SQL database.  It should
# make things faster.
#
# Revision 1.3  1999/06/17 15:15:43  joan
# Corrected a bug where the program kept using the same
# commission rate, despite the fact that senior employees
# have a higher rate.
#
# Revision 1.2  1999/06/17 15:13:49  bjepson
# example6.py now uses an SQL data source instead of a
```

```
# DBM file.
#
# Revision 1.1  1999/06/17 15:13:30  bjepson
# Initial revision
#
```

Reduce Memory Load

When someone is reading your program, she has to juggle a lot of things in her short-term memory. For instance, a reader of your program needs to keep the name of the file, module or class, and procedure in mind. In addition to these chunks of information, the reader also needs to track any variables or control structures that are in the current routine.

The typical American telephone number is a good example of the number of pieces of information that can be reliably kept in short-term memory: seven digits, or seven pieces of information. If there are too many pieces of information that readers of your program need to keep track of, they might have a hard time understanding your program.

McConnell discusses many things you can do to reduce the burden on programmers' short-term memories. The following section discusses a few techniques.

Keep references to variables together. McConnell suggests that you shouldn't spread references to variables all over your program. You can consolidate references to variables by keeping an eye on the *variable span* and *variable live time*.

Variable span measures the distance between references to a variable. If you can minimize the size of the span, you can avoid placing unnecessary burdens on your users. In this example (not counting comments or whitespace), $distance has a span of one (one line between references to $distance) and $time has a span of zero (no lines between references to $time):

```
my $distance = 100;    # distance in miles
my $time = 2.5;        # time in hours

# Calculate speed, in miles per hour.
#
my $speed = $distance / $time;
```

Similar to span is variable live time, which measures how many lines a variable is live. Consider the following example:

```
01    int emp_index = 0;
02    int emp_salary = 0;
```

```
03    int new_salary = 0;
04    int performance_factor = 0;
05    String emp_name = "";
06    for( emp_index = 0;
07        emp_index < employees.length;
08        emp_index++)
09    {
10        emp_name = employees[emp_index].getName();
11        emp_salary = employees[emp_index].getSalary();
12        performance_factor =
13          getPerformanceFactor(employees[emp_index].getID());
14        new_salary =
15          (emp_salary * performance_factor)/10 + emp_salary;
16        System.out.println(emp_name +
17                          " now earns " + new_salary);
18    }
```

The live time for the variables are as follows: emp_index = 13 lines, emp_salary = 14 lines, new_salary = 15 lines, performance_factor = 12 lines, and emp_name = 12 lines. Try to keep the live times down so readers don't have to keep track of more variables than necessary.

Avoid deep nesting. Try to avoid deeply nested statements. Too much nesting can be very confusing to someone reading your source code. If your code has deep nesting levels, chances are it can be broken out into routines or handled in another fashion (some cascading if statements can be easily converted to case statements). Consider this example:

```
for( int emp_index = 0;
     emp_index < employees.length;
     emp_index++)
{

    int emp_id = employees[emp_index].getID();

    if (isManagement( emp_id ) ) {

        /*
         * Complicated processing to calculate
         * a manager's bonus.
         *
         */

    } else if ( isSales( emp_id ) ) {

        /*
         * More complicated processing, this time
         * for a salesperson's bonus.
         *
```

```
        */

    } else if ( isProgrammer( emp_id ) ) {

        /*
         * Slightly less complicated processing,
         * this time for a programmer's bonus.
         *
         */

    }

}
```

There are a few things wrong with this code. First, why do we have to invoke a function to figure out which type of employee a given employee is? Why isn't employee type an attribute of the employee? Second, the cascading if statements could be rewritten as a case statement. Finally, the sections of complicated code (not shown, but believe me, they are complicated) should be broken out into separate routines. Here is the revised code:

```
for( int emp_index = 0;
     emp_index < employees.length;
     emp_index++)
{

    int emp_id   = employees[emp_index].getID();
    int emp_type = employees[emp_index].getType();

    switch ( (emp_type) ) {
      case EMPL_MANAGER:
          calc_manager_bonus(emp_id);
          break;
      case EMPL_SALESPERSON:
          calc_sales_bonus(emp_id);
          break;
      case EMPL_PROGRAMMER:
          calc_programmer_bonus(emp_id);
          break;
      default:
          // unknown type - throw exception
    }

}
```

Boolean tests in control statements. If you've got complicated boolean tests, move them into a separate routine. This serves two purposes: First, it makes the code easier to read, since the reader doesn't have to mull over the boolean test while he is reading the code. Second, by choosing a good name for the boolean test function, you make the intent of the boolean test clear. Consider this example:

```
if ($have_record or ($end_of_file or $beginning_of_file)
    and $curr == $record_count)
{
    # do something...
}
```

If the boolean tests were moved into a subroutine called done_processing_table(), here is how much simpler the code would look:

```
if (done_processing_table() ) {
    # do something
}
```

Algorithms

When you've finished designing your system, what's left? The next step is to develop routines that modules and classes use to operate on their data. A key component of any routine is the algorithm it uses to perform its duties.

An *algorithm* is a series of steps that, given an input, produces a certain output. For example, a sorting algorithm takes a list, performs a series of steps, and produces a sorted list as its output.

How do you discover an algorithm? You can invent them, but you can also find them. In most cases, someone else has already written the algorithm you need. Because of this, treasure troves of algorithms are much sought after.

The classic work is *The Art of Computer Programming* by Donald E. Knuth (Addison-Wesley), a five-volume work-in-progress, three of which are currently completed and in print. The volumes are *Volume I, Fundamental Algorithms*, Third Edition (1997); *Volume II, Seminumerical Algorithms*, Third Edition (1997); and *Volume III, Searching and Sorting*, Second Edition (1998).

Steven S. Skiena's *Algorithm Design Manual* (Springer Verlag, 1997) sports a Catalog of Algorithmic Problems, hundreds of pages in which real-world problems are examined along with algorithmic solutions. Each problem includes pointers to implementations of the algorithms.

Both Skiena and Knuth are valuable resources that should be no more than an arm's length away from any serious programmer!

Algorithm Design Strategies

Skiena offers a great deal of insight for people who need to develop an algorithm. The book is liberally peppered with Skiena's war stories, narratives that describe how certain real-world algorithms were discovered, developed, and incrementally improved. Skiena provides an explicit method for designing certain classes of algorithms in Chapter 3, "User Interface Design." In this chapter, he describes two methods: dynamic programming, and divide and conquer. Both these strategies teach you how to start with a definition of what problem the algorithm is to solve, and work your way to an algorithm in which you can be confident.

One of the most important lessons we learn from Skiena is that we must be able to discern between a problem itself and an instance of the problem. If you're asked to sort a list of customer names, you're dealing with an instance of the problem, not the problem itself, which is sorting a list of string values. You should think about what you're trying to do, and boil it down to the problem itself. Otherwise, you may not recognize the problem as something that's been solved before, and you will end up reinventing the wheel!

Dealing with Recursion

Understanding recursive algorithms is one of the first issues a novice computer programmer struggles with. When you experience this struggle, one of two things will happen: Either complete understanding will come to you in a flash, or you will accept recursion (the property exhibited by recursive algorithms) as a spooky phenomenon. If you follow the latter course, you will probably try hard to avoid recursion in the future, faking it when necessary.

A *recursive algorithm* is an algorithm that is self-referential. At some point in the algorithm, the algorithm invokes itself. A child could use a recursive algorithm to climb a tree by climbing the first branch that looks sturdy, then moving on to successive branches:

```
Climb(branch):
Climb to the branch
For the first sturdy adjacent branch I can reach from the branch I'm on:
    Climb(adjacent branch)
```

It has to end at some point, though. You need a terminal, or basis case. When climbing a tree, you should probably stop when you can't find any more sturdy branches. Otherwise, the child might hang on the last sturdy branch, looking repeatedly at the remaining branches. This is an infinite regress, and it must be avoided by any practical recursive algorithm. Here is one possible solution to the child's infinite regress:

```
Climb(branch):
Climb to the branch
For the first sturdy adjacent branch I can reach from the branch I'm on:
    Climb(adjacent branch)
If there are no more sturdy branches:
    Descend the tree.
```

It's worth pointing out that the algorithm for descending a tree is much simpler:

```
Descend(tree)
    Scream loudly until an adult arrives with a ladder
```

Recursion is not important because it is an efficient way of doing things—very often, it's *not* the most efficient. In some cases, an iterative solution (discussed later in the chapter) may be the most efficient. Each time a function invokes itself, a certain amount of memory must be set aside to store the current state of the variables in the function, as well as the arguments that are passed to the new invocation of the function (this makes recursion expensive). If your function takes complicated objects or data types as arguments, the memory overhead of recursion can become unacceptable. Further, some recursive functions require exponential time to operate. The impact of exponential time is discussed in the next section.

Despite the fact that recursion doesn't always perform best, it prepares you for a way of thinking that is crucial to creating your own algorithms. Once you grasp recursion, you will find that it's easy to solve many problems with a recursive algorithm. Because recursive algorithms can be demanding on system resources, it is helpful to be able to convert recursive algorithms to algorithms that are based on looping constructs such as for and while loops.

In the next section, we'll see an example of an inefficient recursive algorithm that performs much better when it is rewritten as an iterative algorithm. Bryan Flamig's *Practical Algorithms in C++* (Wiley, 1995) includes detailed explanations of how to remove recursion, when to leave things recursive, and when not to leave things recursive. Although oriented toward the C++ programmer, I think the lessons in Flamig transfer well to other programming languages.

Analyzing Time Complexity

The discussion went something like this:

Consultant: "I think we should optimize your system so that it performs well for larger data sets. What would happen if you had 10,000 rows in the table that you are processing? Are you certain that it wouldn't grind to a halt?"

Customer: "I don't care how long it takes for very large data sets. It performs fast enough for 40 rows, I don't think we need to think about 500 or even 1000, let alone 10,000."

How did this story end? You're probably expecting to hear that the customer came running back to the consultant with a requirements change to make the system handle data sets of 10,000 rows. This is not the case. In fact, the system went from 40 to 50 rows, and in the process, went from processing the table in 1 second to processing it in 20 minutes. What happened? To find out, let's take a look at how to model the complexity of an algorithm.

We can predict the number of steps an algorithm will perform on a given input by modeling its complexity. To model the number of steps an algorithm takes, you need to define what a step is, look at the program, and count the number of steps. An example is a recursive algorithm that calculates a Fibonacci sequence, a numerical sequence in which each successive number is the sum of the two preceding numbers, such as 1, 1 (1+0), 2, 3, 5, 8, and so on. The algorithm is defined in Skiena as:

```
F(0) = 0

F(1) = 1

F(n) = F(n - 1) + F(n - 2)
```

In pseudocode, it looks like the following (A, B, and C are reference points we'll refer to when we step through the calculation):

```
Fibonacci(n):
    If n is zero, return zero (A)
    If n is one, return one (B)
    Otherwise:
        Return Fibonacci(i - 1) + Fibonacci(i - 2) (C)
```

Let's walk through the steps to calculate the third Fibonacci number, defining comparison, addition, and subtraction each as one step. Although C takes three steps by itself, it takes a total of five steps to reach and complete: Even if A and B don't return a value, they take up one step each, just for the comparison. These steps are shown graphically in Figure 4.1.

```
F(3) = F(2) + F(1) (A+B+C = five steps)
    F(2) = F(1) + F(0)  (A+B+C = five steps)
        F(1) = 1 (A+B = two steps)
        F(0) = 0 (A = one step)
    F(1) = 1 (A+B = two steps)
```

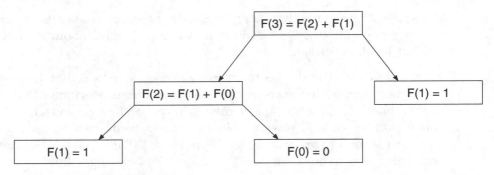

Figure 4.1 Calculating Fibonacci(3).

So, F3 = 1 + 1 = 2. It took us 15 steps to calculate this number. It takes 28 steps to calculate the fourth, and 48 steps to calculate the fifth. What's this? The number of steps is almost doubling each time, as Table 4.4 shows.

As you calculate more Fibonacci numbers, the ratio gradually approaches 1.61803. This is a *bad thing*, because if you find that the number of steps is *increasing by a constant ratio*, you know that the number of steps is increasing *exponentially*. The number of steps is somewhere in the ballpark of 1.6^n (it gets closer to this for larger n), where n is the input, or which Fibonacci number you want to calculate. What you may not know is that this is bad, very bad indeed. For example, when you calculate the 40th Fibonacci number, this algorithm takes over 1 billion steps!

At this point, it should be clear how a poorly designed algorithm can lose the ability to scale, even for seemingly small inputs.

Table 4.4 Hideous Exponential Growth

INPUT	OUTPUT	NUMBER OF STEPS	RATIO TO PREVIOUS NUMBER OF STEPS
1	1	2	N/A
2	1	8	4 to 1
3	2	15	1.88 to 1
4	3	28	1.87 to 1
5	5	48	1.71 to 1
6	8	81	1.69 to 1
7	13	134	1.65 to 1

What do you do with an algorithm that wastes so many CPU cycles? It would be much better if you could get the numbers to increase in a linear, quadratic, or logarithmic fashion. Both Skiena and Flamig include discussions of how to compute the complexity of algorithms. The ideal algorithms will progress at a logarithmic or linear rate. Table 4.5, based on Table 1.1 from *Practical Algorithms in C++*, shows where different progressions can lead.

Functions that have a constant complexity function (not shown in Table 4.5) may also be desirable. These functions take the same number of steps, no matter how large the input. If the constant is small enough (one or two steps would be nice), this level of complexity is desirable. However, if the constant is huge (such as 4 million steps), a constant complexity is less desirable.

As it turns out, it is possible to convert some nasty exponential algorithms to something more manageable. Skiena suggests something similar to the following algorithm:

```
Fibonacci(n):
    If n is zero, return zero (A)
    If n is one, return one (B)
    Allocate an array f[], with length n.
    Set f[0] to 0 (C)
    Set f[1] to 1 (D)
    For i = 2 to n:
        Set f[i] to the sum of f[i - 1] and f[i - 2] (E)
    Return f[n]
```

What does this algorithm do? If you feed it a one or a zero, it gets out of there as soon as possible and returns the value you passed to it. Otherwise, it prepares an array of size n, and sets the first two elements to zero and one, respectively. Then, it iterates over the remaining elements (2 to n) and sets each element to the sum of the two elements before it. When it's done, it returns the final element, which is the Fibonacci number you want.

Table 4.5 The Complexity of Functions, Where n Is the Size of the Input

COMPLEXITY	n = 1	n = 16	n = 64	n = 65536
Linear (n)	1	16	64	65,536
Quadratic (n^2)	1	256	4,096	4,294,967,296
Exponential (2^n)	2	65,536	18,446,744,073,709,551,616	Unbelievably Huge
Logarithmic ($\log_2 n$)	0	4	6	16 (sweet!)

Let's walk through calculating the third Fibonacci number:

```
initial comparisons (A+B = two steps)
f[0] = 0 (C = one step)
f[1] = 1 (D = one step)
f[2] = 1 (E = five steps)
f[3] = 2 (E = five steps)
```

Taking each assignment, comparison, addition, subtraction, and loop iteration as a single step (which is why step E adds up to 5 steps), we can see that this takes 14 steps. At first glance, it doesn't seem much better than the first implementation. But, if you look at Table 4.6, you'll see that this solution does not grow as quickly as the exponential solution. In fact, this solution follows the linear function 4.8n, which grows at a respectable rate. Remember how the original algorithm would take over 1 billion steps to compute the 40th Fibonacci number? According to 4.8n, the new algorithm will compute it in approximately 4.8 * 40 = 192 steps!

Both Skiena and Flamig discuss the Big Oh notation, a formal method of modeling algorithmic complexity that is similar to the informal analysis we used in this section. Also, both books offer strategies for transforming algorithms that don't scale well. Although it's possible to modify some algorithms so they don't become unworkable on large data sets, some classes of problems cannot be fixed in this way. These problems are known as *intractable* or *NP-complete*, and are discussed in Skiena and Flamig. The NP in NP-complete stands for nondeterministic polynomial, which means that there is no solution without human intervention that executes in polynomial time. Putting the big words aside, NP-complete problems are those for which the solution has an exponential complexity, such as the 2^n entry in Table 4.5. Examples of algorithms that execute in polynomial time include linear, quadratic, and logarithmic time.

Table 4.6   Manageable Growth

INPUT	OUTPUT	NUMBER OF STEPS	4.8N
1	1	2	4.8
2	1	9	9.6
3	2	14	14.4
4	3	19	19.2
5	5	24	24
6	8	29	28.8
7	13	34	33.6

Building Routines and Modules

If you know what behaviors your objects must have, and you've designed important algorithms, you can start building routines. Even at the routine level, you need to do a certain amount of design work.

PDL

PDL (Program Design Language) is a tool for designing routines that was developed by the company Caine, Farber, & Gordon. McConnell suggests a generalized version of PDL that is very useful for building routines.

If you've ever written all the comments first and filled in the code later, you've used a form of PDL. PDL is essentially a comments-to-code-to-comments method for writing routines. The following steps to follow when writing a routine using PDL are based on this methodology.

1. Describe the purpose of the routine. What is the routine going to do? What are its input and outputs? You should be able to find the routine's purpose in the specification for the system. If not, the specification needs to be revised. This description becomes the routine's header comment. Here is a description of a sample routine:

   This routine attempts to find the least number among a list of numbers. It is acceptable to have more than one occurrence of a number in the input, but the routine should emit a warning if the least number occurs more than once. This routine returns two values: the least number, and the number of times that number occurs in the input. If the input array is empty, this routine will return undefined values and print a warning.

2. Figure out the name of the routine. As Dr. Evil (Austin Powers' arch-nemesis) might have said were he a programmer, "I shall call him mini_count()."

3. Determine the algorithms and data structures you will use. Jot this down somewhere, and use it as a guide when you write the PDL (we'll also put this into the source code as the description of the routine):

   This routine will sort the input array and store the result in another array. Since the array is sorted, the minimum value will be the first element of the array. Further, if the minimum value occurs more than once in the input, each extra occurrence will be adjacent to the first element of the sorted array. The routine can get a count of extra occurrences by counting these duplicate elements that appear at the beginning of the array.

4. Write the PDL in human language, not in a programming language. The PDL is a direct translation of the algorithm and data structure description into an explicit outline of the steps that the routine takes. Avoid the temptation to use PDL to describe *how* the routine will proceed. Instead, focus on the level of intent: *what* you want the routine to do. What versus how can be a subtle distinction. Here is the PDL:

```
if the array is empty
    set the return values to undefined or null
    print a warning message
else if the array is not empty
    sort the input array numerically into another array
    remove and save element one (the min) of the new array
    set the count to one
    while the top value of the sorted array equals the min
        remove the top element
        add one to the count
    if the count is greater than one
        print out a warning message
return the min and the count
```

5. Check the PDL. Keep checking and refining the PDL until you feel it is time to write the code.

6. Write the routine declaration and opening/closing braces. Indent as appropriate. Use the algorithm and data structure description as the description of the routine:

```
# This routine will sort the input array and store the
# result in another array. Since the array is sorted, the
# minimum value will be the first element of the array.
# Further, if the minimum value occurs more than once in the
# input, each extra occurrence will be adjacent to the first
# element of the sorted array. The routine can get a count
# of extra occurrences by counting these duplicate elements
# that appear at the beginning of the array.
#
sub mini_count {

  if the array is empty
      set the return values to undefined or null
      print a warning message
  else if the array is not empty
      sort the input array numerically into another array
      remove and save element one (the min) of the new array
      set the count to one
      while the top value of the sorted array equals the min
          remove the top element
          add one to the count
```

```
            if the count is greater than one
                print out a warning message
        return the min and the count


    }
```

7. Turn the remaining PDL into comments.

```
# This routine will sort the input array and store the
# result in another array. Since the array is sorted, the
# minimum value will be the first element of the array.
# Further, if the minimum value occurs more than once in the
# input, each extra occurrence will be adjacent to the first
# element of the sorted array. The routine can get a count
# of extra occurrences by counting these duplicate elements
# that appear at the beginning of the array.
#
sub mini_count {

  # if the array is empty
      # set the return values to undefined or null
      # print a warning message
  # else if the array is not empty
      # sort the input array numerically into another array
      # remove and save element one (the min) of the new array
      # set the count to one
      # while the top value of the sorted array equals the min
          # remove the top element
          # add one to the count
      # if the count is greater than one
          # print out a warning message
  # return the min and the count


}
```

8. Fill in the rest of the code, adding variable declarations as necessary. In Perl (unlike many programming languages), parameters are not declared in the function prototype. Instead, arguments are passed in through @_, the parameter list.

```
# This routine will sort the input array and store the
# result in another array. Since the array is sorted, the
# minimum value will be the first element of the array.
# Further, if the minimum value occurs more than once in the
# input, each extra occurrence will be adjacent to the first
# element of the sorted array. The routine can get a count
# of extra occurrences by counting these duplicate elements
# that appear at the beginning of the array.
#
```

```perl
sub mini_count {

    @input_array = @_;  # fetch the argument

    $min_value = 0; # The minimum (return value)
    $min_count = 0; # The count (return value)

    # if the array is empty
    if ( ! @input_array ) {

        # set the return values to undefined or null
        $min_value = undef;
        $min_count = undef;

        # print a warning message
        warn "mini_count() received an empty array!";

    # else if the array is not empty
    } else {

        # sort the input array numerically into another array
        @sorted_array = sort { $a <=> $b } @input_array;

        # remove and save element one (the min) of the new array
        $min_value = shift @sorted_array;

        # set the count to one
        $min_count = 1;

        # while the top value of the sorted array equals the min
        while ($sorted_array[0] == $min_value) {

            # remove the top element
            shift @sorted_array;

            # add one to the count
            $min_count++;

        }

        # if the count is greater than one
        if ($min_count > 1) {

            # print out a warning message
            warn "Minimum value is greater than one.";

        }
    }

    # return the min and the count
```

```
    return ($min_value, $min_count);

}
```

Modularity

In Chapter 5, "Object-Oriented Programming," you will learn about object-oriented programming. The object-oriented approach derives a lot of its power from the fact that it hides information. In a well-designed system, objects are not tightly bound to one another. Instead, they use a carefully defined collection of methods to allow other objects to access their behavior and data. The information that these methods protect is important, as is the information that these methods publicize.

This act of information hiding is a key component of modular programming. A *module* is a group of routines that share common data. Like an object, a module can be looked at as a collection of behaviors and data. Unlike an object, a module doesn't come with inheritance or polymorphism. However, the notions that are fundamental to modular programming can be applied to object-oriented programming as well. In fact, it's useful to look at modular programming without the conceptual baggage of object-oriented programming. Not that there's anything wrong with that baggage, but looking at modularity alone offers the opportunity for some unique insights.

McConnell identifies three components of the modular approach that are key: cohesion, coupling, and information hiding. Of the three, we'll look at information hiding most closely.

Cohesion and coupling are two closely related features of modules. We're not going to say whether a module is cohesive or coupled. Instead, we'll look at *how cohesive* a module is, and *how coupled* a module is to other routines outside the module.

A good module should have high cohesion. When you design a module, try to rank it based on the answers to the following questions. The more strongly you feel that the answer is "yes," the more cohesion the module has.

Do the module's routines clearly belong together? Example: a collection of routines for connecting to, querying, and updating databases.

Does every routine in the module share common data? Example: a module that simulates the gravitational effects of an object. This module would have routines to manipulate such data like the speed, position, and mass of the object.

If the routines in the module don't share data, are the routines conceptually related in another way? Example: A general-purpose library that can concatenate, split, or perform substitutions on strings.

A good module should have low coupling with other modules. Low coupling means that other routines and modules don't have to tinker with the internal structure of the module. In the gravitational effects example, if changing the mass of the object requires you to also change its shape slightly, it's best to have an accessor method PutMass() that sets the mass and updates the shape by invoking a private method that routines outside the module can't access. Thus, the PutMass() method lets the other routines remain loosely coupled to your module in that they don't need to know about the internals of the module. Figure 4.2 shows an example of two objects that are highly coupled, while Figure 4.3 shows two objects that exhibit lower coupling.

Information Hiding

Coupling is closely related to the notion of information hiding. Loosely coupled modules hide internal data and private information well. Information hiding has a lot more depth, though. It is a technique that will make your programs safer, more maintainable, and more understandable to other programmers. One practical benefit of hiding information is that when something changes (such as when you port your application to a different GUI library), you only need to change your code in one place: the module that hid the GUI dependency from the rest of the system.

McConnell refers to the information you hide as "secrets." He goes on to suggest some categories of information that you might want to hide. The following list of categories is based on McConnell's list, but with some changes. In

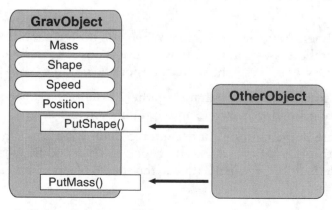

Figure 4.2 High coupling.

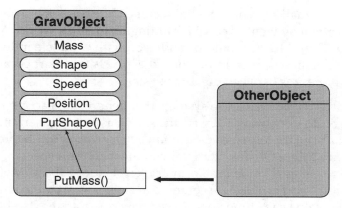

Figure 4.3   Low coupling.

looking at each of these categories, you'll see the virtues of information hiding, and in contemplating how these techniques can be applied to an object-oriented approach, you'll find ways to make your applications stronger.

GUI dependencies. The X Windows system is blessed (or cursed, depending on how you look at it) with a wide variety of GUI toolkits. These include Motif/LessTif, GTK+, QT, Tk, and many others. If you write an application that uses a GUI interface, you should consider isolating the code that deals with the GUI. This will make it easier for you and others to port the application to another GUI toolkit or to systems with radically different sets of fonts and display sizes such as palm devices.

Nonstandard language features. Are you using a language extension or library that is not widely available? If so, isolate the parts of your program that do this in a separate module. It will make it easier to port your application to an environment or platform that does not support the extension or library.

Cutting-edge libraries. Are you using a cutting-edge version of a library that has phrases like "alpha release," "developers only," or "deprecated API" in the documentation? If you think the library is volatile, chances are that the interface will change. It's a good idea to isolate the parts of your application that deal with the library into separate modules.

Business logic. Many applications are used to automate or model certain business processes. These processes are shaped by rules, policies, and laws. If the laws change, so must the program. Do what you can to isolate business logic within modules.

Areas of potential change. If you've identified an area of the system that is very likely to change, make sure to put that part in its own module.

In addition to McConnell's list of potential secrets, there are some secrets that database developers may want to consider hiding. In an ideal world, APIs such as DBI, ODBC, and JDBC would provide you with complete independence from your database server. In practice, these APIs fall short because of the amount of differences between database systems.

There are several aspects of database systems that generic data access APIs cannot address, or do not always fully address. One aspect is generating unique values for primary keys (see *Generating Unique Values* in Chapter 9, "Databases"). With Mini SQL, for example, you must access a special _seq (sequence) field to get new value for a primary key. Under Sybase, MySQL, and other databases, you can declare columns in such a way that they get a unique sequential value each time you insert a new row into the database. To make things more complicated, some database developers choose to make use of a separate table for managing and generating sequential keys.

Does your program rely on features of your database server that are not handled by the database access API? If so, move these parts into a separate module. When it comes time to port your application to a different database, someone will be thankful!

Summary

When you get ready to build something, the first thing you should do is have a look around for reusable components. One of the benefits of all the free software development that goes on is the development of reusable libraries. A perfect example of this is GTK+, which was developed to support the GIMP, but has been used in many other applications.

When you can't reuse, you may need to build something yourself. When you do this, pay attention to issues that affect the readability, design, and modularity of your code. The world needs more modular and readable implementations of robust and fast algorithms. When you develop code for Linux, you can either contribute a new puzzle for people to solve, or another tile in the mosaic of free software.

Object-Oriented Programming

Object-oriented programming is a paradigm that was developed to facilitate the design and development of large and complex projects, to encourage software reuse, and to decrease software maintenance time. The introduction of object-oriented programming is the most significant change in computer science since the introduction of subroutines, and has similar revolutionary and evolutionary characteristics. If you are used to procedural programming, transitioning to object-oriented programming will require a conceptual, rather than tactical, shift. The algorithms that you use to compute a result will remain the same, but the way in which you organize and link those algorithms will change. So, while the bad news is that you will have to adjust to a new way of thinking about programs, the good news is that good procedural design practices (and programming techniques) will be better supported and easier to implement under this new paradigm.

Since the goal of object-oriented programming is to support the development of large and complicated programs, and to reduce the maintenance cost of *all* programs, we can find much direct support in the syntax of object-oriented languages for good design practices. Here we examine the built-in constructs that the object-oriented languages provide to support the design process. In Chapter 8, "Object-Oriented Design," we look at some ways to design object-oriented applications.

Characteristics of Object-Oriented Languages

In this section, we will consider some of the main features of object-oriented languages, including:

Encapsulation. Hiding information and behavior behind an interface.

Classes. Using encapsulation to mirror the behavior of real-world objects.

Interfaces. Defining the types of interactions you can have with an object.

Abstract Classes. Defining behaviors that are shared among different classes.

Inheritance. Sharing behavior much in the same way that organisms share genes.

Polymorphism. Interchanging classes that have the same or similar interfaces.

Encapsulation

One of the main innovations in object-oriented programming is the robust integration of program and data. Each individual object is a combination of attributes (data) and methods (behavior represented by program code). This combination is referred to as *encapsulation* (behavior and data are encapsulated in an object in the same way that pain-relieving chemicals are encapsulated in a gel tab). Encapsulation is extended from one object to another through *visibility modifiers*. An object may declare its attributes and methods Public, Private, or Protected (the names of modifiers vary from language to language). These visibility modifiers govern whether one object may access the attributes or methods of another object. The use of visibility modifiers is called *information hiding*.

As an example, consider a book in a public library loan application. Books are due to be returned two weeks after they are checked out. In a procedural program, you would need the following:

- A location in memory to store the identity of the book.
- The date the book was checked out.
- A function to figure out when the book was due back.
- A way to pass the date when the book was checked out to the function that figures out when the book is supposed to be returned.

Encapsulation lets us create a book object, which:

- Uniquely identifies the book with the book's ISBN number and its title (data).

- Has an attribute that contains the date when the book was checked out (data).

- Has a method, such as getDueDate, that adds two weeks to the check-out date to determine the return date (behavior).

Having used encapsulation to implement the logic of a book loan, you can develop a variety of subsystems for checking books out, without having to concern yourself with how to figure out when the book is due back. In addition, if the library policy changes, and books are to be lent for only one week, rather than two, you only need to change one piece of code (such as the getDueDate method of the book object) to upgrade all of your checkout systems to the new policy.

Let's extend the example to use information hiding. We will declare the attribute, checkedOutDate, to be private, and add a method, setCheckedOutDate, and declare it public. When a subsystem wants to check a book out, it calls the setCheckedOutDate method of the book, and passes it the date when it was checked out, as in setCheckedOutDate("October 1, 2002"). The setCheckOutDate method then updates the checkedOutDate attribute, and the getDueDate method functions as before.

Now let's suppose than the library bought a lot of bar code scanners that are not Y2K compliant. If the scanners had been directly updating the checkedOutDate attribute of the book, the only way you could check books out after December 31, 1999 would be to replace all of the scanners. However, since we used information hiding, rather than having to replace all of the magnetic scanners, all we need to do is update the setCheckedOutDate method to use something such as a Y2K windowing technique to adjust the incorrect dates, and the system will continue to function normally.

Classes

We use *classes* to specify the structure and behavior of sets of these encapsulated objects. This is an organizing principle that facilitates the design of encapsulated objects. A class is a kind of "cookie cutter" for describing and creating sets of objects, or instances of the class, that have a common set of features. In most applications there are many occurrences (or instances) of objects that have the same attributes and methods. Classes are a refinement, and extension, of a structure or record in a procedural language, such as the C language's structs. In fact, the C++ compiler implements C++ classes as C structs.

Classes are a *refinement* of structures, in that they support all the data aspects of structures while incorporating encapsulation and information hiding facilities. Classes are an *extension* of structures in that they support inheritance, which we will cover later in this chapter.

Let's look at two alternate definitions of the Book class, using similar syntax to Java. The first version of the Book class allows external objects to directly manipulate the checkOutDate and name properties by giving them public visibility:

```
class Book {
    public checkOutDate, name;
    public getDueDate() {
        return checkOutDate + 14;
    }
}
```

The second version uses encapsulation, which provides a superior design (for reasons we'll explore througout the chapter). It hides the checkOutDate and name properties, and requires external objects to use the setCheckedOut-Date() and setName() methods to change it:

```
class Book {
    private checkOutDate, name;
    public getDueDate() {
        return checkOutDate + 14;
    }
    public setName(new_name) {
        name = new_name;
    }
    public setCheckedOutDate(pDate) {
    checkOutDate = dateFix(pDate);
    }
    private dateFix(pDate) {
            // Some windowing code that fixes
            // various Y2K problems.
        }
}
```

In a minute, we will explain the definitions of the book objects, but first let us show what the scanner program might look like (scanner1 corresponds to the first version of the Book class while scanner2 corresponds to the second):

```
program scanner1 {
    Book thisBook = new Book();
    thisBook.name = "Valis"
       thisBook.checkOutDate = "01-01-99";
}
```

```
program scanner2() {
    Book thisBook = new Book();
    thisBook.setName("Valis");
        thisBook.setCheckedOutDate("01-01-99");
}
```

Both of these programs do the same thing. Both start by creating an instance of the Book class. After creating the object, the scanner gives it a name, to distinguish this instance of the class Book from any other instance of the class Book. Having gotten an instance of the Book class, the program can begin to operate on the object, by accessing attributes of the object (scanner1) or by calling methods of the object (scanner2).

Now, let's look at the attributes and methods of the Book objects. In the first version, the checkOutDate attribute is public. Any other application can access the checkOutDate attribute, either to read it or to update it.

In the second version, the checkOutDate attribute is private, and may only be accessed by methods of the Book object itself. Also, getDueDate and setCheckOutDate are public methods; and dateFix is a private method. While private methods may only be called by other methods in the object, public methods can be used by external objects/users to access the private data, and the collection of all of the public methods of a class is called its *interface*.

Interfaces

Interfaces are a very important object-oriented design concept. With an interface, you are entering into an agreement describing the services that the object will provide and how an external application can use these services. Interfaces enable large system development by allowing you to share a terse description of a piece of code rather than having to share the source code itself. The ease with which you can develop check-out subsystems around the Book object is entirely dependent on the Book's interface being well designed and widely published.

Interfaces refine and extend the procedural concepts of header files and Application Programming Interfaces (APIs). Interfaces *refine* APIs by implementing function entry points in a more granular and secure way. Interfaces *extend* APIs by allowing programs to work together dynamically, at run time or design time, rather than statically, at compile time.

Object Models

Component object models (such as Mozilla's XPCom, KDE's KParts, and GNOME's Bonobo) and Distributed object models (such as CORBA and RMI) work hand in hand with the run-time binding facilities of interfaces. Actually, there is much overlap in these things—many component object models include some distributed features (GNOME's Bonobo, for example, is based on CORBA, a distributed component architecture that is discussed in Chapter 15, "Introduction to CORBA").

Object models enable the development of large and complex systems and reduce the programming costs associated with such systems. The larger the project you are working on, the more likely it is that someone else has already developed some portion of the system. Taking advantage of these existing programs immediately reduces the programming effort involved in developing your system, and having these programs be supported by the original author reduces the ongoing maintenance costs of your system.

To return to our Book example, there are thousands of libraries in the United States, all of which have to check out and return books. Chances are, there is already a perfectly adequate Book object out there. In fact there may be hundreds. Let's suppose that each publisher, when they ship a book to the library, also ships their version of a Book object. When you write your check-out program, you have no way of knowing which publisher's book is being checked out. Using a component object model, the check-out system could query the Book that is being checked out, asking it what check-out methods it supports, and then call the appropriate check-out method of the Book. Suppose you wanted to enhance your check-out program to include inter-library loans. Using a distributed object model, the check-out program could ask another library in the system to send a copy of the interface that the remote Book object supports, and then call the appropriate check-out method on that interface.

Abstract Classes

Abstract classes are a way of specifying interfaces without supplying the implementation. The previous example assumes that every Book object has an appropriate check-out method. Being able to dynamically query an interface is all fine and good, but if the interface doesn't contain the method you need, you are out of luck. Abstract classes address this situation, by guaranteeing that types of objects support particular methods.

Let's look at how abstract classes enable the development of complex systems. In any large development project (in fact, whenever there is more than one developer working on the project), a number of tasks will have to be completed concurrently. If it takes two months to develop the check-out system, and two months to develop the book object, and you have three months to deliver the entire system, you can't have the check-out developer sitting around until the book developer has completed his work. The solution is that you spend one month designing the Abstract class of Book. It doesn't take the full two months to create the abstract class, because you only describe the interface the Book object needs to support, and you don't have to get into the nitty-gritty algorithms of doing the things a book needs to do. Once you have the abstract class, you can distribute it to the check-out developer and the book implementation developer, who can both work with the guarantee that when they put their separate code bases together, their systems will work as designed.

Here is a Java style definition of the abstract Book class:

```
public abstract class AbstractBook {
    public abstract getDueDate();

    public setName(new_name);
    public abstract setCheckOutDate(pDate);
}
```

As you can see, the abstract class is very simple. So simple, in fact, that it doesn't do anything at all. Because abstract classes are designed to be specifications, rather than implementations, you cannot instantiate an abstract class. The way in which you complete the implementation, and allow your object to be used by other programs, is through *inheritance*.

Inheritance

Inheritance is an object-oriented construct that makes it easier for the programmer to reuse code and organize objects into hierarchies whenever they have similar-features. Here is a Java style definition of the Book class:

```
public class Book extends AbstractBook {
    private checkOutDate;
    public getDueDate() {
        return checkOutDate + 14;
    }
    public setCheckedOutDate(pDate) {
        checkOutDate = dateFix(pDate);
    }
    private dateFix(pDate) {
        // Some windowing code that fixes
        // various Y2K problems.
    }
}
```

When we use the keyword *extends*, what we are saying is that this subclass, Book, inherits all of the characteristics of its superclass, AbstractBook. Because AbstractBook is abstract, any class that inherits from AbstractBook must implement the two methods defined in AbstractBook: getDueDate and setChecked-

OutDate. However, the Book class may go beyond this bare minimum, and implement as many additional methods and attributes as necessary.

The power of inheritance comes from the fact that in addition to inheriting from an abstract class, classes may also inherit from concrete (non-abstract) classes, and when you inherit from a concrete class, the subclass inherits all existing implementations of the methods and attributes of the superclass.

For example, Book is a nice object, but there are many different types of books. There are hardcover books and paperback books and art books and computer books. You could go on indefinitely. However, one thing that all of these books have in common is that they can be checked out of the library. So when you need to create another type of book, all you need to do is inherit from Book. Regardless of any special characteristics of your new type of Book, it can still be checked out, without any additional programming effort.

One benefit of Object inheritance, over say, human inheritance, is that you do not have to blindly accept your genetic limitations, but can pick and choose which characteristics you would like to change. In the same way that a subclass of an abstract class (such as Book) provides its own implementations of the abstract class interface, a subclass of a *concrete class* (that is, a class that can be instantiated, such as Book) can provide its own implementations of the Concrete Class Interface, overriding the implementation of the superclass.

Let's suppose that art books are just like books, except that they can only be checked out for one week, rather than two weeks. To accomplish this, all the artBook class needs to do is provide a new implementation of getDueDate. Here is an example:

```
public class ArtBook extends Book {
    public getDueDate() {
        return checkOutDate + 7;
    }
}
```

Books are not the only materials in a library. Suppose the library wants to start a new policy of lending Digital Video Discs. If you already have a DVD class, what you need to do now is implement check-out logic. All you need to do is define a new class, LoanableDVD, which inherits from both DVD and Book. The new class doesn't need to implement anything at all; every piece of required functionality already exists in the superclasses. The ability to inherit from more than one superclass is called *multiple inheritance*. Multiple inheritance is a little bit of a mixed bag. If you breed a horse and a donkey, you get a mule. If you breed a dolphin and a Chihuahua, you get something else entirely. Not all OO languages support multiple inheritance, and if it is supported, use it with care.

As an alternative to inheritance (and more frequently, multiple inheritance), you can use object nesting. At a very basic level, objects are nothing more than user-defined data types, and you can use objects the same way you use built-in data types. Instead of creating a LoanableDVD class that inherits from both Book and DVD, you can create a new class with two attributes, a Book object and a DVD object. Here is a Java style definition of the object and the scanner program:

```
public class LoanableDVD {
    public Book vBook;
    public DVD vDVD;
    public LoanableDVD {   // constructor
        vBook = new vBook(); // using a book under the hood
        vDVD = new vDVD();   // using a DVD under the hood
    }
}

program scanner3 {
    LoanableDVD item = new LoanableDVD();
    item.vBook.setCheckedOutDate("01-01-99");
}
```

Nested objects are very useful in a number of situations. However, if you use nested objects, rather than inheritance, you do not get the benefits of *polymorphism*.

Polymorphism

Polymorphism refers to the use of objects of different types that share the same methods. In the *Interfaces* section, we talked about the ability to use an object's interface, rather than the specific implementation, to access standard functionality across heterogeneous classes. In the *Inheritance* section, we talked about the possibility of inheriting from the concrete class Book, and using these subclasses of Book to implement library materials that have different attributes can still use existing check-out functionality. Polymorphism is the mechanism that allows us to implement these constructs, and achieve significant code reuse in software development.

In procedural programming, the unique identifier for a function is called its *signature*. Generally, a function signature consists of the function name and the number and data type of the function's arguments. In C, print_value(short) and print_value(long) are two separate functions, with separate implementations, which do (basically) the same thing. We have already discussed the fact that C++ compilers implement object-oriented constructs as C code. Let's look at the implications of function signatures in our check-out example.

Up to this point, we have examined things from the perspective of the book object, rather than the scanner program. Let's turn the example around, and look at things in terms of the scanner program. The scanner program has to set the check-out date on an unknown number of library materials. In a procedural paradigm, we would have to write a different function for every data type that needs to be checked out. So, while inheriting from Book reduces the amount of code we have to write for ArtBook, it increases the amount of code we have to write for Scanner, and when you are looking at things from the point of the Scanner developer, this isn't a very good trade-off at all. However, if we are using an object-oriented language for our scanner development, we can use polymorphism to get around the limitations of function signatures, and bring the same types of code reuse to Scanner that we achieved in Book. Here is a Java-style definition of the new Scanner class:

```
public class Scanner {

    public itemScanned(Book pBook) {
        return pBook.getDueDate();
    }
}

program Scan { // simulates checking out various materials
    Scanner vScanner = new Scanner();
    vScanner.itemScanned(new Book());
    vScanner.itemScanned(new ArtBook());
}
```

With this example, a single method in scanner, with a single implementation, is able to handle all possible check-out scenarios of any class that inherits from Book. The reason you can do this is because the compiler expands the function signature to accept the literal data type of the argument as well as any subclasses of that data type. In addition, the compiler will select the appropriate implementation of the method, so that itemScanned(ArtBook) will return seven days, while itemScanned(Book) will return 14 days.

But then again, who is to say what is appropriate? Suppose I really want the Book version of getDueDate, rather than the overridden version? Maybe Art students are allowed to borrow Art books for two weeks, while the general public can still only take Art books for one week. To access the Book version of the method, all we need to do is *cast* (perform a run-time conversion of one type to another, in this case, a subclass to its parent class) the ArtBook Object to a Book Object, and let the compiler or run-time environment take care of the rest. Here is an example:

```
program Scan1 {
    Scanner vScanner = new Scanner();
```

```
        if (person.isArtStudent()) {
            vScanner.itemScanned( (Book) new ArtBook());
        } else {
            vScanner.itemScanned(new ArtBook());
        }
    }
```

Summary

In this chapter, we introduced the major constructs of object-oriented programming. This is not to be confused with object-oriented design, which is used in the preliminary stages of the conception of a software system. We can easily confuse the two since many software engineers use object-oriented language to describe the more detailed parts of their design. In later chapters we talk in more detail about object-oriented design. In this chapter, we introduced encapsulation, inheritance, polymorphism, and message passing as the major constructs of object-oriented programming. We provided this information in the belief that object-oriented languages, if coupled with good design procedures, can provide more affordable, more complete, and more manageable software systems. In the next chapter, we'll look at the issues involved with software development life cycles, with a particular leaning toward open-source software projects.

Software Engineering

I n the previous chapter we discussed strategies for code reuse using object-oriented (OO) languages. But why is code reuse so important? To understand the push toward OO, and the way in which it encourages code reuse, we need to look at some commonly accepted beliefs in software engineering that were put forth in Frederick P. Brooks' *The Mythical Man-Month* (Addison-Wesley, 1995):

Communication. The complexity and communication costs of a project rise with the square of the number of developers, while work done only rises linearly. While four programmers may get twice as much work done as two, the project becomes six times as expensive and complex, so the extra work you get out of the two programmers is wasted.

Maintenance. The total cost of maintaining a widely used program is typically 40 percent or more of the cost of developing it.

Regression testing. A change to any piece of code requires that, in addition to testing the changed code, every piece of code that interacts with the changed code be retested.

Wheel reinvention. Every experienced programmer has a toolkit of algorithms and routines for common programming tasks. Rarely are these toolkits shared between programmers.

Productivity. A good programmer is more productive than a mediocre programmer by a factor of 10.

Object-Oriented Development to the Rescue?

Object-oriented analysis and design, which is discussed in Chapters 7 and 8, address these concerns very well. UML diagrams, interfaces, and abstract classes reduce the communication costs from designers to programmers as well as between programmers. Inheritance ensures that changes to a base class will be reflected in all subclasses, reducing the amount of code that must be maintained. Using interfaces dramatically reduces regression testing requirements, because you only have to retest the interface, rather than every piece of code that uses the interface. Component Object models (such as GNOME's Bonobo or KDE's KParts) allow a standard set of routines to be used by all programmers on a project. And by allocating base classes to more productive programmers and subclasses to less productive programmers, you can raise the production rates of the entire team.

These techniques should enable software engineers to produce more, higher quality code in less time for a lower cost. Unfortunately, despite the wide-spread adoption of object-oriented approaches in the 1990s, software still took a long time to develop, had bugs, was difficult to maintain, and cost a lot of money. Does the fact that the fundamental problems of software engineering remain, despite demonstratively better tools and approaches, mean that OO is invalid? No, but perhaps it suggests that modern applications are more complex, and in some cases, OO is not being applied correctly.

Is Bigger Better?

Software delivered today, albeit late, buggy, and over-budget, is much more complex, functional, and easy to use than software delivered, late, buggy, and over-budget 10 years ago. In the early 1980s I spent several months writing a program to allow users to draw certain geometric shapes on a screen by typing in a long string of obscure commands. Today, you could render the shapes in 3D, choosing whatever shape you want, with a click of the mouse, and it will still take me a couple of months to write. My skill as a programmer, quadratic equations, and software engineering have not changed, what has changed are the requirements for what a graphing package should do, and my ability to reuse the huge libraries of code already developed.

In some ways, software is a victim of its own success. A good piece of software just raises the bar for what is considered acceptable in that category, and makes users of software in other categories wonder why their program doesn't have those types of features. While this is not a bad problem to have, it is still a problem, and in order to meet the next generation of software complexity requirements, we may have to rethink our whole approach to software engineering.

Two crucial components to success in classical software engineering are communication and regression testing, because they both have exponential, rather than linear, effects. Most of the code reuse strategies in object-oriented programming are based on enabling binary reuse (reusing an object as a component or precompiled library). This eliminates the need to have access to the source code you are reusing, which is good because controlling source code addresses the two nonlinear problems of classical software engineering:

Program correctness. Uncontrolled changes to source code drive quality assurance managers crazy: unless they know exactly which programs were changed, in what order, they have to rerun the entire suite of test cases.

Project management. Giving new developers access to the source code on a project drives project managers crazy. They have to spend days, perhaps weeks, instructing the new programmer in the nuances and stylistic tics of the code base before the new programmer can even start to be productive, which pushes the project farther behind, which causes more developers to be added to the project, and so on.

The typical approach to these two problems was in the makeup of the development team. The classical software engineering team was made up of a single, omnipotent software architect (the Hero), surrounded by a small group of core developers and a huge body of test cases, run by a faceless army of semi-automated drones in the testing department:

Ensuring program correctness. The only way to ensure program correctness was to have a test case for every feature in the program. In some projects, this would mean a test case for every function, and with the demands of regression testing, the only way to make it through all of the test cases was to use drones. The drones would run the test case, record the output, and send it back to development if the output diverged from the test result baseline in any way.

Project management. You couldn't add any new developers later on in the project, so you needed a project manager to constantly monitor the progress of the project. Without this constant monitoring, it became impossible to make up time if there was slippage early in the project: The manager needed to know about slippage as soon as possible to manipulate the feature set to work around the slippage. This often involved splitting the project up into two phases: deliver a subset of functionality by the original ship date, and add the remaining features in a second phase.

Classical software engineering remained constant from procedural programming through object-oriented programming. The fact that the central problems of software engineering remain is not the result of a failure of object-oriented programming (it was only the benefits and efficiencies of OO that allowed software to continue to meet increased requirements). The fact that the central problems of software engineering remain is the result of a failure in classical software engineering and, specifically, the failure of software engineering to incorporate the possibilities of the global Internet.

The Cathedral and the Bazaar

Eric Raymond, in his provocative series of essays, "The Cathedral and the Bazaar," (www.tuxedo.org/~esr/writings/) brings the example of open source, community software, and specifically the development of the Linux operating system, to illustrate how the failure of classical software engineering to address the central problems of software development can be corrected. The crux of Raymond's argument, as it pertains to classical software engineering, is that by opening your source code to the community of developers and users of the global Internet, you can bring sufficient additional resources to bear on its development, testing, and maintenance problems. Further, you not only overcome the exponential issues of communication and regression testing, but create software that has the functions users actually *want*, rather than just those specified in the requirements document and enforced in the body of test cases.

Using the Internet reduces communication costs significantly. Communicating via email is considerably more efficient than communicating face to face. Because you have a quantifiable record of the body of questions and answers over time, you can create a compilation of frequently asked questions (FAQs), which brings the same sort of benefits to software engineering communication that base classes bring to OO programming.

Using a mailing list means that you can effectively clone the project lead. The questions that the project lead previously had to respond to personally can now be answered by anyone on the list who has the answer (and answers to frequently asked questions can make their way on to permanent lists of such answers, called FAQs).

Using the Internet also enormously increases the number of developers available for a project, with a rate of growth that is greater than the growth in the communications cost. If you have five inhouse developers, and you try to add five more inhouse developers, the communications overhead will have a negative impact on the project. However, if you add 50 Internet developers, the overall effect will be positive, despite the increase in communications overhead (which is mitigated by FAQs and mailing lists). In addition, if participation in the project is open to anyone who is interested, you are much more likely to get skilled, motivated programmers from the Internet, whose productivity will likely be 10 times higher than the mediocre, clock-punching programmers you could get inhouse. Often, the reason inhouse programmers are available to be added to a project that is falling behind is because they are not doing anything useful on their current project!

The solution to the testing issues involves a change in the definition of software quality. In classical software engineering, it was a truism that you never test using developers, for they have too much of an understanding of why things can go wrong and too much empathy for the original developers. The thinking went that they will not provide you with objective feedback about the performance of the program. It was also a truism that users and developers often disagree about what constitutes a bug. This leads to the requirement that any user feedback must be filtered by a "responsible" project manager, who would classify and prioritize issues (with the most common classifications being "Functioning as Designed" and "Training Issue" and the most common priority being "On Hold"). If you define software quality as an external metric, rather than the satisfaction of the users, software will always be unsatisfactory. Users don't care about requirements documents or successful test cases, they care about being able to do *what they want to do*.

Once you redefine software quality in this way, it is clear that what you actually want is for your users to become developers and your developers to become testers, at least until an end-user-friendly release of your product ships. Consider Helix Code (www.helixcode.com), who distributes an end-user-friendly release of the GNOME desktop, complete with friendly installation and upgrade wizards. If your users are developers, they will be able to create satisfactory software, because they will be empowered to write the functions that they require, and modify the program to produce the output they desire. If your developers are testers, they will understand what the software is supposed to do, and be able to fix defects during the testing process, rather than putting the requests back into the already backed-up development queue.

This redefinition, along with the introduction of the Internet, again brings logarithmic benefits to the testing process, which overcome the exponential growth in testing requirements. The testing process becomes more efficient, because defects are fixed directly in the testing process, rather than in a separate development process. Adding 50 motivated Internet testers means that you don't have to try and minimize the number of test runs that your five, drone, inhouse testers have to perform; you can just go ahead and run the whole regression suite (by actually running the program) as often as you like. And making users your testers means that the failure to create a test case for every possible usage scenario no longer slips through the cracks, the proof is in the pudding, and if there is a defect, it will be found by some user, somewhere on the Internet, and that feedback will not be swept under the "On Hold" rug.

The Spiral Model, 4GL, and RAD

While Raymond's solution to classical software engineering is novel, the analysis of the fundamental flaws of classical software engineering is not. To rephrase the problem statement: Despite improvements in tools and techniques, software takes a long time to develop, costs too much, and has bugs. To rephrase the analysis: Modifying source code is exponentially difficult and users should be programmers. In the mid 1990s there was a movement in software engineering, which tried to deal with these issues, called Rapid Application Development.

There are two immediate functional problems with implementing a solution using this analysis. The first is that by and large, users are users because they can't or won't be programmers. Especially in the area of productivity tools, users use these tools because the program makes it easier or more convenient to access existing software functionality, not because they need functionality that does not already exist. The second is that although modifying source code takes time and creates bugs, the point of software engineering is to produce software, and that is not possible without code.

RAD attempted to address these problems by using software productivity tools to create and manage source code. They called these tools *Fourth Generation Languages* (4GL), and what these tools attempted to do was enable the creation of software by nonprogrammers, using pre-built components, property pages and drag-and-drop gestures to design, assemble, and compile programs.

Once these 4GL tools (Visual Basic, PowerBuilder, Oracle Forms) were available, it was possible to use a new model of software development. With 3GLs (the programming tools of classical software engineering such as C), most development followed a pattern called the Waterfall Model, which basically went through Requirements Gathering, Functional Specification, Design, Implementation, and Testing. With 4GLs a new pattern, called the Spiral Model, emerged.

In the Spiral Model, you start with Joint Application Design (JAD). Basically, you lock a collection of people from various disciplines (technical, functional, management) in a room together with one of those oversize flip pads and a bunch of magic markers, and don't let them out until they have decided what the software should do. Based on one of these magic marker designs, a developer would go off and use a 4GL tool to generate a prototype. The prototype didn't have to do much, it just had to give the various people from the JAD session an idea of what the software would look like and how it might be used. The developers would then implement the functionality behind the screens and buttons, still using the 4GL tool, and give the application to users to test. Over time, as users provided their feedback about the defects and required functionality of the software, the prototype would be refined, again and again, until users were satisfied with the end product.

RAD addressed the involvement of users and management of source code very well. The users were intimately involved with the requirements, specification, design, implementation, and testing of their application. If they didn't like the application they had no one to blame but themselves, and you would be amazed at how effective that can be in muting dissent. The source code was managed well, because there was, as far as the developers were concerned, no source code to manage. Everything was done by the 4GL, so if there was a defect in the software, it was a problem with the tool, not the developers' program. In addition, 4GLs are very effective at addressing code reuse, since everything is done with a pre-built component or framework, you are guaranteed that none of your programmers will be writing their own version of the quicksort algorithm. The maintenance costs of a RAD approach are higher than in classical software engineering, but are amortized over the life of the project, rather than incurred up front, and are offset by a decrease in requirements gathering and design time.

OO and 4GL

While many 4GL tools, with their abstraction of source code to component palettes, property pages, and dragging gestures, do not fully implement object-oriented techniques, the 4GL tools expose, both implicitly and explicitly, OO capabilities. In fact, 4GL tools were the killer app for the component object models we discussed in Chapter 5, "Object-Oriented Programming."

Problems with RAD

The problem with RAD was that development is a subdiscipline of programming. The applications that you can create using a 4GL are a very limited subset of the applications you can create using a 3GL. As an example, using C, you can create C++, and using C++ you can create Visual Basic, but if you only have Visual Basic, you are at the end of the line. Another consequence of the dependence of 4GLs on 3GLs was that it takes an entire generation of applications for structural innovations to trickle down to the developers.

The fatal example was the growth of the Internet. The most sophisticated pieces of software in the early 1990s (with the exception, perhaps, of the 4GLs themselves) were relational databases. So, 4GLs made it easy to access the functionality inherent in RDBMS software, and lots of people developed lots of applications that let users query tables and update records. But when the Internet became the raison d'etre of application development, it was impossible to access Internet services from 4GL tools, while 3GL tools could work very well with the Internet, and applications written using 3GLs raised the bar of end-user expectations to a place where they could not be fulfilled using existing 4GL tools.

4GLs were also problematic during installation. Because the generated application relied on services from the 4GL, to install an application written using a 4GL you also had to install the runtime of the 4GL on every machine that was going to run the application, and provide technical support at the desktop level to ensure that all of the required libraries were installed and configured properly. This extension of the technical support Help Desk raised serious concerns about the total cost of ownership of these types of applications. The positioning of browsers as a universal client, with a ubiquitous runtime for HTML, JavaScript, and Java made 4GLs seem much less attractive, and started a trend back toward centralization of application deployment.

All this being said, RAD is far from finished. The most recent generation of RAD tools are extremely Internet savvy, and generally, much more complex and capable than the previous releases. There is a huge population of 4GL developers, and because the barrier of entry is much lower to development than programming, that population is growing every day. But most importantly of all, for the right type of application, using a 4GL tool will produce functional software 10 to 20 times faster than using a 3GL tool, which means that you can effectively overcome the productivity difference between good and mediocre programmers by using a RAD approach.

Developers of tools are by and large a very clever bunch, and if we assume that they will continue to address current 4GL technical difficulties (arbitrary complexity limitations, configuration management, generation lagging), two main problems remain. One is that the programming barrier to entry is still too high to achieve the full participation of end users in the development process, and the other is that there is limited code reuse of functionality developed in the 4GL.

As previously stated, users are users because they can't or won't be programmers. Given that the latter is a personal preference, and hence, very difficult to change, 4GL tool developers targeted the former, lowering the programming barrier of entry to allow users who wanted to be programmers, but lacked the background or skill to contribute to the development process.

However, merging developers and programmers into the software engineering process became a project management headache. As a project manager, you really want everyone to use the same tools; otherwise, your testing and integration issues become all consuming. But because you have two different skill sets, you cannot optimize the contributions of each group; if you choose a powerful 3GL, your programmers are happy but your developers are frustrated, if you choose an easy-to-use 4GL your developers are happy but your programmers are frustrated. To bridge this gap, 4GL tools introduced code editors and compilers into the mix. What this did was enable both groups to access the appropriate level of complexity, while working in the same tool and environment. It also enabled some level of code reuse for functionality developed in the 4GL.

However, this design did not address the end users who won't be programmers, and in fact, left them farther removed from the software engineering process than ever before.

Scripting Languages and the Third Way

If I wake up one day and decide to write a full-featured spreadsheet, I'll probably write it in a 3GL such as C, C++, or Java. While this is arguably a matter of preference, these are the languages that many productivity applications are written in. In this day and age, a full-featured spreadsheet needs to be customizable, and one of the best ways to make something customizable is to add support for a scripting language such as Perl or Python (in fact, GNOME's Gnumeric spreadsheet is written in C, and the Python interpreter is embedded for just this purpose: see www.gnome.org/gnumeric).

When I sit down to write my spreadsheet, I will most likely follow all the best practices I can: come up with a good set of requirements (see Chapter 1, "Requirements"), employ a use-case driven analysis of the requirements (see Chapter 7, "Object-Oriented Analysis"), and use patterns for designing the application (see Chapter 8, "Object-Oriented Design"). This is what you'd expect me to do with a large application written in a 3GL: I am writing a program that deals with the general case of a problem, does lots of exception handling, is clearly coded and commented, and is going to be used and reused by other programmers and users (I am wearing the hat of a programmer).

But what happens when I'm working on a spreadsheet, and I need to write a macro subroutine to price my personal stock portfolio? Well, since the spreadsheet has support for a scripting language, I'll probably write something quick and dirty in Perl or Python, because I am writing a script that deals with a specific instance of a problem and I don't care about errors, exceptions, readability or reuse: I am the only person who will ever see or run this code (I am a user, now, using the scripting language to extend existing components and environments).

Some may argue that this is a sloppy way to do things, and that maybe I should consider extending the spreadsheet in a modular way, so that other people can price their stock portfolios. While this may be the case with certain problems, there will always be singular problems that are best fixed with something quick and dirty.

As with RAD, scripting languages let you glue together components created in higher level languages. Unlike RAD, you are not trapped in the box of your development environment. For example, I can:

- Use the Glade user interface tool (see Chapter 13, "GNOME") to design a GTK+ user interface.
- Display the user interface from within a Perl application (see www.glade.perl.connectfree.co.uk/index.html or the Glade home page at http://glade.pn.org).
- Use Perl's DBI (see Chapter 12, "DBI and Perl") to store the user's input into the database.

In this case, I'm using Perl as a scripting language (although Perl blurs the line between scripting languages and a 3GL) to glue together GTK+ and DBI, two large components that have been built by other people. And, if something's not fast enough, I can extend Perl with C, using Perl's open extension API. Scripting languages are a lot like RAD done right!

For an interesting perspective on 3GLs (referred to as system programming languages in the paper) and scripting languages, see John K. Ousterhout's *Scripting: Higher Level Programming for the 21st Century* at www.scriptics.com/people/john.ousterhout/scripting.html.

Tools Selection

So, given that there are two viable software engineering methodologies available to you, how do you decide which one to use? 3GL languages have the benefits that they are powerful and flexible, and have access to the most recent hardware and infrastructure innovations. 3GL applications generally require less support at the Help Desk level, and 3GL compilers and libraries are generally freely available and widely distributed. 3GL languages have the drawbacks that they require an up-front investment of time, both in terms of application design and programmer training, and that they require an ongoing investment in testing over the life of the project.

4GL and scripting languages have the benefit that they are easy to learn and easy to use, can produce usable software in a very short period of time, and keep you from making fundamental mistakes in the software design, because you rely on other people to build major components.

4GL languages have the drawbacks that they are limited in the type and complexity of applications that they can produce, generally have configuration management issues, and 4GL tools and components usually have to be purchased from software vendors. Scripting languages don't have these limitations: The most popular and successful scripting languages are open source, work well with configuration management tools, and are highly extensible.

The Magic Cauldron

In "The Cathedral and the Bazaar," Eric Raymond describes how to run a successful 3GL project (fetchmail, which is at www.tuxedo.org/~esr/fetchmail) as a community software initiative. And by and large, the great success stories (such as Perl, Apache, Linux) of the Open Source movement have been 3GL projects. In his essay "The Magic Cauldron," Eric Raymond discusses how the open source revolution will affect the economics of software development. He starts by describing the qualities a program must have to be a candidate for open source development:

> For purposes of examining this question, it will be helpful to sort kinds of software by the degree of completeness which the service they offer is describable by open technical standards, which is well correlated with how commoditized the underlying service has become. ... As middleware services become commoditized, they will in turn tend to fall into the open-source infrastructure—a transition we're seeing in operating systems right now. [tMC]

What is interesting for our argument is that the criteria Eric describes for a project to be open source are very similar to the criteria for a project to be executed with a scripting language. Open source software requires that the application be a commodity service with open technical standards. Scripting language applications exist as a collection of commoditized components that communicate through open, standards-based interfaces. He goes on to say:

> Finally, we may note that purveyors of unique or just highly differentiated services have more incentive to fear copying of their methods by competitors than do vendors of services for which the critical algorithms and knowledge bases are well understood. Accordingly, open source is more likely to dominate when... key methods (or functional equivalents) are part of common engineering knowledge.[tMC]

Once again, the conditions that create a strong preference for open source are the same conditions that create a strong preference for using a scripting language. The application that turns on your VCR from your Web browser is a unique and highly differentiated service, while the critical algorithms and knowledge bases of double entry accounting are certainly part of common engineering knowledge.

The example of accounting software is an interesting one, because the most successful commercial 4GL programs on the market today are extended accounting packages, sold under the generic name of "Enterprise Resource Planning" (ERP) applications. ERP applications are pathologically closed source; they are tightly controlled by the software vendor, difficult to implement, extremely difficult to customize, very expensive, upgraded infrequently, and always filled with bugs.

> Suppose you open-source that accounting package. It becomes popular and benefits from improvements made by the community. Now, your competitor also starts to use it. The competitor gets the benefit without paying the development cost and cuts into your business. Is this an argument against open-sourcing? [tMC]

The answer to this question is no, and the proof is the Business Process Reengineering (BPR) that generally accompanies the implementation of an ERP package. While the person doing the BPR will probably charge three hundred dollars an hour, and may take (upwards) of a year to get to the point, what he or she will eventually tell you is that instead of trying to customize the ERP package to fit your business processes, you should just *change your business processes* to fit the ERP package. The fact that companies in the same industry, in the same market segment, would spend a lot of time and a lot of money to achieve the same business process as their competitor shows that whether or not another company has the source code to your accounting software, the fact that the other company has the same binary version of your accounting software means that there is *no possible competitive advantage* from the accounting software *in any form*.

One example of this type of a project that could fit well into a BPR model is GnuCash (www.gnucash.org), a personal finance and small business accounting application.

So, for those of you who are thinking of writing a closed-source application, consider the fact that you're not in the business of selling software licenses, and you never will be. Licenses are at least twice removed from the original problem your software will solve; the notion of a software license is far too abstract for most people to grasp, let alone obey to the letter of the law. Get back to the original goal: solving a problem in a context. This certainly involves software, but is executed in the support, customization, and other value-added services. No one said you can't make money off of software, but no one said you had to make it in closed-source licensing.

Summary

If you're convinced that your Next Great Idea should be realized as an open source project, your first question is probably going to be, "how do I get started?"

For starters, check out Eric S. Raymond's writings at www.tuxedo.org/~esr/writings and the Free Software Foundation's philosophy page at www.gnu.org/philosophy/philosophy.html. This will give you two different perspectives on free software, and will help you think about how you will approach the issue of open source.

As far as the infrastructure that a project needs, you don't need to worry about this at all! There are a number of *free* support services for open source projects:

SourceForge (www.sourceforge.net). The SourceForge project is sponsored by VA Linux Systems, and offers configuration management tools (the CVS suite), mailing lists, bug tracking, Web site hosting, and much more (such as a MySQL database).

Freshmeat Server51 (server51.freshmeat.net). Server51 also offers FTP and WWW hosting, CVS, mailing lists, and bug tracking.

More services can be found at the open directory project's Open Source Hosting page, http://dmoz.org/Computers/Open_Source/Hosting/.

One of the advantages of going with a service that specializes in open source projects (aside from the fact that it is free) is that using such a service will draw developers and users to your project, since these services make the community aware of the projects they host. And this one simple thing helps solve the problem of attracting a critical mass. Once you've got this critical mass, you've got to do what you can to energize it!

Object-Oriented Analysis

I n Chapter 4, "Construction," we talked about a host of techniques for building high-quality code. In that chapter, we focused on a subroutine (also known as function or method) as the unit of work. In this chapter, we're going to look at system construction on a much higher level. We'll analyze a formal requirements document and produce some documents that will help in the next chapter as we design classes and look at what's involved in writing code.

This (and the following) chapter bring together many of the activities that fall under object-oriented analysis and design (OOA&D). Keep in mind that the steps we present don't form a rugged, proven process. Instead, these steps represent a *sampling of activities* that are used in industrial-strength OOA&D processes. So, the activities in this chapter form a lightweight process that you could use to build good systems, but you would do yourself a disservice if you didn't look beyond the ideas in this chapter. After you digest the material in this chapter, you would be wise to consult the following books (which we highly recommend), and use them as departure points for further investigation into OOA&D:

- *Applying UML and Patterns* by Craig Larman (Prentice Hall, 1998).
- *UML Distilled Second Edition* by Martin Fowler and Kendall Scott (Addison-Wesley, 1999).

The process presented in this (and the following) chapter is closely patterned after Larman's.

One reason that these two chapters cannot offer a full OOA&D process (besides the fact that it's too darn short for such a thing) is that there really isn't one true process. Instead, there are many activities that can be put together, like a modular system, to build a process that works for you and the organizations you develop software for.

What's the Point?

You may be wondering why we are bothering so much with analysis and design. There are two ways you can use the information in this and the next chapter. First, you can learn all about the analysis and design process, and follow the references to learn much more about it. Second, you can simply learn the notation, and use it as a tool to understand the examples in this book. We think you'll agree that a notation such as UML makes it easier to understand how an application fits together. In the next chapter, we'll look at *patterns*, an idiom that lets you look at the structure of a solution on a very high level.

Whether you agree with the details of the process in these chapters is not important. The most important thing we want to sell you on is the use of UML and patterns as tools for communication.

The Unified Modeling Language

The *Unified Modeling Language* (UML) is a notation for representing problems and specifying the design of systems that deal with the problems. UML has evolved over time from deep roots in object-oriented process and notation, and is recognized as a standard for modeling within OOA&D. It's an interesting sort of standard, because you can choose which parts of UML that are most useful to you. You are not bound by the standard to do things a certain way, or even in a certain order. More details on UML can be found at the UML Resource Center at www.rational.com/uml.

It's important to point out that UML is not a modeling process, but a notation for creating models of systems. However, UML is used *within* modeling processes.

Why Have a Process?

"I hate to say this . . . but this place is getting *to* me. I think I'm getting the Fear."

"Nonsense," I said. ". . . now that we're right in the vortex, you want to quit." I grabbed his bicep and squeezed. "You must *realize* that we've found the main nerve."

"I know," he said. "That's what gives me the Fear."

—Hunter S. Thompson, "Fear and Loathing in Las Vegas"

Writing heaps of notation without a beneficial process becomes an annoying activity that is performed just to add to the mounds of paper in your PHB's (Pointy Haired Boss, of Dilbert fame) office. By beneficial process, we mean a process that helps something or someone. In the case of processes that go hand in hand with UML, that something is your system, and that someone is you (and your fellow programmers and successors). If you use UML within a beneficial analysis and design process, you could write better code, work shorter days, and significantly reduce maintenance costs.

The importance of UML is that it lets us model things. *The UML User Guide* by Booch, Jacobson, and Rumbaugh (Addison-Wesley, 1998) starts out by exploring the reasons that engineers must model things before they build them. Hopefully, that discussion will reassure developers who have been burned by too many documentation efforts whose artifacts gather dust on a shelf. To some, UML diagrams look like flowcharts from the age of big iron, and they are understandably suspicious.

In fact, UML is significantly different from older notations such as flowcharts. UML is used to document more than the flow of an application: A UML diagram can show the relationships between classes, and how those classes interact. When you use patterns (which we'll discuss in the following chapter), you'll organize your classes in ways that are instantly familiar to other developers who are familiar with common design patterns. UML succeeds (in combination with patterns) by communicating vast quantities of information at a glance.

Many systems have sections of code that may as well be marked with "here be dragons" and "abandon all hope, ye who enter here." These are the sections that the people who joined the team toward the end of development (or at the beginning of support) never had time to learn about. These are the sections that strike fear into the hearts of the people who support the system. These people will never learn about that part of the system, because there's this dude, you see, who works in France or something now, but we can call him any time (sure it costs the company $250 an hour), and he'll fix a bug in that part of the system. Well, I've got news for you, Sonny Jim! Your man in France just finished clown college and has joined a travelling circus! He'll never fix a bug in that code again!

In this chapter, we'll look at concepts and techniques that can be used with UML to circumvent many of the problems associated with complex software projects. One of the most amazing results is that you'll be able to communicate many things about the system to programmers who are unfamiliar with it.

This is not your great-grandmother's flowchart!

Terminology

Instead of using jargon and terminology that is fully compliant with a particular version of a process or notation, we'll use terms that are appropriate for an introductory discussion, in the hopes that they will communicate the basic information to you. This should not suggest that there is no reason to pursue correct and widely accepted terms. If you think of this chapter as an introduction to the wider world of software engineering processes and notations, you will learn more, and become more familiar with accepted terminology as you make use of standard references in this area.

In this chapter, we'll perform an analysis of a problem that is stated in a set of formal requirements. We'll use UML to produce *artifacts* (diagrams and associated documents) that communicate this analysis.

First, we'll look at the analysis phase of the process, a phase that enhances your understanding of the problem. In the next chapter, we'll look at some ideas that will help bridge the gap between analysis and design, and then move on to the design phase of the lightweight process. When we have completed analysis and design, we will discuss how to develop code with UML artifacts as a guide.

Using UML in Object-Oriented Analysis

The analysis phase of the process is concerned with enhancing your understanding of the *problem domain* (the area or realm that the problem affects). To that end, analysis seeks to model the problems from the viewpoint of a *domain expert*, someone who understands everything about the problem (usually someone from your user community).

Each part of the process will be presented by example, and the key points will be summarized at the end. Within the analysis phase of the process, we will look at how to generate the following artifacts:

Use cases. Narrative descriptions of interactions involving the system that illustrate and expound upon the requirements.

Conceptual model. A static diagram that shows the relationships between concepts within the problem domain.

System sequence diagrams. A visual representation of individual use cases that define the operations the system must supply.

Contracts. A textual description of the responsibilities of each operation in the system.

One purpose of these artifacts is to enhance your understanding of the problem, so you can build the right system (see Chapter 1, "Requirements"). This understanding will be used in the design stage to assign responsibilities to objects and determine the relationships between objects.

Figure 7.1 shows the relationships between the artifacts we will examine in this chapter.

NOTE

In this chapter, we'll base all the examples on the requirements found in Chapter 2, "Database Design." If you did not read Chapter 2, you should take the time now to read the requirements, which can be found in the section titled *Use the Requirements.*

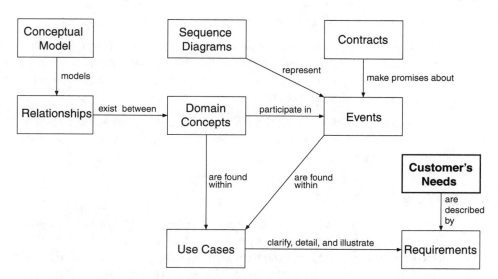

Figure 7.1   Relationships between design artifacts.

Use Cases

A *use case* is a description of the scenarios that follow from interacting with the concepts found in the requirements. For example, if your requirements included concepts such as a cash register, products, and customers, a use case would describe how these concepts interact when someone purchases a product. The purpose of use cases is to enhance the understanding of the requirements. You should use the requirements as a basis for the use cases, but use brainstorming sessions with the customer to develop the use cases.

Use cases tend to follow a common format, but there is no canonical use case format. You can use as much or as little of the format as you'd like, and you can embellish it as you see fit.

Fowler says that "use cases provide the basis of communication between customers and developers in planning the project." At a certain point, you will depart from artifacts that can be easily understood by the users, and will begin focusing on developing artifacts that get closer to code. Because it is so important to get requirements correct before design, make sure you take full advantage of use cases as a communications tool between you and your customers.

Your users can provide what Fowler refers to as domain expertise (knowledge of the area affected by the problem you are trying to solve). Make use of this expertise.

Actors and Events

Use cases are made up primarily of *actors* and *events*.

Actors are the participants in use cases. They represent things (users, operators, pilots, and other intelligent beings) that initiate actions. Actors don't have to be human, though. Computer systems, and electronic devices, for example, can be actors as well.

Events are what happen as the result of something an actor does. Most events will result in other events, and in some cases, the same event may have alternative outcomes.

Identifying Use Cases

How do you start writing a use case? The only constraint is that you must write enough use cases to account for all the requirements that relate to how participants interact with the problem domain. If you have followed a structured format for writing requirements, you can include a reference to the numbered parts of the requirements that a particular use case addresses (such as "1.1," "3.1.1.1," or "4.2").

Within these constraints, though, you still need to decide where to begin. Larman cautions us to avoid writing use cases for individual steps. Instead, look for larger processes that have many steps. For example, you would not model "the system reports total fines" as a use case. Instead, this is a step in the "Pay Fines" use case from our library example.

Larman suggests two methods for identifying use cases:

- Identify all the participants involved with the requirements, and then identify the processes or events they are involved in (actor-based).
- Identify the events that are indicated by the requirements and relate these events to actors and use cases (event-based).

In this example, we'll take an actor-based approach. If you look at the requirements, the only actor that is explicitly mentioned is the Patron. But someone needs to facilitate the Patron's interactions with the system. If you didn't know anything about libraries, you could ask your user (a domain expert) who this is. We're pretty sure they'd tell you that this person is a librarian. As far as we know from looking at the requirements, the system doesn't need to know anything about a librarian (unless that librarian happens to also be a Patron). Nevertheless, the librarian is responsible for coordinating the system processes, such as loaning out a book or generating a report. So, it is clear that the librarian is an actor in the system. To identify actors and events, inspect the requirements. If you can have more than one person involved with this inspection you can compare notes and brainstorm about the list you come up with.

You should write a use case for each event you identify. Based on an inspection of the requirements, here are the actors and the events they initiate:

Actor	Events
Patron	Borrow Books
	Return Books
	Pay Fines
	Toggle Borrowing History (at the Patron's request, turns off tracking all books a patron has borrowed)
Librarian	Generate a Report

Use Case Diagrams

Use case diagrams, while simple, can be useful to illustrate use cases and the actors who participate in them. The actors are shown as stick figures, and the use cases are shown as ovals. This is not too fancy. Eventually, the sequence diagrams will illustrate the details of activities that the use cases describe. For now, the use case diagrams are useful for someone who is unfamiliar with the problem to understand it at a very high level. Figure 7.2 shows the use cases we listed in our actor/event example.

The elements of a use case diagram include:

- Each use case, shown as an oval
- Each actor

For each use case the actor participates in, a line is drawn from each actor to that use case.

Writing Use Cases

As you write use cases, keep the following in mind:

Use cases should enhance your understanding of the problem. If it is particularly illuminating to create a particular use case, then do so.

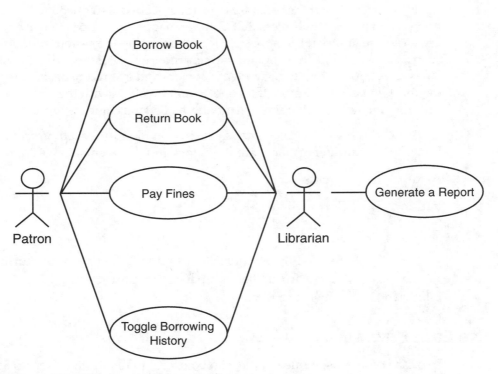

Figure 7.2 Library system use case diagram.

Don't let implementation details affect how you develop a use case. Try to think about the problem in isolation from issues such as whether your language supports multiple inheritance or how you will develop your classes.

The format we'll use here is based on the expanded use case format shown in Larman and the use case format shown in Fowler. This format consists of the use case name, the actors involved with the use case, a description, the reference numbers of the corresponding requirements, and the typical course of events.

Don't be surprised if the example use cases you see here go above and beyond what the requirements state. Remember that use cases are developed to give you an enhanced understanding of the requirements, and part of this may involve getting into things in more detail. In many cases, you will find that the information you discover in the use cases contradicts something in the requirements, and you'll have to change the requirements (if it turns out the use case is correct).

Here's a sample use case for borrowing a book:

Use Case: Borrow Books

Actors: Patron (initiator), Librarian
Reference: 3.1.1, 3.1.1.1, 3.1.1.2

Typical Course of Events

Action	System Response
1. The patron brings one or more books up to the circulation desk.	
2. The librarian asks the patron to present his or her library card.	
3. The patron gives the library card to the librarian.	
4. The librarian identifies the patron to the system.	5. The system acknowledges that it knows about the patron.
6. The librarian records the fact that each book has been borrowed by the patron.	7. Calculate due date for each book and record the fact that the patron must return that book on the due date.
8. When all books have been recorded, the librarian returns the library card.	
9. The patron leaves with the books.	

(Continues)

Use Case: Borrow Books *(Continued)*

Alternatives

Step 3. The patron does not have a library card. Ask the patron to apply for a card. At this point, we would need to branch to another use case, "Apply for a Library Card." When that use case is completed, we'd return to Step 3. However, this use case isn't discussed in the requirements, nor do we treat it in this chapter. You'd need to confer with your users to determine whether it should exist and what steps it consists of.

Step 4. The patron has forgotten the library card. If the patron has another form of identification, try to identify the patron to the system by his or her name.

Step 5. The patron has overdue books. Cancel the transaction, and ask the patron to return the overdue books before borrowing more.

Step 7. The book has already been checked out. Generate an error message.

The following sections describe the remaining use cases.

Use Case: Return Books

Actors: Patron (initiator), Librarian
Reference: 3.1.2, 3.1.2.1

Typical Course of Events

Action	System Response
1. The patron returns one or more books to the library.	
2. The librarian records that the books have been returned.	3. Note the fact that the Patron no longer has the book.
	4. If the book was returned late, calculate any fines at a rate of twenty-five cents per day. Add the fines to the patron's outstanding fines, if any.
5. The librarian returns the book to the shelf.	

Alternatives

Step 2. The book had never been checked out. Generate an error message.

Use Case: Pay Fines

Actors: Patron (Initiator), Librarian
Reference: 3.1.3

Typical Course of Events

Action	System Response
1. The patron arrives at the library to pay fines.	
2. The librarian asks the patron to present his or her library card.	
3. The patron gives the library card to the librarian.	
4. The librarian identifies the patron to the system.	5. The system acknowledges that it knows about the patron.
6. The librarian looks up the total amount of the fines.	7 Report the total amount of fines.
8. The patron gives some money to the librarian.	
9. The librarian accepts the money and records the amount.	10. Deduct the amount from the out standing fines.
	11. Print a receipt.
12. The librarian gives the receipt to the patron.	

Alternatives

Step 4. The patron has forgotten the library card. Try to identify the patron to the system by his or her name.
Step 7. The patron doesn't owe anything. Report this fact, and cancel the transaction.
Step 11. The patron doesn't want a receipt. Don't print it.

Use Case: Generate a Report

Actors: Librarian (initiator)
Reference: 3.2.1, 3.2.2, 3.2.3

Typical Course of Events

Action	System Response
1. The librarian chooses one of three reports: Report of Checked-out Books, Report of Overdue Books, or Historical Report.	2. Let the user choose any report-specific options.

(Continues)

Use Case: Generate a Report *(Continued)*

Typical Course of Events

Action	System Response
3. The librarian selects options.	
4. The librarian asks the system to print the report.	5. Print the report.

Use Case: Disable Borrowing History

Actors: Patron (initiator), Librarian
Reference: 3.2.3.1

Typical Course of Events

Action	System Response
1. Patron asks that the library stop tracking his or her borrowing history.	
2. Librarian disables patron's borrowing history.	3. Disable borrowing history for this patron.

When you have finished writing the use cases, revisit each item in your requirements, and make sure each one has been accounted for in the use cases. Note that satisfying some requirements implicitly satisfies others. For example, if you look at the use cases and see that 3.1.1 and 3.1.2 are satisfied, you can also consider 3.1 to be satisfied, because all of its subordinate requirements are satisfied.

However, if we examined sections 1 and 2 of the requirements and found an actor that wasn't accounted for in the rest of the requirements or the use cases, this would be cause for concern. In such an event, you would need to ask a domain expert why the actor never appears in the requirements, and alter the requirements appropriately (either adding requirements that relate to the actor, or removing the reference to the actor).

The process we follow in this chapter involves a deeper exploration of requirements than we saw in Chapters 2 and 3. If you choose to use an OOA&D process (such as the one described in this and the next chapter), you may want

What about the Data?

All of our use cases were derived from activities that were explicitly stated in the requirements. However, section 2 of the requirements discuss the data that the system needs to maintain. Common sense would suggest that we need, at a minimum, the ability to add, edit, or delete this data! A more complete specification would have included a description of how a patron signs up for a card, how books are entered into and removed from circulation, and how this information is kept up to date. From these requirements, we could develop use cases that handle adding, editing, and deleting a patron or a book. For the purposes of keeping the example simple, our requirements do not address these issues.

to defer database and user interface design until after you have done an initial class diagram, since this artifact can be used as the basis of a database or user interface design. For simple systems, the analysis and design techniques in Chapters 2 and 3 should be sufficient. We'll discuss design issues in more detail in the next chapter.

Use Case Summary

In the example use cases, we saw a number of elements that you should include in use cases you write yourself:

Actors. When you choose the actors for a use case, think of everyone who is involved. You should try to choose one actor who is the initiator. Think about how the process is played out in the real world, and ask yourself, "who started it?"

Reference. This is a cross-reference to the formal requirements. The reference serves two purposes: You can use it to find out where the use case has its origins, and you can also use it as a handy reference when you are verifying that all the requirements have been accounted for.

Typical course of events. This part will tap your storytelling skills. You need to think about how the process should be played out. If you think of exceptions along the way, save them for the Alternatives. You may need to use your imagination, especially as you think about how to phrase the system responses, but avoid the temptation to invent requirements at this point!

Above all, don't talk about how the system will handle the responses, just talk about what the responses must be. For example, notice that we specified "calculate due date." We don't specify how the calculation is to be performed, but we specify that it must be performed. At some point, we'll have to calculate it, and we can either consult a domain expert or the requirements to find out the details.

Alternatives. Use the Alternatives to enumerate the possible things that could alter the typical course of events. Although you don't need to consider every possibility, you should think about things that apply to the task at hand. If the task involves books and library cards, what could go wrong with books and library cards? In other words, you probably don't need to add an alternative for "the Patron remembers she has a copy of the book at home and decides not to check it out."

The Conceptual Model

Once you have completed the use cases, the next step is to create a conceptual model. Use cases help you identify actors and events that occur in the problem domain. The conceptual model provides a graphical representation of the domain elements, as well as the relationships between those elements.

Developing the Conceptual Model

The conceptual model is a diagram that shows the relationships between concepts in the problem domain. Not only does the conceptual model communicate a huge amount of information at a glance, but the process of building it gives you many opportunities to learn more about the problem domain.

We can't give you a complete cookbook approach to developing a conceptual model, because intuition and iteration come into play here. However, we developed the conceptual model in an iterative fashion, and we've added some notes after each item to explain our thinking. Under *concepts*, *associations*, and *attributes*, you'll find lists of items we rejected or that we felt needed more explanation. Most of these were things that were modified during various iterations, and we hope that they give you some examples of the sort of thinking you need to approach this type of analysis.

Nevertheless, there are four distinct activities that go into building the conceptual model: concept identification, diagramming, and discovering associations and attributes. You'll probably find yourself looping between these activities a few times as you build the conceptual model.

Identify Concepts

The first step in building your conceptual model is identifying concepts (ideas or things). The noun phrase identification technique in the section titled *Find the Nouns and Verbs* in Chapter 3, "User Interface Design," is one approach. Larman also suggests using a concept category approach, which lists categories of concepts that you can use to identify concepts within the use cases.

NOTE

Don't feel that you have to wait until you've completed one step to start the next. In fact, you should come up with a draft list of concepts and associations, and then move on to diagramming. If something looks wrong to you, your coworkers, or customers, go back and revise the lists and the diagram. You may need to go back and forth between the lists and the diagram a few times before you get it right!

Let's take a look at Larman's list and all the concepts from the use cases that fit into this list, shown in Table 7.1. Notice that we're turning multiple word concepts into a single identifier, such as BorrowingPolicy. This prepares us for using these concepts in a programming language, most of which do not allow spaces in identifiers.

CONCEPT CATEGORIES WE DIDN'T FIND

Transaction Line Items. If you were to look at the Loan as a single transaction, then you could think of each individual book that is borrowed as a line item on that transaction. However, a loan is really specific to an individual book. Once the books leave the library, they are accounted for on a book-by-book basis, not as a collective. This is not to say that representing it as a line item would be wrong, but we chose not to do so in this example. When you develop a conceptual model, you should choose alternatives based on what you feel is closest to the ideas in your users' heads.

Table 7.1   Concept Categories and Concepts in the Library Problem Domain

CATEGORY	CONCEPT
Physical, tangible objects	Book, Report
Places	Library
Transactions	Payment, Loan, Return
Roles of people	Librarian, Patron
Containers	Library
Things in a container	Book
Abstract noun concepts	Fine
Events	Loan, Return
Rules and Policies	BorrowingPolicy

Manuals/books. Sure, a library system is all about books. But this concept category is used to refer to books or manuals that may have domain-specific behavior or attributes, such as an employee manual.

Records. Our first revision of the conceptual model included a BorrowingHistory, but we discovered it was irrelevant in later iterations. Why is this so? As you will see later, the behavior of the conceptual model tells us that a Loan is created when the Patron borrows the book, and a Return is created when it is returned. Neither of these objects are ever destroyed, so they provide a de facto borrowing history.

Other systems. If the library system were connected to another system, such as a state- or county-wide card catalog system, we would represent that as a concept.

Organizations. If organizations (such as Friends of the Library or funding organizations) were relevant to the system, we would represent these as concepts.

Processes. You could think of BorrowABook, ReturnABook, and PayAFine, but these are addressed in the events Loan, Return, Pay. However, if you find that it is better to explicitly describe these as processes, then you should do so.

Specifications, designs, or descriptions. If we were building a card catalog system (a system to let patrons locate and search for books), we might need a CardCatalogEntry object. This would contain a description of a book, and would fit into this category.

Catalogs. If we were building a card catalog system, the CardCatalog would be found in this category, as well as in the Containers category, since it would contain CardCatalogEntry objects.

CONCEPTS WE REJECTED

CirculationDesk (place, tangible object). In some systems (such as the case study used in Larman), you might find it useful to represent point-of-service equipment (such as a cash register) as a concept. A circulation desk might fit this category, but it doesn't actively participate in any events.

System (tangible object). The system is really just an umbrella for all the services that it provides, so it's not appropriate to consider as a concept. The closest concept to System, however, is Library.

Shelf (tangible object, container). If we were building a library or tracking the location of books on shelves, this object might be interesting to us. However, it is external to the system, and neither initiates nor participates in events.

LibraryCard (tangible object). We're going to make the case that the library card is an attribute of the Patron. It's a means of identification, and is used exactly as a name or social security number. So, we should see it show up again in the attributes later. However, you might disagree, and include the library card in your conceptual model.

CONCEPTS THAT NEED A LITTLE EXPLANATION

Loan. This is a linguistic problem. Loan is just Borrow turned on its head. We can turn the verb *loan*, (as in "the library *loans* a book") into a noun, *loan* (as in "this *loan* is for two weeks"). However, it's not so easy with the verb *borrow*. Another way to look at it is, if a patron wants to borrow a book, the library will loan it to her.

BorrowingPolicy. The rules that govern a loan. It includes such things as the duration of the loan and the amount of fines.

If you want, you can also use the noun phrase identification technique described in Chapter 3. If you do this, eliminate all the concepts that are attributes of another concept. Larman suggests a test: if you think of something as a number or some text, it is probably an attribute. By this thinking, we can eliminate attributes such as fine, title, and phone number.

Here is a list of concepts that are part of the conceptual model:

Book	BorrowingPolicy	Fine	Librarian
Library	Loan	Patron	Payment
	Report	Return	

There is no "right" conceptual model. The idea is to get as close to what is in your users' heads as is possible! The closer you can get, the better. But you will have the opportunity to refine the conceptual model as you work through the analysis and design.

Draw the Model

The next step is to draw the model. At first, we'll just draw all the concepts as boxes that contain the name of the concept. To draw these, you can use a specialized UML tool, such as Dia or Argo/UML, or you can use a vector drawing program such as tgif or xfig. Chapter 10, "Linux Development Tools Catalog," discusses these tools in the section titled *Modeling/Diagramming Tools*.

Figure 7.3 shows the model showing the concepts without the relationships (or associations) between them. In this diagram, the UML class figure (a box) is used to show concepts.

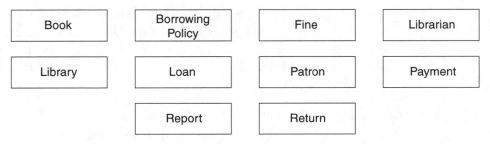

Figure 7.3   Conceptual model, without associations.

Discover and Diagram Associations

Some of the associations (or relationships) may be obvious, such as Patron borrows Book, or Librarian works for Library. In order for associations to be obvious, you need to be knowledgeable in the problem domain. Most of us are familiar with libraries. Unfamiliar problems might not provide such obvious associations.

Larman suggests an approach for discovering associations. The *common associations list* contains a number of categories. You can start out with a blank piece of paper, and write the categories down the left side of the paper. Then, start at the top of the page and look at each category: Examine your requirements and use cases, and fill in each association you can find that fits into that category. As you choose an association, make sure you name it in such a way so that it can be read from left to right (such as *Patron borrows Book*).

Larman also suggests the following:

Select associations that must be preserved for some duration. He refers to these as "need-to-know" associations.

Don't select associations that can be derived. For example, you do not need an explicit relationship between the Library and a Loan. Since a Loan records the loan of a Book, and a Book is contained in the Library, there is an implicit relationship between Library and Loan.

Table 7.2 lists the associations that we found, using a set of categories that are similar to those Larman suggests.

ASSOCIATIONS WE DIDN'T FIND

A is the description of B. If we had a CardCatalog, then the CardCatalog-Entry would be a description of a book.

Table 7.2 Associations in the Library Domain

CATEGORY	ASSOCIATIONS
A is part of (or contained in) B	Books are contained in a Library
A is a line item of a transaction or report B	Loan is a line item of Report
A is known, logged, recorded, reported, or captured in B	Report reports on Loan Loan records loan of Book
A is a member of B	Patron is a member of the Library Librarian works for Library
A uses, manages, owns, or is responsible for B	BorrowingPolicy governs Loan Patron owes Fine Patron initiates Loan Patron initiates Return Librarian approves Loan
A is a transaction related to another transaction B	Return terminates Loan
A is related to transaction B	Patron makes Payment

A communicates with B. Librarian communicates with Patron is derivable through Librarian approves Loan and Patron initiates Loan, so it's not needed.

ASSOCIATIONS WE REJECTED

Patron borrows Book. At first glance, it would probably occur to you to use this association. In an earlier iteration of this list, we did the same thing. However, the Loan object captures the relationship between a patron and a book, and also gives us something that can enjoy relationships with other objects.

Payment reduces Fine. We caught this one while we were writing the contracts. The original thinking was that each Patron will have one Fine that accumulates the total fines. By this thinking, each Payment reduces the amount of the fine. However, this removes the ability to trace the history of fines and payments, which might be needed to resolve disputes. Instead, each Patron will have zero or more fines and zero or more payments. The amount they owe will be the difference between total fines and total payments. In this model, the only relationship a Payment has to a Fine is derived through their respective associations with a Patron. However, a more flexible alternative would be to associate a fine with a particular Loan.

Associations that Need Explanation

Figure 7.4 shows the conceptual model using a UML static structure diagram. The associations are shown as lines between concepts. You should read associations from left to right, or from top to bottom, unless there is an explicit arrow (as with Report reports-on Loan). Some of the associations have been renamed to accommodate the left-right or up-down reading. For example "Librarian works for Library" has been reworded as "Library employs Librarian." Feel free to adjust the relationship names if you feel a change would introduce clarity but would not alter the meaning.

On each side of the association, you may see a number or an expression such as 0..1, 1..*, or 1,2,3. This is used to denote multiplicity. For example, notice that the enumerated association between Patron and Loan shows 1 on the left and * on the right. The * indicates zero or more, and the 1 indicates exactly one. This can be read as "exactly one Patron initiates zero or more Loans." Table 7.3 shows the notation for multiplicity.

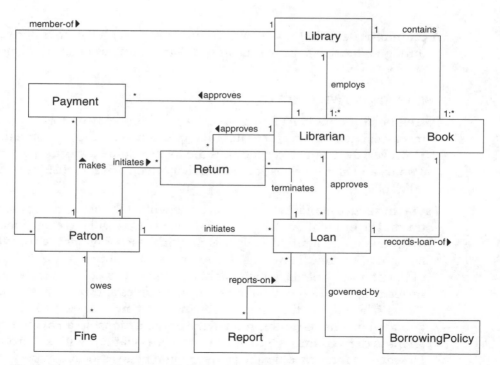

Figure 7.4 Conceptual model with associations.

Table 7.3 UML Multiplicity Notations

NOTATION	MULTIPLICITY
1	Exactly one
*	Zero or more
1..*	one or more
0..1	zero or one (indicates optional association)
n	Exactly n (where n is a number)
n1..n2	Between n1 and n2 (where n1 and n2 are numbers)
n1, n2, n3	either n1, n2, or n3

Add Attributes

Next, we need to add attributes to the diagram. Attributes are data that belong to a concept. Attributes can be thought of in terms of primitive data types: strings, numbers, dates, and other simple values.

There are several categories of attributes that are suggested by a list of common attributes found in Larman. We'll examine these categories, and look in the use cases for attributes that fit them. Because there are no use cases for data maintenance (see the sidebar titled *What about the Data?*), you will need to also look at section 2 of the requirements to find many attributes.

Table 7.4 shows the attributes we discovered. We're using lowercase identifiers with underscores between spaces, since these conform to the way identifiers are often written in many programming languages.

Table 7.4 Attributes in the Library Domain

CATEGORY	EXAMPLE	ATTRIBUTE IN LIBRARY MODEL
Color	Surface color, interior hue	none
Money	Sum owed, line item cost, subtotal	Fine.amount Payment.amount
Geometry	Height, Width, Length	none
Contact information	Email address, phone number, fax number	Patron.phone_number
Identification	Social Security number, name, employee ID, ISBN	Book.title Book.isbn_number Author.name Publisher.name Patron.first_name *(Continues)*

Table 7.4 Attributes in the Library Domain (*Continued*)

CATEGORY	EXAMPLE	ATTRIBUTE IN LIBRARY MODEL
		Patron.last_name Patron.middle_initial Patron.library_card Patron.track_history Report.report_type
Address component	city, state, zip, PO Box, street address, etc.	Patron.home_address
Distinguishing Characteristic	Scar on left cheek	Book.binding_type Book.publication_date Book.publication_city
Primitive Data Type	Date, time, number, code, ID	Book.isbn_number Book.volume Book.edition Publisher.code BorrowingPolicy.duration BorrowingPolicy.fine_per_day
Date	Start date, date of birth, end date	Report.start_date Report.end_date Loan.due_date Loan.borrow_date Return.return_date

ATTRIBUTES WE DIDN'T FIND

Author and Publisher. Author is not a primitive data type. It is not something that can be expressed as a string (although the author's *name* can be expressed as such). So, how do we represent the author of a book? If we're not going to use an attribute, we need an association between a book and an author. This means we need to modify the conceptual model to include Author. The same goes for Publisher.

However, you may decide that Author and Publisher are insignificant enough that they can be represented as simple strings. There is no right choice—the goal is to get as close to the users' conception of the problem as possible.

ATTRIBUTES THAT NEED SOME EXPLANATION

Report Start and End Dates. These were not explicitly stated in the requirements, but are reasonable attributes for a report. This information may have been added during discussion with the users.

Borrowing Policy Fine Per Day and Duration. If there are to be fines and loans, there must be parameters that govern them.

Don't worry about catching all the attributes right now. We may pick more up along the way, especially as we move to the design phase.

Attributes versus Foreign Keys

Larman specifically suggests that we avoid creating attributes for foreign keys, something that you might consider doing based on the information with Chapter 2. Larman warns us that if we include attributes that are foreign keys, we are making a presupposition as to how the relationship will be implemented. It's enough that the associations catch the relationships. For example, the Loan doesn't need an attribute to refer to the book or patron.

Figure 7.5 shows the conceptual model with concepts, associations, and attributes.

NOTE Keep in mind that choosing attributes and their types does not say anything about how the classes will be implemented. We are still studying the problem domain here, and the attributes are just part of the conceptual model, and have no direct bearing on the implementation. Consider the Librarian for example: a concept without attributes or major responsibilities. It's possible that the Librarian will eventually drop out of the model when you move into design or implementation, or perhaps it will be merged with another concept, such as Library. Nothing is set in stone at this stage.

Conceptual Model Summary

Here are the steps we took to build the conceptual model:

1. *Identify concepts.* What are the key concepts (ideas or things) in the problem domain?
2. *Draw the model.* The first draft of the diagram shows the concepts in isolation from each other: no associations or attributes. It is the first step in visualizing the problem domain.
3. *Discover and draw associations.* Find out how concepts are related and diagram this information.
4. *Add attributes.* Find out what data belongs to each concept and add this information to the diagram.

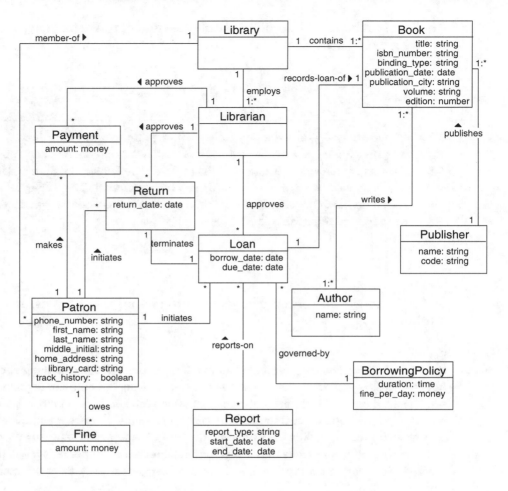

Figure 7.5 Completed conceptual model.

System Sequence Diagrams

Now that you have devised the use cases and conceptual model, it's time to move on to *system sequence diagrams* (SSDs). This is the stage where you start to think in terms of the events that the system handles. When we go on to contracts, we're going to think about the results of these events.

System sequence diagrams model the behavior of the concepts in the conceptual model.

At this stage, we're going to look at the system as a *black box*. All we want to model is the interactions that the user has with the system. So, we'll use the

SSDs to show the events that the user generates, but we won't show how the system reacts to these events.

SSDs are fairly straightforward interpretations of the *Typical Course of Action* from the use cases. You can inspect each action to see if it implies an interaction with the system. If there is a system response to the action, it's a sure sign that the corresponding action implies an interaction with the system.

Figure 7.6 shows the SSD for the Borrow Books use case. The two participants in this diagram are an actor that represents the Librarian (shown as a stick figure), and a box that represents the system. Beneath Librarian and the system, a dashed line (the *lifeline*) represents the progression of events through time (from top to bottom). For each event, an arrow from the Librarian lifeline leads to the system's lifeline.

When you need to make up the names for a system event (also called a message), you should choose names that are descriptive and that conform to the programming style guidelines you are using; eventually, these messages will become method names.

This is a simple example that illustrates a simple use case. It shows the Librarian sending two messages (or generating two events) to the system. We don't show how the system responds, because we are using the SSD only to figure out what events the system is responsible for.

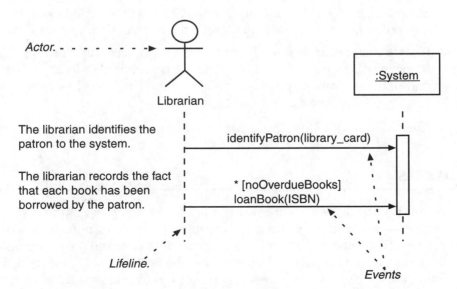

Figure 7.6 Borrow Books system sequence diagram.

Overpowered by Minutia?

Why does the word *System* have a colon in front of it? Why is it underlined?

In the Conceptual Model, we looked at concepts, whose nearest equivalents on the implementation level are classes. In the System Sequence Diagrams, we are modeling behavior, and we discuss this behavior in terms of concrete entities: objects. The underlining and colon in front of the word System specifies an unnamed (anonymous) object of the System class. If we gave it a name, such as my_system, it would be represented as <u>my_system: System</u>.

Developing the Diagrams

To develop the system sequence diagrams, you can follow this simple method, adapted from Larman:

Represent actors and the system. For each diagram, put the actor at the left and the system at the right. The actor will generate events that the system responds to. Don't get fancy at this point; you should not try to show the domain objects, such as a Patron or Book. Just show the system as a black box.

Illustrate each event. Examine the use cases for system interactions. Try to group things at the level of intent, not at the level of how things should be carried out. For example, you should not make loanBook() and setDue-Date() two separate system operations. Instead, you can assume that loanBook() takes care of setting the due date. This will be stated explicitly in the contracts, which we will explore in the next section.

Annotate each event. You might find it helpful to decorate the system sequence diagrams with text from the use case. It makes it easy to see what part of the use case a system operation is taking responsibility for. This may help you write the contracts.

Figures 7.7 through 7.10 illustrate the remaining use cases.

Contracts

At this point, we are almost ready to proceed to the design of the system. Before we can do this, we need to determine what the responsibilities of the system are. Contracts, which were originated by Bertrand Meyer in the Eiffel language, offer us a way to describe what those responsibilities are, without having to specify how they are carried out. The format we use for contracts in this chapter is based on the format presented by Larman.

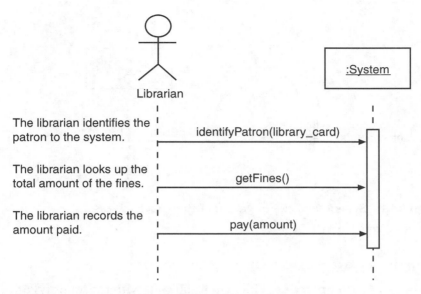

Figure 7.7   System sequence diagram for Pay Fines use case.

Writing Contracts

You must write a contract for each system operation in the SSDs. Then you need to figure out what the responsibilities of that operation are, what must be satisfied before the operation can occur, and what effect the operation has on the system.

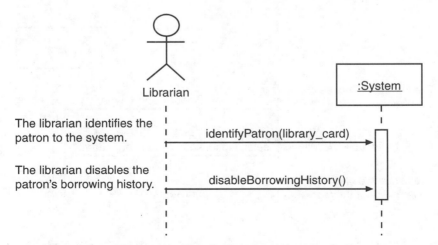

Figure 7.8   System sequence diagram for Disable Borrowing History use case.

Figure 7.9 System sequence diagram for Return Book use case.

Here are some of the steps suggested by Larman:

Represent each operation. First, we'll start out with the identifyPatron() operation.

Determine responsibilities. Describe the purpose of the operation. The purpose of identifyPatron() is fairly clear by its name: it needs to locate a Patron in the system.

Determine the state of the system after the operation (post-conditions). The state of the system is represented by a set of post-conditions. Larman

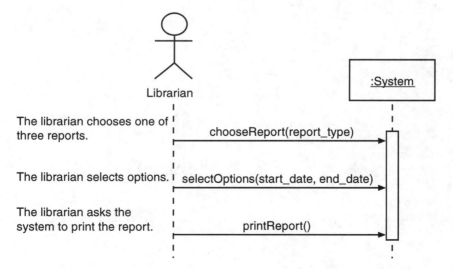

Figure 7.10 System sequence diagram for Generate Report use case.

suggests the following categories of post-conditions: Creating and deleting instances, modification of attributes, forming and breaking associations.

What is the result of identifying the patron? Don't consider how it's to be done; otherwise, you'll say something like "the patron is retrieved from the database." This is wrong because it is a description of how the results are achieved. In this case, it's much simpler: A Patron is created. We could change this slightly to reflect the fact that the system already knows the Patron, and say "A Patron is found and instantiated." This is desirable because "created" implies the creation of something new, and it is understood that the Patron already exists. Are there any associations formed? No. This operation does not form associations. We'll see examples of forming associations in later operations.

Declare what the state of the system must be before the operation (pre-conditions). What assumptions must hold in order for this operation to be performed? The use cases talk about the fact that the Patron must be known to the library, so this is definitely something that should be included. Do we need to include that the Patron must have a library card? Not necessarily, because the use case allows us to identify the Patron by other means. We can capture this by allowing either the library card or patron's name as parameters to this operation.

Determine exceptions. According to Fowler, pre-conditions are technically the responsibility of the system or whoever invokes the operation, so they can't be relied upon to provide error or exception handling. If there are any exceptional conditions that can occur when the operation is invoked, you should list them in the Exceptions section.

In the case of the Patron, an exception would occur if the system could not find the Patron. This reinforces the pre-condition that states the Patron must be known to the Library.

Other items. Larman also suggest using a section labeled Notes to include any design decisions, such as an algorithm you would use to solve a particular problem.

Here is the contract for identifyPatron:

IDENTIFYPATRON

Contract: identifyPatron.

Parameters: Library card or Patron's name (first, last, middle).

Refers to use case(s): Borrow Books, Pay Fines.

Responsibilities: Locate a Patron.

Exceptions:

- If the Patron cannot be located, generate an error.

Pre-conditions:

- Patron must be known to the Library.

Post-conditions:

- A Patron was found.
- That Patron was instantiated.
- The Patron was associated with the System. Until we do responsibility assignment in the next chapter, we don't know a specific object that the Patron will be associated with, so the System is a sort of placeholder.

Remaining Contract

In the next chapter, we'll only look at the design of one use case (Borrow Books), so we won't write contracts for the operations in all the use cases. Instead, we'll just look at the remaining operation from the Borrow Books use case:

LOANBOOK

Contract: loanBook.

Parameters: ISBN, Patron.

Refers to use case(s): Borrow Books.

Responsibilities: Loan a book to a patron, and record when the book is due.

Exceptions:

- If a Patron has not been associated with the System, generate an error.
- If the Patron has overdue books, generate an error.
- If the Book that corresponds to the ISBN number cannot be found, generate an error.
- If the Book has already been checked out, generate an error.

Pre-conditions:

- A Patron was associated with the System.
- The book has not already been checked out.
- The Patron has no overdue books.
- The ISBN is known to the Library.
- A Patron has already been found and instantiated.

Post-conditions:

- A Book was found.
- That Book was instantiated.
- A new Loan was created.
- A borrowing policy was created.
- Loan.borrow_date was set to the current day.
- Loan.due_date is set to the current date plus BorrowingPolicy.duration.
- An association was formed between the Patron and Loan.
- An association was formed between the Book and Loan (because the book is already associated with the Library, we don't need to form an association between the Loan and Library).

Summary

In this chapter, we looked at how to analyze and model the problem domain. In the next chapter, we'll look at the issues involved with designing and building the application logic. This will draw on the model we created in this chapter. Also, the next chapter will raise questions and provide answers as to how OOA&D can work in conjunction with the design and development of the user interface and database.

Object-Oriented Design

In the previous chapter, we analyzed the formal requirements for a library
system, and produced some artifacts (use cases, conceptual model, system
sequence diagrams, and contracts) that will help us design the system. In this
chapter, we'll create an object-oriented design and look at the issues involved
with turning it into an application. As with the previous chapter, the process
followed in this chapter is closely patterned after Craig Larman's *Applying
UML and Patterns* (Prentice Hall, 1998), but is highly condensed, and does not
delve into the issues as deeply.

This design addresses application logic (the domain tier), storing data in a
database (the persistence tier), and the user interface (the presentation tier).
The domain tier is the central focus of the object-oriented design, and is in
the driver's seat. The design of the other two tiers will be based on the analysis and design that went into the domain tier.

Three-Tier Architecture

A traditional client-server architecture is usually thought of as a two-tier application: The front-end is the *user interface*, while the back-end is the *database*.

While this approach had its moment in the sun, it caused more problems than
it solved. In a client-server system, the front-end often became responsible for

a lot of processing, and architects often thought of how much they could offload to the back-end. The result of this was that domain logic was spread between the database and user interface.

In a three-tier architecture, the presentation tier (or user interface) relies on another layer (the domain tier) to make decisions about information, perform processing, and worry about where data goes after you click OK. The domain tier, in turn, uses the persistence tier, which is often a database system, to permanently store objects. Figure 8.1 shows this architecture graphically.

You will often hear about three-tier systems as systems with distinct processes for each layer. In Web applications, the presentation layer is usually a Web browser with some HTML forms, the domain layer is an application server, and the persistence layer is a relational database. This is an example of a three-tier system with three physically separate tiers. While this is a common three-tier implementation model, it is not the only one. In this chapter, we're going to focus on the logical separation of tiers, rather than the physical separation.

Two benefits you can derive from a three-tier architecture are *reuse* and *scalability*. When you separate your application into logical tiers, you end up with a more modular design, which is a foundation of reusability. If you build applications in an environment that supports distributed objects, you can easily distribute components across multiple processes on the same machine, or even across different machines, providing you with many alternatives for scaling your application. CORBA, which works very well on Linux, can be used as the foundation of a distributed architecture. We'll discuss CORBA in Chapter 15, "Introduction to CORBA."

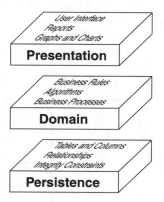

Figure 8.1 A three-tier architecture.

Designing for a Three-Tier Architecture

In earlier chapters, we considered the UI and database design issues in total isolation from object-oriented design. This allowed us to present the techniques that were specific to each of those activities, which will prepare you for the material in this chapter. These activities, however, generally don't occur in isolation. In some ways, they conflict with each other. UI design often takes a human-centered approach, database design often takes a data-centered approach, and object-oriented design often takes a responsibility-driven approach. As a consequence, each design produces results (see Figure 8.2) that may not merge with each other when you need to build an application.

The problem is artificially complicated by the fact that we looked at each design in isolation. In fact, it can be partially simplified by using the class diagram (see *Class Diagrams,* elsewhere in this chapter) to drive the design of the user interface and database. If you use this technique, you can at least guarantee that you will start out each design process with the same assumptions.

These issues will be explored in the following section *UI and Database Design in Context*.

The issues involved with bridging the presentation and domain layers are relatively simple. However, the real problem lies in the persistence layer. Somehow, we need to store domain objects in this persistence layer, and as needed, rematerialize them.

From Domain to Persistence

Why is going between the domain layer and persistence layer so complicated? Just to give you a taste of why it's problematic, let's remember how a database represents a part-whole association between two entities, such as an

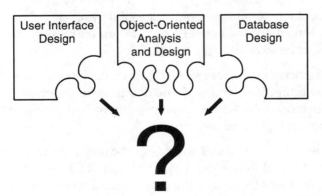

Figure 8.2   Can you assemble the pieces of this puzzle?

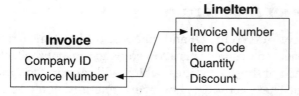

Database Representation: Reference goes from LineItem to Invoice.

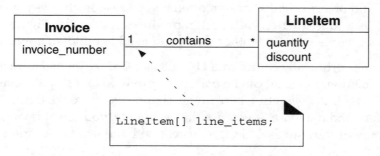

OO Representation: Reference goes from Invoice to LineItem.

Figure 8.3　Database and OO Representations, compared.

invoice and a line item: Each line item has a foreign key that corresponds to a row in the invoice table. You can find out which line items belong to a given invoice, such as invoice S1000, by selecting the line items that have S1000 as the value of the invoice number foreign key.

Now, let's consider how an association is handled in object-oriented design: The invoice object would contain a collection (such as an array or vector) that contains instances of all its line items. Figure 8.3 shows the differences. If you think about the differences between the two, you'll probably think of some ways to solve this problem, or at least some ways to approach it. The point is, there is not a one-to-one mapping between objects and entities in a database. Some work must be done to resolve the differences.

In this chapter, we'll focus on a responsibility-driven design that, for the moment, ignores the issues involved with the database and user interface requirements. The responsibility-driven design will produce a design that accounts for the domain logic, and *nothing else*.

It might seem insane not to consider the needs of the database and user interface, but it's actually helpful in the end. Ultimately, we'll address the presentation and persistence layers by examining patterns and tools that take into account the user interface and database.

Patterns for Object-Oriented Design

In the previous chapter, we used contracts to get a sense of the responsibilities that a system will need to fulfill. The next step is to identify how those responsibilities are assigned.

Patterns, which were first defined in Christopher Alexander's *A Pattern Language* (Oxford University Press, 1977), are solutions to recurring architectural problems. In the 1980s, Kent Beck and Ward Cunningham applied Alexander's concepts to object-oriented design, and presented their results to the world. Patterns were highly popularized by Gamma, Helm, Johnson, and Vlissides' *Design Patterns: Elements of Reusable Object-Oriented Software* (Addison Wesley-Longman, 1995).

The primary function of a pattern is to pass on knowledge from experts to their fellow practitioners. Patterns distill experience into a form that can be easily applied to new instances of familiar problems.

Although patterns have been written to solve many problems, including how the design process itself should be carried out, we'll look at a specific type of pattern in this chapter, *design patterns*. Design patterns are immensely helpful when you need to decide how responsibilities are assigned (Larman, 1998). Design patterns are not algorithms, reusable code, or data structures. They are descriptions of objects and collaborations that you can apply in a specific context.

Elements of a Pattern

A minimalist description of a pattern consists of:

Name. This is a descriptive name that should communicate a lot of information about the pattern. The idea is to increase your vocabulary with words that communicate complex concepts quickly.

Problem. The problem describes the context in which the pattern should be applied.

Solution. The solution describes the objects, relationships, responsibilities, and collaborations that are part of the pattern. It is essentially an abstract template that can be applied to the problem in context. You can superimpose the solution on your problem to light the way toward an implementation.

There are numerous variations on this formalized description.

Observer

Suppose you are building a system to handle auctions. In any given auction, you have one object to represent the Item, and any number of objects to represent the

Bidders. When the price of the auction changes, how do you notify each Bidder of the new price without coupling the Bidders too closely to the Items?

The Observer pattern (Gamma) can be applied in a situation such as this. This pattern can be applied where you want changes in one object (the subject) to result in notifications being sent to other objects (the observers).

In the Observer pattern, you have one subject and many observers. A typical way to handle this is to define a Subject and Observer class, and let your implementations inherit from those classes.

The following is a more formal description of the Observer pattern.

Problem

How do we define a one-to-many relationship between objects in such a way that changes in one object result in notification to the others (without unnecessarily increasing coupling)?

Solution

The Subject. The Subject class should define something similar to the following methods:

METHOD	PURPOSE
addObserver(Observer)	Attach an observer
removeObserver(Observer)	Remove an observer
notify()	For each observer, send a subjectChanged() message

You can define a class, such as Item, to be a subclass of Subject. This way, Item inherits the methods just described. Through polymorphism (see Chapter 5, "Object-Oriented Programming"), we can say that an Item is also a Subject.

The Observer. The Observer class only needs a subjectChanged() method. One way to implement this is to define a class, such as Bidder, as a subclass of Observer.

It's up to you to define how the Bidder (or any Observer) will respond to the subjectChanged() message. More likely than not, the Observer will invoke one of the subject's methods, such as getPrice().

What's the point of all this observing? The Observer pattern decreases coupling: The Observer (Bidder) needs to know about the Subject (Item), but the

Subject doesn't need to know anything about the true identity of the Observer. Item knows it is being watched by a bunch of Observers, but it doesn't know who they are.

NOTE

The notification that is sent to each observer shouldn't carry extra information: It should only tell observers that something has changed. It's up to the observers to discover whatever data they need. If the Item communicated its price to the Observer instead, coupling would be increased. The Subject shouldn't know what the Observer wants—as far as the Item is concerned, the Observer might be interested in something else, such as the starting bid or some other piece of data.

The Observer pattern is ideal in circumstances where the Observer already knows about the Subject. By applying this pattern, you solve the notification problem without increasing coupling.

Figure 8.4 shows a class diagram that shows the Item, Bidder, and Observer classes. The filled diamond in some of the relationships indicates composition, that one object contains the other (for example, the Subject contains Observers). The hollow triangle indicates inheritance: Item is a subclass of Subject, and Bidder is a subclass of Observer.

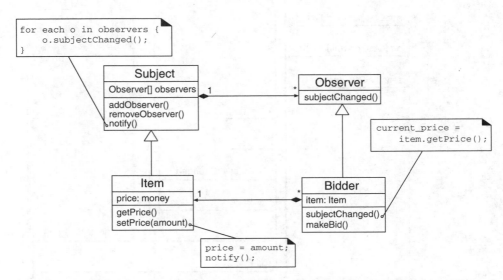

Figure 8.4 Objects and relationships in a sample application of the Observer pattern.

To use this pattern, first create an Item object. Then, as you create each Bidder object, register the Bidder with the Item's addObserver() method. When the price changes:

- The Item sends itself a notify() message.
- The Item sends the subjectChanged() message to each Observer.
- Each Observer decides to invoke the Item's getPrice() method.

Figure 8.5 shows the Observer pattern in action.

You can also use the Observer pattern when you don't know the type of the observer. For example, if your subject was a Directory object that represents a

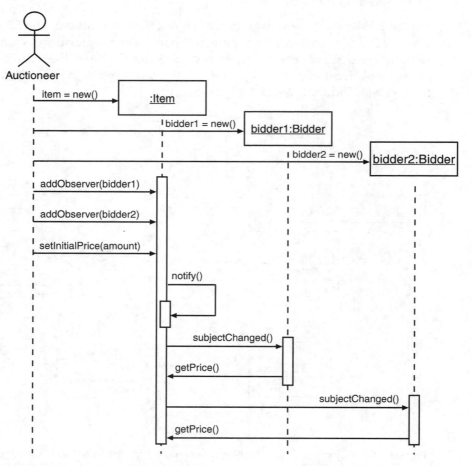

Figure 8.5   A system sequence diagram for a sample application of Observer.

directory of files on a file system (such as /home/bjepson), you could have multiple Observers, as long as they were subclasses or implementations of Observer. For example, you might have observers such as DiskUsageChart or HTMLContents. If the contents of the directory changed, the Observers would need to know about it. Figure 8.6 shows a representation of this relationship.

The Value of Patterns

Remember, a pattern is a solution, but it is not meant to be treated as reusable code. Patterns often include examples to aid in explanation, but there is no reason you need to implement the solution using the same class names and methods in the example. Patterns are more abstract than implementations; they suggest the classes and collaborations that make up a potential solution. You can then superimpose this suggestion on your problem to create a solution.

Patterns make systems easy to explain—using patterns, two programmers can communicate about a system on a high level, but express enough to be able to understand the innards. Patterns also provide a way to codify and communicate programmers' experiences to share with others, or recollect themselves at a later date (Gamma, et al).

Patterns help us break problems down by recognizing several places where patterns can be applied within complex problems. This makes systems easier to understand because we can look at a system as an applied set of patterns. Patterns free us to think about complex systems on a higher level.

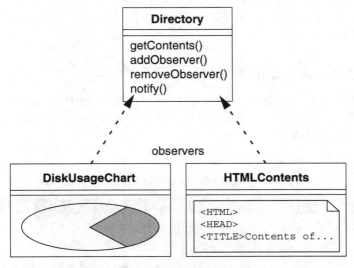

Figure 8.6   Observing a directory's contents.

Choosing Patterns

How do you choose which patterns to use? There are many ways to approach this. The first question you need to ask is, when is it appropriate to use a pattern? To answer this question, you need to think about the problem you are trying to solve.

To assign responsibilities in our design, we're using Larman's General Responsibility Assignment Software Patterns (GRASP). We're not going to describe each pattern here. Instead, we'll bring them up as we use them. To get you thinking about how you'd use them, here's a table of Pattern names, and the categories they fit into. Table 8.1 lists some of the GRASP patterns.

Using UML in Object-Oriented Design

The artifacts in the previous chapter are aids to comprehension. The artifacts that are produced in this section describe software constructs. In this chapter, we'll build two artifacts that will directly help you in writing code: A Collaboration Diagram and Class Diagram. When those are completed, we'll discuss techniques to deal with the user interface and database issues. By deferring consideration of these issues, we can concentrate on the domain logic, and achieve a purer design of our classes.

In this chapter, we're going to design for only one of the use cases. In practice, you will assign one or more use cases to a given iteration, and develop a prototype for that use case. As you proceed through successive iterations, you will gradually take on more use cases. For example, if you did *Borrow Books* in the first iteration, you might do *Borrow Books* and *Return Books* in the second iteration.

Baggage from Previous Iterations

When you move into the next iteration, what can you keep? Do you have to throw away all the artifacts and implementations from the previous iteration? Let's consider both scenarios:

Table 8.1 Patterns Used in This Chapter (from Larman's GRASP Patterns)

PATTERN	DESCRIPTION
Controller	Who is responsible for handling a system operation?
Expert	What is the most basic technique we can use to delegate responsibility?
Creator	Who should be responsible for creating an instance?

Collaboration and class diagrams. If a system operation, such as identifyPatron, occurs in more than one use case, you should make sure you have only one current version of the identifyPatron collaboration diagram. It's okay to archive the version from the first iteration, but when you are in the second iteration, your diagram for identifyPatron should satisfy the needs of both use cases. If you need to update identifyPatron in some way to support Return Books, you will need to propagate this change through the collaboration diagram and probably the class diagram, as well.

In short, if the artifacts from the previous iteration are consistent with the responsibility assignments you decided on for the current iteration, you may be able to reuse them.

Implementations. If you have implemented classes in a modular fashion, you may be able to reuse them in subsequent implementations. However, if you end up seriously changing the responsibilities of a class in a given iteration, you should strongly consider reimplementing that class. If you changed the collaboration and class diagram that apply to that class, you'll almost certainly need to reimplement it.

Collaboration Diagrams

We're going to tackle each of the system operations that apply to the Borrow Books use case. We'll develop one collaboration diagram for each operation.

Before we develop the diagram, we need to determine how responsibility is assigned. We can assign responsibilities to a concept (which we should start thinking about as a class since we are moving from analysis to design) that we discovered in the conceptual model, or we can assign it to a new class. Some of the patterns we'll look at will suggest new classes, others will encourage us to use classes from the conceptual model.

Developing Collaboration Diagrams

To develop collaboration diagrams for a specific use case:

Represent each operation. Develop a separate collaboration diagram for each system operation. The system operations are shown visually in the system sequence diagrams, and you should also have a contract for each system operation.

Figure out who's in charge. When you are beginning to develop a collaboration diagram for a system operation, the first question you have to ask is "who is in charge?" The Controller pattern is a means for discovering this information and is a logical starting point for any system message.

Make good on all the promises in the contract. After you've figured out who is in charge of the operation, look at each of the promises in the contract (post-conditions), and use patterns to assign the responsibility for fulfilling those promises.

Collaboration Diagrams for Borrow Books

Let's develop a collaboration diagram for each of the system operations in the Borrow Book use case. The system sequence diagrams let you see, at a glance, all the operations that go into a use case. Use the contracts to get to the specific details of the operation.

The identifyPatron() Operation

Let's take care of the first operation in Borrow Books: identifyPatron().

We start by looking at who is in charge. Let's look at Controller, which is one of Larman's GRASP Patterns. This is not the full description of the pattern, but is instead a discussion of the pattern in the context of the problem we are solving. A more complete description of the pattern can be found in Larman.

Classes versus Instances (Objects)

When we work with an instance of a class, such as Patron, we write :Patron instead of Patron. UML makes a distinction between classes and instances of classes: ClassName represents the name of a class, :ClassName represents an instance of ClassName (an object), and myObject:ClassName represents a named instance of ClassName (the object named myObject).

Who Is in Control? (Using the Controller Pattern)

Let's use the Controller pattern to figure out who is responsible for system operations. We'll examine some variations on the pattern that may be useful.

Problem. In the previous chapter, we assigned a number of operations to the system, which represents the system as a whole. Who is responsible for handling a system operation? The Controller pattern answers this.

Solution. Consider one of the following choices:

1. *Façade Controller.* Do you create an object that represents the overall system or the organization as a whole? If so, using an object such as CirculationSystem or Library might be a good choice.

2. *Role Controller.* Should you use something that represents an active agent in the real world? If so, Librarian would be a good choice.

3. *Fabricated Entity.* Should you create a controller for the use case or a collection of use cases? If so, a handler class (a class whose sole purpose is to handle a sequence of operations) like BorrowBooksHandler would be appropriate. You could also create a handler to take care of related use cases, such as LoanHandler, which could handle the Borrow Books use case and Return Books use case.

Restrictions. Use the same controller for all operations in a given use case.

Considerations. Both the Façade and Role controller carry with them the possibility of becoming a single class that has too much responsibility (see the *Poltergeist and Blob AntiPatterns* sidebar). Adding a handler for each use case, such as BorrowBooksHandler, runs the risk of creating too many classes with similar responsibilities. Consequently, we are going to use a fabricated entity (LoanHandler) to handle all use cases related to borrowing or returning books.

General Notes on the Application of a Pattern:

- Show the system operation as a message being sent to an instance of the class you chose. Use an arrow as shown in Figure 8.7 to show the direction of the message.

- If a parameter corresponds to an attribute of another object, make sure you write the parameter in the same form as you did in the conceptual model. For example, this operation can take a Patron's last name as a parameter. We wrote last_name in the conceptual model, so you should use that, not "last name", LastName, or some other variation. Be consistent!

- If there are alternative parameters for the message, show all of them using alternative messages. In the case of identifyPatron, you can either identify a Patron with either the library card ID or the Patron's first and last name. Find an economical way to express the condition that constrains the alternatives, and use braces to express it, as in [has card] and [forgot card].

Figure 8.7 shows the first draft of the diagram.

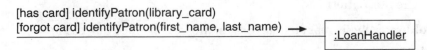

[has card] identifyPatron(library_card)
[forgot card] identifyPatron(first_name, last_name) → :LoanHandler

Figure 8.7 The identifyPatron operation, step one.

Cleanup tasks. If we were covering another iteration of development, we'd update the Conceptual Model to include LoanHandler and use this revised conceptual model when we begin the next iteration.

We're not done yet! Next, we need to make good on all the promises of the identifyPatron() contract.

A Patron Was Found (Using the Expert Pattern)

The contract for identifyPatron() specifies that a Patron was found. We need to ask some object to find a Patron for us, given the patron's library card code or the patron's first and last name.

Who is responsible for knowing a Patron by name or library card? Larman's Expert pattern (one of the GRASP patterns) can help us answer this question:

Problem. What is the simplest technique we can use to delegate responsibility?

Solution. Assign responsibility to the object that has the information required to solve the problem.

Considerations. Look at the conceptual model to find objects that contain, record, or otherwise know about Patron. While a Patron has relationships with several objects, Library appears to be a clear candidate, since a Patron is a member of a Library.

Application of the pattern (see also, *General Notes on the Application of a Pattern*):

- Show the operation as a message being sent to an instance of the class you chose. Use an arrow as shown in the figure to show the direction of the message. In this case, we'll show two alternative messages, findPatron(library_card) and findPatron(first_name, last_name), being sent to Library. Who sends this message? The only object we have defined so far, and the only object that knows library_card or first_name and last_name, is the LoanHandler. So, both by default, and by Expert, LoanHandler becomes the object that sends the message to Library.

Figure 8.8 shows the application of this pattern.

A Patron Was Instantiated (The Creator Pattern)

Now, we have the problem of creating the Patron we found. This is a job for the Creator pattern.

Problem. Who is responsible for creating an instance of a class?

Solution. Assign this responsibility to whoever contains, aggregates, records, closely uses, or has initializing data for objects of that class.

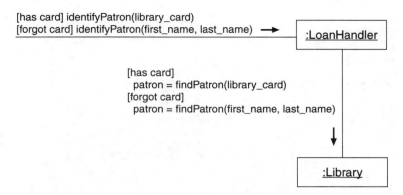

[has card] identifyPatron(library_card)
[forgot card] identifyPatron(first_name, last_name) ⟶   :LoanHandler

[has card]
 patron = findPatron(library_card)
[forgot card]
 patron = findPatron(first_name, last_name)

:Library

Figure 8.8   The identifyPatron operation, step two.

Considerations. As with the previous step, Library is the clear choice, since a
Patron is a member of a Library.

**Application of the pattern (see also, *General Notes on the Application
of a Pattern*):**

- Up until now, we have been looking at associations, such as *member-of*,
  as abstract connections between objects. However, in order to fulfill
  this association, Library must contain all the Patrons it is responsible
  for. For now, we must represent this as a collection of Patrons. Since
  there are two ways we can access the data, we'll represent it as two collections: a collection of Patrons ordered by name (called byName) and
  a collection of Patrons ordered by library_card (called byCard). A collection is represented as a *multiobject*, two boxes stacked on top of each
  other, shown in Figure 8.9.

- In an actual implementation of this design, we'd need to tie this to the
  database somehow. In that case, we'll have to choose a general architecture for the database layer, and adapt this particular collaboration to
  fit it. So, consider the two collections as placeholders for the database:
  For now, they need to be added to the Library class diagram as two
  array objects (see Figure 8.13, later in this chapter).

The Patron Was Associated with the System (Expert)

At this point, we come across the area of incompleteness: Somehow, the
Patron must be remembered (associated with the system) to satisfy the pre-
conditions of the loanBook() contract. Which object will represent the system? Remember that the restrictions on the Controller pattern tell us to use
the same controller for all operations in a use case, so the LoanHandler will
be available for the duration of the use case. Also, since the Library returns

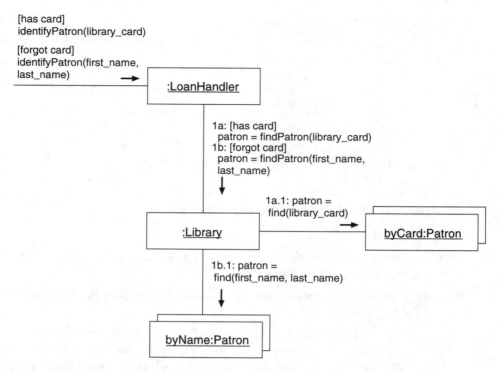

Figure 8.9 The completed identifyPatron operation.

the patron instance to the LoanHandler, the Patron is already associated with the LoanHandler.

So, the LoanHandler is the ideal representative for the system, and no further change is needed to the diagram. Figure 8.9 shows the completed identifyPatron collaboration diagram.

What's this 1a and 1b stuff? This figure introduces notation that lets you trace execution paths through the collaboration diagram. In a collaboration diagram without alternatives, you'll see numbers next to every message except the initial one. Typically, they will be numbered in sequence, indicating the order of execution, as shown in Figure 8.10.

If a message to one object causes the object to send another message, these messages are numbered differently, as shown in Figure 8.11.

Messages 1.1 and 1.2 are messages that resulted from message 1, and message 1.2.1 was the result of message 1.2. The execution order is:

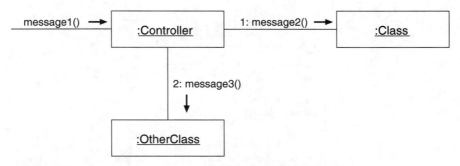

Figure 8.10 Tracing execution through a collaboration diagram.

1

1.1

1.2

1.2.1

2

2.1

The loanBook() Operation

Let's take a quick look at the next operation in the Borrow Books use case. After each post-condition, we list the pattern and the steps that are shown in Figure 8.12.

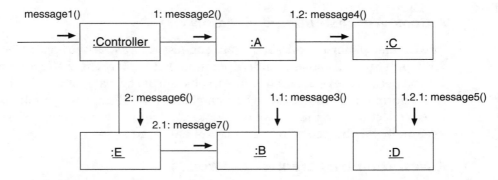

Figure 8.11 Slightly more convoluted execution.

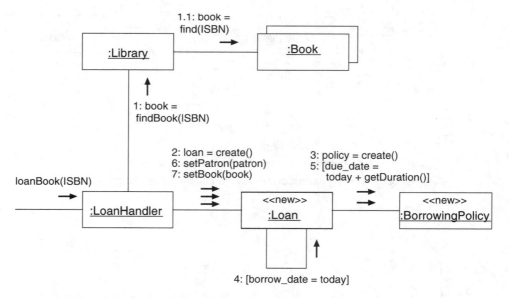

Figure 8.12 Collaboration diagram for loanBook.

Who Is in Control? (Controller)

The first step is to identify a controller. In the previous system operation, we identified a controller called LoanHandler. Because the Controller pattern tells us to use the same controller for all operations in the use case, we'll use LoanHandler again.

A Book Was Found (Expert, 1)

As with identifyPatron(), Expert comes in handy here. Because the Library contains books, it is the expert with regard to Book.

A Book Was Instantiated (Creator, 1.1)

The Creator pattern applies here, and suggests Library as the creator. Although this is listed as a find() operation on the diagram, we're looking at it as a special case of creation, since an object is instantiated after it is found: It lies dormant in storage (such as a database) until it's needed. Again, we'll use a collection to represent all the Books the Library knows about. This will eventually be plugged into some form of data access.

A New Loan Was Created (Creator, 2)

Who is responsible for creating an instance of a Loan? The Creator pattern suggests that we can use whatever class contains the initializing data for

Loan. In this case, it is clear that the LoanHandler has this information (it has knowledge of both the book and the patron), so it will create the Loan.

A Borrowing Policy Was Created (Creator, 3)

The *governs* relationship between Loan and BorrowingPolicy can be interpreted to suggest that Loan uses BorrowingPolicy in some way, so we'll let Loan create the BorrowingPolicy.

Borrow Date Was Set to the Current Date (Expert, 4)

The Expert pattern suggests that Loan, which knows the most about its own attribute (borrow_date), is responsible for this.

Due Date Was Set to the Current Date Plus Duration (Expert, 5)

Again, the Expert pattern suggests that Loan should initiate this message (since it is setting its own attribute, due_date).

Loan Was Associated with Patron and with Book (Expert, 6 and 7)

By the Expert pattern, we see that LoanHandler knows the most about a Book, a Loan, and a Patron. LoanHandler, by Expert will be responsible for associating a Loan with a Patron and a Book. Figure 8.12 shows the completed collaboration diagram.

The Poltergeist and Blob AntiPatterns

AntiPatterns: Refactoring Software, Architectures, and Projects in Crisis by Brown, Malveau, McCormick, and Mowbray (Wiley, 1998) includes two AntiPatterns, the Poltergeist and the Blob, which represent the dark side of controller or handler classes.

The Poltergeist is a software controller that has a transient lifespan, no internal state, and is usually called into being to temporarily use other classes.

The Blob is a controller that monopolizes the operation of the application, lacks a clear reason for having its responsibilities, and contains many unrelated attributes and operations.

You can avoid creating the Poltergeist and Blob by using controllers sparingly, making sure they have a clear reason for their existence, and making sure that they take on closely related responsibilities.

Class Diagrams

The next step, class diagrams, will take you very close to the code. To develop class diagrams, you should reflect upon the conceptual model and collaboration diagrams. The class diagram will look somewhat like a subset of the conceptual model, but it will have more details and any extra classes you defined when you wrote the collaboration diagrams.

To develop class diagrams, we'll use a technique based on the one found in Larman:

Identify all classes. Examine the collaboration diagrams, and find all the classes. For economy, we will show the byName and byCard collections as attributes, since they are explicitly used in the collaboration diagrams (we'll also add a byISBN collection to support searching for books by ISBN). Library has a relationship with Patron, and showing a relationship between Library and a Patron collection would be redundant.

Diagram the attributes. For each class you found in the previous step, look up its attributes in the conceptual model. Start a diagram of classes with these attributes. As you can see in Figure 8.13, these classes have an extra box at the bottom to hold methods.

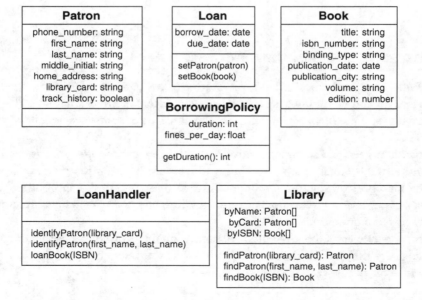

Figure 8.13   Borrow Books class diagram with classes, attributes, and methods.

As with the conceptual model, don't worry about foreign keys. For example, you don't need a Patron and Book attribute on Loan, because we will capture this as relationships between Loan and the other two classes.

Diagram the methods. Look at all the messages that are sent to each class in the collaboration diagrams. For each message sent to the class, add a method, its parameters, and its return type to the class diagram. Methods appear in the lower box, as shown in Figure 8.13. Unless you have constructors that take arguments, don't show constructors. Unless they are specifically referenced in the collaboration diagrams, don't show accessor (get and set) methods (methods for getting or setting attributes). The existence of the class implies a constructor, and every attribute implies accessor methods. If you included get and set methods for every attribute, the more important methods might be lost in the clutter. For example, setPatron and setBook set the implied Book and Patron attribute of the Loan. We'll include them in the diagram because they increase clarity.

Diagram the associations. Examine the collaboration diagrams (not the conceptual model), to see if there are any associations that would imply an attribute. These include situations such as:

- One class sends a message to another
- One class is passed to another as a parameter
- One class creates another

One further clarification. Only choose things that need to be maintained over time. This excludes things that would only be represented as temporary variables (such as the patron and book that LoanHandler creates before passing them to the Loan). Table 8.2 lists the associations we found.

Figure 8.14 shows the diagram with attributes, methods, and associations.

Table 8.2 Associations in the Borrow Books Class Diagram

ASSOCIATION	RATIONALE
LoanHandler looks-in Library	The LoanHandler needs to have access to the Library across multiple messages (the Library is used in both identifyPatron and loanBook).
Library contains Book Library contains Patron	These are required because the Library is used as an expert in two places (identifyPatron [Figure 8.9] steps 1a and 1b and loanBook step 1).
Loan captures-loan-of Book Patron is a borrower with respect to a Loan	In order to complete a loan, the book and patron must be associated with the Loan object (loanBook steps 3 and 4).

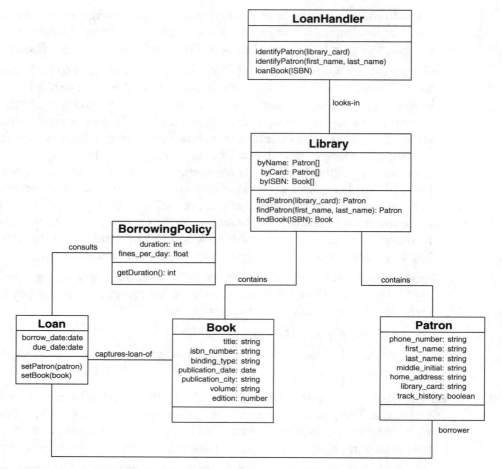

Figure 8.14 The class diagram, now with associations.

Diagram dependencies. We'll use dependencies (lightly dashed lines) to capture any temporary dependencies between objects. These include situations where one class needs to know about another, but not through an attribute. Table 8.3 lists the corresponding dependencies.

Diagram visibility. At one end or another (or both) of an association or dependency, an arrow indicates the direction of visibility. This tells us which object knows about the other, and can be derived through the associations and dependencies. Since a LoanHandler knows about a Loan, there will be an arrow along the dependency pointing at Loan. The reverse is *not* true: The Loan does not and should not know about the LoanHandler (otherwise, Loan would be coupled to LoanHandler, and it's in our interests to keep coupling to a minimum).

Table 8.3   Dependencies in the Borrow Books Class Diagram

DEPENDENCY	RATIONALE
LoanHandler and Loan	The LoanHandler creates a Loan (loanBook step 2).
LoanHandler and Book	The LoanHandler gets a Book from Library.findBook() and passes it to Loan (loanBook steps 1 and 7).
LoanHandler and Patron	The LoanHandler gets a Patron from Library and passes it to Loan (identifyPatron and loanBook step 6).

Figure 8.15 shows the class diagram with classes, attributes, methods, associations, dependencies, and visibility.

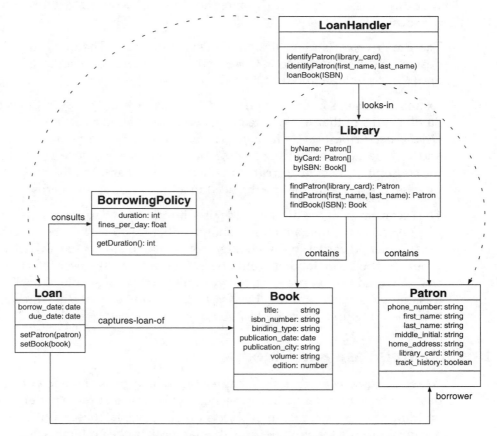

Figure 8.15   The finished class diagram for the Borrow Books use case.

UI and Database Design in Context

Earlier chapters on database and UI design presented design strategies outside of the context of the OO analysis and design process. Although this approach enabled us to focus on the core issues without coupling the details of those issues to OO analysis and design, we did not generate design documents that capture the level of detail that the OO analysis and design did. In fact, the design strategies discussed in those chapters are ideal for smaller projects. On larger projects, it makes sense to begin with object-oriented design, and proceed to UI and database design.

Designing the User Interface

Now that we have a collaboration diagram and a class design, we need to develop a user interface. The two questions we need to answer are "how do we design the user interface?," and "how do we incorporate it into our current design?"

There are two parts to the design of the user interface. The first is the GUI design, which is discussed in Chapter 3, "User Interface Design." How do we graft this technique into the OOA&D process?

Examine the steps in the section titled *The Development Process* in Chapter 3. Steps 4 and 5 of that section are discussed in detail in the section titled *Develop and Refine the UI Prototype*. That section suggests identifying nouns and verbs, and then building an object-attribute tree. However, you can use the conceptual model we created in the previous chapter as the basis of this process, possibly eliminating the need to identify nouns and verbs.

The second part of the design of the user interface is adapting the user interface objects to the domain objects shown in Figure 8.15. The Observer pattern, discussed earlier in this chapter, gives us a great way to solve this problem: The LoanHandler would be the subject, and the user interface classes would be observers. There are other patterns available to deal with this issue. Larman examines the *Model-View Separation* pattern, which is helpful in hooking up a user interface to domain objects.

Bridging Database and Objects

As we discussed earlier in this chapter, bridging objects and a relational database can be very difficult. In this section, we'll glance at some patterns for building frameworks that map objects to relational databases. Building such a framework is a lot of work (probably larger than the system itself!).

The point of this section is to educate you about object-relational mapping and expose you to some frameworks that others have built. Unless you are responsible for building an object-relational framework that's going to be widely reused, it is probably more trouble than it's worth: Use one of the solutions listed in the next section. All of the object-relational mapping tools discussed are open source software, so if the solution doesn't fit your needs, you should customize or port it. This will certainly be less effort than building from scratch!

NOTE

As of this writing, no object-relational framework exists specifically for GNOME or KDE, so if you're looking for some way to contribute to the free software community, perhaps this section will inspire you.

Patterns for Object-Relational Mapping

There are a number of pattern languages (collections of cooperating patterns) that address the issue of object-relational mapping. Many of these are listed on the Cetus Links Object-Relational Mapping page at www.cetus-links.org/oo_db_systems_3.html.

Let's take a look at some of the patterns in one of the most popular pattern languages, *Crossing Chasms* (Brown and Whitenack, *Pattern Languages of Program Design* Volume 2, Addison-Wesley, and online at www.ksccary.com).

Table Design Time. According to this pattern, the best time to design a table is after you have created a first pass of your object model (this is the class diagram as shown in Figure 8.15, not the conceptual model). The Table Design Time pattern suggests that doing a database design first will result in a design that does not work well with an object-oriented approach.

Representing Objects as Tables. This pattern depends on the Foreign Key Reference, Object Identifier, and Representing Collections patterns. Otherwise, it suggests that many attributes can map cleanly to columns.

Representing Collections in a Relational Database. This pattern suggests using an extra table to represent one-to-many relationships, as we did with many-to-many relationships in Chapter 2, "Database Design." This approach allows visibility from the parent object, instead of from the child (see *From Domain to Persistence* earlier in this chapter).

Object Identifier (OID). This pattern suggests using unique IDs for each persistent object. If you read Chapter 2, this should not be much of a surprise. However, primary keys are usually only unique within a given table. A unique OID should be unique throughout the entire database. That way, if you use two tables to represent subclasses of a parent class (such as Student-Patron and ChildPatron), you won't have objects with duplicate OIDs if you cast them to their superclass.

Foreign Key Reference. The Foreign Key Reference pattern suggests storing a reference to the foreign instance's OID, as is done in relational database design.

Broker. A broker is a special class that knows how to talk to the database. It is responsible for creating instances of domain objects from the database, and for updating the database when an object changes. See *Tangram: Object-Relational Mapping in Perl* in Chapter 12, "DBI and Perl," for an example of a framework that uses a broker, the Tangram::Storage class.

Crossing Chasms is a complete pattern language that includes many other patterns. We've presented a glance at some of the patterns here to give you a taste of it, but it would be best if you read the entire pattern language if you plan to implement any of it.

Object-Relational Mapping Tools

Here are some free tools that may help you with object-relational mapping:

Tangram. Tangram is an object-relational mapping framework for Perl. The section titled *Tangram: Object-Relational Mapping in Perl* provides an introduction to Tangram, and can be found in Chapter 12.

Enterprise Java Beans (EJB). EJB is a component technology for Java that is used to develop your domain objects (business objects). It includes many features, including persistence via an object-relational mapping. Roesch Consulting AG distributes an EJB implementation (RC-EJB) under the GNU General Public License. More information is available at www .roesch-ag.ch/ejb/en/download.html.

GNUStep. GNUStep is a free implementation of OpenStep, a suite of enterprise application frameworks developed by Sun and NeXT. GNUStep includes GNUStep-db, an implementation of EOF (Enterprise Objects Framework), which supports object-relational mapping to a number of SQL databases. More information can be found at www.gnustep.org.

JORA. Konstantin Knizhnik's home page is at www.ispras.ru/~knizhnik/. Among other things related to object-oriented database development, you can find JORA (Java Object-Relational Adapter) there, which helps you map Java classes to database tables.

From Design to Code

Once you have completed a design for your system, and taken the database and user interface into account, you should map your design to code. This is a straightforward translation from your design artifacts. Let's walk through the implementation of the Loan class:

1. *Define classes with the methods and attributes shown in the class diagrams.* Include accessor methods (get and set methods) for all attributes.

2. *Add attributes to support visibility inherent in the model.* If the multiplicity of an association is greater than one, you need to use a collection class. Add any accessor methods that are needed. For example, since Patron and Book are visible to Loan, there are two attributes of the Loan class: a Patron called *patron*, and a Book called *book*.

3. *Add the constructor.* Write the constructor for the class. If you need to create any instances of attributes you added in Step 1 or 2 (such as the Library or BorrowingPolicy), do so within the body of the constructor.

4. *Use the collaboration diagrams to write the body of the method.* Start with message 1 and follow it to 1.1, 1.1.1, etc. Then move on to message 2, and so forth.

5. *Inspect the contracts (see Chapter 7, "Object-Oriented Analysis") to decide what error and exception handling is needed.* You may find that the classes do not support the functionality necessary to implement all the exceptions. See the two FIXME notes in the LoanHandler listing—these suggest the need for boolean methods such as Patron.hasOverdueBooks() and Book.isLoanedOut(). When this happens, you should go back to your class and collaboration diagrams, and add these methods: they are important enough that they need to be shown in the diagrams. In such cases, we see the need for iterative development: much is learned each time we go around.

Let's look at the listings for a Java implementation of Loan and LoanHandler. The comments in the code are accompanied by step numbers, which correspond to the steps in the preceding list. Some comments also include a reference to the system operation (either loanBook—Figure 8.12, or identifyPatron—Figure 8.9) and the corresponding message number. Because we only show implementations for two of the classes, only some of the messages are implemented (identifyPatron 1a, 1b; loanBook 1, 2, 3, 4, 5, 6, and 7).

Here is the listing for the Java implementation of Loan:

```java
import java.util.*;

// A Loan class for the library system.
//
public class Loan {

  // When the book was borrowed. (Step 1)
  GregorianCalendar borrow_date;

  // When the book is due. (Step 1)
  GregorianCalendar due_date;

  // Attributes to support visibility in the model.
  // (Step 2)
  //
  Patron patron; // The patron who borrows the book
  Book book;     // The book that is borrowed.

  // The Constructor. (Step 3)
  //
  public Loan() {

      // Create a borrowing policy. (Step 4)
      // Operation: loanBook(), message 3
      //
      BorrowingPolicy policy = new BorrowingPolicy();

      // set borrow date to today (Step 3)
      // Operation: loanBook(), message 4
      //
      borrow_date = new GregorianCalendar();

      // Set the due date. (Step 4)
      // Operation: loanBook(), message 5.
      //
      due_date = new GregorianCalendar();
      due_date.add(Calendar.DAY_OF_WEEK,
                   policy.getDuration());

  }

  // Set the Patron who borrows the book.
  // (Step 1 - defined in class diagram)
  //
  public void setPatron(Patron the_patron) {
      patron = the_patron;
  }

  // Get the Patron who borrowed the book.
  // (Step 2)
```

```java
    //
    public Patron getPatron() {
        return patron;
    }


    // Set the Book that the Patron borrows.
    // (Step 1 - defined in class diagram)
    //
    public void setBook(Book the_book) {
        book = the_book;
    }


    // Get the Book that the Patron borrowed.
    // (Step 2)
    //
    public Book getBook() {
        return book;
    }


    // Set the borrowed date.
    // (Step 1)
    //
    public void setBorrowDate(GregorianCalendar the_date) {
        borrow_date = the_date;
    }


    // Get the borrowed date.
    // (Step 1)
    //
    public GregorianCalendar getBorrowDate() {
        return borrow_date;
    }


    // Set the due date.
    // (Step 1)
    //
    public void setDueDate(GregorianCalendar the_date) {
        due_date = the_date;
    }


    // Get the due date.
    // (Step 1)
    //
    public GregorianCalendar getDueDate() {
        return due_date;
    }

}
```

Here is the listing for the Java implementation of LoanHandler:

```java
// A Loan handler class for the library system.
//
public class LoanHandler {

  Library library;        // The library (Step 2)
  private Patron patron;  // The patron (Step 4)
                          // (needed to remember the patron
                          //  between identifyPatron() and
                          //  loanBook().)

  // The constructor. (Step 3)
  //
  public LoanHandler() {
      library = new Library();
  }

  // Identify a Patron by library card.
  // (Step 1)
  //
  public void identifyPatron(String library_card) {

      // Use the library to find a Patron.
      // (Step 4)
      // Operation: identifyPatron(), message 1a
      //
      patron = library.findPatron(library_card);

      // Make sure we got a patron. (Step 5)
      //
      if (patron == null) {
          System.err.println("No patron found for " +
                             "card " + library_card);
          System.exit(0);
      }
  }

  // Identify a Patron by name. (Step 1)
  //
  public void identifyPatron(String first_name,
                             String last_name)
  {
      // Use the library to find a Patron.
      // (Step 4)
      // Operation: identifyPatron(), message 1b
      //
      patron = library.findPatron(first_name,
                                  last_name);
      // Make sure we got a patron.
```

```
        // (Step 5)
        //
        if (patron == null) {
            System.err.println(first_name + " " + last_name +
                            " is not a Patron.");
            System.exit(0);
        }
    }

// Loan a book. (Step 1)
//
public void loanBook(String ISBN) {

    // Make sure we have a patron. (Step 5)
    //
    if (patron == null) {
        System.err.println("There is no patron. " +
                        "Did you call identifyPatron()?");
        System.exit(0);
    }

    // FIXME: How do we find out if the Patron has
    // overdue books? (Step 5)

    // Use the library to find the Book. (Step 4)
    // Operation: loanBook(), message 1
    //
    Book book = library.findBook(ISBN);

    // Make sure we got a book. (Step 5)
    //
    if (book == null) {
        System.err.println("No book found for " +
                        "ISBN " + ISBN);
        System.exit(0);
    }

    // FIXME: How do we find out if the book is
    // already checked out? (Step 5)

    // Create a loan and set the patron and book.
    // (Step 4)
    //
    Loan loan = new Loan(); // Operation: loanBook(), message 2

    // messages 3,4, and 5 are handled inside Loan.

    loan.setPatron(patron); // Operation: loanBook(), message 6
    loan.setBook(book);     // Operation: loanBook(), message 7
```

```
        // OK to forget about the patron now.
        //
        patron = null;

        // We're finished, but here's something to help
        // with debugging.
        //
        System.out.print("The book " + book.getTitle());
        System.out.print(" is due on ");
        System.out.println(loan.getDueDate().getTime());

    }

}
```

Finally, here are some "dummy" implementations of the other classes, and a main() method that can be used to test Loan and LoanHandler. This should give you an idea of how you can use mocked-up classes to test as you work on the other classes (as we did with Loan and LoanHandler):

```
// Dummy class definitions.
//
class Patron { }

class Book {
  public String getTitle() {
      return "Naked Lunch";
  }
}

class Library {
  Patron findPatron(String c) {
      return new Patron();
  }
  Patron findPatron(String f, String l) {
      return new Patron();
  }
  Book findBook(String i) {
      return new Book();
  }
}

class BorrowingPolicy {
  int getDuration() {
      return 14;
  }
}

// Simple test program.
```

```
//
public class Test {

  public static void main(String[] argv) {

      LoanHandler lh = new LoanHandler();
      lh.identifyPatron("000-111-333");
      lh.loanBook("0802132952");
  }

}
```

Here is the output of running the Test program:

```
The book Naked Lunch is due on Sun Jan 02 20:21:51 EST 2000
```

Summary

In this chapter, we saw how the artifacts from object-oriented analysis can be used to create an object-oriented design. However, we only scratched the surface of the issues involved with turning this design into code. While seasoned programmers may find it easy to take this final step, less experienced programmers may thirst for more details. For a complete discussion of this topic, we defer to Larman's *Applying UML and Patterns*, which provides a treatment of design-to-code issues that are outside the scope of this book.

Implementation

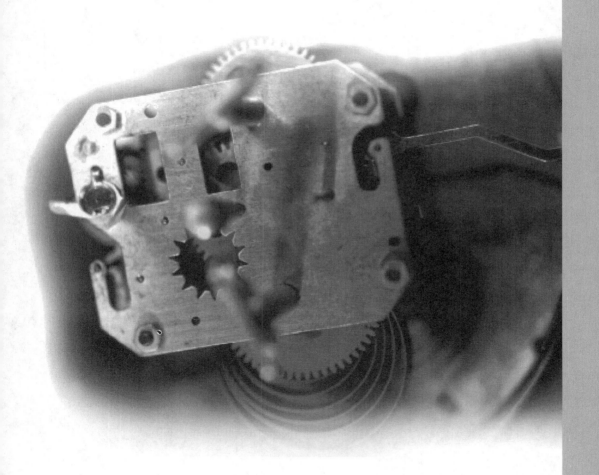

Databases

Chapter 2, "Database Design," introduced you to the logical structure of a relational database: A collection of related tables that are composed of rows and columns. The goal of this chapter is to look at the services that a Relational Database Management System (RDBMS) provides. By the end of this chapter, you should be able to answer these questions:

- How does an RDBMS make information available to applications?
- What do I need to do to get started with one of these databases?
- What sort of neat stuff can I do with the information stored in an RDBMS?
- What are the differences between the various RDBMSs that are available for Linux?

What Is an RDBMS?

If a relational database is a collection of related tables, what is an RDBMS? In *Fundamentals of Database Systems* (Addison-Wesley, 2000), Elmasri and Navathe define a database system as "a *general-purpose software system* that facilitates the processes of *defining*, *constructing*, and *manipulating* databases for various applications."

What do we need to add to this definition to address our expectations of an RDBMS? Assuming that Chapter 2 presented a comprehensive overview of relational features, we could say that an RDBMS is a database system that supports those features: The data is organized into tables that can be manipulated with commands such as SELECT, UPDATE, INSERT, and DELETE. Further, tables can be linked to one another using the WHERE clause (this feature is covered in the section titled *Joins* in Chapter 2).

As it turns out, this is very close to the three criteria that Elmasri and Navathe propose:

Data is stored in relations (tables). Further, these tables are organized in such a way that every column can be identified by its name (as in *SELECT first_name FROM customer*), and the way in which rows are ordered in the table is not important (however, see *Ordering Result Sets* in Chapter 2).

Operations are relational operations. The operations that the system provides should generate new tables from old tables. For example, the *SELECT name, id FROM customer* statement should create a new table as its result (albeit a table that is unnamed) and that is a subset of the old table (customer).

Joins must be supported. A relational database system must support a join operation, as described in the section titled *Joins* in Chapter 2.

Relational Databases and the PC

Some database programmers who come to Linux bring with them certain assumptions from a Windows-based PC background. As a result, some of what these new users find is a little bewildering. This is due to the fact that most of the SQL databases for Linux are client-server. There is a tradition in Windows of having application development and database features presented as a single (monolithic) tool. Examples of this are FoxPro, Access, and FileMaker. Although these tools can work with client-server databases, they also have their own database engines, and as such, there is a more complete integration between parts of the program such as GUI builders and an SQL database. Figure 9.1 shows the structure of such a system.

With most databases for Linux, however, there are at least three components to contend with: the database server, a client API for connecting to the database, and the language you use to build applications. If you need to build a graphical user interface for your applications, it can get even more complicated: Now you have a widget tool kit and the X server to worry about. Figure 9.2 shows one possible arrangement of these components.

So, for those of you coming from a client-server database background, please pardon the parts of this chapter that seem elementary (some of us have a bit of catching up to do).

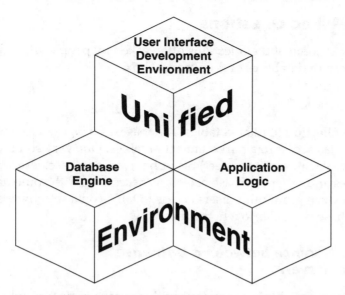

Figure 9.1   Monolithic, unified database development system.

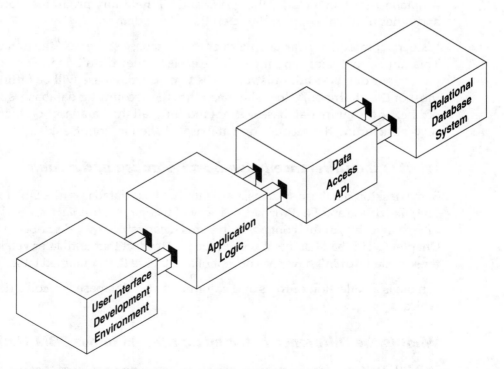

Figure 9.2   Modular database development architecture.

Some Frequently Asked Questions

Let's take a look at some of the questions often asked by people who are starting to work with databases on Linux and Unix.

What Is a Database?

A database is a collection of related tables. Databases can be used as a way of controlling who has access to a particular set of tables. One very common practice is to give each user (or project) his or her own database. Users can then create tables and other database objects as necessary. With some database servers, they can grant other users access to tables on a selective basis. In this way, a database is similar to a home directory.

What Is the Difference between a Database and Database Server?

A database server is roughly synonymous with a database system, which we described earlier. A database server is the daemon that runs in the background and manages the data itself, as well as access to the data from clients. A database system includes the server and all the utility programs, libraries, and other files that support the operation of the database.

It's very common to hear people refer to a database server as "the database." This can be confusing, and it would be easier if they didn't do it. For example, if your database administrator tells you "the database will be offline most of the afternoon," does she mean that the accounting database is going offline, or the entire database server (and thus, all the databases on that server, including the accounting database)? When in doubt, ask!

What Is the Difference between a Database and a Table?

Some desktop database systems, particularly Xbase databases (the DBF file format) like dBase and FoxPro, had a history of using the terms *database* and *table* interchangeably; in this context, both terms mean table as we described it in Chapter 2. This bad habit was encouraged by the fact that until later versions, those systems didn't have the concept of a database that contained tables.

A table is a collection of rows and columns, and a database is a collection of tables.

What Is the Difference between an RDBMS and a DBM File?

DBM (Database Manager) is a library for managing databases that consist of key/value pairs. DBM files are essentially hash tables. So, each entry in the

DBM file has the equivalent of two columns: One is the *key* (a unique ID) and the other is the *value*. Although some programmers have overloaded DBM to support retrieving multiple values by a single key, DBM is not a replacement for an SQL database server. However, DBM is very powerful and useful, and if your database requirements are very simple, you should consider using DBM. For documentation on the GNU implementation of DBM, type 'man gdbm' at the shell prompt.

How Do I Seek on a Table in an RDBMS?

In desktop database products that are Xbase-compatible, a common paradigm for reading rows from a table was:

- Open the table for reading:

```
USE invoices
```

- Set the current index to the field you are interested in:

```
SET INDEX TO customer_name
```

- Seek the first occurrence of some value:

```
SEEK 'Big Company'
```

- Scan through the database until the match fails:

```
SCAN WHILE customer_name = 'Big Company'
    ? inv_no
END SCAN
```

With SQL, you don't deal with the data in this way. Instead, you use one statement to retrieve all the matching rows, which creates a result set. You can think of a result set as a temporary table, or cursor, that contains all the data you asked for. Here is an example that retrieves the same data:

```
SELECT inv_no
    FROM invoices
    WHERE customer_name = 'Big Company'
```

So, the question becomes, how do I process each row in my programs? It differs from one programming language to another. In the chapters that follow, we'll answer that question in a variety of programming languages.

What Is SQL?

SQL is the Structured Query Language, a language for accessing and manipulating relational databases. While SQL has been standardized, there are few implementations that come close to the standard. Chapter 2 introduces some basic SQL, and this chapter also looks at some special topics in SQL. An SQL reference can be found in Appendix A, "SQL Reference."

How Does SQL Get from My Program to the RDBMS?

Just as Linux applications need to link to /usr/lib/libc.so in order to gain access to system calls, database applications must also link against a library that provides access to the database. This library (a data access API) does a number of things on your behalf, including:

- Opening a TCP/IP connection to the database server that is used to send data to and receive data from the server
- Performing whatever handshaking is needed to authenticate you to the server
- Sending SQL commands to the server for you
- Parsing the output of the SQL commands and converting them into objects or data structures that you can work with in your program

What Format Is the Data Stored in?

The short answer is, *it doesn't matter*. Once upon a time, it was important to consider whether a database was compatible with Xbase, Access, or some other such database format. The reason this was important was that people needed some way to connect other programs (such as word processors and spreadsheets) to the database. A common format like Xbase made it easy to do this.

But, because we are dealing with networked database servers, it's more important to ask, "how can I connect my programs to the database?" Because what you are really trying to figure out is how you're going to get data in and out of it.

Because all the databases we're looking at support SQL, you can pump data in and out of them using SQL. Most databases also have a dump utility that lets you import and export in a delimited format, such as comma or tab delimited. Most applications that need to deal with a lot of data (such as a spreadsheet or desktop database) can import from and export to such a format. See the *Bulk Data Operations* section, later in this chapter, for more details.

You could also use a database independence API, such as ODBC (C or C++), DBI (Perl), or JDBC (Java), and write your own programs to move data from one place to another.

What Is a Database Independence API?

All of the database systems we are looking at can be accessed from C or C++, by using the native database API. This API is a collection of headers and libraries that are installed on the server along with the database itself.

Because most native database APIs are not compatible with each other, most people prefer to use a *database independence API*, which unifies the different APIs. Essentially, a database independence API makes all the database APIs look the same, regardless of what database you are using.

For example, ODBC is used by C and C++ programmers as a bridge to a variety of databases. Whether a programmer is using Sybase, Oracle, PostgreSQL, MySQL, or Mini SQL, the programming API is still ODBC; what's different is the special driver program that glues ODBC to native API. Figure 9.3 shows how ODBC can connect C to Sybase's CT-Lib, which uses the network to communicate to a SQL Server. We'll briefly touch on ODBC in some of the following chapters.

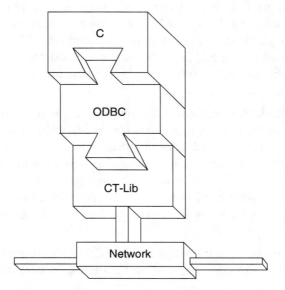

Figure 9.3 Using ODBC to connect to a database.

Getting Started with an RDBMS

In this section, we'll take a brief look at some of the database systems available for Linux, and what you need to do to get started with them. This section is not meant to be a substitute for the documentation that accompanies the system, but is meant to help get you to the point where you can execute your first SQL query.

PostgreSQL

PostgreSQL is a highly advanced, robust open source database system that is based on POSTGRES, a research database developed at the University of California. PostgreSQL runs on many varieties of Unix, and includes many of the features you would find in a commercial database system like Oracle or Sybase. PostgreSQL should be strongly considered when a high-end database is needed.

You can download the latest version from www.postgresql.org (please use a local mirror site, if possible, since this will help avoid network congestion on the main server).

Before You Install

Before you install PostgreSQL, you should consider the following:

Where to find the documentation. Most Linux distributions include PostgreSQL. The documentation for PostgreSQL is usually installed into /usr/doc/postgresql-x.y.z, where x.y.z is the version number of PostgreSQL. When you install PostgreSQL from source code, the documentation is installed into ~postgres/doc (where postgres is the name of the PostgreSQL superuser).

Source versus binary installation. Although PostgreSQL is included with most Linux distributions, you may choose to install it by building it from source. The PostgreSQL source distribution includes a README and INSTALL file. Read both these documents to learn how to install PostgreSQL from source code. We don't believe that there is any advantage to building it from source; whenever possible, you should install the version that came with your Linux distribution, or look for binary releases at the PostgreSQL home page.

Upgrading an older installation. The PostgreSQL INSTALL document includes instructions for upgrading an existing PostgreSQL installation.

After You Install

After you install PostgreSQL, you should consider the following:

Startup and shutdown. If your Linux distribution included PostgreSQL, it should be already configured to start and stop on shutdown. If you installed PostgreSQL from source, you should look in the contrib/linux subdirectory of the source distribution for an initialization script that can start and stop PostgreSQL.

For more details on how to install such a script, see the *Automatic Startup and Shutdown* sections, later in this chapter.

Setting up your environment. If your Linux distribution included PostgreSQL, your environment should be set up to use it. If you installed PostgreSQL from source, the INSTALL document explains all the steps necessary to use PostgreSQL, including setting necessary environment variables.

Sending SQL to the server. PostgreSQL includes an interactive tool called psql that you can use to send SQL commands to the server and view the results of queries. To log on to psql, simply run the program from the Linux shell. If you have created a user and database for yourself (see the entries *Adding a user* and *Creating a database* later in this section), you will be logged on and connected. To use psql, type an SQL statement followed by \g or a semicolon, and then press Enter (to exit, type \q and then press Enter).

Here is a sample session:

```
[postgres@oscorb pgsql]$ psql
Welcome to the POSTGRESQL interactive sql monitor:
  Please read the file COPYRIGHT for copyright terms of POSTGRESQL

   type \? for help on slash commands
   type \q to quit
   type \g or terminate with semicolon to execute query
 You are currently connected to the database: postgres

postgres=> select * from sample\g
name                 | id
---------------------+---
Brian                |100
Joan                 |110
Ty                   |120
(3 rows)
postgres=> \q
```

Logging on to psql as the PostgreSQL superuser. The PostgreSQL superuser is usually the account postgres. In many installations, the postgres Linux user does not have a password (as opposed to having a blank password, which means you can log on without typing a password) by default, which means you cannot log on to that account with telnet or at the console.

So, you should either log on as root and then use the command *su - postgres*, or log on as root and set a password for the user postgres before logging on as postgres. In general, it is a good idea to *not* set a password for this user, so that you have one less account to worry about from a security standpoint (in which case you'll always need to use *su* to become the postgres user).

Once you have su'd to or logged on as postgres, start the psql utility to issue commands as the PostgreSQL superuser. You can also use the -u option to have psql prompt you for a user name (type postgres at this prompt) and password if you are logged on as a different user.

Adding a user. PostgreSQL relies on the operating system to authenticate users. This means that if you are logged on as a user, PostgreSQL will trust you. This extends to processes that run as you: If a CGI script is running under your user id, and it makes a connection to PostgreSQL, the PostgreSQL database server will trust that process as though it were you.

However, PostgreSQL doesn't know about a user until the PostgreSQL superuser has run the createuser script. To add a user under PostgreSQL:

1. Log on to Linux as the PostgreSQL superuser.
2. Run the command *createuser username* (for example, *createuser bjepson*). The createuser program starts running, and asks you a few questions:

   Enter user's postgres ID or Return to use unix user id. In general, you should use the Unix user id. See the createuser man page for details on this option.

   Is user "username" allowed to create databases? If you want the user to be able to create databases, answer yes to this question.

   Is user "username" allowed to add users? If you want the user to be able to add other users, answer yes to this question.

   Shall I create a database for "username"? If you want this user to have his own database (which is most likely the case), answer yes to this question.

Once you have answered these questions, the new user is created.

NOTE You can use the destroyuser command to delete this user and all the databases owned by that user.

By default, PostgreSQL is very trusting of users on the local machine. For more details, see the section titled *The Security of Initial Accounts* later in this chapter.

Creating a database. To create a database for a PostgreSQL user (only if you did not create a database when you created the user):

1. Log on to Linux as the PostgreSQL superuser (usually the user postgres).

2. Run the command *createdb username* (as in *createdb bjepson*). The createdb program creates the database for you.

After this database is created, the user bjepson can connect to the database and issue queries by starting the psql program from the Linux shell.

Mini SQL

Mini SQL is a lightweight SQL system that was originally designed as a back-end for a suite of network management applications. It became very popular for use with Web applications, and has also been used in desktop application development. Mini SQL supports a small subset of SQL that makes large application development a little tricky. However, it is small and fast, which appeals to a lot of developers.

Mini SQL is distributed in source code form, but it is somewhere between free software and shareware. If your organization is a school, church, or other charitable institution, you may use Mini SQL for no charge. Others have to pay a fee, which includes support.

You can download Mini SQL from www.hughes.com.au.

Before You Install

Before you install Mini SQL, consider the following:

Where to find the documentation. Installation instructions are included with the source distribution in the files README and INSTALL. After you install Mini SQL, the user documentation will be in /usr/local/Hughes/doc.

Source versus binary installation. Mini SQL is typically distributed in source code form. The source code distribution can be found at www.hughes .com.au.

Upgrading an older installation. Unless you are upgrading a much older installation, there are not usually any extra steps that must be taken to upgrade. However, consult the README and INSTALL documents for details.

After You Install

After you install Mini SQL, consider the following:

Startup and shutdown. Mini SQL can be controlled with a simple script. The msql2d program starts Mini SQL, and the msqladmin program can be used to shut it down. Here is a sample script (see *Automatic Startup and Shutdown* later in this chapter):

```
#! /bin/sh
#

case "$1" in
  start)
        echo -n "Starting Mini SQL: "
        /usr/local/Hughes/bin/msql2d &
        echo
        ;;
  stop)
        echo -n "Stopping Mini SQL: "
        /usr/local/Hughes/bin/msqladmin shutdown
        echo
        ;;
  *)
        echo "Usage: minisql {start|stop}"
        exit 1
esac

exit 0
```

Setting up your environment. After you have installed Mini SQL, you should add the directory /usr/local/Hughes/bin to the path of any user who needs to use it.

Creating a database. To create a Mini SQL database:

1. Log on to Linux as the Mini SQL administrative user (usually root).
2. Run the command *msqladmin create databasename*, as in:

```
msqladmin create bjepson_db
```

Adding a user. Mini SQL uses a very simple authentication system that is tied into the Linux permissions. The file /usr/local/Hughes/msql.acl controls whether a given user or host has access to a database. By default, Mini SQL does not have a msql.acl file. To give a user exclusive access to a database:

1. Log on to Linux as the Mini SQL administrative user (usually root).
2. Create or edit the /usr/local/Hughes/msql.acl file and add the following lines:

```
database=DATABASE
read=USER
write=USER
access=local
```

where DATABASE is the name of a database, and USER is the name of a Linux user. The following example gives bjepson (and no one else) local access to the bjepson_db database. Local access implies that bjepson cannot connect from a remote machine, which is the recommended setting:

```
database=bjepson_db
read=bjepson
write=bjepson
access=local
```

3. Make sure msql.acl is owned by the msql user, not root:

```
chown msql /usr/local/Hughes/msql.acl
```

4. Use msqladmin to tell Mini SQL to reload the permissions table:

```
msqladmin reload
```

For more details about permissions and msql.acl, see the Mini SQL documentation.

Sending SQL to the server. Mini SQL includes an interactive monitor program called msql, which is installed into /usr/local/Hughes/bin by default. To use the msql program:

1. Log on to Linux as a user who has access to the database you want to connect to.

2. Start msql with the name of the database you want to connect to as an argument.

3. After you type each SQL command, make sure it is terminated with \g, and press Enter.

4. To exit, type \q and then press Enter.

Here is an example session:

```
[bjepson@oscorb bjepson]$ msql bjepson_db

Welcome to the miniSQL monitor.  Type \h for help.


mSQL > SELECT * FROM invoice\g

Query OK.  2 row(s) modified or retrieved.
```

```
+--------+----------------------+
| inv_no | customer_name        |
+--------+----------------------+
| 001    | Big Company          |
| 002    | Little Co., Inc.     |
+--------+----------------------+


mSQL > \q


Bye!
```

MySQL

MySQL is a database server that offers fast performance (especially on large data sets), while offering many SQL features, locking, and a flexible authentication mechanism. The MySQL developers offer a feature comparison at www.mysql.com/crash-me-choose.htmy. At this page, you can choose one or more database servers, and see which features they support.

For most purposes, you do not need to pay for a MySQL license. Also, older versions of MySQL are released under the GPL. You can find MySQL at www.mysql.com (use a mirror site if possible for downloads of the source or binary distributions).

Before You Install

Before you install MySQL, take the following into consideration:

Where to find the documentation. Documentation for MySQL is available online at www.mysql.com. However, this documentation covers the latest (sometimes beta or alpha) version of MySQL. The source code distribution includes user documentation in the Docs subdirectory.

If you install MySQL from a binary distribution, the documentation should install into /usr/doc, in a directory named something similar to /usr/doc/MySQL-3.23.11-alpha (the exact name will depend on the version of MySQL you installed).

Instructions on installing MySQL can be found in the source code distribution, which includes two files, INSTALL-SOURCE, and INSTALL-SOURCE-GENERIC. You should read these before trying to compile MySQL.

Source versus binary installation. The MySQL Web site includes source code and binary distributions. If you need more control over the configuration of MySQL, you might want to install from source. Otherwise, the binary distributions are recommended.

Client-only installation. If you want to install only the MySQL client libraries, you can either download the client RPMs (binary distribution) from the MySQL Web site, or you can add the flag—*without-server* to the configure script before you compile MySQL (see the INSTALL-SOURCE and INSTALL-SOURCE-GENERIC files in the MySQL source distribution for details).

Upgrading an older installation. When you upgrade MySQL, you may need to run some scripts to bring your databases up to the latest version. See the MySQL documentation and installation documents for more details.

After You Install

After you install MySQL, take the following into consideration:

Startup and shutdown. The MySQL binary distribution includes a startup and shutdown script, which is installed by default.

If you installed MySQL from source, you will need to set up your own script (see also the mysql.server.sh script in the *support-files* subdirectory of the MySQL source distribution).

The MySQL server is started with the safe_mysqld program, and can be shut down with the mysqladmin program. The following init.d script can start and stop MySQL (see the section titled *Automatic Startup and Shutdown*, later in this chapter):

```
#! /bin/sh
#

case "$1" in
  start)
        echo -n "Starting MySQL: "
        /usr/local/bin/safe_mysqld &
        echo
        ;;
  stop)
        echo -n "Stopping MySQL: "
        /usr/local/bin/mysqladmin shutdown
        echo
        ;;
  *)
        echo "Usage: mysql {start|stop}"
        exit 1
esac

exit 0
```

Setting up your environment. Once you have installed MySQL, there are no special changes you need to make to your environment. However, there are some steps you may wish to follow that are described in the INSTALL-SOURCE file, in the section "Post-installation setup and testing."

Sending SQL to the server. MySQL includes an interactive SQL monitor called mysql. To log on to mysql, simply run it from the Linux shell. If you have created a user id and password (see below), you can log on as that user. The mysql monitor attempts to log you on as whichever Linux user you are currently logged on as. If that mysql account has a password, you must start mysql with the -p option. Although you can include your password as an argument to -p, it is recommended that you let the mysql program prompt you for your password.

You can also put your password in the .my.cnf file (which must reside in your home directory). For example, you can specify your password with the following lines in the .my.cnf file:

```
[client]
password=open_sesame
```

To use the mysql program:

1. Run the mysql program with the database name as an argument. Include the -p option if the user has a password. If you want to log on as a different user than the one you're logged on as, use the -u option to specify a user.

2. For each SQL statement you type, you must follow the statement with a semicolon (or \g or \G), and then press Enter.

3. Type quit and then press Enter to exit the mysql program.

Here is an example session (note that there can be no space between -p and your password):

```
[bjepson@oscorb bjepson]$ mysql -popen_sesame bjepson_db
Reading table information for completion of table and
column names You can turn off this feature to get a quicker
startup with -A

Welcome to the MySQL monitor.  Commands end with ; or \g.
Your MySQL connection id is 8 to server version: 3.22.27

Type 'help' for help.

mysql> select item_description from line_item;
+------------------+
| item_description |
+------------------+
```

```
|  Widget           |
|  Troubadorio 55x  |
|  Fancy Hat        |
|  Telephone        |
+-------------------+
4 rows in set (0.00 sec)

mysql> quit
Bye
```

Logging on to mysql as the MySQL superuser. You can log on to mysql as the superuser in one of two ways:

1. Log on to Linux as root (or su to root).

2. Start mysql as described in *Sending SQL to the Server*, earlier in this section.

or

1. Log on to Linux as a mortal user.

2. Start mysql with the *-u root* option. If the root user has a password, you will also need to use the -p option, as described in *Sending SQL to the Server*, earlier in this section.

Here is an example of the MySQL root user logging on to the mysql database (the mysql database is the master database where configuration activity, such as adding users, must be performed):

```
[bjepson@oscorb bjepson]$ mysql -u root \
                          -psecret_password mysql
Reading table information for completion of table and
column names You can turn off this feature to get a quicker
startup with -A

Welcome to the MySQL monitor.  Commands end with ; or \g.
Your MySQL connection id is 9 to server version: 3.22.27

Type 'help' for help.

mysql> show tables;
+-----------------+
| Tables in mysql |
+-----------------+
| columns_priv    |
| db              |
| func            |
| host            |
| tables_priv     |
| user            |
+-----------------+
6 rows in set (0.01 sec)
```

Creating a database. To create a database:

1. Log on to mysql as the MySQL superuser.

2. Issue the create *database db_name* command, as in *create database bjepson_db*.

Adding a user. Unless you have set a password for a given user, mysql is very trusting. You can use the -u username flag with mysql, and unless that user has a password, mysql lets you log on and gives you all the privileges for that user. If you don't use the -u flag, mysql looks for a mysql user with the same name as the Linux user you are logged on as.

- To create a user and assign them ownership of a given database:

1. Log on to mysql as the mysql superuser.

2. Issue the GRANT command. The following GRANT statement gives bjepson access to all the objects in bjepson_db, with the password open_sesame:

```
GRANT ALL PRIVILEGES ON bjepson_db.*
    TO bjepson@localhost
    IDENTIFIED BY 'open_sesame';
```

If you include the WITH GRANT OPTION, then the user can give other users access to objects in the database (see the MySQL documentation for more information on the GRANT statement):

```
GRANT ALL PRIVILEGES ON bjepson_db.*
    TO bjepson@localhost
    IDENTIFIED BY 'open_sesame'
    WITH GRANT OPTION;
```

Oracle

The Oracle database server is the Oracle corporation's flagship product. It is a database server with advanced capabilities, including object-relational functionality, an embedded Java virtual machine, and extensive support for multimedia storage and retrieval.

Unfortunately, it is the one of the most difficult database servers to install. The installation suffers from many flaws:

- The installer requires huge amounts of runtime memory.

- Despite the fact that it has a friendly graphical interface, the installer requires you to complete numerous steps at a shell prompt before, during, and after installation.

- The default settings consume much more disk space than other databases (over 700MB).

However, once it is installed, it becomes reasonably easy to manage and use. Evaluation downloads of Oracle 8i can be found at http://technet.oracle.com.

Before You Install

Before you install Oracle, consider the following:

Where to find the documentation. The Oracle binary distribution comes with installation instructions, and some administrative reference material. However, the bulk of the Oracle documentation can be found online at http://technet.oracle.com.

Source versus binary installation. Oracle is distributed only in binary form, and as of this writing, only for Intel-based Linux.

Client-only installation. When you run the Oracle installer, you have the option of only installing the client components. You can use this option to install the Oracle client components on workstations that need to access the server.

After You Install

After you install Oracle, consider the following:

Startup and shutdown. The Oracle installation documentation includes a sample script (dbora) that you can use in the manner described in the section titled *Automatic Startup and Shutdown*, later in this chapter. However, this script does not automatically start a listener service, nor does it automatically start all databases you have configured. The listener service is needed if you want remote clients to access Oracle, or if you want to use a data access API such as ODBC or DBD::Oracle.

To configure a database so it can be started automatically, you may need to edit the /etc/oratab file:

1. Log on to Linux as the oracle user (usually named oracle).

2. Open the /etc/oratab file in an editor. Find the line that corresponds to the database you created during installation, such as:

```
ORCL:/u01/app/oracle/product/8.1.5:N
```

3. If the last letter is an N, the database will not be started automatically. If so, change the last N (for no, don't start automatically) to a Y (for yes):

```
ORCL:/u01/app/oracle/product/8.1.5:Y
```

4. Save and close the /etc/oratab file.

It is suggested that you use the dbora script suggested by Oracle, with two modifications. First, make sure the *start* section of the document starts the listener before it starts Oracle. This step is essential to make sure that the Oracle database can register itself with the listener service. Second, make sure the listener service is shut down before Oracle is shut down. Here is an example:

```sh
#!/bin/sh

# The same as the ORACLE_HOME user environment variable.
ORACLE_HOME=/u01/app/oracle/product/8.1.5

# The user who owns the oracle installation.
ORACLE_OWNER=oracle

case "$1" in
  start)

    echo -n "Oracle:"

    # su to the oracle owner and start the listener.
    su - $ORACLE_OWNER -c "$ORACLE_HOME/bin/lsnrctl start"

    # su to the oracle owner and start the database.
    su - $ORACLE_OWNER -c $ORACLE_HOME/bin/dbstart &
    touch /var/lock/subsys/dbora
    echo
    ;;

  stop)

    echo -n "Oracle:"

    # su to the oracle owner and terminate the listener.
    su - $ORACLE_OWNER -c "$ORACLE_HOME/bin/lsnrctl stop"

    # su to the oracle owner and shut the database down.
    su - $ORACLE_OWNER -c $ORACLE_HOME/bin/dbshut &
    rm -f /var/lock/subsys/dbora
    echo
    ;;

esac
```

In summary, the following steps should be completed on startup:

1. Start the listener service with *lsnrctl start*.

2. Wait for the listener service to start, then start Oracle with the dbstart script.

The following steps should be completed on shutdown:

1. Stop the listener service with lsnrctl stop.
2. Wait for the listener service to stop, then stop Oracle with the dbshut script.

NOTE Future releases of Oracle may automate the installation of the listener service. Please consult the Oracle documentation for more details.

Setting up your environment. There are a number of environment variables that should be set for each user who will use Oracle. You can set these variables in each user's login scripts (such as .bash_profile or .cshrc).

These variables are documented in the Oracle installation manual, and an example is shown in the following listing for the bash shell:

```
export ORACLE_BASE=/u01/app/oracle
export ORACLE_HOME=$ORACLE_BASE/product/8.1.5
export ORACLE_SID=ORCL
export PATH=$PATH:$ORACLE_HOME/bin
```

Here is an example setting for csh:

```
setenv ORACLE_BASE /u01/app/oracle
setenv ORACLE_HOME ${ORACLE_BASE}/product/8.1.5
setenv ORACLE_SID ORCL
setenv PATH ${PATH}:${ORACLE_HOME}/bin
```

If you want to use Oracle's Java features, you should add the following to your CLASSPATH environment variable:

```
$ORACLE_HOME/jlib:$ORACLE_HOME/product/jlib
```

These are just sample settings. You should consult your Oracle documentation for the exact values, because the names of the directories change with each version (the version number is part of the directory name).

Sending SQL to the server. Oracle includes an interactive query tool called sqlplus that you can use to send SQL to the server and retrieve formatted results. You can start and log on to sqlplus in two ways:

1. Start sqlplus from the shell prompt. When you are prompted for your Oracle user name and password, supply the correct values, and then sqlplus will start.
2. Start sqlplus with the userid and password as an argument, by typing *sqlplus username/password*, as in *sqlplus scott/tiger*.

After you type each SQL statement, terminate it with a semicolon and press Enter. Type quit and press Enter to exit sqlplus. The following is an example session:

```
[oracle@oscorb oracle]$ sqlplus scott/tiger

SQL*Plus: Release 8.1.5.0.0 - Production on Sun Oct 10 19:39:21 1999

(c) Copyright 1999 Oracle Corporation.  All rights reserved.


Connected to:
Oracle8i Enterprise Edition Release 8.1.5.0.1 - Production
With the Partitioning and Java options
PL/SQL Release 8.1.5.0.0 - Production

SQL> SELECT * from DEPT;

    DEPTNO DNAME          LOC
---------- -------------- -------------
        10 ACCOUNTING     NEW YORK
        20 RESEARCH       DALLAS
        30 SALES          CHICAGO
        40 OPERATIONS     BOSTON
SQL> quit
Disconnected from Oracle8i Enterprise Edition Release 8.1.5.0.1
With the Partitioning and Java options
PL/SQL Release 8.1.5.0.0 - Production
```

Adding a user. To add a user:

1. Log on to sqlplus as a user with DBA permissions, such as the SYSTEM user—the default password is usually manager, but consult your Oracle documentation to be sure.

2. Issue the CREATE USER command.

3. Use the GRANT command to set up that user's permissions.

For example, to create a user named bjepson with the password open_sesame, you could issue these two commands:

```
CREATE USER bjepson
   IDENTIFIED BY open_sesame
   QUOTA 10M ON system
   PASSWORD EXPIRE;
GRANT CREATE SESSION, RESOURCE TO bjepson;
```

The QUOTA clause allows bjepson to use up to 10 megabytes of storage, and the PASSWORD EXPIRE clause forces bjepson to choose a new password the first time he logs on. The GRANT statement gives bjepson the RESOURCE role and ability to create a session, which is needed to log on and work with the database system. The RESOURCE role lets bjepson create and own various objects, such as tables and stored procedures.

Creating a database. Creating a database under Oracle is complicated, and involves fundamental changes to the configuration of Oracle itself. When you install Oracle, a database is usually created for you. If you must create a database, use Oracle's Database Assistant program, dbassist.

Fortunately, you shouldn't need to create another database under most circumstances. Like Sybase (which is discussed next), Oracle puts all the objects created by each user into a separate schema (a schema is a logical organization of tables and other database objects). So, when the user bjepson creates a table called *test_table*, and a user *joan* creates a table of the same name, these tables are created within separate schemas. So, you could select all the rows from joan's table with the command *SELECT * FROM joan.test _table*, and all the rows from bjepson's with *SELECT * FROM bjepson .test_table*.

If you would like to create a separate work area for a given user, you should use a tablespace, which is a unit of storage in which you can create database objects such as tables. You can create a tablespace with the CREATE TABLESPACE command. Consult the Oracle documentation for more details.

Sybase Adaptive Server Enterprise

Sybase is a relational database system that includes advanced data management features such as stored procedures, triggers, and declarative referential integrity. Sybase was one of the first major database vendors to recognize Linux. Although they did not port their server to Linux as quickly as some of us would have liked, they offered a free download of their client libraries, enabling Linux programmers to develop applications to access Sybase servers on other platforms.

Before You Install

Before you install, consider the following:

Where to find the documentation. After you install Sybase, you can find some documentation in the ~sybase/doc directory. More documentation can be found online at http://sybooks.sybase.com/.

Source versus binary installation. Sybase is distributed only in binary form, and as of this writing, only for Intel-based Linux.

Client-only installation. The Sybase installation should include an Open-Client RPM, such as sybase-openclient-11.1.1-1.i386.rpm. Install this RPM, as well as the sybase-common RPM (which is named something similar to sybase-common-11.9.2-1.i386.rpm), to get the Sybase client libraries.

After You Install

Before you can use your newly installed version of Sybase, you must log on as the user *sybase*. This user is created when you install the Sybase rpms. The root user will need to give this user a password before you can log directly on to this account.

The first time (and only the first time) you log on to this account, your login scripts attempt to run the program *srvbuild*, which configures the Sybase installation. If this script fails, you may need to start it by logging on as the sybase user and running srvbuild from the shell prompt. However, since installation procedures with any product are subject to change, consult the Sybase documentation for specific details.

As of this writing, srvbuild requires the X Windows System, so the sybase user's login scripts fail to start it on machines that do not log directly on to X. To get around this, log on as the sybase user, start the X Windows system, then run *srvbuild*. See the Sybase documentation for instructions on using the srvbuild utility.

Startup and shutdown. The Sybase installation creates the /etc/rc.d/init.d/sybase script that you can use as directed in *Automatic Startup and Shutdown*, later in this chapter.

Setting up your environment. Sybase generally installs itself in /opt/sybasedir, where sybasedir is the release name of the version of Sybase you are running. Since this is the same as the sybase user's home directory, you can use ~sybase as a shortcut for this directory.

To use Sybase, you should add ~sybase/bin to your PATH, and create the SYBASE environment variable. You should also set the DSQUERY variable to the name of the Sybase server you created when you installed Sybase (you can find the name of the server in the ~sybase/interfaces file).

You can add the following lines to your .bash_profile script, and these variables will be automatically set the next time you log on. Here is an example for a Sybase server named oscorb:

```
export PATH=$PATH:~sybase/bin
export SYBASE=~sybase
export DSQUERY=oscorb
```

Change oscorb to whatever you named your Sybase server. To do the same under csh, add the following to your .cshrc:

```
setenv PATH ~sybase/bin:$PATH
setenv SYBASE ~sybase
setenv DSQUERY oscorb
```

In some Linux environments, the environment variables LANG and LC_ALL may be configured with locale-specific settings that Sybase does not recognize. If this is the case, you will need to unset them prior to running isql (see *Sending SQL to the Server*, elsewhere in this section). Since other applications probably rely on these settings, you may want to create a shell script to run isql, and store it in /usr/local/bin:

```
#!/bin/sh

export PATH=$PATH:~sybase/bin
export SYBASE=~sybase
export DSQUERY=SYBASE

unset LC_ALL
unset LANG

# Start isql and pass it all of this script's arguments.
$SYBASE/bin/isql $@
```

NOTE

The UnixODBC open-source ODBC implementation (www.unixodbc.org) comes with a program called isql. By default, the UnixODBC isql program is installed into /usr/local/bin. The isql program is similar to the Sybase program of the same name, but they are not compatible. If you installed UnixODBC and Sybase on the same system, we suggest that you rename the UnixODBC isql program to something different, or that you put ~sybase/bin in your path before /usr/local/bin.

Sending SQL to the server. Sybase includes an interactive SQL monitor called isql. To use this, run the command *isql*. You can specify your userid with the -U option, and the password with the -P option. After each batch of SQL statements, you should send the GO command and press Enter. Type quit and then press Enter to quit. Here is an example session:

```
[bjepson@oscorb bjepson]$ isql -Ubjepson -Popen_sesame
1> use pubs3
2> GO
1> SELECT au_fname, au_lname FROM authors
2> GO
 au_fname             au_lname
 -------------------- ------------------------------------
```

```
Abraham            Bennet
Reginald           Blotchet-Halls
Cheryl             Carson
[f] and so on [f]

(23 rows affected)
1> quit
```

Starting isql as the Sybase superuser. By default, the Sybase superuser name is sa, with a blank password. To log on to isql as the Sybase superuser, run *isql* with the *-Usa* and *-Ppassword* options, where password is the password for the Sybase superuser. If the password is blank, use """, as in *isql -Usa -P""*.

Creating a database. Use the CREATE DATABASE statement to create a database. If you want to create a database for each user, create the database and then create the user. The next section, *Adding a User*, explains how to give a user ownership of his or her own database.

To create a database:

1. Start *isql* as the Sybase superuser.

2. Make sure you are in the master database:

```
USE master
GO
```

3. Issue the CREATE DATABASE command: *CREATE DATABASE dbname ON DEFAULT=size*, where size is the size of the database in megabytes. To create a 4MB database named bjepson_db, you could issue this command:

```
CREATE DATABASE bjepson_db
ON DEFAULT=4
GO
```

For more information on the CREATE DATABASE command, see the Sybase documentation.

Adding a user. To add a user to the system:

1. Start isql as the Sybase superuser.

2. Use the sp_adduser stored procedure to add the new user (issue this command within the master database). You should supply the user_name, password, and default database as parameters. The default database is the database that the user automatically uses when he or she logs on to isql. This example adds the user bjepson, with the password open_sesame, and with bjepson_db as the default database:

```
USE master
GO
sp_addlogin bjepson, open_sesame, bjepson_db
GO
```

3. If you want to give the user ownership of a database, use the sp_changedbowner command. First, change to the database you want to change ownership of, and then execute the command:

```
USE bjepson_db
GO
sp_changedbowner bjepson
GO
```

Now, when the user bjepson logs on to isql, he will have bjepson_db as his default database, and he will be able to create database objects, such as tables and stored procedures.

Common Database Issues

Rather than simply give you a shopping list of all the features of an RDBMS, we'll look at the problems that come up in the day-to-day life of an RDBMS. We'll look at the features that high-end database systems use to address the problems, and what you can do to deal with the problems if you are using a lightweight database that lacks such features.

Invalid Values

If you're going to store data in a relational database, you should do what you can to store the data as accurately as possible. Let's look at the things that can go wrong with this, and what you can do to protect your data.

Problem. How do we keep human and computer errors from putting invalid data values in the database?

Example. Consider a system that must track customer addresses. The user interface has been infallible in catching all human errors. However, somewhere between the user interface and database, a data conversion has been turning all zip codes from strings to numbers. As a result, all zip codes that start with 0 are missing the leading zero (for example, 02881 becomes 2881). So, there are many zip codes in the database that have only four digits, and this is causing some confusion at the post office!

The designers of the system knew the rule that each zip code must have five digits (we're ignoring zip+4 for this example). How could a problem like this be avoided?

Solution. Create a set of rules that must be met before the database will accept new data. For example, if a US zip code is entered that does not have five digits, reject it and send the error back to the user. This way, there is no way that invalid data can be entered in the database.

Implementation. It is not sufficient for you to implement these rules in the user interface, or even in the domain layer. All too often, databases are manipulated by feeds from other systems, automated processes, and administrators performing direct updates to the database by hurriedly typing SQL when the system is corrupted. There are too many places where invalid data can be entered, and the best place to catch it is at the database itself: Don't let anything in that's not right.

The SQL Way

When you create a table, you can specify constraints using the CONSTRAINT clause. The CONSTRAINT clause takes the form CONSTRAINT constraint _name CHECK (condition). If we want to verify that a character value has a certain number of characters, we can use the CHAR_LENGTH( ) function do so. Because some strings may be padded on either side with white space, it is suggested that you use LTRIM and RTRIM on the value, which makes for a funny expression: *CHAR_LENGTH(LTRIM(RTRIM(value)))*. The following is a CREATE TABLE statement that defines an address table where all zip codes must be five characters long:

```
CREATE TABLE address
    (street_address CHAR(35),
     city CHAR(35),
     state CHAR(2),
     zip CHAR(5),
     CONSTRAINT check_zip
         CHECK (CHAR_LENGTH(LTRIM(RTRIM(zip))) = 5)
    )
```

NOTE

Some implementations of SQL do not support the CHAR_LENGTH function. You may want to see if LENGTH is implemented instead.

The CONSTRAINT clause is supported in Oracle, PostgreSQL, and Sybase. See the database server documentation for specific notes on how to use this feature. For database systems that do not support this clause, you'll have to fake it.

Faking It

If your database system does not support constraints, you don't have much recourse on the server side. One option is to agree not to directly access the database in your code, and instead, go through an access layer that uses a set of rules to determine whether the data is okay.

You can encode these rules in the database as tables, or store them in some other fashion. The most important thing is to make sure that 1) the rules are not forgotten, and 2) they are easily updateable. Table 9.1 shows a set of rules that specify constraints on various tables.

Then, instead of going directly through an API such as ODBC, you can write a data access layer that sits between your program and an API such as ODBC. Here is some PDL (see the section *PDL*, in Chapter 4, "Construction") that describes how this is handled in the data access layer (with an SQL statement as input). You could use this to write an application in a language such as Perl or Java:

```
Open the rules table.
For each row in the rules table where table_name is 'address':

    Examine the value in the SQL statement that corresponds to
    rules.column_name.

    If the value is not at least as wide as minimum_size:
        Display an error

If no errors were encountered:
    Submit the SQL statement to the ODBC, JDBC, or DBI driver.
```

Another advantage of this rules-based approach is that you can use the same rules to develop quality checks for your system. For a given table, you could write a program that interprets the rules and applies them to the database. Here is an example:

```
Open the rules table.
Open the address table.
For each row in the address table:
```

Table 9.1 Data-Driven Constraints

TABLE_NAME	COLUMN_NAME	MINIMUM_SIZE
users	password	6
address	state	2
address	zip_code	5

```
For each row in the rules where table_name is 'address':

    Examine the column value in the address table
    that corresponds to rules.column_name.

    If the value is not at least as wide as minimum_size:
        Display an error.
```

Generating Unique Values

When you use a primary key, you need a way to come up with values for it each time you insert a new row. Each database server has a different way of dealing with generating these values.

MySQL. Under MySQL, you can declare a primary key column with the auto_increment attribute:

```
CREATE TABLE people
    (name CHAR(20),
     id   INTEGER AUTO_INCREMENT PRIMARY KEY);
```

Then, when you insert a value into the table, make sure you specify NULL for the primary key:

```
INSERT INTO people (name, id) VALUES ('Brian', NULL);
INSERT INTO people (name, id) VALUES ('Oscar', NULL);
```

This automatically increments the primary key column for each insert:

```
mysql> SELECT * FROM people;
+-------+----+
| name  | id |
+-------+----+
| Brian | 1  |
| Oscar | 2  |
+-------+----+
2 rows in set (0.00 sec)
```

PostgreSQL. Under PostgreSQL, create the table as you normally would, but also create a sequence object for that table:

```
CREATE TABLE people
    (name CHAR(20),
     id   INTEGER PRIMARY KEY);

CREATE SEQUENCE people_seq;
```

Then, when you insert a row, use NEXTVAL(*sequence-name*) to get the next id:

```
INSERT INTO people (name, id)
    VALUES ('Brian', NEXTVAL('people_seq'));

INSERT INTO people (name, id)
    VALUES ('Oscar', NEXTVAL('people_seq'));
```

As you can see, the sequence is automatically incremented for each insertion:

```
bjepson=> SELECT * FROM people;
name                  |id
----------------------+--
Brian                 | 1
Oscar                 | 2
(2 rows)
```

Mini SQL. Under Mini SQL, you must also create a sequence, but it is associated with a table. You must also specify its starting value and the step to increment it by each time you get a sequence:

```
CREATE TABLE people
    (name CHAR(20),
     id   INTEGER)\g
CREATE UNIQUE INDEX ix_people ON people (id)\g

CREATE SEQUENCE ON people STEP 1 VALUE 1\g
```

To get a value, you need to first select the sequence and store the value in your client application (see the Perl, Java, and GNOME chapters for information on processing result sets and acquiring values):

```
mSQL > SELECT _seq FROM people\g

Query OK.  1 row(s) modified or retrieved.

    +----------+
    | _seq     |
    +----------+
    | 2        |
    +----------+
```

Then, you have to create an SQL statement that uses the sequence value you obtained (there is no tight integration with the INSERT statement as there is in PostgreSQL). As you can see, this requires you to generate SQL statements that specify the value you got from the sequence:

```
mSQL > INSERT INTO people (name, id)
    ->      VALUES('Brian', 2)\g
```

Oracle. Oracle is very similar to PostgreSQL. As with PostgreSQL, create a table and a sequence:

```
CREATE TABLE people
   (name  CHAR(20),
      id   NUMERIC PRIMARY KEY NOT NULL);

CREATE SEQUENCE people_seq;
```

Then, when you insert data into the table, use the NEXTVAL pseudocolumn (in PostgreSQL, NEXTVAL is implemented as a function) to get the next value from the sequence:

```
INSERT INTO people (name, id)
   VALUES ('Brian', people_seq.NEXTVAL);

INSERT INTO people (name, id)
   VALUES ('Oscar', people_seq.NEXTVAL);
```

And, you can see, the sequence values were inserted:

```
SQL> SELECT * FROM people;

NAME                        ID
-------------------- ----------
Brian                        1
Oscar                        2
```

Sybase. Under Sybase, you must define a numeric column with the identity attribute. You should also specify that it is a primary key, and that it will not accept NULL values:

```
CREATE TABLE people
   (name  CHAR(20),
      id   NUMERIC identity PRIMARY KEY NOT NULL);
```

Then, you can issue inserts, but do not specify the column name in the insert:

```
INSERT INTO people (name) VALUES ('Brian');
INSERT INTO people (name) VALUES ('Oscar');
```

Next, you can see how the values were automatically inserted:

```
1> SELECT * FROM people
2> GO
 name                 id
-------------------- --------------------
```

```
Brian                                    1
Oscar                                    2

(2 rows affected)
```

For a complete discussion of unique keys under Sybase, see document id 860 at http://techinfo.sybase.com.

Orphaned Data

Earlier, we looked at what we can do to avoid getting invalid values in a database. While this is an important part of data integrity, another key part is the integrity of the relationships between tables.

Problem. Relational databases depend on the connections between tables that are represented by foreign keys. What happens when there is data in a child table that has no corresponding parent record?

Example. Suppose you have an invoice system that includes two tables, invoice and line_item. The relationship between the invoice and line_item table can be expressed as *line_item.invoice_number = invoice.invoice_number*.

What happens if an invoice is deleted, but (perhaps through an error) the corresponding rows in the line_item table are not deleted? These line_item rows have been orphaned, and can be a real nuisance. Suppose that you sum up all the line_items to figure out how much product you have shipped? You'll end up with an incorrect total, because you'll count line items that shouldn't be there!

Solution. You need a way to declare the relationships between tables, and have the data server enforce these relationships. In the case of the line items and invoices, the system could either require the user to delete all line items before deleting the invoice, or automatically delete all the line items when the user deletes an invoice.

Implementation. There are two ways to address this situation, as suggested in the solution. The easiest way (and probably the safest) is the first option: Don't let the user delete a parent record as long as it still has child records. This has the added benefit of avoiding accidents (imagine a cascading deletion that wipes out 90 percent of your data!).

Declarative Referential Integrity

The CREATE TABLE clause supported by some implementations of SQL includes a REFERENCES constraint, that lets you explicitly state that one table is dependent on another. The following is an SQL statement that creates the invoice table. The PRIMARY KEY constraint specifies that invoice_number is the primary key for this table:

```
CREATE TABLE invoice
    (inv_no CHAR(3) UNIQUE, customer_name CHAR(20));
```

Next is an SQL statement that creates the line_item table. The REFERENCES clause takes the form REFERENCES table(column), where table is the name of a table, and column is the name of a column within that table that has a unique index. Since a primary key has a unique index, you can reference a primary key in this way:

```
CREATE TABLE line_item
    (inv_no CHAR(3) REFERENCES invoice(inv_no),
     item_description CHAR(20),
     quantity INT);
```

If you attempt to delete an invoice that still has line items, you'd get an error message that this would violate referential integrity.

The REFERENCES constraint is supported by Oracle and Sybase. Although MySQL and PostgreSQL recognize the keyword, it is ignored by the server (the keyword is only there to make it easier to port SQL from other servers).

Triggers

You can also use a *trigger* to customize how the database will react to an operation such as a deletion. A trigger is a special type of procedure that is invoked whenever certain database events occur.

To install a trigger in your database, you can send it to the server as you would any SQL statement (see the sections titled *Sending SQL to the Server* under each database section in this chapter).

If you would rather delete all the line items when an invoice is deleted, you can use a trigger to cascade the deletion to all the child tables. In other words, whenever you delete a row from the invoice table, you want the trigger to execute the command *DELETE FROM line_item WHERE line_item.inv_no = old.inv_no* (where old.inv_no is the invoice number of the row you are deleting from the invoice table).

Cascading Deletes with Oracle Triggers

Here is a trigger in Oracle's PL/SQL that cascades a delete on the invoice table down to the line_item table:

```
1 CREATE OR REPLACE TRIGGER line_item_check
2     BEFORE DELETE ON invoice
3     FOR EACH ROW
4     BEGIN
5         DELETE FROM line_item
6             WHERE line_item.inv_no = :old.inv_no;
7     END;
```

Line 1. CREATE OR REPLACE TRIGGER creates a trigger with the specified name. If a trigger with the same name already exists, it is replaced (overwritten).

Line 2. This specifies that the trigger must execute before the delete occurs.

Line 3. This specifies that the trigger should be fired for each row that is deleted (one SQL delete statement may affect many rows).

Lines 4 and 7. The BEGIN and END signal the start and finish of the trigger itself.

Lines 5 and 6. This is a DELETE statement that removes the line items. *:old* is the name of a pseudo-table that contains the row being deleted from invoice. In this example, we use it as we would a table name or alias, using the SQL syntax tablename.column (:old.inv_no).

This assumes that you don't have a referential integrity constraint such as the one shown in the previous section. Now, when you delete an invoice, all of its line items are deleted.

NOTE
Use cascading deletes with caution (or not at all), since a cascading delete can ripple through a parent-child hierarchy, deleting lots of data!

Cascading Deletes with Sybase Triggers

Sybase's implementation of triggers is very similar to the Oracle implementation shown earlier. However, where you could simply refer to a row in the old table with tablename.column under Oracle, you need to be more explicit under Sybase. Sybase creates a temporary table called *deleted* that contains all the rows that are about to be deleted from the table.

So, instead of saying: *DELETE FROM child_table WHERE child_table.foreign_key = :old.primary_key*, you need to involve the deleted table in the FROM clause of a query. An easy way to do this is to use a subquery with the IN keyword:

```
1   CREATE TRIGGER line_item_check ON invoice FOR DELETE
2   AS
3     DELETE FROM line_item
4       WHERE line_item.inv_no IN (SELECT inv_no FROM deleted)
```

Lines 1 and 2. Creates a trigger named line_item_check on the invoice table. The trigger is only fired when someone tries to DELETE a row from invoice.

Lines 3 and 4. Use a subquery on the deleted table to find all the rows in the line_item table that should be deleted. The IN keyword makes the WHERE clause only match rows in the line_item table that have the same inv_no as the rows in the subquery.

Again, use this approach with caution: Cascading deletes in this way can have a large-scale rippling effect, and may delete lots of data!

Blocking Deletes with PostgreSQL Triggers

PostgreSQL supports triggers, as well. To get the most out of triggers (as well as stored procedures), you should enable the embedded procedural language PL/pgSQL. This language is an extension to PostgreSQL that allows you to extend the database in many ways. If you built PostgreSQL from source, PL/pgSQL should be available to you. If you installed PostgreSQL from a binary distribution, you may or may not have received a package for PL/pgsql. Under the Debian potato distribution (which was frozen at the time of this writing), this package is called postgresql-pl.

PL/pgSQL is not enabled by default. *The PostgreSQL Programmer's Guide* (part of the PostgreSQL online documentation) includes a description of how to enable PL/pgSQL in Chapter 42, "Procedural Languages."

There are two parts to writing a trigger: writing the function itself, and then setting up the trigger. Here is the SQL source code you need to set up a trigger that prevents you from deleting an invoice that still has line items:

```
1   CREATE FUNCTION line_item_block()
2   RETURNS opaque
3   AS 'BEGIN
4     IF COUNT(*) > 0 FROM line_item
5        WHERE line_item.inv_no = old.inv_no
6     THEN
7       RAISE EXCEPTION
8         ''Cannot delete invoice when line items exist.'';
9     END IF;
10    RETURN old;
11  END;'
12  LANGUAGE 'plpgsql';

13  CREATE TRIGGER invoice_trigger
14      BEFORE DELETE ON invoice
15      FOR EACH ROW
16      EXECUTE PROCEDURE line_item_block();
```

Line 1. Creates a function named line_item_block().

Line 2. This line states the return value of the function, which is *opaque* (meaning it returns the row that triggered the function call). Functions that will be used for triggers must return an opaque value.

Lines 3 and 11. BEGIN and END; start and finish the source code for the function. Notice that everything between and including BEGIN and END; are captured within single quotes. This is because the PL/pgSQL source code is stored in the database as a string, and is passed to the PL/pgSQL engine when it is invoked.

Lines 4 and 5. This is a modified version of the SQL SELECT statement that returns true if one or more rows were found in the line items table whose parent is the invoice you are trying to delete. old is an alias for the row you are trying to delete.

Lines 6 through 9. If there are any child line items, this code raises an exception. This exception prevents the DELETE from succeeding.

NOTE

On line 8, there are two double quotes on either side, rather than one single quote or one double quote. This is needed because we are using single quotes inside a string that is already in single quotes (see notes on Lines 3 and 11). Some languages use \' to use a single quote within a single-quoted string, but PL/pgSQL uses doubled-up single quotes.

Line 10. Returns the row that triggered the function. This is required for functions that will be used with a trigger.

Line 12. Specifies that this function is written in PL/pgSQL.

Line 13. Creates a trigger named invoice_trigger.

Line 14. Specifies that the trigger should be executed before a row is deleted from the invoice table.

Line 15. This specifies that the trigger should be fired for each row that is deleted (one SQL delete statement may affect many rows).

Line 16. Specifies that the trigger should call the function line_item_block().

Cascading Deletes with PostgreSQL Triggers

Here are a function and trigger that cascades the DELETE, so that whenever you delete an invoice, all its line items are deleted (as we mentioned earlier, cascading deletes can ripple through your system causing many deletions, and should be used with extreme caution):

```
CREATE FUNCTION line_item_cascade()
RETURNS opaque
AS 'BEGIN
  DELETE FROM line_item
    WHERE line_item.inv_no = old.inv_no;
  RETURN old;
END;'
LANGUAGE 'plpgsql';

CREATE TRIGGER invoice_trigger
    BEFORE DELETE ON invoice
    FOR EACH ROW
    EXECUTE PROCEDURE line_item_cascade();
```

Faking It

Because database systems such as Mini SQL and MySQL don't support triggers or declarative referential integrity, the best you can do (at first) is look for problems that have occurred.

One proactive measure you can take is to develop your applications to always delete rows first from child tables, and then move on up to the parents, your applications will usually be faster (since you avoid the overhead of triggers), and you don't need to worry about maintaining the integrity on the server. This won't offer protection from mistakes made when you issue ad-hoc SQL updates, but it is a good first line of defense.

High-end database systems like Oracle, Sybase, and PostgreSQL use database tables (the system catalog) to keep track of meta-information that concerns the relationships between tables. You can do the same thing in your own system, by creating these tables by hand. The following is an example table called syskeys, that captures the parent-child relationship. Table 9.2 shows that the line_item table has a reference to the invoice table on the line_item.invoice_number column.

To periodically check for orphaned data, you could use the following algorithm to write an application in a language such as Perl or Java:

```
Open the syskeys table.
For each row in the syskeys table:
    Open the table (child table) in syskeys.table_name.

    For each row in the child table:
        Open the table (parent table) in syskeys.parent_table.
        Search for a row with a primary key value equal to the
        child table's foreign key value.
        If no such row exists:
            Display an error.
```

Table 9.2 Data-Driven Foreign Key References

TABLE_NAME	FOREIGN_KEY	PARENT_TABLE
line_item	invoice_number	invoice

Although the example shown here merely demonstrates a reactive solution, there are ways that you can use a system catalog to make your system more robust, and less prone to data integrity problems.

The solution involves departing from the practice of writing SQL statements by hand, and instead, using the data in the system catalog to guide your programs. For example, instead of issuing a DELETE FROM invoice WHERE invoice_number = '001', you could use something like the following delete_something() routine, shown in PDL:

```
function delete_something(table, id)

Open the syskeys table.
For each row where syskeys.parent_table = table:
    Open the table specified in syskeys.table_name.

    If there are any rows where the foreign key (such as
    line_item.invoice_number) equals id:
        Display an error.

If there were no errors:
    Delete all rows from table where the primary key equals id.
```

Using this technique, you can ensure that any delete statements do not violate referential integrity.

Lost Updates

When you have more than one user working with the database system at the same time, most operations proceed as they would in a single-user situation. However, there are some situations where multiuser access creates complicated situations.

Problem. A multi-user database system can process many changes concurrently. How do we keep changes submitted by one user from colliding with changes made by another user?

Example. Consider a system that tracks inventory. Two sales are made at roughly the same time. User A reads the current inventory and updates the value. Unfortunately, User B read the current inventory before User A's

	User A	User B	Current Value in Database
Time	Read the current inventory. temp = 25		25
		Read the current inventory. temp = 25	25
	Decrease the inventory by 5. temp = 20		25
		Increase the inventory by 5. temp = 30	25
	Update database. Set quantity = 20		20
		Update database. Set quantity = 30	30!?

Figure 9.4 The lost update.

changes were committed. When User B calculates the new inventory, User A's update will be completely lost! Figure 9.4 shows this situation.

Solution. Provide some method of grouping several operations into a logical unit and giving them exclusive access to a table or to some rows within a table. Until these operations are complete, don't let anyone else access the data.

Figure 9.5 shows a possible solution, with User B's read attempt being blocked until User A is finished.

	User A	User B	Current Value in Database
Time	Read the current inventory. temp = 25	Try to read the current inventory. Blocked!	25
	Decrease the inventory by 5. temp = 20	Try to read the current inventory. Blocked!	25
	Update database. Set quantity = 20	Try to read the current inventory. Blocked!	20
		Read the current inventory. temp = 20	20
		Increase the inventory by 5. temp = 25	20
		Update database. Set quantity = 25	25

Figure 9.5 Blocking another user to isolate a transaction.

Implementation. The solution can be implemented using locks and/or transactions. A lock places a hold on a row or table, which prevents other users from making changes until you are finished. A transaction groups a collection of statements into a unit, and uses locks in the following way: If you acquire a lock during a transaction, it is held until the transaction is completed. Transactions offer other benefits, such as all-or-nothing completion: If one of the elements in the transaction fails, all the pending changes can be automatically rolled back, or undone.

The SQL Way

Let's look at how different database servers address this problem using SQL:

PostgreSQL. After you begin a transaction, you must explicitly place any locks you will need. Until you release the locks, no other user may read from the table:

```
BEGIN TRANSACTION;
LOCK inventory;
SELECT quantity FROM inventory WHERE item='widget';
[...] some calculations that result in 30 [...]
UPDATE inventory SET quantity = 30;
COMMIT;
```

Oracle. Like PostgreSQL, Oracle gives you the ability to lock a table. The SHARE ROW EXCLUSIVE lock will allow other users to view data, but won't let them acquire a lock on the table (which is required to change data). Oracle implicitly creates a transaction, so there is no need for a BEGIN TRANSACTION statement. Here is an example where we lock the inventory table in SHARE ROW EXCLUSIVE MODE, and then perform a select and an update:

```
LOCK TABLE inventory IN SHARE ROW EXCLUSIVE MODE;
SELECT quantity FROM inventory WHERE item='widget';
[...] some calculations that result in 30 [...]
UPDATE inventory SET quantity = 30;
COMMIT;
```

Sybase. The HOLDLOCK keyword in a SELECT statement will lock a portion of a table within a transaction. When the transaction is complete, the lock is released, which allows other users to retrieve data:

```
BEGIN TRANSACTION
   SELECT quantity FROM inventory HOLDLOCK
   WHERE item = 'widget'
   [...] some calculations that result in 30 [...]
   UPDATE inventory SET quantity = 30 WHERE item = 'widget'
COMMIT TRANSACTION
```

The Sybase solution to the problem may seem a little unusual. If two of these transactions execute simultaneously, one of them is forced to fail. This is because this solution leads to a deadlock situation. When User A issues the SELECT statement, a shared lock is acquired. If User B comes in and issues the SELECT statement, User B also gets a shared lock. The deadlock occurs when the two users try to issue the UPDATE: The first user to issue the UPDATE statement waits to acquire an exclusive lock, but cannot get it until the shared lock is released. When the second user issues the UPDATE statement, Sybase detects the deadlock and chooses to terminate one of the transactions.

Doing without Transactions

As of this writing, the current version of MySQL (version 3.23) does not support transactions. However, it supports explicit locking and unlocking of tables. Use the LOCK TABLES statement to lock one or more tables, which should appear as a comma-separated list or tables and lock modes (READ or WRITE):

```
LOCK TABLES table_one WRITE, table_two READ
```

Here is a MySQL solution to the lost update problem:

```
LOCK TABLES inventory WRITE;
SELECT quantity FROM inventory WHERE item='widget';
UPDATE inventory SET quantity = 30;
UNLOCK TABLES;
```

Version 3.24 of MySQL will have support for transactions.

NOTE
You must lock all tables that you are going to use. MySQL uses this assumption to guarantee that you won't have to worry about deadlocks. If you don't lock a table that you use, you may run into a deadlock situation.

If you really wanted to use transactions with a database that doesn't support them (such as Mini SQL or MySQL), you would need to build a broker (a component that acts as a mediator for requests) between your applications and the database. In order to do this, the broker would need to implement some features, such as:

- A client/server protocol so your applications could make requests
- Some form of caching to hold uncommitted objects before they are sent to the database

- An undo mechanism, which would allow uncommitted objects to be restored to an earlier state in case of an error
- An internal mechanism to represent locks

With a scheme like this, you would not be able to have your applications talk to the database directly. All database access would have to be through the broker to ensure that the locks are respected.

Words of Caution

Be careful when using transactions! If you use a transaction that might block another operation, make sure to follow two rules:

- Don't let the program pause for user input during a transaction.
- Do your thing as quickly as possible, and get out of there and release your locks.

Also, make sure that all parts of your program are following the same rules. If you are using shared locks in some places that perform updates, and no locks in others, it may be possible for lost updates to occur. If you are updating data, make sure you acquire locks in the same way each time, to ensure that the database server does the correct thing.

Administrative Issues

To use your freshly installed database without hassle, you need to take care of some issues. This section does not address ongoing security or maintenance concerns, but points out issues that will come up sooner or later. You will find that there are some server-specific discussions of other issues in the database-specific sections earlier in this chapter. This section is intended as a supplement to those discussions.

Bulk Data Operations

Sometimes you need to move data in and out of your database in large quantities. There are two ways to do this. The first is to use SQL. The SQL monitor for your database is capable of sending batches of SQL to the server, and most databases have a method to dump the contents of a database or table as a table. This SQL will include the commands necessary to create the tables and other database objects.

Table 9.3 Dumping Databases and Tables as SQL

DATABASE	DUMP DATABASE	DUMP TABLE
PostgreSQL	pg_dump -D dbname	pg_dump -D -t tablename dbname
Mini SQL	msqldump -c dbname	msqldump -c dbname tablename
MySQL	mysqldump -ppassword -c dbname	mysqldump -ppassword -c dbname tablename

Table 9.3 shows the commands used to dump SQL from a database, and example invocations for dumping a database or table to standard output. You should redirect this output to a file.

To import this data, use the SQL monitor program for the target database. If you plan to import it into a different database system, you may need to modify the end-of-command delimiters (such as Sybase's GO, Mini and MySQL's \g, or the semicolon). Conversion may be complicated if you use an SQL feature or some SQL syntax that is not supported by the target database system.

The sample invocations in Table 9.3 generate CREATE TABLE statements for each table and complete SQL INSERT statements for each row in the table. The -D option(PostgreSQL) and the -c option (MySQL and Mini SQL) causes the dump to include INSERT statements with explicit column names.

Many of these utilities have extended options. Please see the documentation for your database for more details. The output of these utilities may not include DROP statements for tables, but they will include CREATE TABLE statements. As such, you cannot load the output into a database without dropping those tables first. (mysqldump is an exception: it supports the *--add-drop-table* command-line switch).

You can also export and import data in a delimited format, such as tab-delimited. To do this, the table you want to import into must already exist.

Table 9.4 contains the commands that you would need to issue to export the contents of a table in tab-delimited format. Many other options are available (including alternative delimiters), so consult your documentation for more details.

NOTE

<TAB> refers to a literal tab character. To type this under the bash shell, type ^V and then press the TAB key. For users of other shells, consult the man page for your shell.

Table 9.5 shows the commands you would issue to import data in a tab-delimited format. Again, consult the database server's documentation for more options, including alternative delimiters.

Table 9.4 Exporting Data in Tab-Delimited Format

DATABASE	EXPORT TABLE
PostgreSQL	`\copy tablename to file.out` (use within the psql utility)
Mini SQL	`msqlexport -s "<TAB>" dbname tablename`
MySQL	`mysqldump -T dirname -ppassword dbname` (dirname is a directory. This creates one .txt and one .sql file in dirname/ for each table in dbname)
MySQL	`SELECT * INTO OUTFILE 'file.out' FROM tablename;` (use within the mysql utility, when logged in as the MySQL superuser)

Examples

Let's take a look at some example bulk import/export sessions. Text between *<<EOF* and *EOF* is a sort of multi-line quoting that is known as a *here-document* (see the man page for your shell for more details). These statements should be typed into your shell as shown:

Mini SQL. Dump the invoice table from the bjepson_db database into the file /tmp/msqldump.txt:

```
msqldump -c bjepson_db invoice > /tmp/msqldump.txt
```

Mini SQL. Load the /tmp/msqldump.txt dump into the bjepson_db database. Drop the invoice table, because the file msqldump.txt contains CREATE TABLE statements, and you will get an error if you try to create a table that already exists:

```
msql bjepson_db <<EOF
DROP TABLE invoice
\g
EOF
```

Table 9.5 Importing Tab-Delimited Data

DATABASE	IMPORT TO TABLE
PostgreSQL	`\copy tablename from file.in` (use within the psql utility)
Mini SQL	`msqlimport -s "<TAB>" dbname tablename < file.in`
MySQL	`LOAD DATA LOCAL INFILE 'file.in' INTO TABLE tablename;` (use within mysql utility)
MySQL	`mysqlimport dbname tablename.in` (filename must start with the name of the table)

```
msql bjepson_db < /tmp/msqldump.txt
```

Mini SQL. Export the invoice table in comma-delimited format. The msqlexport utility is privileged, and should be run as the Mini SQL admin user, usually root. Note that the , (comma) in "Little Co., Inc" is escaped with \ in the dump, to differentiate it from a delimiter:

```
bash2-2.03$ su -c 'msqlexport -s"," bjepson_db \
            invoice > /tmp/msqldump.txt'
Password: ********
bash2-2.03$ cat /tmp/msqldump.txt
001,Big Company
002,Little Co.\, Inc.
```

MySQL. Dump the line_item table into a tab-delimited file and its definition into an SQL file. Display each file with cat, but use the -vt option to show the tabs as ^I in /tmp/dumps/line_item.txt. Notice that we are logging on with the MySQL root user name and password. If your MySQL user account does not have privileges to dump a database, you may need to be the root user to perform this operation:

```
bash2-2.03$ mkdir -p /tmp/dumps
bash2-2.03$ mysqldump -T/tmp/dumps -uroot \
            -psecret bjepson_db line_item

bash2-2.03$ cat -vt /tmp/dumps/line_item.txt
001^IWidget^I25
001^IBlivet^I12
002^IWidget^I25
002^IBlivet^I10
bash2-2.03$ cat /tmp/dumps/line_item.sql
# MySQL dump 6.4
#
# Host: localhost    Database: bjepson_db
#--------------------------------------------------
# Server version        3.22.27

#
# Table structure for table 'line_item'
#
CREATE TABLE line_item (
  inv_no char(3),
  item_description char(20),
  quantity int(11)
);
```

MySQL. Load the dump we just created back into the line_item table. Note that we first delete all the rows in the table. Otherwise, we would duplicate every row in the table:

```
mysql -popen_sesame bjepson_db <<EOF;
DELETE FROM line_item;

LOAD DATA LOCAL INFILE '/tmp/dumps/line_item.txt'
    INTO TABLE line_item;
EOF
```

PostgreSQL. Dump the contents of bjepson's database into the file dump.out:

```
pg_dump -D bjepson > dump.out
```

PostgreSQL. Drop the invoice and line_item tables (assuming they are the only tables in bjepson's database) and reload the database from dump.out:

```
psql <<EOF
DROP TABLE line_item;
DROP TABLE invoice;
EOF

psql < dump.out
```

Sybase

Sybase does not have a utility that can dump SQL statements for creating tables and their contents. However, SybPerl (www.perl.com/CPAN/modules/by-module/Sybase) includes a utility, dbschema.pl, that can dump SQL statements for creating tables and other objects. To move the actual data in and out of the database, you can use the bcp utility, which can import and export data in various formats.

To export a table using bcp, you should issue the command *bcp database-name.owner.table out filename*, as shown in the following bcp session (note that we use dbo as a shortcut for the user name, which specifies the owner of the database). When you start bcp, it interrogates you about the structure of the table. While the defaults are generally OK, you should consult the Sybase documentation for more details.

The following bcp session exports bjepson_db.invoice as tab-delimited, with line feeds to separate lines:

```
$ bcp bjepson_db.dbo.invoice out /tmp/invoice.bcp \
  -t \\t -r \\n -Ubjepson -Popen_sesame

Enter the file storage type of field inv_no [char]:
Enter prefix-length of field inv_no [0]:
Enter length of field inv_no [3]:
Enter field terminator [\t]:
```

```
Enter the file storage type of field customer_name [char]:
Enter prefix-length of field customer_name [0]:
Enter length of field customer_name [20]:
Enter field terminator [\n]:

Do you want to save this format information in a file? [Y/n]

Host filename [bcp.fmt]: invoice.fmt

Starting copy...

2 rows copied.
Clock Time (ms.): total = 1  Avg = 0 (2000.00 rows per sec.)
bash2-2.03$ cat -vt /tmp/invoice.bcp
001^IBig Company
002^ILittle Co., Inc.
```

The following bcp session imports a tab-delimited file into the invoice table:

```
$ bcp bjepson_db.dbo.invoice in /tmp/invoice.bcp \
  -f invoice.fmt -t \\t -r \\n                    \
  -Ubjepson -Popen_sesame

Starting copy...

2 rows copied.
Clock Time (ms.): total = 1  Avg = 0 (2000.00 rows per sec.)
```

Note that you must enable the select into/bulkcopy/pllsort option for the database that you are bcp'ing data into. To do this, you must be the database owner, and you must be in the master database. Here is an example that shows how to set this option for the bjepson_db database:

```
bash2-2.03$ isql -Ubjepson -Popen_sesame
1> use master
2> go
1> sp_dboption bjepson_db,
2>    "select into/bulkcopy/pllsort", true
3> go
Database option 'select into/bulkcopy/pllsort' turned ON for database
'bjepson_db'.
Run the CHECKPOINT command in the database that was changed.
(return status = 0)
1> use bjepson_db
2> checkpoint
3> go
```

Oracle

Unfortunately, Oracle does not have a utility that can be used to create SQL dumps from a database, or to easily create delimited dump files that can be loaded into other systems. A crude methods of achieving a tab-delimited dump is shown next, where the | | (concatenation) operator is used to concatenate the field values with the tab character.

You should save these commands into a file called export_invoice.sql (type <TAB> as a literal tab character—make sure your editor does not replace tabs with spaces!):

```
rem
rem ECHO OFF      - Supresses echoing of commands
rem                 as they are executed
rem FEEDBACK OFF - Suppresses record count reports
rem HEADING OFF  - Supresses column headings
rem NEWPAGE OFF  - Don't send formfeeds or blank
rem                  lines between pages.
rem TERMOUT OFF  - Don't display output of
rem                  commands.
rem TRIMSPOOL ON - Trim trailing blanks in output.
rem
SET ECHO OFF;
SET FEEDBACK OFF;
SET HEADING OFF;
SET NEWPAGE NONE;
SET TERMOUT OFF;
SET TRIMSPOOL ON;

rem
rem Spool the results to an output file with
rem columns delimited by a tab character.
rem
SPOOL /tmp/invoice.out

SELECT inv_no || '<TAB>' || customer_name
    FROM invoice;

SPOOL OFF;

QUIT;
```

Then, load this script into SQL*Plus, as shown in this example:

```
sqlplus bjepson/open_sesame @export_invoice.sql
```

Then you can see that tabs have been inserted into the output:

```
bash2-2.03$ cat -vt /tmp/invoice.out
001^IBig Company
002^ILittle Co., Inc.
```

The Security of Initial Accounts

Many database systems come with one or more well-known default users and passwords. In order to secure the state of your database, you should change the passwords or delete the users.

PostgreSQL. PostgreSQL comes with one account by default, which corresponds to the Unix user id of the user that manages and runs the database. This user is usually named postgres.

If you do not make any changes to its configuration, PostgreSQL allows any user on the local machine to connect to the database as any user, including the postgres account. That is, PostgreSQL does not use passwords to authenticate a user; it trusts any user on the local system.

To secure your installation, you should examine the pg_hba.conf (or pg_hba.conf.sample) file that comes with PostgreSQL, and select a level of authentication you are comfortable with. If you installed PostgreSQL from a source distribution, this file needs to reside in /usr/local/pgsql/data /pg_hba.conf. Some versions of Linux (such as RedHat 6.0) may store this file in /usr/lib/pgsql/pg_hba.conf.

For more details, read the pg_hba.conf and pg_passwd man pages (type 'man pg_hba.conf' and 'man pg_passwd').

MySQL. By default, MySQL comes with a root user that has no password. After you install MySQL, you should set a password for this account with the command:

```
mysqladmin -uroot password secret
```

(replace *secret* with the password you want to use).

From that point on, you may only use mysqladmin or other mysql utilities by using the -p command line argument to specify a password. The -u command is useful if you are running the command as another user. For example:

```
bash2-2.03$ mysqladmin -uroot -psecret ping
mysqld is alive
```

In general, you should be cautious about putting passwords on the command line, since they can be seen by utilities such as ps. A safer way to do this is to use -p without the password, and you will be prompted for a password:

```
bash2-2.03$ mysqladmin -uroot -p ping
Enter password: *******
mysqld is alive
```

Also, see the discussion of .my.cnf under the section *MySQL*, elsewhere in this chapter.

Oracle. Three accounts that come with Oracle are potential security holes. The *SYS, SYSTEM*, and *scott* accounts come with widely known passwords that should be changed when you install the server (the *scott* account is installed by certain demos, and may not be installed on every server).

To change these passwords, log on to sqlplus and issue the *ALTER USER username IDENTIFIED BY newpassword* command, as shown here:

```
bash2-2.03$ sqlplus SYSTEM/manager

SQL*Plus: Release 8.1.5.0.0 - Production on Wed Oct 20 14:55:53 1999

(c) Copyright 1999 Oracle Corporation.  All rights reserved.


Connected to:
Oracle8i Release 8.1.5.0.0 - Production
With the Java option
PL/SQL Release 8.1.5.0.0 - Production

SQL> ALTER USER SYS IDENTIFIED BY secret;

User altered.

SQL> ALTER USER SYSTEM IDENTIFIED BY secret;

User altered.

SQL> ALTER USER scott IDENTIFIED BY secret;

User altered.
```

Of course, you should not use the password (secret) shown in the preceding code, nor should you use the same password for all three users!

Sybase. By default, the Sybase super user, sa, does not have a password. You should change this immediately after a new installation. Log on to isql as the sa user, and change the password:

```
bash2-2.03$ isql -Usa -P""
1> sp_password NULL, secret
2> go
```

```
Password correctly set.
(return status = 0)
```

Automatic Startup and Shutdown

How do you configure Linux so that it starts the database when the computer boots and shuts the database down when you shut down the computer? Some database systems make the necessary changes to your operating system files, but we'll review these changes here.

Modern versions of Linux, such as RedHat, Debian, and others, use an initialization scheme inherited from Unix System V. Under this scheme, the system has up to seven runlevels, or as we like to think of them, states of consciousness:

Runlevel 0. Halted. Nothing is happening, no programs are running.

Runlevel 1. Single-user mode. This is useful for performing system maintenance that requires root to be the only user logged on.

Runlevel 2. Multiuser, with no NFS.

Runlevel 3. Full multiuser mode.

Runlevel 4. Unused.

Runlevel 5. Boot up and start the X Windows System.

Runlevel 6. When the system enters this mode, it reboots.

When the system boots up, it enters the default runlevel specified in /etc/inittab (you can imagine why you might not want to specify 0 or 6). As it enters a runlevel, the system looks in a directory that corresponds to the new runlevel (rc0.d, rc1.d, rc2.d, rc3.d, rc4.d, rc5.d, or rc6.d). For RedHat systems, these directories are found in /etc/rc.d. For Debian systems, these directories are found in /etc.

The rc*.d directories contain a whole bunch of scripts whose names follow the format S*nn*Name or K*nn*Name, where *nn* is a number from 00 to 99. The S prefix indicates that the operating system should run that script with the argument *start*, and the K prefix indicates that the operating system should run the script with the argument *stop*.

K scripts are run first, followed by the S scripts. As you can imagine, there are generally more K scripts in rc0.d and rc6.d than there are in the other directories. The scripts are usually symbolic links from files in the /etc/init.d (Debian) or /etc/rc.d/init.d (RedHat) directories (the init.d directory should contain all the scripts needed to stop and start processes). Here is an example script, called hellogoodbye:

```
#!/bin/sh

case "$1" in
    start)
        echo Hello!
    ;;

    stop)
        echo Goodbye!
    ;;

    *)
        echo "Usage: $0 {start|stop}"
        exit 1
    ;;
esac

exit 0
```

If you created a symbolic link from /etc/init.d/hellogoodbye to /etc/rc3.d/S99hellogoodbye, then, as the system is coming up:

- The system will invoke this with the command *S99hellogoodbye start*.
- The script will say "Hello!"

If you created a symbolic link from /etc/init.d/hellogoodbye to /etc/rc0.d/K01hellogoodbye, then, as the system is shutting down:

- The system will invoke this with the command *K01hellogoodbye stop*.
- The script will say "Goodbye!"

RedHat Users

RedHat systems use the /var/lock/subsys directory to keep track of which processes have been started. It is vitally important that you use this feature correctly. If you do not, your processes will be started but not stopped. If you bring the system down to single-user mode or reboot it without stopping the database processes, they may die an abrupt death, leaving your database in a corrupt state.

To use this feature, you need to do two things:

- When the script is started, touch /var/lock/subsys/script_name.
- When the script is ended, remove /var/lock/subsys/script_name.

When RedHat sees a file in /var/lock/subsys that has the same name as a script in /etc/rc.d/init.d, it knows to shut it down when the system is brought down. Here is a modified version of hellogoodbye for RedHat systems:

```
#!/bin/sh

case "$1" in
    start)
        touch /var/lock/subsys/hellogoodbye
        echo Hello!
    ;;

    stop)
        rm -f /var/lock/subsys/hellogoodbye
        echo Goodbye!
    ;;

    *)
        echo "Usage: $0 {start|stop}"
        exit 1
    ;;
esac

exit 0
```

NOTE

Under RedHat, the chkconfig utility can be used to automatically install a startup/shutdown script, and to automatically create symbolic links. For more details, see the chkconfig man page.

Database Features Quick Reference

In this section, we're going to take a quick look at some of the features of each database system. We're presenting this information in tabular format, in the hopes that it will make it easier to find the information you need, and easier to compare the different database systems.

General Overview

Let's look at some of the general information about each database. Table 9.6 shows a summary of this information.

Home Page. This is where you can find information, documentation, and latest releases.

Table 9.6   Overview of Each Database System

DATABASE SYSTEM	HOME PAGE	DATA ACCESS API	DAEMON	LICENSE
PostgreSQL	www.postgresql.org	libpq	postmaster	Open Source.
Mini SQL	www.hughes.com.au	libmsql	msql2d	Free to use for some, shareware for others.
MySQL	www.mysql.com	libmysqlclient.so	safe_mysqld	Open Source (with some exceptions); older versions are released under the GPL.
Oracle	www.oracle.com/linux	libclntsh.so	oracle	Proprietary.
Sybase	linux.sybase.com	libct.so	dataserver	Proprietary.

Data Access API. The shared library that client programs use to connect to the database server.

Daemon. The name of the server process.

License. The type of license used by the creators of the software.

Data Types

Although the SQL standard includes a standard set of data types, not all of the database servers adhere to that standard. Table 9.7, the Data Type Cross-Reference table, is included here as a guide to the differences. This is not a complete list of data types supported by each server, but a common convergence point to make it easier to port from one to another.

Boolean. A true or false value. Some databases support a bit type, which can be 0 or 1.

Character(len). A string of length len. Often abbreviated as char.

Character Varying(len). A variable string of maximum length len. Often implemented as varchar.

Date. A date value. Some implementations combine date and time into one data type. In Oracle, this is the date data type. In Sybase, it is datetime.

Table 9.7 Data Type Cross-Reference Table

SQL-92 DATA TYPE	POSTGRESQL	MINI SQL	MYSQL	ORACLE	SYBASE
boolean	bool		bit		bit
character(len)	*	*	*	*	*
character varying(len) or varchar(len)	*	text(len)	*	*	*
date	*	*	*	*	datetime
decimal(prec, scale)	*		*	*	*
decimal(9, 0)	decimal		decimal(9,0)	decimal(9,0)	decimal(9,0)
double precision	float8		*	*	*
float(prec)	float4/float8		*	*	*
integer	int4/integer	*	*	*	*
numeric(prec, scale)	*		*	*	*
numeric(9, 0)	numeric				
smallint	int2		*	*	*
real	float8	*	*	*	*
time	*	*	*	date	datetime
timestamp	*		*		

* indicates it is the same as SQL-92

Decimal(prec, scale). An exact numeric value. The number of digits is specified in prec. The number of those digits that are reserved for the decimal portion are specified in scale. For example, decimal(5, 2) could hold a maximum value of 999.99. Older versions of MySQL counted the decimal point, but current versions do not. With the older versions (3.22 and earlier), the maximum for decimal(5,2) would be 99.99.

Double Precision. An approximate floating-point value. This is generally eight bytes wide, so you can put some pretty big numbers in there.

Float(prec). An approximate floating-point value with the specified precision (prec). Depending on the precision, this will be either four or eight bytes wide.

Integer. An integer in the range from -2,147,483,648 to 2,147,483,647. Often abbreviated as int.

Numeric(prec, scale). See Decimal(prec, scale).

Smallint. A small integer value that ranges from -32,767 to 32,768.

Real. An approximate floating-point value that is generally four bytes wide.

Time. A time expression of the form HH:MM:SS, such as '06:45:00' or '23:59:59'. Some implementations combine date and time into one type. Sybase uses the datetime type, which can be assigned a time value (such as '23:59:59') without a date component (such as 'Dec 31, 1999 23:59:59'). You cannot assign a time value without a date component to an Oracle date column. However, before you do this, you may want to select your date format, as shown in this example:

```
CREATE TABLE time_test
    (start_date DATE);
ALTER SESSION
    SET NLS_DATE_FORMAT='DD-MON-YYYY HH24:MI:SS';
INSERT INTO time_test
    VALUES(TO_DATE('01-Dec-1999 23:59:59'));
```

Timestamp. A timestamp value that combines date and time. On systems that support this, timestamp columns are automatically updated whenever a row is changed. This is usually used to check the last time a row was modified, rather than for storing time and date values. Databases that combine date and time into a single type (see Date) don't need a timestamp data type. You should consult your database server documentation for more information.

Date formats can be a tricky thing. Many database systems are somewhat flexible in the date formats that they support, but not all systems agree on the same format. Table 9.8 shows some of the common date formats that are supported by each database system, along with examples that can be used in SQL statements. Delimiters such as single quotes and dashes should be taken literally when you create an SQL statement.

Although this table states that Oracle only supports the first format, this is not entirely true. You can reconfigure Oracle to support almost any date format you can imagine, but by default, it only recognizes the first format.

SQL Monitors

Table 9.9 summarizes the interactive SQL programs that come with each database system. For more details, see the *Sending SQL to the Server* sections for each database system throughout this chapter.

Table 9.8 A Sampling of Date Formats

FORMAT	EXAMPLE	POSTGRESQL	MINI SQL	MYSQL	ORACLE	SYBASE
DD-MMM-YYYY	'01-Dec-1999'	Yes	Yes	No	Yes	Yes
MMM DD, YYYY	'Dec 01, 1999'	Yes	No	No	No	Yes
MM-DD-YYYY	'12-01-1999'	Yes	No	No	No	Yes
MM/DD/YYYY	'12/01/1999'	Yes	No	No	No	Yes
YYYY-MM-DD*	'1999-12-01'	Yes	No	Yes	No	Yes

* the SQL standard date format

Table 9.9 SQL Monitors

DATABASE	MONITOR	GET HELP ON MONITOR	INVOKE EDITOR	SEND A COMMAND	QUIT
PostgreSQL	psql	\?	\e	\g or ;	\q
Mini SQL	msql	\h		\g	\q
MySQL	mysql	help	\e	\g or ; or go	\q
Sybase	isql		vi	go	quit
Oracle	sqlplus	help	edit	;	quit

Oracle Users

To use the edit command, you must have the environment variable EDITOR set before you start SQL*Plus. Otherwise, you will end up in the line-mode editor ed, or possibly much worse. Also, in order to use the *help* command, you must install the SQL*Plus help database, which is found in the $ORACLE_HOME/sqlplus/admin/help directory.

To install it, you'll need to execute the following commands (replace secret with SYSTEM's password):

```
cd $ORACLE_HOME/sqlplus/admin/help
sqlplus SYSTEM/secret < helptbl.sql
sqlplus SYSTEM/secret < helpindx.sql
sqlldr userid=SYSTEM/secret control=plushelp.ctl
```

Summary

There are many responsibilities a database server can take on. These responsibilities are determined in part by the complexity of the system you are writing, but are also determined by the need to maintain consistency in any set of data.

By now, you should be able to do some simple work with one or more of the database servers discussed in this chapter. In the chapters that follow, we'll look at how to write programs that connect to these databases, and take advantage of many of the features we discussed in this chapter.

Linux Development Tools Catalog

Before you start hacking on your own database applications, you should find tools that might save you time. In this chapter, we'll look at a selection of tools that can help you develop database applications and manage your database server.

Database Tools

It can be tricky getting the database end to cooperate with a front-end you are trying to write. The following are examples of when you might want to have a closer relationship with the data server:

- Debugging an SQL statement
- Optimizing the performance of an SQL statement
- Examining the impact of various indexing alternatives
- Examining the database for data quality problems (invalid values and relational integrity violations)
- Routine database administration

In situations such as these, you might turn to your trusty SQL monitor program (see the section titled *SQL Monitors* in Chapter 9, "Databases"), if you didn't know of the alternatives. However, there are many database administration tools that make dealing with the database a lot easier than would be possible with a command-line client.

Multi-RDBMS

Many of the database administration tools support more than one RDBMS. Although each of these tools favors the features of one particular RDBMS, they all represent progress toward centralized administration tools for multiple database systems.

Katabase

Katabase is the desktop database component of Koffice, KDE's office suite. At the time of this writing, Katabase was still in the planning stages. Although Katabase is planned to be similar to tools such as Access or Paradox, the designers want to make it support as many databases and data formats as possible. It seems that in some ways, it will be similar to GNOME-DB (see Chapter 13, "GNOME"). You can find out more about it at http://koffice.kde.org/katabase/.

KSQL

KSQL (formerly KMySQL) is an open source graphical database client for various SQL databases. In its original incarnation, it only supported MySQL. More recent releases are based on a plug-in architecture (the database connection is handled by a plug-in for a specific database server), which makes it easy for KSQL to support other database systems. As of this writing, KSQL supports plug-ins for MySQL, Mini SQL, Sybase, and PostgreSQL. However, many of the features described next are only available for MySQL. Over time, they may be available for the other supported databases.

Installation. KSQL is available in source and binary (RPM) form at http://ksql.sourceforge.net/. You can also obtain plug-ins and documentation at this site.

Connecting to a database server. To start KSQL, type kmysql in an xterm (or other X shell) and press Enter. If you are using KDE, there may be an option for KSQL on your KDE menu, under Applications (at the time of this writing, the name of the binary had not yet changed from kmysql to ksql—if it changes in future versions, you might need to run ksql instead of kmysql).

After you start KSQL, choose Add Server from the Server menu. The Add Server dialog appears, shown in Figure 10.1. Select the type of database server you want to connect to, and provide the required parameters, such as username, password, and database. You can have multiple connections open at once, and you can explore the database using the explorer view as shown in Figure 10.2.

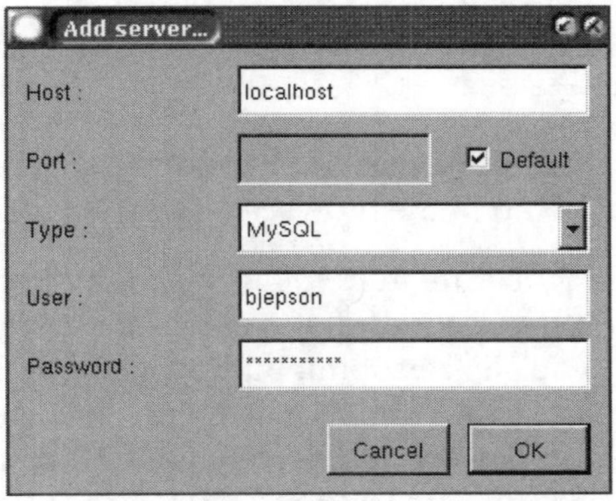

Figure 10.1 The KMySQL Add Server dialog.

Fetching data. KSQL offers a number of features for getting data from the database. To fetch all the rows in a table, simply double-click on the table's name in the explorer view, and the contents of the table appear as shown in Figure 10.2. You can print the results of queries or generate an HTML file from the results by choosing the corresponding option from the View menu.

Static queries. You can also create static queries in the database. These are simply queries that have been associated with a given name (they are similar to the views discussed in Appendix A, "SQL Reference"). In Figure 10.2, the query Static_Sample is displayed in the explorer view, just above the list of tables. This query was defined as:

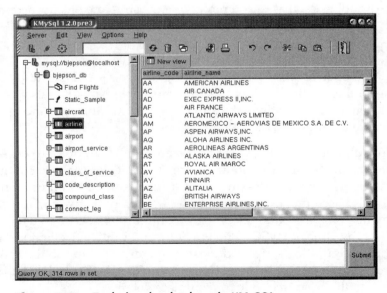

Figure 10.2 Exploring the database in KMySQL.

```
SELECT flight.flight_code,aircraft.aircraft_type
    FROM flight,aircraft
    WHERE flight.aircraft_code=aircraft.aircraft_code
```

You can double-click on Static_Sample just as you would with a table, and the results of that query will show up in the browser view.

Forms. Perhaps the most compelling feature in KSQL is the ability to create custom forms. The form editor offers a handful of widgets and a simple (but powerful) function: When you click a submit button, a query of your choice is executed using values from the form. For example, you could create a form that lets you choose a departure and destination city. Your choice is bound to the variables $from_city$ and to_city. When you click OK, the following query is executed and shown in the view:

```
SELECT flight_number, category, departure_time, arrival_time
    FROM flight, aircraft
    WHERE flight.aircraft_code = aircraft.aircraft_code
    AND     from_airport = '$from_airport$'
    AND     to_airport = '$to_airport$'
    ORDER BY departure_time
```

Figure 10.3 shows this form in action. You could also use other SQL queries, such as an INSERT statement. While this feature may seem simple, you'll appreciate its value the first time you need it! At the time of this writing, the custom forms only work with the MySQL server.

Administration. KSQL includes support for creating and dropping tables, creating and dropping databases, and modifying the structure of existing tables.

dbMetrix

dbMetrix is an open source tool for exploring databases and executing SQL. At the time of this writing, dbMetrix supports Oracle, MySQL, PostgreSQL, Solid, and Mini SQL. Over time, the author of dbMetrix plans to incorporate administrative features and data export support.

Installation. dbMetrix is available at www.tamos.net/sw/dbMetrix/. As of this writing, only source distributions are available. It is easy to configure and compile the source code, since dbMetrix includes a configuration script that is based on GNU autoconf (www.gnu.org/software/autoconf/). You may need to pass parameters to the configuration script to tell it the location of the Oracle, MySQL, PostgreSQL, and Mini SQL client libraries. After the configuration script is done, you merely need to run the *make* utility to compile the application. Consult the README and INSTALL files that come with the source code for complete details.

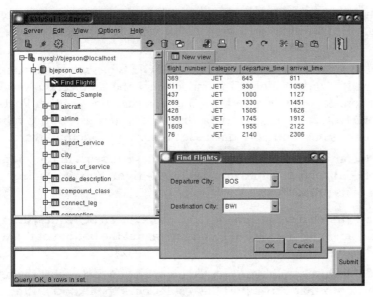

Figure 10.3 A KSQL custom form.

Connecting to a database server. To start dbMetrix, type the command *dbmetrix* in an xterm (or other X shell) and press Enter. To connect to a server, click the Connect button or choose New Data Source from the File menu. When the Add Data Source dialog appears, choose the type of database server, and provide the host name, user name, password, and other options. If your database server is on the local machine, you may want to try leaving options such as Host, Port, and Socket File blank, unless you are sure you need to supply a value. If you leave the values blank, the client API may try to use sensible defaults.

You can have more than one connection open at once. When you are connected, you can explore the database, as shown in Figure 10.4.

Fetching data. You can type an SQL query into the query window, and then click the Execute button to send the query to the database server. The results of the query appear in a window, as shown in Figure 10.4.

gtkSQL

gtkSQL is an open source SQL query tool for PostgreSQL and MySQL. It offers an easy way to inspect the structures of tables, execute SQL statements, and export result sets to a variety of formats.

Installation. gtkSQL is available at www.multimania.com/bbrox/GtkSQL/. At the time of this writing, gtkSQL is available in source form only.

Although the version we used (0.3) did not include an autoconfigure script, the README file had simple instructions for configuring and compiling the source code.

Connecting to a database server. To start gtkSQL, type *gtksql* in an xterm (or other X shell) and press Enter. To connect, click the Connect button. The Database connection dialog appears, and you can choose either PostgreSQL or MySQL. To connect to the database, you must supply values for options such as host and port, database name, login, and password.

When you connect to the database, a query field appears in the left pane, and a tabbed display of tables appears on the right. You can click on a table name to see its properties.

Fetching data. To fetch data from the database, type an SQL query into the query field, and click Send. The results appear at the bottom of the window, as shown in Figure 10.5.

Exporting data. Once you have executed a query, you can export the results to a variety of formats. To export the results, click the Export button. A dialog appears that lets you choose a file name and file type (text or HTML). If you choose to save it to an HTML document, you will be prompted to choose how many records to display per page, and other options. If the

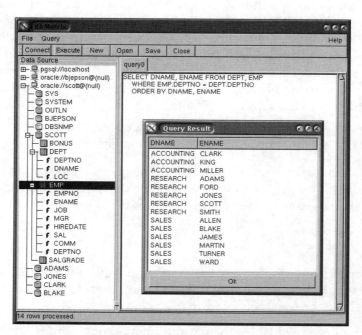

Figure 10.4 Exploring databases with dbMetrix.

HTML document overflows the page, it will be saved as several numbered files, such as export000.html, export001.html, and so on.

If you choose to export the data as text, you can choose a delimiter, such as tab, space, comma, and others. gtkSQL does not escape delimiters that appear in the contents of fields, so you should be careful to choose a delimiter that does not appear in the result set.

dbMan

dbMan is an open source SQL query tool written in Perl. It uses the Perl DBI module to connect to the database, and the Tk module for a graphical user interface. To use dbMan, you should install the Perl DBI, as well as DBD drivers for any database you want to connect. For details on setting this up, see the DBI discussion under *Drivers and Driver Managers* later in this chapter.

Installation. dbMan is distributed as an RPM package, and is also available in source form. dbMan can be obtained from the dbMan homepage at http://dbman.linux.cz/. This site features an installation how-to document that will help if you need to install it from source.

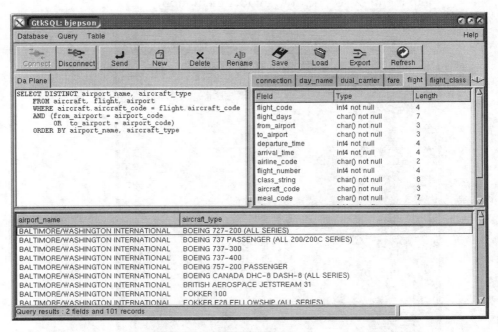

Figure 10.5 Querying the database with gtkSQL.

Connecting to a database server. You can start dbMan as an X application, or as a text-only console application. To start it under X, type dbman in an xterm (or other X shell) and press enter. To start it as a console application, type *dbman -l* (that's a lowercase L, not the number 1) at the shell prompt, and press Enter.

On startup, dbMan prompts you for the host name, port, DBD driver, database name, login, and password. Supply the requested values to connect to a database (for information on DBI connections, see Chapter 12, "DBI and Perl").

Fetching data. dbMan's user interface is simple, and you can use the same commands with the console version that you can with the graphical version. In the graphical version, simply type an SQL statement into the field marked *SQL*, and click *Do* or press Ctrl+Enter. The results appear in the scrolling window region, as shown in Figure 10.6.

dbMan has some extended features, including the ability to describe the structure of tables, display the output of SQL queries in a browser grid, and edit the contents of a table in a browser grid. dbMan also includes the useful \ex command, which dumps table definitions and their contents as SQL. For a complete list of dbMan's features, select *In-line Commands Index* from the Help menu or see the dbMan documentation.

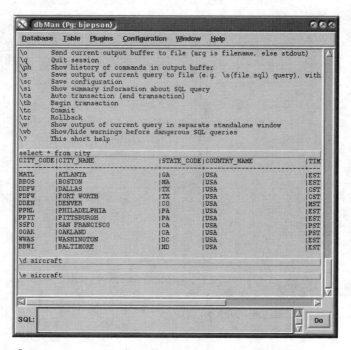

Figure 10.6   Executing an SQL statement with dbMan.

Gnome Transcript

Gnome Transcript is a graphical environment that allows you to define tables and data entry forms. You can then use the forms to add, edit, and delete data from your tables. At the time of this writing, Gnome Transcript supports PostgreSQL and MySQL. More information, including downloads, can be found at http://gtranscript.sourceforge.net/.

PostgreSQL Tools

Let's take a look at some of the tools that are available specifically for PostgreSQL.

kpsql. This is a graphical query tool for sending SQL to a PostgreSQL database server, and for viewing the results. This tool features SQL Syntax highlighting, and lets you generate output in a variety of formats, including HTML and delimited text. You can obtain kpsql at www.mutinybaysoftware.com/kpsql.html.

PgAccess. This tool is a sophisticated database development environment written in Tcl/Tk. It has many features styled after Microsoft Access, including a form builder, report designer, schema design tool, and powerful scripting capabilities. The PgAccess home page is at www.flex.ro/pgaccess.

Oracle Tools

The following are some tools designed specifically for Oracle:

OraSoft Application Suite. The OraSoft Oracle Applications for Linux page, at http://oracle.mattshouse.com, is home to a development effort to build a full-featured suite of tools for working with Oracle on Linux. At the time of this writing, this suite includes a table browser, visual query tool, stored procedure editor, a server monitoring tool, and the powerful Object Manager.

ora_explain. The DBD::Oracle database driver (see the section titled *Installing Database Drivers (DBDs)* in Chapter 12 for where to get this) includes the powerful ora_explain tool. This is a visual tool for inspecting Oracle query plans, which show you how the Oracle engine will handle a given query. ora_explain also lets you monitor and visualize the query plans for all the SQL that the server is currently processing (even for other users). Query plans are a complicated facet of database servers, but they can be indispensable when you need to optimize a query. ora_explain takes a lot of the mystery out of this process.

Orac. Orac is a powerful database administration tool written in Perl. It includes a vast array of features that help support, maintain, and tune an Oracle site.

Orac uses the DBI module for database connectivity and Tk for the graphical user interface. Although Orac was originally geared toward Oracle database servers, contributors have been adding support for other systems, and the Orac developers plan to make it as database and platform agnostic as possible. The Orac home page is at www.kkitts.com/orac-dba/index.html.

MySQL Tools

The following are a couple of tools that work with MySQL:

MySQLGUI. MySQLGUI is a graphical front-end to MySQL that is distributed at the *Downloads* page on the main MySQL site (www.mysql.com). MySQLGUI includes features for administering MySQL and working with data in a database.

KMySQLAdmin. This is an administration tool for MySQL that you can use to monitor the server, modify user permissions, create and modify tables, and export data. It includes a table browser that has some neat features, including a visual interface for querying tables and the ability to export in text, HTML, or LaTeX. The KMySQLAdmin page is at www.webeifer .de/alwin/Programs/KMySQLAdmin/index.html.

Sybase Tools

Now let's look at some tools designed for Sybase:

sqsh. sqsh is a fantastic replacement for the isql program that comes with Sybase. Where isql is a useful batch tool for sending SQL to Sybase, sqsh is a full-featured SQL shell that includes job control, variables, redirection, and many other features. The sqsh homepage is at www.voicenet.com/~gray/.

Like Sybase central. This tool is a comprehensive administration tool for Sybase. It includes features for managing users, databases, tables, and many other aspects of a Sybase server. It's a very impressive management tool, and is available at http://perso.wanadoo.fr/laserquest/linux/.

Drivers and Driver Managers

If you are writing a program that needs to connect to a database, what's the best way to make that connection? Just as a graphical application needs to link against the X Windows System libraries (such as libX11.so.6), an application that needs to connect to a MySQL database needs to link against libmysqlclient.so. As with MySQL, every database system includes headers and libraries that you can use to connect to the database. PostgreSQL has libpq.so, Oracle has libclntsh.so, and the list goes on and on.

In general, it's not a good idea to get involved with these client libraries, because you will end up writing an application that only works with one database. Instead, you should use a database independence API such as ODBC (C and C++), DBI (Perl), or JDBC (Java). There are many reasons why this is advantageous:

- With a database independence API, your programs are more portable to other platforms and database servers.
- Every client library does essentially the same thing: It facilitates accessing, querying, and modifying data stored in the database. Why should you learn a different client library for every database?

If you use ODBC (or DBI or JDBC) to develop a MySQL application, you can turn it into a PostgreSQL, Oracle, Mini SQL, or Sybase application by using a different database driver. Your programs connect to the driver manager, which acts as a broker between your program and the database. The driver manager uses one of the drivers on your system to actually issue calls to the database. As the programmer, you only need to bother with the ODBC (or DBI or JDBC) API, and you don't need to think about the client API for whichever database you want to connect to.

However, a database independence API, such as ODBC, only frees you from concerns that affect the underlying mechanics of how your program connects to and interacts with the database. If you choose to use vendor-specific extensions to SQL, you may introduce additional complications that make your application less portable. For example, MySQL supports a REPLACE statement, which combines DELETE and INSERT into one operation. Other database servers do not support this, and JDBC, ODBC, or DBI will not be able to help translate your SQL.

ODBC

ODBC is one of the venerable ancestors of data access APIs. It is a standard API for developing portable applications that need to connect to SQL database systems. ODBC was initially developed on the Microsoft Windows platform, but is available for many other platforms. ODBC applications are commonly written in C or C++. We won't be looking at any ODBC specific examples in this book, but there are bridges to ODBC from other languages, including Java (JDBC-ODBC bridge) and Perl (DBI::ODBC). Also, GNOME-DB can connect to ODBC data sources. So, even if you don't learn to program the ODBC API in this book, you can learn how to set up ODBC drivers, and use them from Java (see Chapter 11), Perl (see Chapter 12), or GNOME-DB applications written in C (see Chapter 13).

There are two freely redistributable ODBC kits for Linux: *iODBC* and *unixODBC*. These kits include the ODBC driver manager, which acts as a mediator between your database and an ODBC driver. The ODBC driver does the actual work of connecting to the database server. In addition to the driver manager, both ODBC kits include the headers and libraries you need to develop ODBC applications and drivers. The unixODBC package also includes several ODBC drivers.

iODBC

iODBC is an ODBC driver manager and software development kit that is maintained by OpenLink Software (www.openlinksw.com). You can find information about iODBC, as well as downloads for the latest versions, at www.iodbc.org.

Installation. You can download binary or source releases of iODBC. The source release includes a README and INSTALL file that has instructions on how to compile and install it. The automatic configuration script makes it easy to prepare the source code before you compile it.

Installing drivers. Once you've installed iODBC, you'll need to get some ODBC drivers, which let you connect to a database. iODBC should be compatible with any ODBC driver for Linux, including the free drivers that come with unixODBC. To find an ODBC driver for a specific database server, consult the homepage for that server (see Table 9.6 in Chapter 9 for a list of some database homepages). OpenLink Software, the maintainers of iODBC, has commercial driver offerings for many database servers. Other vendors may have similar offerings.

Once you have obtained an ODBC driver you want to use with iODBC, consult the iODBC documentation for details on how to install a driver. As of this writing you will need to edit the iODBC configuration files manually (but the developers are working on graphical configuration tools).

unixODBC

The unixODBC project features an ODBC driver manager, several ODBC drivers, and graphical utilities for configuring ODBC. In addition, unixODBC also includes a driver template, which is designed to make it easier to write new drivers. The unixODBC homepage is at www.unixodbc.org, where you can download the unixODBC source code and browse the online documentation.

Installation. The unixODBC source code includes a README and INSTALL file to help you get ready for compilation and installation. The autoconfigure script that comes with unixODBC takes care of most of the work, so installation should be smooth. Once you have installed unixODBC, you need to configure it. Where configuring ODBC on Linux was once a big headache, unixODBC has vastly simplified this with the ODBCConfig program, which has a user interface that should be familiar to ODBC users on Windows.

Adding drivers. The unixODBC distribution includes several drivers. To configure your installation to use these drivers:

1. Log on as the root user.

2. If it is not already started, start the X Windows System.

3. From the shell prompt, run the ODBCConfig program. The ODBC Data Source Administrator appears, as shown in Figure 10.7.

4. Select the Drivers tab. At first, there will be no drivers in the list. Click Add, and the New Driver dialog appears (see Figure 10.8).

5. You can give the driver any name and description you want. In this example, we'll use the PostgreSQL driver, so type PostgreSQL for the Name, and "PostgreSQL ODBC Driver" for the description.

6. A driver consists of two shared libraries: one is the driver itself, and the other is the setup code used to add a new data source for that driver. You must read the unixODBC documentation for the location of these two shared libraries. In Figure 10.8, they are libodbcpsql.so.1.0.0 (the driver) and libodbcpsqlS.so.1.0.0 (setup), both of which are located in /usr/local/lib/.

7. Click OK to add the driver.

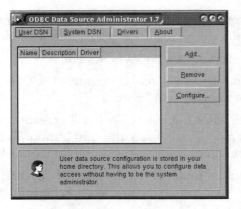

Figure 10.7 The unixODBC Data Source Administrator.

Figure 10.8 ODBC driver setup with the New Driver dialog.

Adding data sources. After you have installed a driver, you can configure as many data sources as you need. A data source is a named resource that associates a set of parameters with a driver. Each data source is named by a Data Source Name (DSN).

You can use data sources to create logical entry points into your database servers. For example, the data source PRODUCTION could use the PostgreSQL driver to connect to the PostgreSQL server on oscorb.as220.org, in the database that corresponds to the live system. You could also have the DEVELOPMENT data source, which connects to the same server, but uses a different database, which corresponds to the system that is under development. When it comes time to deploy the system under development, you can tell your program to start using the PRODUCTION data source.

Before you add a data source, you should decide if it should be a user data source (only available to one specific user) or a system data source (available to all users on the system). To add a data source:

1. Log on as the user who should have access to the data source. If you want to create a system data source, log on as the root user.

2. If it is not already started, start the X Windows System.

3. From the shell prompt, run the ODBCConfig program. The ODBC Data Source Administrator appears (see Figure 10.7).

4. To create a user data source, click the User DSN tab. To create a system data source, click the System DSN tab. Click the Add button. The Adding a New Data Source dialog appears, as shown in Figure 10.9.

5. Choose the ODBC driver to use (such as the PostgreSQL driver). Click OK. The New Data Source dialog appears, as shown in Figure 10.10.

6. Depending on which ODBC driver you choose, the New Data Source

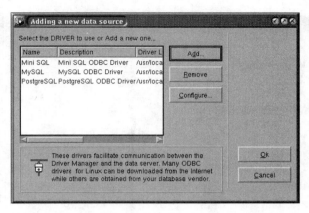

Figure 10.9   Adding a new data source with ODBCConfig.

dialog will vary. Check the documentation that came with unixODBC or with the driver for details on this dialog.

7. Supply any values required for the new data source, and click OK to create the new data source.

DataManager. unixODBC includes a graphical utility called DataManager. You can run this program by starting the X Windows System, and running the command DataManager from a shell prompt. The DataManager utility,

New Data Source	
Name	Sample Database
Description	PostgreSQL
Driver	PostgreSQL
Trace	No
TraceFile	>
Database	bjepson
Servername	localhost
UserName	bjepson
Password	
Port	5432
Protocol	6.4
ReadOnly	No
RowVersioning	No
ShowSystemTables	No
ShowOidColumn	No
FakeOidIndex	No
ConnSettings	
Ok	Cancel
Ready	

Figure 10.10   The New Data Source dialog.

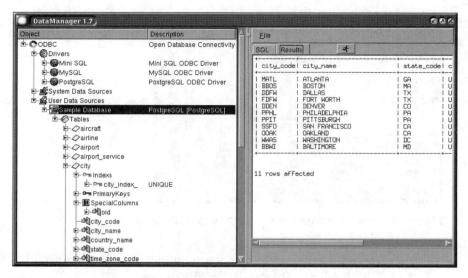

Figure 10.11 unixODBC's DataManager utility.

shown in Figure 10.11, allows you to navigate your data sources, examine the database structure, and issue SQL queries.

Finding drivers. Although unixODBC comes with a number of drivers, you may need to locate other drivers on your own. The unixODBC Web site includes a link to a *Drivers* page that lists all the drivers included with unixODBC, as well as all the drivers that the unixODBC developers know about. This is a good place to start your search. You may also want to consult the homepage for the database server, since they may have links to sources of ODBC drivers as well.

DBI

DBI is the database independence API used by Perl. It has many similarities to ODBC, but it is a higher-level interface that is designed to be more accessible than ODBC. Some Linux distributions include the DBI and at least one driver (a DBD), but you may need to install it on some systems. Chapter 12 provides more details on installing and using the DBI.

If you are using Orac or dbMan, you may need to use a DBI connection string to specify which database to connect to. See Chapter 12 for a discussion of the various connection strings that are used for different servers.

JDBC

JDBC is a database independence API for Java. It bears some resemblance to ODBC, but like DBI, it exposes its functionality on a high level, which frees programmers from having to worry about many of the details of connecting to a database. More details on JDBC are available in Chapter 11.

Modeling/Diagramming Tools

Here are some diagramming and modeling tools you may find useful:

Dia. Dia is a diagramming tool that is similar to the commercial Visio product. You can use Dia to draw practically any kind of diagram, either by using the built-in shapes, or by creating your own. Dia includes an extensive set of shapes for UML diagrams, as well as for network diagrams, entity-relationship diagrams, and flowcharts. The Dia homepage can be found at www.lysator.liu.se/~alla/dia/.

Argo/UML. The goal of the Argo/UML developers is to produce a system that provides cognitive support for object-oriented design. Although it looks like another UML design tool on the surface, Argo/UML analyzes and critiques your design as you develop it, maintains a to do list of outstanding tasks, and provides a variety of design representations to aid in your comprehension of your design. The Argo/UML homepage is available at www.argouml.org.

DOME. This remarkable tool is a system for developing and using CASE (Computer Aided Software Engineering) software models. It includes support for a variety of existing notations (such as UML), and is highly extensible. You can use DOME to develop new notations, or to develop diagrams written using any supported notation. At the time of this writing, work was underway to add support for entity-relationship diagrams to DOME, but this work had not yet been integrated into the core package. The DOME homepage is at www.htc.honeywell.com/dome/.

tgif. Most of the drawings for this book were made using tgif, an interactive vector drawing tool that can be used to produce a variety of diagrams. While there is no specific support for UML or entity-relationship diagrams, tgif makes it easy to develop such diagrams. It also has hypergraphic editing and browsing capabilities that are integrated with the World Wide Web. Frankly, we find this frightening, yet awe-inspiring. The tgif homepage is at http://bourbon.cs.umd.edu:8001/tgif/.

Summary

This chapter looked at many of the tools available for database development under Linux. It doesn't stop there, though. There will be more tools written, and many tools will evolve into newer things. How can you stay on top of this changing world? The Freshmeat site, at www.freshmeat.net, catalogs many open source tools, and maintains pointers to the lists of changes to these tools. Also, www.linuxdev.net posts articles of interest to Linux developers.

Java, Swing, and JDBC

J ava is a convenient language for database development, and an ideal choice for beginners to SQL application development. The standard Java SDK includes JDBC, a data access API that is powerful and easy to learn. Also, Java's user interface offerings have matured to the point where you can build powerful applications even without a visual user interface builder.

Linux and Java are a great combination, as well. There are several high-quality Java implementations for Linux that are freely available, including some open source implementations. Table 11.1 lists these Java implementations.

In this chapter, we'll look at the building blocks of Java database programming, and show you how to put them together to build your own systems. This chapter expects some familiarity with programming in Java, as well as an understanding of how Java locates classes and uses jar files (archives of Java classes).

JDBC

JDBC is a database access API for Java. You can use it to open a connection to a database server. Then, you can use the connection to send SQL to the database server and retrieve the results of any SQL statements that you execute.

Figure 11.1 shows a high-level view of the major JDBC components (this figure was inspired by the interactive diagram on the About tab of the unixODBC utility ODBCConfig). Let's look at each of these components before we get any closer to JDBC.

Table 11.1 Java Implementations Available on Linux

DISTRIBUTION	ARCHITECTURES	LICENSE	COMPATIBILITY	HOMEPAGE
Kaffe	M68K, Alpha, PowerPC, SPARC, Intel, MIPS, ARM	Open Source	PersonalJava 1.1, some JDK 1.2	www.kaffe.org
Blackdown Java 2 (Based on Sun's original non-Linux Java source)	SPARC, Intel	Sun License	JDK 1.2	www.blackdown.org
Blackdown Java 1.1 (Based on Sun's original non-Linux Java source)	SPARC, Intel, PowerPC, ARM, Alpha	Sun License	JDK 1.1	www.blackdown.org
IBM Java for Linux	Intel	Sun License	JDK 1.1	www.ibm.com/developer/linux
Japhar	Intel	Open Source	JDK 1.1, some JDK 1.2	www.japhar.org
Sun Microsystems (based on Blackdown Java)	Intel	Sun License	JDK 1.2	http://java.sun.com/

Application. The Application is a program written in Java that needs to connect to the database. It is armed only with a JDBC URL, such as jdbc:postgresql:accounting_db. The Application relies on the Driver Manager to connect it to the database.

Driver Manager. The Driver Manager is responsible for managing a registry of JDBC drivers and helping the Application connect to a driver.

JDBC Driver. A JDBC Driver is a collection of classes that implement the JDBC API and have the capability to communicate with a database system. When the Driver Manager connects an Application to a Driver, it asks the Driver to create an instance of a java.sql.Connection subclass. The Application uses this object to get the full JDBC API, without needing to know the real identity of this object. Here is polymorphism in action: The Application thinks it is talking to an instance of java.sql.Connection, when in reality it is talking to something like postgresql.Connection (the connection object from the PostgreSQL driver) or org.gjt.mm.mysql.Connection (the connection object from the MySQL driver).

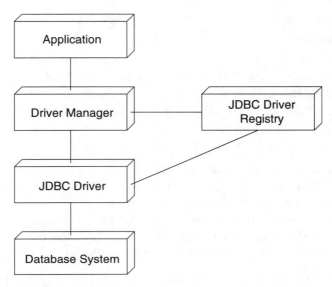

Figure 11.1 Components that make up the JDBC world.

JDBC Driver Registry. This registry is a collection that holds all the JDBC drivers that are available. When the Application gives the Driver Manager a JDBC URL, the Driver Manager looks in the registry to find a driver that is capable of interpreting the URL. The registry is most commonly a list of drivers that is specified in the program, or listed in the command line when you start the program (see *Running the Example Programs*, later in this chapter).

Database System. This is a database server, such as PostgreSQL, Sybase, Oracle, Mini SQL, or MySQL.

To write Java database applications, you need to have the following ingredients:

- A database server (see Chapter 9, "Databases," for an overview of some servers)
- A Java Development Kit
- A JDBC Driver for the database

Installing JDBC Drivers

JDBC is a standard part of the Java Development Kit (JDK), but it only includes one driver, the JDBC-ODBC bridge. You can use the JDBC-ODBC bridge to connect to any ODBC data source as though it were a JDBC data source. In general, it is better to find a driver that is specific to the database you want to connect to.

For example, if you use the JDBC-ODBC bridge to connect to MySQL, then your programs need to load the JDBC-ODBC driver, which is written partially in C. Then, the JDBC-ODBC driver connects to the ODBC Driver Manager, which uses the MySQL ODBC driver to connect to the database. Note that this is just an example; if you wanted to connect to MySQL from Java, you'd most likely use one of the type 4 JDBC drivers available for MySQL.

Not only do you avoid an extra level of indirection by using a JDBC driver, but you can often find a JDBC driver that is written in 100-percent Java (these are called type 3 and type 4 drivers, discussed later in this section). If you use a pure Java JDBC driver, it is more likely that your applications will benefit from Java's cross-platform capabilities. Using a driver that is a mix of Java and native code, such as the JDBC-ODBC bridge, presents a significant barrier to portability.

Sun Microsystems maintains a list of JDBC drivers with links to Web sites where you can download (or purchase) the drivers. This list is available at http://java.sun.com/products/jdbc/drivers.html.

JDBC drivers are divided into four categories:

Type 1: A JDBC-ODBC bridge. This type of JDBC driver, such as the one that ships with the JDK, uses a locally installed ODBC Driver Manager to connect to databases. If you use this driver, you will also need to configure your ODBC driver manager, as described in Chapter 10, "Linux Development Tools Catalog." You may need to do some additional configuration to your Java installation to make it aware of the ODBC driver manager.

Type 2: Hybrid Driver. This is a driver that is written partially in Java and partially in C. These drivers generally use a database-specific client API to connect to the database.

Type 3: 100-percent Java using a Network Protocol. This is a JDBC driver that is written in 100-percent Java. However, it does not connect directly to the database server. Instead, it connects to a middleware server that acts as a broker between the type 3 driver and the database.

Type 4: 100-percent Java with Native Protocol. This type of driver is written in 100-percent Java, and uses the database server's network protocol to connect directly to the database server. This is usually a Java implementation of the client API. It eliminates the need to link against the C API.

Table 11.2 lists information about JDBC drivers for several databases, including where you can locate the JDBC drivers, and the name of the jar file you will need to install. Note that as version numbers change, so may the names of these files, so please consult the Web site listed (or the Java JDBC driver list) for the latest information.

Table 11.2 Some JDBC Drivers

DATABASE	JAR FILE NAMES	DOWNLOAD DRIVER
PostgreSQL	Postgresql.jar jdbc6.5-1.2.jar (RedHat 6.1 package)	www.postgresql.org: see the src/interfaces/jdbc/ subdirectory of the PostgreSQL distribution. It also comes with RedHat 6.1 as the package postgresql-jdbc.
MySQL	Mysql_comp.jar mysql_uncomp.jar	www.worldserver.com/mm.mysql/ www.mysql.com/Contrib/
Mini SQL	Msql-jdbc-1-1b1.jar (JDK 1.1) msql-jdbc-2-0b5.jar (JDK 1.2)	www.imaginary.com/Java/Soul/
Oracle	(distributed as .class files)	technet.oracle.com
Sybase	Jconn2.jar	www.sybase.com/java
FreeTDS (Sybase and MS SQL Server)	Freetds_jdbc.jar	www.freetds.org

Most JDBC drivers are packaged in jar (the Java archiving utility) files. Jar files are very simple to install, and the installation method depends on which version of the JDK you use. However, you should consult the information that accompanies the JDBC driver for details on additional steps that may be necessary. For more details on how to properly set your CLASSPATH, check the documentation that came with the version of the JDK you are using.

Installing a JDBC Driver Under JDK 1.1.x

Under JDK versions 1.1.x, the installation generally involves:

1. Copying the jar file to a shared location, such as /usr/local/classes.
2. Adding the location of the jar file to your CLASSPATH environment variable.

For example, the PostgreSQL JDBC driver that ships with RedHat 6.1 is called jdbc6.5-1.2.jar, and is located in the directory /usr/lib/pgsql/. To add this jar file to your CLASSPATH, you could put one of the following statements in your startup scripts (such as .cshrc or .bash_profile).

Under the bash shell:

```
export CLASSPATH=$CLASSPATH:/usr/lib/pgsql/jdbc6.5-1.2.jar
```

Under the csh shell:

```
if ($?CLASSPATH) then
    setenv CLASSPATH \
        "${CLASSPATH}:/usr/lib/pgsql/jdbc6.5-1.2.jar"
else
    setenv CLASSPATH "/usr/lib/pgsql/jdbc6.5-1.2.jar"
endif
```

Installing a JDBC Driver under JDK 1.2.x

Under JDK 1.2, you can simply copy the jar file to the /jre/lib/ext/ sub-directory of your JDK installation, such as /usr/local/jdk1.2/jre/lib/ext/. For example, under RedHat 6.1, you can simply copy the jar file from the postgresql-jdbc package:

```
[root@oscar /root]# rpm -ql postgresql-jdbc    # where's that driver?
/usr/lib/pgsql/jdbc6.5-1.1.jar
/usr/lib/pgsql/jdbc6.5-1.2.jar  # Copy this one, since it's newerf
[root@oscar /root]# cp /usr/lib/pgsql/jdbc6.5-1.2.jar \
                    /opt/jdk1.2.2/jre/lib/ext/
```

Running the Example Programs

If you would like to run some example programs as you read through the *Using JDBC* section of this chapter, here are example programs (which are available from the companion Web site at www.wiley.com/compbooks/jepson) that accompany each subsection:

ConnectDemo.java. Makes a connection to the database, and does nothing else. Since this demo doesn't do much, it also prints out a String representation of the Connection class that it creates (see the JDK documentation for java.lang.Object.toString()). Related subsection: *Open a Connection*.

SendSQLDemo.java. Sends some SQL to the database that creates a table and puts data in it (it first drops the table if it exists). Related subsection: *Send SQL to the Server*.

ResultSetDemo.java. Fetches the data inserted in the previous program. Related subsection: *Process Result Sets*.

The example programs in the *Swing* section have their own instructions.

These programs are similar to the ones shown in the text, but have some additional processing and error-checking to support the command-line arguments. To run any of these programs, invoke them with the command:

```
java -Djdbc.drivers=DRIVERCLASS PROGRAM URL USER PASS
```

where:

PROGRAM. The name of the Java program, *without* the .java suffix.

DRIVERCLASS. The JDBC driver class name of the JDBC Driver you want to use (refer to Table 11.3).

URL. The JDBC URL for the database server (refer to Table 11.4).

USER. The user name.

PASS. The password.

For example, this should work with most out-of-the-box postgreSQL installations, provided that you run it on the same machine that the PostgreSQL server is running on:

```
java -Djdbc.drivers=postgresql.Driver ConnectDemo  \
    jdbc:postgresql:postgres postgres ''
```

(Note: The last two characters are two single quotes, not one double quote.)

If you have trouble connecting:

- Recompile the class file using either javac or jikes. This may reveal configuration errors you are not aware of, such as necessary classes that are not installed on your system.

- Make sure you can connect to the database server from another program (see *SQL Monitors* in Chapter 9).

- Verify that you are using the correct JDBC driver class and JDBC URL.

- Consult technical support resources for the JDBC driver or database server you are using. The best place to start is the home page listed in Table 11.2.

Using JDBC

When you write a program using JDBC, you will generally do the following:

1. Open a connection to the database server.
2. Send SQL commands to the server.
3. Process any result set generated in response to the SQL command.

Let's look at each one of these steps in more detail. The most complicated and error-prone step in this process is establishing the connection, partly because

JDBC drivers are very sensitive to the syntax of the connection string you use. Other problems, such as the inability to connect to the database at all, may arise because of database configuration issues. Some databases, such as Mini SQL, must be configured to accept remote connections (see Chapter 9 for a discussion of configuration issues for various database servers).

Open a Connection

In order to make a connection to the database, your program must:

- Import the JDBC classes.
- Register at least one JDBC Driver with the Driver Manager.
- Invoke the Driver Manager's getConnection() method with a JDBC URL, user name, and password.

Import the JDBC Classes

To import the JDBC classes, include the following line in your program:

```
import java.sql.*;
```

Register a Driver

Next, register all the drivers you plan to use in your application. You can either register it on the command line, or hard-code the driver name in your program. If you hard-code the driver name in your program, you will need to modify the source code and recompile it to use a different driver.

To register a driver on the command line, use the -Djdbc.drivers switch to specify the class name of the driver. This must appear before the program name. For example, if your program is called Sample.java, and you want to use the PostgreSQL driver, you can run it with this command:

```
java -Djdbc.drivers=postgresql.Driver Sample
```

See the section titled *Running the Example Programs* for an example of this usage. For a list of all driver class names, see Table 11.3. Keep in mind that as new versions and variants of drivers are released, these names may change. Consult your JDBC driver's documentation or home page (see Table 11.2) for the latest details.

To hard-code a driver name in your program, you should use Class.for-Name("DRIVER_NAME") to register the driver. The following code shows an example of this with the PostgreSQL JDBC driver. Because this statement can throw an exceptions, it is caught in the code:

```
try {
    Class.forName("postgresql.Driver");
} catch (ClassNotFoundException e) {
    System.err.println( e.getMessage() );
    System.exit(-1);
}
```

Using Class.forName() in this manner runs the static initialization code in the driver class, which registers the driver with the driver manager. Table 11.3 shows the class names for various JDBC drivers.

NOTE

If you use Class.forName(DRIVERNAME) and your programs get the error message "No suitable driver," try tacking on newInstance(), as in:

```
Class.forName("postgresql.Driver").newInstance();
```

Invoke getConnection()

Now that the driver is registered with the driver manager, you must make a connection to the driver. To do this, you must ask the DriverManager class to create a connection object. There are three variables that you must supply to make the connection:

JDBC URL. This is a connection string that identifies the type of database server you want to connect to, and specifies various options that the driver supports.

User Name. This is the user name to use when connecting to the database.

Password. This is the password for the user.

Table 11.3   JDBC Driver Classes

DATABASE	DRIVER CLASS
PostgreSQL	postgresql.Driver
MySQL	org.gjt.mm.mysql.Driver
Mini SQL	com.imaginary.sql.msql.MsqlDriver
Oracle	oracle.jdbc.driver.OracleDriver
Sybase	com.sybase.jdbc2.jdbc.SybDriver
JDBC-ODBC Bridge	sun.jdbc.odbc.JdbcOdbcDriver

Table 11.4   Some JDBC URLs

DATABASE	JDBC URLS
PostgreSQL	jdbc:postgresql:DATABASE jdbc:postgresql://HOST/DATABASE jdbc:postgresql://HOST:PORT/DATABASE
MySQL	jdbc:mysql:///DATABASE jdbc:mysql://HOST/DATABASE jdbc:mysql://HOST:PORT/DATABASE
Mini SQL	jdbc:msql://HOST/DATABASE jdbc:msql://HOST:PORT/DATABASE
Oracle	jdbc:oracle:thin:SID jdbc:oracle:thin:@HOST:PORT:SID
Sybase	jdbc:sybase:Tds:HOST:PORT jdbc:sybase:Tds:HOST:PORT/DATABASE (you can find the host name and port number in ~sybase/interfaces)
JDBC-ODBC Bridge	jdbc:odbc:DSN

Table 11.4 shows the basic JDBC URLs for various drivers, where:

HOST is the name of the host on which the database server resides. If host is not given, most JDBC drivers assume *localhost.*

DATABASE is the name of the database (not the database server) you want to use when you are connected. For an explanation of the difference between a database and database server, see the section titled *What Is the Difference between a Database and Database Server?* in Chapter 9.

SID is the Oracle system identifier that can be found in /etc/oratab. This is only applicable to Oracle database servers.

PORT is the TCP/IP port to connect to. The JDBC driver usually assumes that the database server was installed with the default port, so unless it was not, you should not need to use the PORT.

DSN is the ODBC data source name. You must configure this using the ODBC driver manager as discussed in Chapter 10.

The getConnection() method can throw an SQLException, so you must use a try...catch construct to handle this exception.

Let's consider an example where we want to connect to a database named postgres on a PostgreSQL server. In the example, we'll connect as a user named postgres, with a blank password. Although it is not required, we have included the host name and port number in the following example.

To make this connection, use the URL, userid, and password as arguments to getConnection(), as shown in this example:

```
String url = "jdbc:postgresql://localhost:5432/postgres";
String user = "postgres";
String pass = "";
try {
    Connection conn =
        DriverManager.getConnection(url, user, pass);

} catch (SQLException e) {

    System.err.println( e.getMessage() );
    System.exit(-1);
}
```

Summary of Steps

Here is an example that performs all the steps we just described:

```
// Step 1. Import the JDBC classes.
//
import java.sql.*;

public class ConnectSteps {

  public static void main(String[] argv) {

      // Step 2. Register the driver. If you use
      // -Djdbc.drivers on the command line, this
      // block of code is not needed.
      //
      try {
          Class.forName("postgresql.Driver");
      } catch (Exception e) {
          System.err.println( e.getMessage() );
          System.exit(-1);
      }

      // Step 3. Invoke getConnection() to create the
      // connection object.
      //
      String url = "jdbc:postgresql://localhost/postgres";
      String user = "postgres";
      String pass = "";

      Connection conn;
      try {
          conn =
              DriverManager.getConnection(url, user, pass);
```

```
        } catch (SQLException e) {
            System.err.println( e.getMessage() );
            System.exit(-1);
        }

    }

}
```

Example Connections

Let's look at a few sample connections. In these examples, we'll only show the URL, user name, and password. You should assume that these are used as shown in the previous example.

MySQL with Local Server. Here, the user name is sales, password 7strat001, and the database name is instruments. The database resides on a MySQL server on the localhost. The three slashes are required, because the HOST-NAME is blank:

```
url = "jdbc:mysql:///instruments";
user = "sales";
pass = "7strat001";
```

MySQL with Remote Server. In this example, the user name is controller, password homer, and the database name is ATIS. The database resides on a MySQL server running on the host frobozz:

```
String url = "jdbc:mysql://frobozz/ATIS";
String user = "controller";
String pass = "homer";
```

Mini SQL with Local Server. In this example, the user name is bjepson, and the database is dungeon_data residing on the local server:

```
url = "jdbc:msql://localhost/dungeon_data";
user = "bjepson";
pass = "";
```

Mini SQL with Remote Server. Here, we connect to the gallery database on the server datacenter.as220.org, using the user name bjepson:

```
url = "jdbc:msql://datacenter.as220.org/gallery";
user = "bjepson";
pass = "";
```

PostgreSQL with Local Server. This example connects to the inventory database on the local PostgreSQL server as the user named manager. There is no password:

```
url = "jdbc:postgresql:inventory";
```

```
user = "manager";
pass = "";
```

PostgreSQL with Remote Server. In this example, we are connecting to the library database on the PostgreSQL server running on a host named frobozz. The user name is librarian, with no password:

```
url = "jdbc:postgresql://frobozz/library";
user = "librarian";
pass = "";
```

Oracle with Local Server. This example connects to the local Oracle server (referenced by the orcl SID) as the user scott, password tiger:

```
url = "jdbc:oracle:thin:orcl";
user = "scott";
pass = "tiger";
```

Sybase. Unlike other Sybase tools and utilities, the Sybase JDBC driver does not use the ~sybase/interfaces file to look up server names. As a result, you must specify the host name and port of the Sybase server. You may have trouble using localhost, even when you are trying to connect from the same machine that's running the Sybase server.

Your best bet is to look at the ~sybase/interfaces file yourself; if you can connect to one of these entries using isql, you should be able to use the host name and port number you find in the interfaces file. Here is an example that connects to the bjepson_db on the Sybase server running on the host oscorb (port 4100). The user name is bjepson, and the password is open_sesame:

```
url = "jdbc:sybase:Tds:oscorb:4100/bjepson_db";
user = "bjepson";
pass = "open_sesame";
```

Common Connection Problems

If you have trouble connecting, look into the following:

Bogus connection string. Check your JDBC URL carefully. Are there spaces, trailing characters, or delimiters where they don't need to be? Pay special attention to Table 11.4, and consult the documentation that came with the driver.

Local versus remote access. If you are trying to connect to a remote server, does that server allow remote connections? Some servers are configured to only allow local connections by default. You may either need to configure the server to allow remote connections or specifically grant access to a user at a particular remote host. Consult Chapter 9 as well as the database server documentation for details.

Send SQL to the Server

After you've made the connection to the database server, you can send SQL statements to it. To send SQL to the server:

Create a Statement object. To create a Statement object, use the Connection's createStatement() method. If something goes wrong, this will throw a SQLException, so you need to catch it, just in case:

```
Statement stmt = null;
try {
    stmt = conn.createStatement();
} catch (SQLException e) {
    System.err.println( e.getMessage() );
    System.exit(-1);
}
```

Invoke executeUpdate(). Invoke the Statement object's executeUpdate() method (this also can throw an SQLException):

```
try {
    String sql = "INSERT INTO statement_demo    " +
                    "(name, id) VALUES('test', 100)";
    stmt.executeUpdate(sql);
} catch (SQLException e) {
    System.err.println( e.getMessage() );
    System.exit(-1);
}
```

If you want to send an SQL SELECT statement, or some other SQL statement that returns results, see the upcoming section, *Process Result Sets*.

Close the statement and connection. When you are done with the statement and the connection, you should close them:

```
stmt.close();
conn.close();
```

Prepared Statements

If you plan to use the same (or similar) SQL statement many times, you can use a prepared statement. Some database servers can compile or cache the query on the server, which may speed things up a bit.

You can also use a prepared statement to create placeholders in an SQL statement. For example, if you wanted to insert three rows into the contact table, you could create a prepared INSERT statement with placeholders (question marks) for the values:

```
String insert = "INSERT INTO userinfo  " +
                "   (username, userid)" +
                " VALUES(?, ?)";
PreparedStatement pstmt =
    conn.prepareStatement(insert);
```

Then, you can use the PreparedStatement's setXXX() methods (such as set-String() and setInt()) to set the value for each parameter, and then execute the statement:

```
pstmt.setString(1, "scrotus");
pstmt.setInt(2, 702);
pstmt.executeUpdate();
```

Sending SQL Example

Let's look at a complete example that creates a table and inserts some data (to keep things brief, we've put a lot of the code in the same try...catch block):

```java
import java.sql.*;

public class SendStatement {

  public static void main(String[] argv) {

      try {
          Class.forName("postgresql.Driver");
      } catch (Exception e) {
          System.err.println( e.getMessage() );
          System.exit(-1);
      }

      String url = "jdbc:postgresql://localhost/postgres";
      String user = "postgres";
      String pass = "";
      try {

          // Open the connection.
          //
          Connection conn =
            DriverManager.getConnection(url, user, pass);

          // Create a statement object.
          //
          Statement stmt = conn.createStatement();

          // Use the statement to create a table and add
          // some rows.
          //
```

```
String sql;
sql = "CREATE TABLE userinfo " +
        "(username CHAR(10), userid INT)";
stmt.executeUpdate(sql);

// Create a prepared statement.
//
String insert = "INSERT INTO userinfo  " +
                    "    (username, userid)" +
                    " VALUES(?, ?)";
PreparedStatement pstmt =
    conn.prepareStatement(insert);

// Insert bjepson
pstmt.setString(1, "bjepson");
pstmt.setInt(2, 700);
pstmt.executeUpdate();

// Insert oscorb
pstmt.setString(1, "oscorb");
pstmt.setInt(2, 701);
pstmt.executeUpdate();

// Insert scrotus
pstmt.setString(1, "scrotus");
pstmt.setInt(2, 702);
pstmt.executeUpdate();

System.out.println(
    "The database has been updated.");

// Close the statement and the connection.
//
stmt.close();
conn.close();

} catch (SQLException e) {
    System.err.println( e.getMessage() );
    System.exit(-1);
}

    }

    }
```

Process Result Sets

Some SQL statements, such as the SELECT statement, produce a result set that is a collection of rows and columns. Others, such as INSERT and

UPDATE, don't produce a result set. For many applications, the result set is the heart of the matter. For example, you might use a result set to:

- Format values for printing in a report
- Summarize values and display them on a screen
- Use the values in a pop-up menu that the users make a choice from
- Put the values in a data structure that will be used elsewhere in your application

If the SQL command you send to the server produces results, you'll need to do the following (after you have created a Statement object as discussed in the previous section):

Invoke executeQuery() and store the ResultSet. The executeQuery() method returns a java.sql.ResultSet, which you should store so you can reference it in the next step:

```
String sql = "SELECT * FROM userinfo";
ResultSet rs = stmt.executeQuery(sql);
```

Loop through the ResultSet. To loop through the result set, you should repeatedly call its next() method until it returns false.

Get the values. While you are in the loop, you can grab column values with the various getXXX() functions. The getXXX() methods, such as getString() and getInt() will do their best to interpret the column value as the value that corresponds to the method name. Here is an example that grabs the *uname* column as a String and the *uid* column as an integer:

```
String uname = rs.getString("username");
int uid = rs.getInt("userid");
```

Processing Result Sets Example

Here is a complete example that queries the *userinfo* table that we created in the previous section:

```
import java.sql.*;

public class ProcessResult {

  public static void main(String[] argv) {

      try {
          Class.forName("postgresql.Driver");
      } catch (Exception e) {
```

```java
            System.err.println( e.getMessage() );
            System.exit(-1);
    }

    String url = "jdbc:postgresql://localhost/postgres";
    String user = "postgres";
    String pass = "";
    try {

        // Open the connection.
        //
        Connection conn =
          DriverManager.getConnection(url, user, pass);

        // Create a statement object.
        //
        Statement stmt = conn.createStatement();

        // Ask for all the rows in the userinfo table.
        //
        String sql = "SELECT * FROM userinfo";
        ResultSet rs = stmt.executeQuery(sql);

        // Loop through the result set
        //
        while ( rs.next() ) {

            // Get the column values from the current row.
            //
            String uname = rs.getString("username");
            int uid = rs.getInt("userid");

            System.out.print("Name: " + uname);
            System.out.println("ID: " + uid);

        }

        // Close the statement and the connection.
        //
        stmt.close();
        conn.close();

    } catch (SQLException e) {
        System.err.println( e.getMessage() );
        System.exit(-1);
    }

    }

    }
```

Swing

Swing is a set of components that are part of the Java Foundation Classes (JFC). You can use Swing to build graphical user interfaces from the ground up. With Swing, you build a hierarchical system of components. For example, a window may contain one or more panels, which in turn contains buttons and text fields. Swing includes many components, and many combinations are possible. Figure 11.2 shows an exploded view of one such possibility.

A Frame, a Field, and a Button

Let's take a look at a very simple Swing application. This application has one Frame (a main Window), one text entry field, and one button. We'll look at the simplest case first (no event handling), and then add event handling to the example. At that stage, we will use event handling to respond to a button click and to requests to close the window.

To create this simple application, we need to perform the following steps, which are necessary for most simple Swing applications:

1. Import the Swing and AWT classes:

```
import javax.swing.*;
import java.awt.*;
import java.awt.event.*;
```

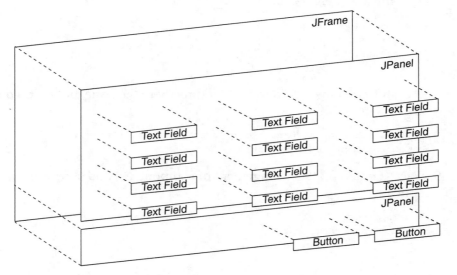

Figure 11.2 A component hierarchy.

2. Create a JFrame, which is your top-level window (the argument "Simple Swing Demo" is the title of the window):

```
JFrame demo_frame = new JFrame("Simple Swing Demo");
```

3. Instead of putting all the components directly into the JFrame, you must create a container (such as a JPanel) to hold the components you want to create:

```
JPanel contents = new JPanel();
```

4. Use a layout manager to control how the container is laid out. This 2x2 grid layout puts each successive element into the next grid cell, starting at the upper left cell:

```
contents.setLayout(new GridLayout(2, 2));
```

5. Create the components. Here, we create a label, a field, and a button:

```
JLabel label = new JLabel("Name:");
JTextField textfield = new JTextField(10);
JButton button = new JButton("OK");
```

6. Do everything you can to add accessibility support. In this example, we tell the label that it belongs to the text field. This could help users who are using a non-visual user interface, such as a voice-driven user interface:

```
label.setLabelFor(textfield);
```

7. Add the components to the container you created in step 3. Notice that we use a blank label to fill the lower-left grid cell, which forces the button into the lower-right cell:

```
contents.add(label);
contents.add(textfield);
contents.add(new JLabel(""));
contents.add(button);
```

8. Add the container. We don't add it directly to the pane, but to its content pane:

```
Container content_pane = demo_frame.getContentPane();
content_pane.add(contents);
```

9. Pack (tighten up the arrangement of components) and show (display) the frame:

```
demo_frame.pack();
demo_frame.show();
```

Event Handling

Although those nine steps are enough to put a simple user interface on screen, they are not enough to build something that is actually useful. If you wrote a program following only those steps, it would become annoying the second you clicked the Close button. The frame would disappear, but the program would not exit. This is because the system generates an event when the frame is closed. The JFrame gets the event and does the right thing, but it ends there.

It's up to you to decide what to do when the window is closed. This is a good thing, because you can check to see if your program is ready to exit well before you let the window close.

Java handles events, such as button clicks, using something similar to the Observer pattern. In this pattern, the *subject* of the event is a Swing component, such as a JButton or a JFrame. The *observers* are classes, such as WindowAdapter, that you register with the subject. When certain events occur (such as when a window is closed), the subject sends a message to all registered observers. Figure 11.3 shows some of the methods of the JFrame and WindowAdapter objects. When you write your own custom event handlers, you create a subclass as WindowAdapter that overrides some or all of its methods. One such subclass is shown in Figure 11.3 as MyWindowAdapter.

To add a window listener to a Frame, follow these steps (these are also shown as a collaboration diagram in Figure 11.4):

1. Create a JFrame object.
2. Define a subclass of WindowAdapter, and override any methods you need to, such as windowClosing(), then create an instance of that class.
3. Register that class with the JFrame using addWindowListener().

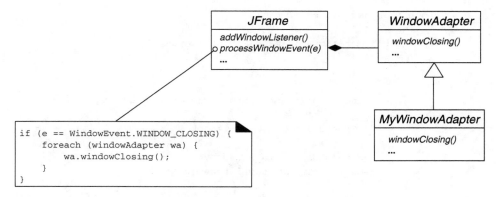

Figure 11.3 Observer pattern in Swing.

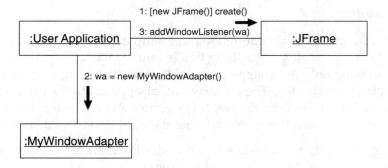

Figure 11.4 Adding a window listener.

When the user closes the window, the JFrame invokes the windowClosing() event of all the classes you registered through addWindowListener(), as shown in the collaboration diagram in Figure 11.5. Here is how you could implement these concepts in Java:

```java
import javax.swing.*;
import java.awt.*;
import java.awt.event.*;

// Define a class to handle the windowClosing event.
//
class MyWindowAdapter extends WindowAdapter {

    public void windowClosing(WindowEvent e) {
        System.out.println("Exiting...");
        System.exit(0);
    }

}

public class ListenerDemo {

    public static void main(String[] argv) {

        // Create a JFrame.
        //
        JFrame demo_frame = new JFrame("Simple Swing Demo");

        // Create a new MyWindowAdapter.
        //
        MyWindowAdapter wa = new MyWindowAdapter();
        demo_frame.addWindowListener(wa);

        // Size and show the frame.
```

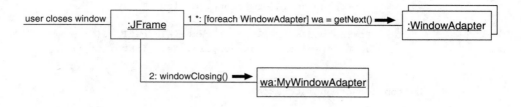

Figure 11.5   Closing a window.

```
        //
        demo_frame.setSize(200, 200);
        demo_frame.show();
    }

}
```

In this chapter's examples, you won't need to deal with the WindowEvent
parameter that's passed to windowClosing(). However, you must include it
in the declaration of your method, or it won't get invoked at all.

Event handling for a Window. As we saw earlier, you can use a WindowAdapter to customize how your application should behave when the
JFrame is closed. You can subclass WindowAdapter on the fly, by creating
an anonymous subclass.

An anonymous subclass declaration is a standard constructor, such as new
WindowAdapter(), followed by a block containing the definition of any
methods you want to override. That block must be terminated with a semicolon, as shown in the following code. Because the anonymous subclass is
defined within another class, it is referred to as an inner class:

```
WindowAdapter wa = new WindowAdapter() {
    public void windowClosing(WindowEvent e) {
        System.out.println("Exiting...");
        System.exit(0);
    }
};
demo_frame.addWindowListener(wa);
```

Event handling for the Button. The event handling for components follows
the same pattern: Create an instance of the observer class, and register it
with the component. When someone clicks OK, this example pops up a
dialog with a personalized message:

```
ActionListener al = new ActionListener() {
    public void actionPerformed(ActionEvent e) {
```

```
                    // Pop up an informational dialog.
                    //
                    String msg = "Hello, " + textfield.getText();
                    JOptionPane.showMessageDialog(demo_frame, msg);
                }
            };
            button.addActionListener(al);
```

Inner Classes and Object References

In order to pop up the dialog box shown in the previous listing, we need to refer to the JFrame as the dialog's parent, and refer to the text of the JTextField (so we can say "Hello, NAME"). Since this reference occurs within an inner class, the two objects (demo_frame and textfield) must be declared final:

```
final JFrame demo_frame = new JFrame("Simple Swing Demo");
final JTextField textfield = new JTextField(10);
```

When you use the final keyword, you are promising the compiler that you won't change the object that the identifier points to. This won't prevent you from invoking methods that change the data that belongs to that object, but it will prevent you from changing it to an entirely different object later, such as:

```
final JFrame demo_frame = new JFrame("Simple Swing Demo");
[... time passes ...]
demo_frame = new JFrame("Some Other Frame"); // bzzzt! No can do!
```

Putting It All Together

Here is an example that follows the steps outlined in A Frame, a Field, and a Button, but adds extra steps for the WindowAdapter and ActionListener:

```
// Step 1. Import the Swing and AWT classes.
//
import javax.swing.*;
import java.awt.*;
import java.awt.event.*;

public class SimpleSwingWithEvents {

    public static void main(String[] argv) {

        // Step 2. Create a JFrame.
        //
        final JFrame demo_frame =
            new JFrame("Simple Swing Demo");
```

```java
// Step 3. Create a Panel to hold the components.
//
JPanel contents = new JPanel();

// Step 4. Lay out components in the JPanel with
// two columns, two rows.
//
contents.setLayout(new GridLayout(2, 2));

// Step 5. Create a label, text field, and button.
//
JLabel label = new JLabel("Name:");
final JTextField textfield = new JTextField(10);
JButton button = new JButton("OK");

// Step 6. Associate the label with its corresponding
// component.
//
label.setLabelFor(textfield);

// Step 7. Add the components to the panel.
//
contents.add(label);
contents.add(textfield);
contents.add(new JLabel(""));
contents.add(button);

// Step 8. Add the container you created in step 3
// to the JFrame's content pane.
//
Container content_pane = demo_frame.getContentPane();
content_pane.add(contents);

// Step 9. Create a WindowAdapter to handle the
// windowClosing event, and add it to the Frame.
//
WindowAdapter wa = new WindowAdapter() {
    public void windowClosing(WindowEvent e) {
        System.out.println("Exiting...");
        System.exit(0);
    }
};
demo_frame.addWindowListener(wa);

// Step 10. Create an actionListener to handle
// the button press.
//
ActionListener al = new ActionListener() {
    public void actionPerformed(ActionEvent e) {

        // Pop up an informational dialog.
        //
```

```
                          String msg = "Hello, " + textfield.getText();
                          JOptionPane.showMessageDialog(demo_frame, msg);
                  }
            };
            button.addActionListener(al);

            // Final Step. Pack and show the frame.
            //
            demo_frame.pack();
            demo_frame.show();
      }


    }
```

To run this example, you must first compile the source with the command *javac SimpleSwingWithEvents.java.* Then, you can run the command *java SimpleSwingWithEvents.* The main window appears—type your name and click OK. The results are shown in Figure 11.6.

Layout Managers

Layout managers are possibly the most confusing aspect of using Swing. What's worse, you'll encounter layout managers in other places, such as the Abstract Window Toolkit (AWT), the basic graphics toolkit on which some of Swing is based. We'll do our best to make this aspect of Java easy to understand.

A layout manager simply controls the way components are added to a frame. Without a layout manager, a frame could only hold one component. There are many layout managers that Swing supports, and each one varies in complexity and flexibility.

Figure 11.6   The Swing application says hello.

To use a layout manager, you must create an instance of it (for example, with *LayoutManager lm = new FlowLayout()*). Then, you must set a container's layout to this object (for example, *myframe.setLayout(lm)*).

One of the simplest layout managers is the FlowLayout, which is part of the java.awt.* package. The FlowLayout arranges components from left to right as they are added. Here is a short example:

```java
import java.awt.*;
import javax.swing.*;

public class FlowLayoutDemo {

    public static void main(String[] argv) {

        JFrame myframe = new JFrame("Flow Layout Demo");
        Container contents = myframe.getContentPane();

        contents.setLayout( new FlowLayout() );

        contents.add( new JButton("Left")   );
        contents.add( new JButton("Center") );
        contents.add( new JButton("Right")  );

        myframe.pack();
        myframe.show();

    }

}
```

To run this example, you must first compile the source with the command *javac FlowLayoutDemo.java*. Then, you can run the command *java FlowLayoutDemo*. The main window appears, as shown in Figure 11.7.

The BoxLayout, which is part of the javax.swing.* package, strikes a balance of flexibility and ease of use. It arranges components from left to right or from top to bottom. You can use a combination of BoxLayouts to create visually pleasing user interfaces. Here are some ways to work with BoxLayout:

Create the layout. The first argument to the BoxLayout constructor is the container you want to lay out, and the second is whether to lay out components

Figure 11.7 A FlowLayout arrangement.

from left to right (BoxLayout.Y_AXIS) or from top to bottom (BoxLayout.X _AXIS). After you create the BoxLayout, use the container's setLayout method to apply it. Here's a JPanel with components laid out from left to right:

```
JPanel demo1 = new JPanel();
LayoutManager left2right_1 =
    new BoxLayout(demo1, BoxLayout.X_AXIS);
demo1.setLayout(left2right_1);
```

Set borders. A little white space can make your screens more readable. Import the javax.swing.border.* package, and use the BorderFactory's createEmptyBorder(top, left, bottom, right) to create a Border object. Then, set the border of your container:

```
Border border =
        BorderFactory.createEmptyBorder(5, 10, 5, 10);
demo1.setBorder(border);
```

Add components. When you add components to a container that is managed by a box layout, the components are laid out according to whether you specified X_AXIS or Y_AXIS (see the previous code). If you want some horizontal or vertical spacing between components, add a strut with Box.createHorizontalStrut() or Box.createVerticalStrut(). Specify the pixel width of the strut as shown here (5-pixel strut):

```
demo1.add(but2);
demo1.add(Box.createHorizontalStrut(5));
demo1.add(but3);
```

If you add components of different sizes, you might be able to achieve balance by setting each component's Y alignment or X alignment. Here are two components that are centered along a horizontal line:

```
JLabel  lab1 = new JLabel("Type Something:");
lab1.setAlignmentY(Component.CENTER_ALIGNMENT);

JTextField text1 = new JTextField(20);
text1.setAlignmentY(Component.CENTER_ALIGNMENT);
```

If you want to force components to the left or right side of a container, you can add glue on either side of them (you can also add glue between components). Here is an example where we use glue to shove two buttons to the right side of the container:

```
demo2.add(Box.createHorizontalGlue());
demo2.add(but2);
demo2.add(but3);
```

Here is an example that demonstrates these techniques (note that this example doesn't have any special event handling for buttons):

```java
import java.awt.*;
import java.awt.event.*;
import javax.swing.*;
import javax.swing.border.*;

public class BoxDemo {

    public static void main(String[] argv) {

        JFrame myframe = new JFrame("Box Layout Demo");

        // Get the content pane.
        //
        Container contents = myframe.getContentPane();

        // Create a top-level panel to hold the other
        // two panels.
        //
        JPanel top = new JPanel();
        LayoutManager top2bottom =
            new BoxLayout(top, BoxLayout.Y_AXIS);
        top.setLayout(top2bottom);

        // Create the first and second panels.
        // Components that are added are laid
        // out from left to right.
        //
        JPanel demo1 = new JPanel();
        LayoutManager left2right_1 =
            new BoxLayout(demo1, BoxLayout.X_AXIS);
        demo1.setLayout(left2right_1);

        JPanel demo2 = new JPanel();
        LayoutManager left2right_2 =
            new BoxLayout(demo2, BoxLayout.X_AXIS);
        demo2.setLayout(left2right_2);

        // Give both of the panels a nice border.
        //
        Border border =
            BorderFactory.createEmptyBorder(5, 10, 5, 10);
        demo1.setBorder(border);
        demo2.setBorder(border);

        // Add the panels to the top-level panel,
        // and add the top-level panel to the
        // contents pane.
```

```
        //
        top.add(demo1);
        top.add(demo2);
        contents.add(top);

        // Create three controls and center them
        // horizontally. This is useful when you
        // are mixing different-sized controls on
        // the same line.
        JLabel  lab1 = new JLabel("Type Something:");
        lab1.setAlignmentY(Component.CENTER_ALIGNMENT);

        JTextField text1 = new JTextField(20);
        text1.setAlignmentY(Component.CENTER_ALIGNMENT);

        JButton but1 = new JButton("Test");
        but1.setAlignmentY(Component.CENTER_ALIGNMENT);

        // Add each control to the first panel, with
        // 5-pixel spacing between each.
        //
        demo1.add(lab1);
        demo1.add(Box.createHorizontalStrut(5));
        demo1.add(text1);
        demo1.add(Box.createHorizontalStrut(5));
        demo1.add(but1);

        // Create two buttons that are right justified.
        //
        JButton but2 = new JButton("OK");
        JButton but3 = new JButton("Cancel");

        // Use some horizontal glue to force the buttons
        // all the way to the right.
        //
        demo2.add(Box.createHorizontalGlue());

        // Add the buttons to the second panel with a
        // 5-pixel spacer between them.
        //
        demo2.add(but2);
        demo2.add(Box.createHorizontalStrut(5));
        demo2.add(but3);

        // Handle window closing events.
        //
        WindowAdapter wa = new WindowAdapter() {
            public void windowClosing(WindowEvent e) {
                System.exit(0);
            }
        };
```

```
            myframe.addWindowListener(wa);

            // Pack and show the frame.
            //
            myframe.pack();
            myframe.show();

    }

}
```

To run this example, you must first compile the source with the command *javac BoxDemo.java*. Then, you can run the command *java BoxDemo*. The main window appears, as shown in Figure 11.8.

Separating Content and Presentation

When you are working with data, it is helpful if you can separate the content from its presentation, because you end up with a more loosely coupled design.

In this section, we'll look at how you can put the results of an SQL query into the Swing JTable component, which is a sort of grid control.

JTable and TableModel

The JTable component can use the Observer pattern (see the section titled *Observer* in Chapter 8, "Object-Oriented Design") to keep the content and presentation separate. This lets us build reusable code without restricting the look and feel of the component. The presentation (look and feel) is taken care of by the JTable component, while the data is encapsulated in a TableModel object.

When you first set up the JTable, it consults the TableModel to find out the structure of the table, and the data that the table contains. If the model changes, it notifies the JTable, which in turn re-reads all the relevant information. Your table model must implement at least the following methods, which the JTable uses to get information:

getRowCount(). This method is used to discover how many rows are in the data set.

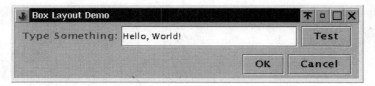

Figure 11.8 Using BoxLayout.

getColumnCount(). Returns the number of columns in the data set.

getValueAt(row_index, column_index). Fetches the value at the specified row and column.

getColumnName(column_index). Returns the name of the column at the given column index (optional).

There are more methods that the TableModel supports. See the JDK API documentation for more details. Here is a simple example table model. It has four rows and two columns:

```java
// SimpleModel.java - a Simple Table Model.
import javax.swing.table.*;

public class SimpleModel extends AbstractTableModel {

    // The names of the columns.
    String[] column_list = {"Name", "City"};

    // The data set.
    String[][] data = { {"Brian",  "Kingston"    },
                        {"Oscorb", "Providence" },
                        {"BB",     "Providence" },
                        {"Lotor",  "Kingston"    } };
    /**
     * Return the number of rows.
     */
    public int getRowCount() { return data.length; }

    /**
     * Return the number of columns.
     */
    public int getColumnCount() { return column_list.length; }

    /**
     * Return the value at the specified row and column.
     */
    public Object getValueAt(int row_index, int column_index) {
        return data[row_index][column_index];
    }

    /**
     * Return the name of the column at the specified column
     * index.
     */
    public String getColumnName(int column_index) {
        return column_list[column_index];
    }

}
```

On its own, this table model doesn't do anything. Now, we need to use this table model in a JTable. The basic steps are:

1. Create an instance of the table model:

```
SimpleModel myModel = new SimpleModel();
```

2. Create an instance of JTable. Pass the table model as the argument to JTable's constructor:

```
JTable table = new JTable(myModel);
```

3. Create a scrolling pane to hold the table. If the table gets too large, the scrollpane lets the user scroll up and down in the table. Instead of using the scrolling pane's add() method, as you do with other containers, pass the table to the scrolling pane's constructor:

```
JScrollPane scrollPane = new JScrollPane(table);
```

4. Create a top-level Frame, add the scrolling pane to it, and give it a handler for window events:

```
// Create a top-level window for everything, add the
// pane, and an event handler.
//
JFrame myframe = new JFrame("Simple Table Demo");
myframe.getContentPane().add(scrollPane);

WindowAdapter wa = new WindowAdapter() {
    public void windowClosing(WindowEvent e) {
        System.exit(0);
    }
};
myframe.addWindowListener(wa);
```

5. Finally, pack and show the frame:

```
myframe.pack();
myframe.show();
```

Here is a complete example that performs these steps. Compile this example with the command *javac TestSimpleModel.java*, and run it with the command *java TestSimpleModel*. The display is shown in Figure 11.9:

```
import java.awt.*;
import java.awt.event.*;
import javax.swing.*;
```

```java
public class TestSimpleModel {

    public static void main(String[] argv) {

        // Create an instance of our model.
        //
        SimpleModel myModel = new SimpleModel();

        // Create a JTable that uses the specified model.
        //
        JTable table = new JTable(myModel);

        // Create a scrolling pane to hold the table.
        //
        JScrollPane scrollPane = new JScrollPane(table);

        // Create a top-level window for everything, add the
        // pane, and an event handler.
        //
        JFrame myframe = new JFrame("Simple Table Demo");
        myframe.getContentPane().add(scrollPane);

        WindowAdapter wa = new WindowAdapter() {
            public void windowClosing(WindowEvent e) {
                System.exit(0);
            }
        };
        myframe.addWindowListener(wa);

        // Pack and show the frame.
        //
        myframe.pack();
        myframe.show();
    }

}
```

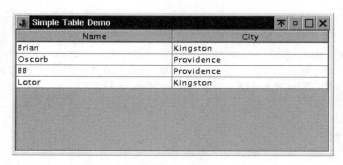

Figure 11.9 A simple table model.

A Table Model for JDBC

Now, let's build a table model that uses JDBC and SQL to get its data. In the interest of keeping things simple, this table model will operate in read-only mode. That is, you won't be able to edit any of the columns, so there is no way to propagate changes back to the database. However, the companion Web site at www.wiley.com/compbooks/jepson includes an example program, JDBCTableModel.java, that does provide read-write capabilities. In addition to the responsibilities of a table model outlined earlier, the JDBC table model will:

Open a connection to the database server. To facilitate this, we'll make the constructor for the class take a JDBC URL, a user name, and a password as arguments. In the constructor, we'll create a connection, and assign it to a field named Connection.

Issue a query and store the results. This is handled in the fetchData() method. The fetchData() method takes an SQL query as an argument, and uses the Connection created in the previous step to send the query to the server. To put this data into a form that can be easily used by the model, fetchData() performs the following steps:

1. *Issue the query and get the result set.* See the earlier section *Process Result Sets* for more details on how this works.

2. *Get a ResultSetMetaData object from the result set.* This object contains a lot of information about the result set, such as the names of all the columns.

3. *Store the column names.* Use the ResultSetMetaData object to put all the column names into a Vector called column_list. Before this, remove any elements in that vector that may be left over from a previous query.

4. *Store the result set's data.* Put the results into a data structure similar to the multidimensional array we saw in the SimpleModel example. You won't know the number of rows until ResultSet.next() returns false, so it's easiest to use the Vector object, which is a growable array that you can add elements to on the fly.

   A Vector can contain any type of object. To store a result set, use one Vector element for each row. To store all the column values for that row, you need to use another Vector for each element. For example, to fetch a value from the Vector named rows, you'd like to do something like:

   ```
   String val = rows[1][2]; // Get the 2nd column from row 1.
   ```

   Instead, you need to first get the Vector that corresponds to the row:

```
Vector row = (Vector) rows.elementAt(1); // get 1st row
```

and then fetch the column from that row:

```
String val = (String) row.elementAt(2); // get 2nd column
```

NOTE

The Vector object returns all elements as Objects. When you want to refer to one of those elements, you will usually need to cast it to another object, as in (String) row.elementAt(2).

5. *Send notifications.* After you perform these steps, you should call the fireTableStructureChanged() and fireTableDataChanged() notifications, which tell the JTable that the table model has changed.

Here is the source code for a table model, JDBCTableModelRO that follows the steps outlined in this section (RO stands for Read-Only):

```java
// JDBCTableModelRO.java - a read-only table model for JDBC
// data sources.
//
import java.sql.*;
import java.util.*;
import javax.swing.table.*;

public class JDBCTableModelRO extends AbstractTableModel {

    Vector column_list = new Vector(); // all column names
    Vector rows = new Vector();        // all the row contents
    Connection conn;                   // the JDBC connection

    /**
     * Create a new JDBC table model.
     */
    public JDBCTableModelRO(String url,
                        String user, String pwd) {

        try {

            // Make the connection to the data source.
            //
            conn =
                DriverManager.getConnection(url, user, pwd);
        } catch (SQLException e) {

            e.printStackTrace();
            System.out.println(e.getMessage());
            System.exit(-1);
        }
```

```
        }

/**
 * Issue the query and put the data into the model.
 */
public void fetchData(String query) {

    try {

        // See Chapter 11 for an explanation
        // of each step.

        // Step 1.
        Statement stmt = conn.createStatement();
        ResultSet rs = stmt.executeQuery(query);

        // Step 2.
        ResultSetMetaData rmd = rs.getMetaData();

        // Step 3.
        column_list.removeAllElements();
        for (int i = 1; i <= rmd.getColumnCount(); i++) {

            // Add the name of the column to the
            // vector of column names (column_list).
            //
            String name = rmd.getColumnName(i);
            column_list.addElement(name);

        }

        // Step 4.
        rows.removeAllElements();
        while (rs.next()) {

            // Create a Vector to hold all the data in
            // this row.
            //
            Vector row = new Vector();

            // Process each column.
            //
            for (int i=1; i <= column_list.size(); i++) {

                // Get the column's string value and
                // add it to the Vector for the current
                // row.
                //
                String value = rs.getString(i);
                row.addElement(value);
            }
```

```
                    // Add this row to the rows Vector.
                    //
                    rows.addElement(row);
            }

            // Step 5.
            fireTableStructureChanged();
            fireTableDataChanged();

            stmt.close(); // close the statement.

        } catch (SQLException e) {
            System.out.println(
                "SQL Error: " + e.getMessage());
        }
    }

    /**
     * Return the number of rows.
     */
    public int getRowCount() {
        return rows.size();
    }

    /**
     * Return the number of columns.
     */
    public int getColumnCount() {
        return column_list.size();
    }

    /**
     * Return the value at the specified row and column.
     */
    public Object getValueAt(int row_index,
                             int column_index) {

        // Get the Vector that corresponds to the row index.
        //
        Vector row = (Vector) rows.elementAt(row_index);

        // Return the column within row that corresponds
        // to the column index.
        //
        // There is no need to cast the element to a String or
        // any other object, because JTable wants to get it as
        // an Object.  Once JTable has this value, it will
        // either cast it to the appropriate type, or simply
        // call its toString() method.
        //
        return row.elementAt(column_index);
```

```
    }

    /**
     * Return the name of the column at the specified column
     * index.
     */
    public String getColumnName(int column_index) {
        return (String) column_list.elementAt(column_index);
    }

}
```

Using the JDBC Table Model

In the first JFrame example, we showed how you can put a table and some data in a window. In this example, we'll go a little bit further. Let's create an application that has a text input field where a user can type any SQL statement. Then, we'll add a button to submit that SQL and show the results in a grid.

To make this happen, we need to:

Register at least one JDBC driver. You can skip this step if you plan to include the -Djdbc.drivers argument on the command line (as described in the section *Running the Example Programs*). Otherwise, make sure your program loads a JDBC driver as described in the earlier section *Register a Driver*.

Create an instance of JDBCTableModelRO. Make sure you pass the JDBC URL, user name, and password as an argument. We'll also declare this *final*, so we can refer to it within the event handler for the button.

Create a JTable that uses the model. Create an instance of JTable, and pass in myModel as the argument to the constructor.

Create a top-level frame. This frame will hold all the components, including the table.

Create a panel for the button and field. We'll use a separate panel for the button and field, so we can exert more control over how they are laid out. This panel has a BoxLayout along the X_AXIS (items are centered horizontally and given as much space as they need).

Create a text field. The user can type some SQL into this text field.

Create a button. When the user presses this button, it calls the myModel .fetchData() method to fill the grid with the SQL results.

Add all the controls to the panel. Add the text field and the button to ctrl_panel, so they are laid out from left to right.

Create a scrolling pane for the table. The scrolling pane is best for a table, since it will automatically add a scrollbar if the table goes off the visible area.

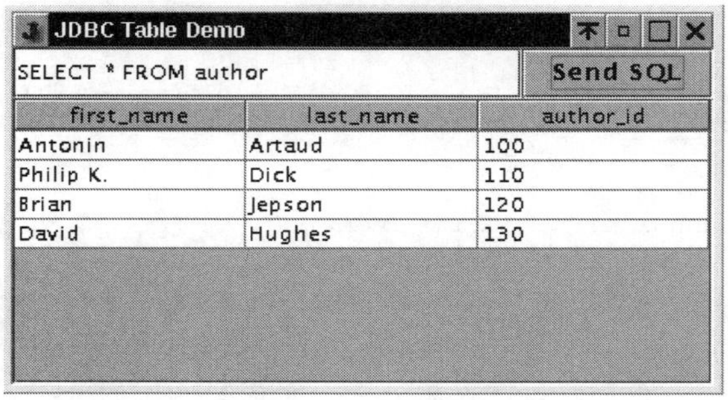

Figure 11.10 The JDBCGrid in action.

Add the panel and the scrolling pane to the frame, then pack and show the frame. When these steps are performed, the table appears as shown in Figure 11.10.

The following listing shows the complete example, JDBCGrid.java:

```java
import java.awt.*;
import java.awt.event.*;
import javax.swing.*;

public class JDBCGrid {

  public static void main(String[] argv) {

      // Register at Least One JDBC Driver.
      // No need to register the driver, since the
      // user should use -Djdbc.drivers to set it.

      // Check the arguments.
      //
      if (argv.length < 3) {
          usage();
      }
      String url  = argv[0];
      String user = argv[1];
      String pass = argv[2];

      // Create an instance of JDBCTableModelRO.
      //
      final JDBCTableModelRO myModel =
          new JDBCTableModelRO(url, user, pass);

      // Create a JTable that Uses the Model.
      JTable table = new JTable(myModel);

      // Create a Top-Level Frame.
```

```java
JFrame myframe = new JFrame("JDBC Table Demo");
WindowAdapter wa = new WindowAdapter() {
    public void windowClosing(WindowEvent e) {
        System.exit(0);
    }
};
myframe.addWindowListener(wa);

// Create a box for the button and field.
//
JPanel ctrl_panel = new JPanel();
ctrl_panel.setLayout(
    new BoxLayout(ctrl_panel, BoxLayout.X_AXIS));

// Create a Text Field.
//
final JTextField sql_field = new JTextField(36);
sql_field.setAlignmentY(Component.CENTER_ALIGNMENT);

// Create a Button.
//
JButton sql_button = new JButton("Send SQL");
ActionListener sendSQLListener = new ActionListener() {
    public void actionPerformed(ActionEvent e) {
        myModel.fetchData(sql_field.getText());
    }
};
sql_button.addActionListener(sendSQLListener);
sql_button.setAlignmentY(Component.CENTER_ALIGNMENT);

// Add the Controls to the Panel.
//
ctrl_panel.add(sql_field);
ctrl_panel.add(sql_button);

// Create a Scrolling Pane for the Table.
//
JScrollPane scrollPane = new JScrollPane(table);

// Get the content pane and have it use a box layout.
//
Container contents = myframe.getContentPane();
contents.setLayout(
    new BoxLayout(contents, BoxLayout.Y_AXIS));

// Add the Panel and ScrollPane to the Frame.
//
contents.add(ctrl_panel);
contents.add(scrollPane);

// Pack and Show the Frame.
```

```
            //
            myframe.pack();
            myframe.show();
        }

    static void usage() {

            System.err.println("Usage:");
            System.err.print("java -Djdbc.drivers=DRIVERCLASS ");
            System.err.println("JDBCGrid URL USER PASS");
            System.exit(-1);

        }

    }
```

To run this example, you should use the -Djdbc.drivers option to specify a JDBC driver, and pass in the JDBC URL, user name, and password, as in:

```
java -Djdbc.drivers=postgresql.Driver JDBCGrid \
     jdbc:postgresql:postgres postgres ''
```

You will need to change the JDBC URL (jdbc:postgresql:postgres) to a JDBC URL appropriate for your system (see Table 11.4). You will also need to change the user id (postgres) and the password ('') to something correct for your system.

Summary

We looked at a lot of stuff in this chapter: Swing and JDBC are two big pieces of Java that go together well. Swing represents a massive improvement over the user interface components in earlier releases of the JDK. The data-driven table model is a great example of how Swing makes it easy to integrate your user interface with a data source.

Although we took a close look at both Swing and JDBC, there is much more to both of these APIs. As you develop applications of your own, we suggest that you use the Java API reference, which is available online. You can find links to the JDBC documentation at http://java.sun.com/products/jdbc/, and you can find links to the Swing documentation at http://java.sun.com/products/jfc/.

DBI and Perl

P erl is no stranger to database programming. In fact, it's probably the most commonly used language for Web database development. Perl also has a long history of being run from the shell, used in CGI scripts, or used in shell scripts. This stdout/stdin legacy should not shackle it, though, because Perl has many pretty faces. In fact, two of the GUI applications (dbMan and Orac) featured in Chapter 10, "Linux Development Tools Catalog," are written in Perl. So, if you have some hang-ups about using Perl for a graphical database application, try to check them at the door. If you can't, we'll do our best to rid you of them. This chapter expects some familiarity with the Perl programming language. Familiarity with Perl references (see the *perlref* man page) will also be helpful.

The Perl DBI

The Perl DBI is a high-level interface to various database systems. It provides database independence by using a single API for every supported database. You can use the DBI interface to connect to databases, issue SQL statements, and retrieve result sets.

Figure 12.1 shows the architecture of a typical DBI application. The following is a breakdown of each component:

Application. The application is a program written in Perl that needs to interact with a database server. It will use a DBI connection string to tell the DBI module which database it wants to connect to (we'll talk more about connection strings later in this chapter).

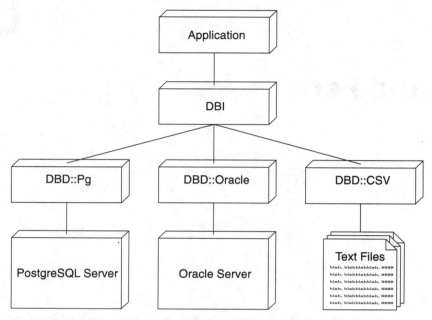

Figure 12.1 DBI application architecture.

DBI. DBI is a driver manager that handles requests for a database connection. It passes requests on to a database driver (DBD), which handles the actual work of interacting with the database.

Database Driver (DBD). A DBD is a module that implements the DBI specification. It is essentially an adapter that bridges the DBI interface with the vendor-specific API that is supported by the database server. The DBD has the ability to connect to a database server, send SQL statements, and obtain result sets.

Database System. This is a database server, such as PostgreSQL, Sybase, Oracle, Mini SQL, MySQL, or even a non-SQL data source such as a comma-delimited file.

Installing the DBI

There are two ways you can install the DBI: Use a precompiled package or build it from the source code. In either case, you need to get the package from the CPAN archive, or from your Linux distribution media.

CPAN

Perl's one-stop repository, the Comprehensive Perl Archive Network (CPAN), contains a huge collection of peer-reviewed modules that cooperate well with each other. If you want to build an application with database access, a user interface, and automatic graph generation, you can find freely redistributable source code on CPAN that is trustworthy.

CPAN consists of a collection of more than 100 cooperating Web and ftp sites that mirror the content of the main archive. You can learn more about CPAN by visiting the CPAN dispatcher at www.perl.com/CPAN (no trailing slash), which you can use to find a CPAN site close to you.

Installing CPAN Modules

There are two ways you can install a CPAN module such as DBI: use a precompiled package or build it from the source code. Before you do either, check to see if the module is already installed on your system (some Linux distributions install various modules by default). To check for the existence of a module, try loading it with the -M switch to Perl and confirmation script specified with -e:

```
perl -MMODULE_NAME -e 'print "OK\n";'
```

For example, you could check for the existence of the DBI module with:

```
perl -MDBI -e 'print "OK\n";'
```

If this program prints OK, the module is installed. If you see an error message, it is not installed.

If the module is not installed, use one of the methods described next to install it. When you are done installing the module, you should read its documentation. To read a module's documentation, issue this command from the shell:

```
perldoc MODULE_NAME
```

as in:

```
perldoc DBI
```

Precompiled package. Many Linux distributions come with Perl modules, or include utilities that know how to find a module. If you are running a variant of the Debian distribution, use Debian's dselect program to locate and install the module.

If you are running an RPM-based Linux system, use an application that is capable of locating RPMs on the Web, such as gnorpm or rpmfind. You should search for and install the RPM (RedHat Package Manager) file that contains the module. RPMs containing Perl modules are usually titled Perl-MODULE_NAME, as in Perl-DBI.

Building from source. Perl includes the CPAN module, a utility that makes it easy to browse and install the optional modules on CPAN. To use this utility, first read the documentation by issuing the following command from the shell prompt:

```
perldoc CPAN
```

When you are ready to begin, log on or su to root, and run the command:

```
perl -MCPAN -e shell
```

If this is the first time you have run CPAN, it will ask you for a lot of configuration information. Once it is finished, you will find yourself at the CPAN prompt, which looks like:

```
cpan shell -- CPAN exploration and modules installation (v1.48)
ReadLine support enabled

cpan>
```

Before you install a module, first view the README by issuing the CPAN shell command:

```
readme MODULE_NAME
```

as in:

```
readme DBI
```

If you are satisfied that you meet all the requirements, install it with the command:

```
install MODULE_NAME
```

as in:

```
install DBI
```

When the CPAN module is finished, the module will be installed on your system, and you can exit the CPAN utility by typing "quit" and pressing Enter.

After Installing DBI

When you are done installing DBI, read the instructions and FAQ before proceeding (you don't need to read the whole thing, but please browse it, since it will help you a lot!). To read the documentation, issue this command at the shell prompt:

```
perldoc DBI
```

To read the DBI FAQ, run this command from the shell:

```
perldoc DBI::FAQ
```

Installing Database Drivers (DBDs)

As with other modules, you can either install a DBD from source, or from a precompiled package (see the instructions in the *CPAN* section of this chapter). If the database server you are using came with your Linux distribution (as PostgreSQL does), you should be able to install a precompiled package for the DBD. If you installed from source, or from a third-party distribution, you may want to install the DBD from source, because some DBDs are sensitive to the version of the database server you are using.

The name of a DBD is always of the form DBD::DRIVERNAME, such as DBD::Pg or DBD::mSQL. Table 12.1 lists some of the DBDs available. After you install a DBD, you should read the documentation using the command *perldoc DBD::DRIVERNAME*, as in *perldoc DBD::Pg*.

If You Have Trouble

If you have trouble building DBI or a DBD, please examine the DBI README again, or visit the DBI FAQ at www.symbolstone.org/technology/perl/DBI/doc/faq.html, and see the section *Compilation Problems*.

Table 12.1   Servers and Drivers

DATABASE SERVER	DBD NAME
Sybase	DBD::Sybase
Oracle	DBD::Oracle
PostgreSQL	DBD::Pg
Mini SQL	DBD::mSQL
MySQL	DBD::mysql
Legacy XBbase (*.DBF) files	DBD::XBase
DBI-ODBC Bridge	DBD::ODBC
Informix	DBD::Informix
DB2	DBD::DB2

Using the DBI

To use the DBI, you need to first connect to a database server. Once you have made the connection, you can send a SQL statement to the server, and process the result set, if any is returned.

Connecting to a Database

To connect to a database server, you need to use the *DBI->connect(DSN, USER, PWD)* method, where:

DSN is a DBI data source, or connection string. The DBI connection string is a combination of the DBD name suffix from Table 12.1 (everything after DBD::) and information that the driver uses to locate the database server and connect to it. For example, to connect to the *inventory* database on the PostgreSQL server on the local host, using DBD::Pg, the connection string would be "dbi:Pg:dbname=inventory".

USER is the user name.

PWD is the password.

Table 12.2 lists some drivers, and the basic connection strings that the driver supports, where:

DATABASE is the name of the database.

HOST is the name of the machine the database server is running on.

Table 12.2   Connection Strings for Various Drivers

DATABASE	DRIVER	CONNECTION STRING
PostgreSQL	DBD::Pg	dbi:Pg:dbname=DATABASE dbi:Pg:dbname=DATABASE;host=HOST dbi:Pg:dbname=DATABASE;host=HOST;port=PORT
Sybase	DBD::Sybase	dbi:Sybase:database=DATABASE dbi:Sybase:database=DATABASE;server=SERVER
Oracle	DBD::Oracle	dbi:Oracle:SID dbi:Oracle:host=HOST;sid=SID
Mini SQL	DBD::mSQL	dbi:mSQL:database=DATABASE dbi:mSQL:database=DATABASE;host=HOST dbi:mSQL:database=DATABASE;host=HOST;port=PORT
MySQL	DBD::mysql	dbi:mysql:database=DATABASE dbi:mysql:database=DATABASE;host=HOST dbi:mysql:database=DATABASE;host=HOST;port=PORT

PORT is the TCP/IP port that the database server uses. Unless you have configured the database to use a non-standard port, you will not usually need this.

SID is the Oracle System Identifier that you can find in the /etc/oratab file.

SERVER is the Sybase server name designated in the ~sybase/interfaces file.

To connect to the database, you should follow these three steps:

1. Import the DBI module.
2. Invoke the DBI->connect() method with the DSN, user name, and password. This gives you a database handle, named $dbh in the examples that follow.
3. Check for connection errors.

When you are done with the connection, you should disconnect. This example (connect.pl) makes a connection to a PostgreSQL database server:

```perl
#!/usr/bin/perl

# Step 1. Import the DBI module.
#
use DBI;

# Step 2. Create a connection.
#
my $dsn  = 'dbi:Pg:dbname=postgres';
my $user = 'postgres';
my $pass = '';
my $dbh = DBI->connect($dsn, $user, $pass);

# Step 3. Check for errors.
#
unless (defined $dbh) {
    die $DBI::errstr;
} else {
    print "Connection successful.\n";
}

# Final Step. When you are done with the database
# connection, disconnect.
#
$dbh->disconnect;
```

To run this example, simply change to the directory containing the Chapter 12 examples (you can get the example programs at this book's companion Web site at www.wiley.com/compbooks/jepson). Then, run the command *perl connect.pl*. You may need to change the $dsn, $user, and $pass variables for your system. If this example runs correctly, you will see the message "Connection successful." If not, you will see an error message. If you get an error message, you should resolve it before attempting to go any further in this chapter. For help on connection problems, see the DBI FAQ at www .symbolstone.org/technology/perl/DBI/doc/faq.html for resources that you may find useful in diagnosing the problem (such as mailing list archives and the FAQ itself).

Sample Connection Strings

Let's take a look at some sample connection strings. In this chapter's example programs, you'll need to change the $dsn, $user, and $pass variables to something appropriate for your configuration.

MySQL with Local Server. This example connects to a database called instruments as the user *sales*, with the password *7strat001*. The database resides on the MySQL server running on the local host:

```
my $dsn  = 'dbi:mysql:database=instruments';
my $user = 'sales';
my $pass = '7strat001';
```

MySQL with Remote Server. In this example, we connect to the ATIS database, which resides on the host named frobozz. The user name is *controller*, and the password is *homer*:

```
my $dsn  = 'dbi:mysql:host=frobozz;database=ATIS';
my $user = 'controller';
my $pass = 'homer';
```

Mini SQL with Local Server. Here, we connect to the dungeon_data database on the local Mini SQL server, as the user *bjepson* with a blank password:

```
my $dsn  = 'dbi:mSQL:database=dungeon_data';
my $user = 'bjepson';
my $pass = '';
```

Mini SQL with Remote Server. This example connects to the gallery database running on the server datacenter.as220.org. The user name is *bjepson*, and the password is blank:

```
my $dsn  =
  'dbi:mSQL:host=datacenter.as220.org;database=gallery';
my $user = 'bjepson';
my $pass = '';
```

PostgreSQL with Local Server. This example connects to the inventory database on the local PostgreSQL server. The user name is *manager*, the password is blank:

```
my $dsn  = 'dbi:Pg:dbname=inventory';
my $user = 'manager';
my $pass = '';
```

PostgreSQL with Remote Server. Here, we connect to the library database on the host frobozz. We connect as the user *librarian*, with a blank password:

```
my $dsn  = 'dbi:Pg:host=frobozz;dbname=library';
my $user = 'librarian';
my $pass = '';
```

Oracle with Local Server. This example connects to the local Oracle instance as the user *scott*, with the password *tiger*:

```
my $dsn  = 'dbi:Oracle:host=localhost;sid=ORCL';
my $user = 'scott';
my $pass = 'tiger';
```

Sybase with Local Server. In this example, we connect to the database bjepson_db on the local Sybase server. The user name is *bjepson*, and the password is *open_sesame*:

```
my $dsn  = 'dbi:Sybase:database=bjepson_db';
my $user = 'bjepson';
my $pass = 'open_sesame';
```

Connection String Discovery

If you have trouble finding a valid connection string, you can write a program that uses the data_sources() method to query a driver for all the data sources it knows about. Just because a driver doesn't report any data sources does not mean that there aren't any, but it's worth checking anyhow. Most of the data sources you retrieve should be usable as connection strings on your system, but there is no guarantee that this is the case.

The following program (dbi_info.pl) uses the DBI module, and then locates all the known drivers. For every driver it finds, it checks to see what data sources the driver knows about and displays the connection string for those drivers:

```
#!/usr/bin/perl

use DBI;

# Get a list of all drivers.
#
my @driver_names = DBI->available_drivers;

# Check each driver for available data sources.
#
foreach $driver (@driver_names) {
```

```
        print "Found the $driver driver.\n";

        my @data_sources = DBI->data_sources($driver);

        # If the driver knows about any data sources, print
        # out the corresponding connection string.
        #
        if (@data_sources > 0) {

            print "DBI knows about these $driver data sources:\n";
            foreach $data_source (@data_sources) {
                print "\t$data_source\n";
            }

        }
        print "\n";

    }
```

To run this example, simply change to the directory containing the Chapter 12 examples. Then, run the command *perl dbi_info.pl*.

Executing a SQL Statement

If you want to execute a SQL statement, simply use the $dbh->do method, as in:

```
$rc = $dbh->do("INSERT INTO contacts
                    VALUES('Brian', 'Jepson', 'FrobCo')");
```

The $rc value is the return code of the command. If $rc is zero, the do() method failed, and you should look for an error message in the $DBI::errstr variable.

The next example uses the do() method to create a table called contacts. It will drop it before it creates it, so if you run this program, make sure you don't already have a contacts table that you need to keep. In this example, we perform the following steps:

1. Import the DBI module.
2. Create a connection and check for any error that might have occurred.
3. Set the database handle's PrintError attribute to 0, which suppresses the automatic printing of errors. This program explicitly checks for errors, and formats them in its own way.
4. Use the do() method to drop the contacts table. An error will occur if the table does not exist. This is OK, since the table won't exist the first time you run the program, but the program prints the error as a warning.

5. Use the do() method to create the contacts table. If an error occurs, use the die() method to print the error and exit. The \n at the end of the string keeps die() from reporting the line number and program name, which makes for a more readable error message in some cases. If you were debugging your code, you might not want to suppress this behavior.

6. Close the connection.

Here is the source code for this example (send_sql.pl):

```perl
#!/usr/bin/perl
#

# Step 1. Import the DBI module.
#
use DBI;

# Step 2. Create a connection and check for an error.
#
my $dsn  = 'dbi:Pg:dbname=postgres';
my $user = 'postgres';
my $pass = '';
my $dbh = DBI->connect($dsn, $user, $pass);
unless (defined $dbh) {
    die $DBI::errstr;
}

# Step 3. Don't automatically print every error. We'll
# check for them.
#
$dbh->{PrintError} = 0;

# Step 4. Before we create the test table, let's try to drop
# it, just in case it already exists.
#
my $rc;
$rc = $dbh->do("DROP TABLE contact");
unless ($rc) {
    print "Warning (probably unimportant): $DBI::errstr\n";
}

# Step 5. Create the contact table.
#
$rc = $dbh->do("CREATE TABLE contact
                        (first_name   CHAR(20),
                         last_name    CHAR(20),
                         company      CHAR(20))");
unless ($rc) {
    # Print the error and exit. The \n at the end keeps die()
```

```
    # from reporting the line number and program name, so
    # the error is formatted a little more nicely.
    #
    die "Database error: $DBI::errstr\n";
}
print "Table created successfully.\n";

# Step 6. Close the connection.
#
$dbh->disconnect;
```

To run this example, simply change to the directory containing the Chapter 12 examples. Then, run the command *perl send_sql.pl*.

Prepared Statements

If you anticipate that you will be using the same SQL statement many times, you can use a prepared statement. Some database servers may compile the query on the server, which can produce a performance benefit if you call it multiple times.

You can also use a prepared statement to create placeholders in a SQL statement. For example, if you wanted to insert three rows into the contact table, you could create a prepared INSERT statement with placeholders (question marks) for the values:

```
my $sth = $dbh->prepare("INSERT INTO contact
                        (first_name, last_name, company)
                        VALUES(?, ?, ?)");
```

That gives you a statement handle, $sth. You can call the statement handle's execute() method with the values that should go into the placeholders. The database driver or back-end server takes care of putting quotes around values that need them.

```
$sth->execute('Brian', 'Jepson', 'FrobCo');
```

The preceding command is the equivalent of issuing the following INSERT statement:

```
INSERT INTO contact
    (first_name, last_name, company)
    VALUES('Brian', 'Jepson', 'FrobCo')
```

Not only is this convenient, but it can also be much faster, especially if the statements occur inside a loop that is executed many times. Here is an example (prepared.pl) that inserts three rows into the contact table (the second insert uses *undef* to insert a NULL company name):

```perl
#!/usr/bin/perl
#

# Import the DBI module.
#
use DBI;

# Create a connection and check for an error.
#
my $dsn  = 'dbi:Pg:dbname=postgres';
my $user = 'postgres';
my $pass = '';
my $dbh = DBI->connect($dsn, $user, $pass);
unless (defined $dbh) {
    die $DBI::errstr;
}

# Don't automatically print every error. We'll
# check for them.
#
$dbh->{PrintError} = 0;

# Create a prepared statement.
#
my $sth = $dbh->prepare("INSERT INTO contact
                            (first_name, last_name, company)
                            VALUES(?, ?, ?)");

# Use the prepared statement to insert three rows.
#
$sth->execute('Brian', 'Jepson', 'FrobCo')
    or die $DBI::errstr;

$sth->execute('Oscorb', 'Beestie', undef)
    or die $DBI::errstr;

$sth->execute('Lotus', 'Frodus', 'Bleemzor')
    or die $DBI::errstr;

print "The data was inserted.\n";

# Close the connection.
#
$dbh->disconnect;
```

To run this example, simply change to the directory containing the Chapter 12 examples. Then, run the command *perl prepared.pl*.

Processing Result Sets

The DBI is very flexible when it comes to getting data out of the database. To issue a query and process its results, you should take the following steps:

1. Use prepare() to create a statement handle, and execute() to execute the statement.
2. Fetch each row in the result set.
3. Invoke the finish() method.

Prepare and Execute

Use the prepare() method to get a statement handle, and then use the execute method to execute the statement:

```
$sth = $dbh->prepare("SELECT * FROM contact")
   or die $DBI::errstr;

$sth->execute()
   or die $DBI::errstr;
```

Fetch the Rows

Next, you can get the result set using one of the following statement handle methods:

fetchrow_array(). Fetches the next row as an array of values:

```
while ( my @values = $sth->fetchrow_array) {
    my ($first, $last, $company) = @values;
    print "$first $last works for $company.\n";
}
```

fetchrow_arrayref(). This fetches the next row as a single reference value to an array. The DBI documentation says that this is the fastest way to fetch data:

```
while ( my $array_ref = $sth->fetchrow_arrayref) {
    my ($first, $last, $company) = @$array_ref;
    print "$first $last works for $company.\n";
}
```

fetchrow_hashref(). This fetches the next row as a hash of values using the column names as a key. While this is very convenient, it does not perform as well as the alternatives:

```
while ( my $row = $sth->fetchrow_hashref) {

    foreach $column (keys %$row) {
        print "$column: $$row{$column}, ";
    }
    print "\n";
}
```

fetchall_arrayref(). This fetches all the rows in the result set as a reference to an array. Each element of that array contains an array of references to the values of each row:

```
my $rows = $sth->fetchall_arrayref();
foreach $array_ref (@$rows) {
    my ($first, $last, $company) = @$array_ref;
    print "$first $last works for $company.\n";
}
```

Within the array that each method returns, NULL values are represented as undefined values.

Finish

After you've finished with the result set, you should invoke the finish() method:

```
$sth->finish;
```

Putting It All Together

The next example performs all three steps (Prepare and Execute, Fetch the Rows, and Finish). Since many databases return values with padding (spaces often fill the values out to the maximum size of the column), we are using a regular expression substitution to clean up the values that fetchrow_array returns.

We also check each row to see whether it contains an undefined company. If so, we skip that person. We have to do this check before we use the substitution to clean up the data, since the substitution has the side effect of defining the value when it modifies it. Here is the example (select.pl):

```
#!/usr/bin/perl
#

use DBI;

my $dsn  = 'dbi:Pg:dbname=postgres';
my $user = 'postgres';
my $pass = '';
```

```perl
my $dbh = DBI->connect($dsn, $user, $pass);
unless (defined $dbh) {
    die $DBI::errstr;
}
$dbh->{PrintError} = 0;

# Step 1. Create a statement that fetches all rows from
# the contact table, and execute that statement.
#
my $sql = "SELECT first_name, last_name, company
              FROM contact";
$sth = $dbh->prepare($sql) or die $DBI::errstr;
$sth->execute()
  or die $DBI::errstr;

# Step 2. Fetch all the results.
#
while ( my @values = $sth->fetchrow_array) {

    # Only list people who have a company. If
    # company is NULL, skip that person.
    #
    unless (defined $values[2]) {
        next;
    }

    # Remove trailing spaces from each array element.
    grep(s/\s*$//, @values);

    my ($first, $last, $company) = @values;
    print "$first $last works for $company.\n";
}

# Step 3. Finish the statement.
#
$sth->finish;

$dbh->disconnect;
```

To run this example, simply change to the directory containing the Chapter 12 examples. Then, run the command *perl select.pl*.

User Interfaces in Perl

There is an impressive array of modules for developing user interfaces in Perl. In fact, CPAN has a separate categorization for user interface modules, which can be found at www.perl.com/CPAN/modules/by-category/08 _User_Interfaces.

Of the modules in that category, Perl/Tk is the most mature, popular, and platform-independent user interface module for Perl. There are other excellent user interface modules in that category, such as Gtk and PerlQt. In fact, you can even build user interfaces for Perl and Gtk using the popular UI builder, glade (http://glade.pn.org). Chapter 13, "GNOME," looks at Glade from a C programmer's perspective, but the information there will be useful for people who want to use Perl with Glade.

Perl/Tk

Perl/Tk is a collection of object-oriented modules that bring the Tk toolkit to Perl. Tk (www.scriptics.com) is the graphical user interface toolkit that is distributed along with the Tcl scripting language. Perl/Tk is based on source code from the Tcl/Tk distribution, but does not need an existing installation of Tcl/Tk in order to function.

You can use Perl/Tk to develop applications with a sophisticated graphical user interface. Perl/Tk has an intuitive object-oriented syntax for building interfaces, and includes a good selection of graphical components you can use in your applications.

Installing Perl/Tk

The Perl/Tk distribution is contained in the Tk archive on CPAN. In this chapter, the section titled *CPAN* explains how to install an optional module with Perl. Use these instructions to install Tk, which is a large archive containing many modules related to Perl/Tk. To get documentation on Perl/Tk, you should start by issuing this command at the shell prompt:

```
perldoc Tk::UserGuide
```

You may also find it instructive to look at the interactive widget demo. This demo is contained in a script called *widget*, which is installed into either /usr/bin or /usr/local/bin. Run this script by logging on to X and issuing the command *widget* at a shell prompt. Because you can view demos along with their source code, the widget demo is a powerful learning tool.

Creating a Simple Form

As with many other user interface tool kits, Tk arranges components hierarchically. A top-level window contains all the components, such as buttons, text fields, and frames. Some components, such as a frame, can contain other components. Figure 11.2 in Chapter 11, "Java, Swing, and JDBC," shows the hierarchical arrangement of components in Java's Swing. This model is applicable to Tk, as well.

To create a basic Tk application, you need to do the following:

1. Use (import) the Tk module:

   ```
   use Tk;
   ```

2. Create a main window. Use the -title attribute to specify a window title:

   ```
   my $main = MainWindow->new( -title => 'Tk Demo' );
   ```

3. Add at least one frame to the window. Use the frame to hold components. To create a frame, invoke the main window's Frame() method. Then you must invoke the pack() method to make sure the frame is packed into the Window correctly:

   ```
   my $top = $main->Frame();
   $top->pack();
   ```

   You can specify where you want pack() to anchor the frame by including the -side attribute:

   ```
   $top->pack(-side=>'top');
   ```

   The next chunk of code creates two frames—the first is anchored to the top of the window. The second frame is anchored to the right of the window, and appears below the first frame:

   ```
   my $top    = $main->Frame();
   my $bottom = $main->Frame();
   $top->pack(-side=>'top');
   $bottom->pack(-side=>'right');
   ```

4. Add components to the frames. It's very easy to add a component to anything in Perl/Tk. Just as we added a frame to a window by calling the window's Frame() method, you can add a text label to a frame by calling the frame's Label() method:

   ```
   my $label = $top->Label(-text => 'Name:');
   $label->pack(-side=>'left');
   ```

   If you don't plan to refer to an object that you create, you can invoke the pack() method on the same line of code you use to create the object (although this can rapidly become unreadable with complicated forms). We'll call this an *anonymous component* (as compared to a named component, as shown in the preceding code):

```
$top->Label(-text => 'Name:')->pack(-side=>'left');
```

You can associate commands with certain components, such as a button. To create a command, set the command attribute when you create the object. This code destroys the main window when the Cancel button is pressed, thereby terminating the application:

```
my $btn = $bottom->Button(-text => 'Cancel',
                          -command => [$main => 'destroy']);
$btn->pack(-side=>'left');
```

You can also create commands that call subroutines. Notice here that we also refer to a named instance of a text entry field. The say_hello() subroutine can call $entry->get() to get the current value:

```
$bottom->Button(-text => 'OK',
                -command => sub { say_hello($entry) }
                )->pack(-side=>'left');
```

5. When you have added all the components, put Tk into its main loop. At this point, you give control up to Tk until the main window is destroyed. Here is the command to start the main loop:

```
MainLoop;
```

Component Constructors

When you create an object, as with $top->Label, you are in effect calling the constructor for an object called Tk::OBJECT_TYPE, as in Tk::Label. Since you call it through another object, such as the frame called $top, you are also associating it with that object.

Component Attributes

The attributes that are passed to the constructor (such as -text, -command, etc.) are a special kind of list notation. The => is a synonym for a comma. So, "-text => 'Cancel'" is equivalent to "-text, 'Cancel'", but the former makes it clear that the two values are associated with each other. This notation is often used to assign variables to hashes as well. See the Tk::options man page (perldoc Tk::options) for a list of standard attributes you can use with some widgets. See the widget's man page for a list of options the widget supports.

Here is a simple example (tkdemo.pl) that follows the steps just described, and prints out a greeting when you click OK (Figure 12.2 shows this program in action):

```perl
#! /usr/bin/perl -w
use strict;  # enable restrictions on unsafe code

# Step One. Use the Tk module.
#
use Tk;

# Step Two. Create the main window.
#
my $main = MainWindow->new( -title => 'Tk Demo' );

# Step Three. Add frames to the main window.
#
my $top    = $main->Frame();
my $bottom = $main->Frame();
$top->pack(-side=>'top');
$bottom->pack(-side=>'right');

# Step Four. Add components to the frames.
#
#     Add a text label.
#
$top->Label(-text => 'Name:')->pack(-side=>'left');
#
#     Add a text entry field as a named component.
#
my $name = $top->Entry(-width => 20);
$name->pack(-side=>'right');
#
#     Add an OK button that calls the say_hello handler.
#
$bottom->Button(-text => 'OK',
                -command => sub { say_hello($name) }
               )->pack(-side=>'left');
#
#     Add a Cancel button that closes the window.
#
$bottom->Button(-text => 'Cancel',
                -command => [$main => 'destroy']
               )->pack(-side=>'right');

# Step Five. Start the main loop.
#
MainLoop;

# This is the say_hello handler.
```

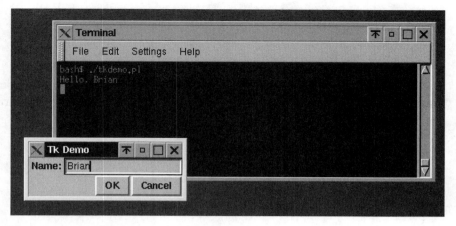

Figure 12.2   Hello from Perl's Tk module.

```
#
sub say_hello {
    my $entry = shift;
    print "Hello, ", $entry->get(), "\n";
}
```

To run this example, simply change to the directory containing the Chapter 12 examples. Then, run the command *perl tkdemo.pl*.

Variable Binding

Instead of using get() to retrieve the current text in a widget, you can bind that widget to a variable. When you do this, you can often avoid using a named instance of a widget, and rely on the bound variable. To bind a variable to a Tk::Entry object, you should first create the variable, and then supply a reference to that variable in the -textvariable attribute. A reference is created by prefixing the variable with a \ character.

Consider these changes to the button and entry field in the preceding example shown:

```
#     Add a text entry field.
#
my $name = "";
$top->Entry( -width => 20,
            -textvariable => \$name
        )->pack(-side=>'right');
#
#     Add an OK button that calls the say_hello handler.
#
```

```
$bottom->Button(-text => 'OK',
                -command => sub { say_hello($name) }
              )->pack(-side=>'left');
```

Instead of passing a reference to the Tk::Entry object itself, we're now just passing the bound variable, which contains the value. So, say_hello can be rewritten as:

```
# This is the say_hello handler.
#
sub say_hello {
    my $name = shift;
    print "Hello, $name.\n";
}
```

Some Widgets

Here are some of the widgets we'll be using in the next examples. Figure 12.3 shows all of these widgets in a single window. For more details on any of these, use *perldoc* or *man* at the Linux shell to read the documentation, as in one of the following:

```
perldoc Tk::Label
man Tk::Label
```

Tk::BrowseEntry. This is a specialized version of the Tk::Entry widget that is similar to a combo box control (a combination of a text field and pull-down menu). With Tk::BrowseEntry, the user can type in his or her own selection, or choose from a number of choices.

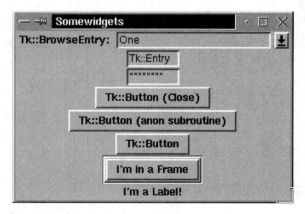

Figure 12.3 Several Tk widgets.

To use this widget, you should specify at least the following attributes: -label (an instructive prompt), -choices (a reference to an array of possible selections), and -variable (a variable to bind the choice to). Here is an example that offers the choices in the array *@choices*, with the first element in *@choices* as the default:

```
my @choices = ('One', 'Two', 'Three');
my $choice = $choices[0];  # default to 1st choice.
$main->BrowseEntry( -width => 25,
                    -variable => \$choice,
                    -label => 'Tk::BrowseEntry: ',
                    -choices => \@choices
                  )->pack();
```

Tk::Entry. A simple text entry field. You should at least specify the -textvariable attribute (a variable to bind to). Here is an example:

```
$main->Entry( -width => 8,
              -textvariable => \$text,
            )->pack();
```

You may also use the -show attribute to specify a character that appears as users type in the field. This overrides what they really type, and is useful for hiding password entry (in Figure 12.3, this is the field containing a sequence of asterisks):

```
$main->Entry( -width => 8,
              -textvariable => \$pass,
              -show => '*'
            )->pack();
```

Tk::Button. A push button that can have an action associated with it. You should at least specify the -text (button label) and -command (action) attributes. The command can be a reference to a list (which uses the [and] delimiters) containing a component/message pair of values. The first value is a component, such as the top-level window, and the second value is the message you want to send to that component, such as *destroy*:

```
$main->Button( -text    => 'Tk::Button (Close)',
               -command => [ $main => 'destroy' ]
             )->pack();
```

The command can also be a reference to some code that you want it to execute. One easy way to do this is to create an anonymous subroutine with sub { ... }:

```
$main->Button( -text    => 'Tk::Button (anon subroutine)',
               -command => sub { print "Hello, World.\n" }
             )->pack();
```

but you can also use the \& prefix to create a reference to an existing subroutine:

```perl
sub hello {
    print "Hello, World from hello().\n";
}
$main->Button( -text    => 'Tk::Button',
               -command => \&hello
             )->pack();
```

Tk::Frame. A component to hold other components. The frame grows to accommodate whatever you put in it. Useful attributes include -relief (raised, sunken, flat, ridge, solid, and groove) and -borderwidth (border width in pixels). Here is a Frame that contains a button:

```perl
my $frame = $main->Frame( -relief => 'groove',
                          -borderwidth => 3
                        )->pack();
$frame->Button( -text => "I'm in a Frame" )->pack();
```

Tk::Label. A simple text label. At a minimum, you should include the -text (text of the label) attribute:

```perl
$main->Label( -text => "I'm a Label!" )->pack();
```

Tk::Scrolled (not shown in Figure 12.3). A scrolled widget. The usage of this is a little different from the other widgets. You might expect that you would first create a scrolled widget, and then add a component to it. Instead, you pass the name of the widget to the special Scrolled's constructor, as in:

```perl
$top->Scrolled( 'Pane');
```

You can specify the location of the scrollbars with the -scrollbar attribute. Use compass points, such as n (north), s (south), e (east), and w(west), You can prefix any of the compass points with an o, which specifies that the scrollbar should only be displayed if it is needed (that is, if the widget is bigger than the enclosing window). This creates a scrolled pane that has a scrollbar on the west (left) side, and an optional scrollbar on the south (bottom) side, with a geometry of 200x200:

```perl
$top->Scrolled( 'Pane',
                -scrollbars => 'ose',
                -height => 200,
                -width  => 200)->pack();
```

Displaying Data in a Grid

When you have a lot of tabular data, it can be useful to display it in a grid format. Although it is not the most elegant way to present data, it is familiar to many users, since it follows the format of spreadsheets and many printed reports. If you are looking for a way to explore data, particularly data that lends itself well to hierarchical exploration, you should look at the following section, where data is explored in a tree format.

Let's look at the Tk::Columns module, which doesn't let you edit the contents of the grid, but is somewhat nice for displaying a read-only grid. If you need to create an editable grid, you should look at Tk::Table. However, large tables created with Tk::Table can consume a lot of memory.

Tk::Columns is not part of the standard Perl/Tk distribution. It is contained within the Tk-DKW distribution, which you can install as described in the section titled *CPAN*. If you use the CPAN utility, you can simply ask it to install Tk::Columns, and it will automatically figure out that it's part of Tk-DKW.

Using Tk::Columns

Tk::Columns is very easy to use, and it integrates well with the DBI. To create a Tk::Columns widget, use the Columns method. Before you create it, you should know your column headers. If these are in an array, you should pass them in as a reference using the -columnlabels attribute:

```
@columns = ('Column A', 'Column B', 'Column C');
$grid = $main->Columns( -columnlabels => \@columns );
```

Once you have created the grid, add rows to it using the insert() method. The insert method takes a positional argument (where you want the row to be added, usually "end"), and a list of values for the row:

```
$grid->insert('end', 'Value for A', 'Value for B', 'Value for C');
```

Before you call MainLoop, you should call pack on the object:

```
$grid->pack;
```

Let's look at a short program that demonstrates the use of Tk::Columns. As you look at the code, take note of the integration of DBI and Tk::Columns. In this example, we use the DBI to get two chunks of data that we use to create the TK::Columns object. The first is the list of column headers; these are obtained from a regular statement handle ($sth) by examining the NAME attribute, which is a reference to an array of column names that we use for the -columnlabels attribute:

```
my $cols = $sth->{NAME};
```

The second chunk of data is, naturally, all the rows in the result set. Since Tk::Columns::insert expects an array of values, we use the *$sth->fetchrow _array* method to get this:

```perl
while (my @columns = $sth->fetchrow_array) {
    $grid->insert('end', @columns);
}
```

The following listing contains the source code for the sample program, dbigrid .pl. Figure 12.4 shows the program in action.

```perl
#!/usr/bin/perl -w

use strict;

# Import the modules we need.
#
use DBI;
use Tk;
use Tk::Columns;
use Tk::BrowseEntry;

# Exempt the $grid variable from the restrictions
# imposed by 'use strict'. In other words, make it
# a global variable.
#
use vars qw($grid);

# Create a top-level window.
#
my $main = Tk::MainWindow->new();

# Create a frame to hold the connection information.
#
my $dbi_frame = $main->Frame();
$dbi_frame->pack();

# Get a list of all known data sources, and store
# the first one in $dsn.
#
my @data_sources = get_data_sources();
my $dsn = $data_sources[0];

# Add a combo box to choose the connection string.
# The user may type one in, or choose from one of
# the data sources.
#
$dbi_frame->BrowseEntry( -width => 32,
                         -variable => \$dsn,
```

```
                              -label => 'Connection String: ',
                              -choices => \@data_sources
                          )->pack( -side => 'left' );

# Add a field for the user name.
#
my $user = $ENV{USER}; # default to current user

$dbi_frame->Label( -text => 'User: ')->pack( -side => 'left' );
$dbi_frame->Entry(-width => 8,
                   -textvariable => \$user
                  )->pack( -side => 'left');

# Add a field for the password.
#
my $pass;
$dbi_frame->Label( -text => 'Password: ')->pack( -side => 'left' );
$dbi_frame->Entry( -width => 8,
                   -textvariable => \$pass,
                   -show => '*'
                  )->pack( -side => 'left');

# Add a frame for the SQL statement and execute
# button.
#
my $sql_frame = $main->Frame();
$sql_frame->pack();
# Add a field for the SQL statement.
#
my $sql = "SELECT * FROM "; # sensible default

$sql_frame->Label(
    -text => 'SQL: ')->pack( -side => 'left' );
$sql_frame->Entry( -width => 50,
                   -textvariable => \$sql
                  )->pack(-side=>'left');

# Add a button to execute the SQL.
#
$sql_frame->Button(
    -text    => 'Execute',
    -command => sub { exec_sql($dsn, $user, $pass, $sql) }
  )->pack( -side => 'right');

# Start the main event loop.
#
MainLoop();

# Execute the SQL statement and put the results into
# a grid using Tk::Columns.
#
```

```perl
sub exec_sql {

    # Get the arguments that were passed to this
    # routine.
    #
    my $dsn = shift;
    my $user= shift;
    my $pass = shift;
    my $sql= shift;


    # If the global variable $grid refers to a
    # Tk::Columns object, destroy it before
    # creating the new grid.
    #
    if (ref $grid eq 'Tk::Columns') {
        $grid->destroy;
    }

    # Try to connect to the database. If the connection
    # fails, print a message and give the user a chance
    # to try again.
    #
    my $dbh = DBI->connect($dsn, $user, $pass);
    if (!defined($dbh)) {
        print "SQL Error: $DBI::errstr\n";
        print "Check your connection string.\n";
        return;
    }

    # Try to execute the SQL statement. If it fails,
    # print the error message and give the user a
    # chance to try again.
    #
    my $sth = $dbh->prepare($sql);
    if (!defined($sth) or !$sth->execute()) {
        print "SQL Error: $DBI::errstr\n";
        print "Check your SQL.\n";
        return;
    }


    # Get the list of columns, and create a Tk::Column
    # object with those columns as headers.
    #
    my $cols = $sth->{NAME};
    $grid = $main->Columns( -columnlabels => $cols );
    $grid->pack(-expand => 'true',
                -fill => 'both' );
```

```perl
        # Add each row to the Tk::Columns object.
        #
        while (my @columns = $sth->fetchrow_array) {
            $grid->insert('end', @columns);
        }

        # Close the statement and database handles.
        #
        $sth->finish;
        $dbh->disconnect;
}


# Return an array containing all the data sources
# that DBI knows about.
#
sub get_data_sources {

    # Get a list of all drivers.
    #
    my @driver_names = DBI->available_drivers;

    # Check each driver for available data sources.
    #
    my @data_sources;
    foreach my $driver (@driver_names) {
        push @data_sources, DBI->data_sources($driver);
    }
    return @data_sources;

}
```

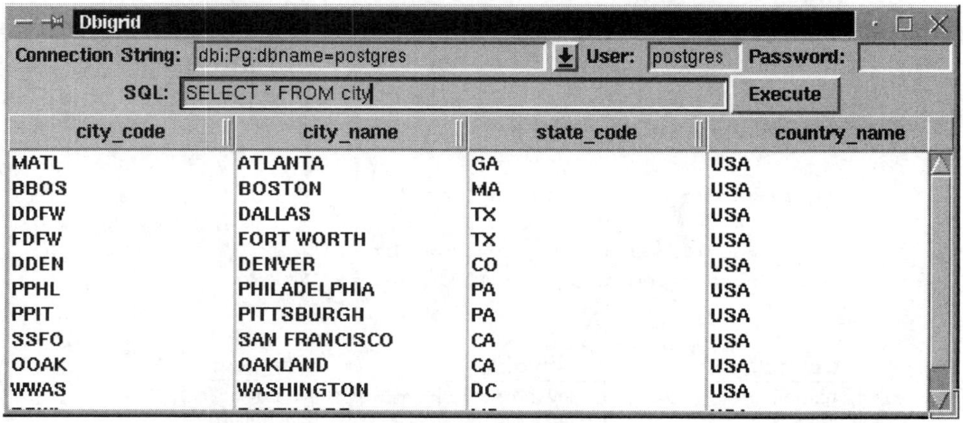

city_code	city_name	state_code	country_name
MATL	ATLANTA	GA	USA
BBOS	BOSTON	MA	USA
DDFW	DALLAS	TX	USA
FDFW	FORT WORTH	TX	USA
DDEN	DENVER	CO	USA
PPHL	PHILADELPHIA	PA	USA
PPIT	PITTSBURGH	PA	USA
SSFO	SAN FRANCISCO	CA	USA
OOAK	OAKLAND	CA	USA
WWAS	WASHINGTON	DC	USA

Figure 12.4 The dbigrid.pl application with some data.

To run this example, simply change to the directory containing the Chapter 12 examples. Then, run the command *perl dbigrid.pl*.

Displaying Hierarchical Data

A hierarchical display, such as the tree display used in many file system explorers, is a visual tool that involves the user and expresses the relationships between data. There are many circumstances in which a tree display can make the ideas in your applications clearer.

For example, if you have many tables with cascading relationships, such as you might find in customer->invoice->line item tables, the tree view provides an excellent way to explore this data. Consider such a relationship, shown in Figure 12.5.

We can use the Tk::Tree module to make this happen. To use Tk::Tree, you should create a scrollable tree (see Tk::Scrolled, in the earlier section *Some Widgets*). Tk::Tree assembles the hierarchy by looking at raw node strings that are similar to directory listings.

For example, "food" could be a top-level item, while "food/meat" is a child node of food. Similarly, "food/bread/sticks" is a child node of "food/bread". When you create the Tk::Tree object, you should specify the separator to use, and any options, such as -scrollbars, -height, and -width:

```
my $tree = $top->Scrolled( 'Tree',
                           -separator  => '/',
                           -scrollbars => 'se',
                           -height => 20,
                           -width  => 30);
```

After you create the tree, you should pack it, and then you can add nodes to it using the add() method. You should supply the raw node string, as shown in the preceding code, as well as a label by using the -text attribute, since the node strings aren't user friendly:

```
$tree->add("food", -text => "Food");

$tree->add("food/dairy",-text => "Dairy");
$tree->add("food/dairy/milk",  -text => "Milk");
```

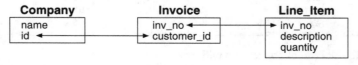

Figure 12.5 The invoice schema.

After you add the nodes, call the autosetmode() method to add collapse and expand controls (+ and – buttons, as shown in Figure 12.6).

Before you call autosetmode(), you can use the hide() method to hide nodes. These nodes will appear if the user clicks + to expand the parent node. The hide() method takes an option parameter, which is the type of node to hide (currently only "entry" is supported), and the raw node path:

```perl
$tree->hide('entry', "food/fruit/citrus");
```

Here is a complete example (tree.pl) that displays a food tree, as shown in Figure 12.6:

```perl
#!/usr/bin/perl -w

use strict;

# Import modules.
#
use Tk;
use Tk::Tree;

# Create a new main window.
#
my $top = new MainWindow( -title  => "Tree" );

# Create a scrollable Tree widget.
#
my $tree = $top->Scrolled( 'Tree',
                           -separator  => '/',
                           -scrollbars => 'se',
                           -height => 20,
                           -width  => 30);
$tree->pack();

# Fill the tree with information.
#
$tree->add("food", -text => "Food");

$tree->add("food/dairy",-text => "Dairy");
$tree->add("food/dairy/milk",  -text => "Milk");
$tree->add("food/dairy/cheese",-text => "Cheese");
$tree->add("food/dairy/yogurt",-text => "Yogurt");

$tree->add("food/meat",  -text => "Meat");
$tree->add("food/meat/pork",    -text => "Pork");
$tree->add("food/meat/beef",    -text => "Beef");
$tree->add("food/meat/poultry",-text => "Poultry");
```

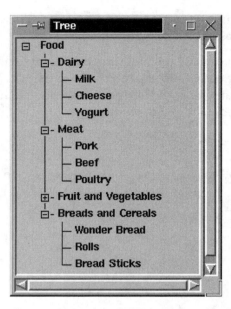

Figure 12.6   The oft-forgotten four food groups.

```
$tree->add("food/fruit", -text => "Fruit and Vegetables");
$tree->add("food/fruit/berries", -text => "Berries");
$tree->add("food/fruit/ketchup", -text => "Ketchup");
$tree->add("food/fruit/citrus",  -text => "Citrus");

# Collapse these entries by default:
#
$tree->hide('entry', "food/fruit/citrus");
$tree->hide('entry', "food/fruit/ketchup");
$tree->hide('entry', "food/fruit/berries");

$tree->add("food/breads",-text => "Breads and Cereals");
$tree->add("food/breads/wonder",-text => "Wonder Bread");
$tree->add("food/breads/rolls", -text => "Rolls");
$tree->add("food/breads/sticks",-text => "Bread Sticks");

$tree->autosetmode(); # Add collapse/expand controls.


MainLoop();
```

To run this example, simply change to the directory containing the Chapter 12 examples. Then, run the command *perl tree.pl.*

Now, how can you turn the invoice schema into a tree view? The technique is not substantially different from what we said with the food tree. With the related tables from the invoice schema, we'll create a level for each table, as shown in this description of the basic algorithm:

```
For each company:
    Add a node to the tree labeled with the company name.
    For each invoice for that company:
        Add a node labeled with the invoice number.
        For each line item of that invoice:
            Add a node labeled with the line item detail.
```

For maximum portability, it's best to avoid opening multiple statements at the same time. Because of this, we are going to finish each statement before we issue the next. This more detailed explanation of the algorithm is shown here:

```
Create a statement to get all the rows from company.
Store all the results in an array (fetchall_arrayref).
Finish the statement.
For each company:

    Add a node to the tree labeled with the company name.

    Create a statement to get all the invoices for that company.
    Store all the results in an array (fetchall_arrayref).
    Finish the statement.
    For each invoice for that company:

        Add a node labeled with the invoice number.

        Create a statement to get all the line items for that invoice.
        Store all the results in an array (fetchall_arrayref).
        Finish the statement.
        For each line item of that invoice:

            Add a node labeled with the line item detail.
```

To work with Tk::Tree, we'll need to introduce some delimiters into the data. When you add a node for a company, you can use its name as the raw node id:

```
$tree->add("FrobCo", -text => "FrobCo")
```

But when you add an invoice for that company, you'll need to introduce the delimiter:

```
$tree->add("FrobCo/001-C", -text => "Invoice 001-C");
```

The same goes for a line item:

```
$tree->add("FrobCo/001-C/Widget", -text => "Widget (24)");
```

Here is a complete example (invoice_tree.pl) that expands the invoice schema into a tree, as shown in Figure 12.7:

```perl
#!/usr/bin/perl -w

use strict;

# Import modules.
#
use DBI;
use Tk;
use Tk::Tree;

# Create a new main window.
#
my $top = new MainWindow( -title  => "Invoices" );

# Create a scrollable Tree widget.
#
my $tree = $top->Scrolled( 'Tree',
                           -separator => '/',
                           -scrollbars => 'se',
                           -height => 20,
                           -width  => 30);
$tree->pack();

# Fill the tree with data.
#
add_nodes($tree);

# Set up the collapse/expand controls
#
$tree->autosetmode();

MainLoop();

# Add nodes for all the companies, invoices, and
# line items.
#
sub add_nodes {

    my $tree = shift; # tree object

    # Connect to a datasource.
    #
    my $dsn  = "dbi:mysql:dbname=bjepson_db";
    my $user = "bjepson";
    my $pass = "open_sesame";
    my $dbh = DBI->connect($dsn, $user, $pass)
        or die $DBI::errstr;
```

```perl
# First, fetch all the company names and ids.
#
my $sql = "SELECT name, id FROM company ORDER BY name";

my $sth = $dbh->prepare($sql);
if (!defined($sth) or !$sth->execute()) {
    die $DBI::errstr;
}
my $companies = $sth->fetchall_arrayref;
$sth->finish;

# Add a node for each company.
#
foreach my $company (@$companies) {

    my $name = $$company[0]; # company name
    my $id   = $$company[1]; # company id

    # Add the company node.
    $tree->add("$name",
               -text => $name);

    # Fetch all the invoices for this company.
    #
    my $sql = "SELECT inv_no
                    FROM invoice
                    WHERE company_id = $id";
    my $sth = $dbh->prepare($sql);
    if (!defined($sth) or !$sth->execute()) {
        die $DBI::errstr;
    }
    my $invoices = $sth->fetchall_arrayref;
    $sth->finish;

    # Add a node for each invoice.
    #
    foreach my $invoice (@$invoices) {
        my $inv_no = $$invoice[0];

        # Add the invoice node.
        #
        $tree->add("$name/$inv_no",
                   -text => "Invoice $inv_no");

        # Keep it hidden by default.
        $tree->hide('entry', "$name/$inv_no");

        # Now, get all the line items for this
        # invoice.
```

```
        #
        my $sql = "SELECT description, quantity
                        FROM line_item WHERE
                        inv_no = '$inv_no'";
        my $sth = $dbh->prepare($sql);
        if (!defined($sth) or !$sth->execute()) {
            die $DBI::errstr;
        }
        my $line_items = $sth->fetchall_arrayref;
        $sth->finish;

        # Add a node for each line item.
        #
        foreach my $line_item(@$line_items) {
            my $desc = $$line_item[0];
            my $qty  = $$line_item[1];
            $tree->add("$name/$inv_no/$desc",
                        -text => "$desc ($qty)");

            # Keep it hidden by default.
            $tree->hide('entry', "$name/$inv_no/$desc");
        }

    }
    }
    $dbh->disconnect;
}
```

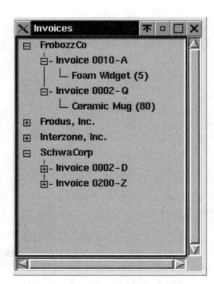

Figure 12.7 Exploring the invoice schema.

Running This Example

Before you run this example, you'll need some sample data. The following SQL statements will create the invoice schema. These can be found in the file invoice_schema.sql on the companion Web site (www.wiley.com/compbooks/jepson) in the Chapter 12 section:

```
CREATE TABLE company (
  name char(20),
  id int
);

INSERT INTO company VALUES ('SchwaCorp',1);
INSERT INTO company VALUES ('FrobozzCo',2);
INSERT INTO company VALUES ('Frodus, Inc.',3);
INSERT INTO company VALUES ('Interzone, Inc.',4);

CREATE TABLE invoice (
  inv_no char(10),
  company_id int
);

INSERT INTO invoice VALUES ('0001-C',4);
INSERT INTO invoice VALUES ('0002-D',1);
INSERT INTO invoice VALUES ('0010-A',2);
INSERT INTO invoice VALUES ('0002-Q',2);
INSERT INTO invoice VALUES ('0213-D',3);
INSERT INTO invoice VALUES ('0200-Z',1);
INSERT INTO invoice VALUES ('6124-P',4);

CREATE TABLE line_item (
  inv_no char(10),
  description char(20),
  quantity int
);

INSERT INTO line_item VALUES ('0213-D','3\' Surgical Tubing',12);
INSERT INTO line_item VALUES ('0001-C','Scalpel',5);
INSERT INTO line_item VALUES ('0002-D','Ceramic Mug',144);
INSERT INTO line_item VALUES ('0010-A','Foam Widget',5);
INSERT INTO line_item VALUES ('0002-Q','Ceramic Mug',80);
INSERT INTO line_item VALUES ('0200-Z','Bug Pillow',19);
INSERT INTO line_item VALUES ('0200-Z','Shower Radio',7);
INSERT INTO line_item VALUES ('0213-D','Rubber Gloves',93);
INSERT INTO line_item VALUES ('0002-D','Medium Flask',1200);
```

Before you run this program, you should modify the $dsn, $user, and $pass variables in the add_nodes method of invoice_tree.pl. To run the program, simply execute perl invoice_tree.pl from the shell prompt.

Object-Oriented Perl

In the next section, we'll look at the Tangram framework, which makes it easy to move objects between Perl and relational databases. Before we talk specifically about Tangram, let's look at some of the object-oriented features of Perl. Before you read this, make sure you are comfortable with object-oriented concepts (see Chapter 5, "Object-Oriented Programming").

A Class definition in Perl is stored in a *package*, which contains code that is isolated from other code. There is more to Perl's object-oriented capabilities, but packages provide a fundamental feature: isolation of data and behavior into logical groups.

Packages

If you have the package Foo, and it contains a variable called $x, that variable is different from $x that is contained within another package:

```
package Foo;
$x = 100;
package Bar;
$x = 3000;
```

By default, Perl code goes into a package called *main*. If you've included other packages definitions (such as package Foo), you can switch back into main with:

```
package main;
```

You can even create your own $x that belongs to main:

```
$x = 30;
```

If you want to refer to your $x, you don't need to do anything fancy, but if you want to refer to the other $x variables, you need to put the package name and two colons (::) between the $ and the variable name:

```
print $x, "\n";
print $Foo::x, "\n";
print $Bar::x, "\n";
```

Packages can also contain subroutines, such as:

```
package Foo;
sub test {
```

```
   print "Testing.\n";
}
```

You can execute test() from another package as:

```
Foo->test;
```

Modules

A module is a file that contains a Perl package, and has the same base name as the package it contains. For example, if the module Foo is contained in Foo.pm, you can import this module with the command:

```
use Foo;
```

You have seen this syntax in many examples in this chapter.

Classes

To create a class, you need to write a constructor method. This is responsible for creating a value that represents the object. This value must be a reference to a basic Perl data structure, such as a scalar variable, array, or hash. The hash is the most flexible, partly because you can easily store properties in it:

```
$ref = {}; # create a hash reference.

# Set the properties.
#
$ref->{name} = "Brian";
$ref->{city} = "Kingston";

# Retrieve the properties.
#
print $ref->{name}, " lives in ", $ref->{city}, "\n";
```

As with the preceding example, an object's constructor creates a reference to a hash with {}, but, as we'll see in the following code, a constructor performs an additional step: It invokes the bless function on the reference. The bless function causes the reference to remember the package that it was created in, so it can find its methods. When you invoke a constructor, Perl makes sure to pass in the name of the class as an argument, so this is also passed to bless, as shown in this constructor:

```
package OODemo;
sub new {
   my $class = shift;      # get the class name
```

```
    my $self = {};          # create a hash reference
    bless ($self, $class);  # bless the hash reference into the class
    return $self;           # return the hash reference
}
```

Notice that we use the *my* operator to ensure that the $self and $class variables are scoped within the enclosing block. This ensures that each time you invoke the constructor, you don't accidentally touch an old instance of the object—as soon as the return statement executes, Perl forgets that $self refers to an object. The only way to get it back is to call one of the object's methods. Create a method the way you would any other subroutine, but make sure that you grab the first argument and put it into a variable called $self. Even if you don't pass any other argument to the method, Perl makes sure that there is at least one argument (the object itself):

```
sub print_name {
    my $self = shift;
    my $name = $self->{name};
    print "My name is: $name\n";
}
```

To create an instance of the object, call the constructor as shown here, where we create two OODemo objects:

```
$object1 = OODemo->new();
$object2 = OODemo->new();
```

You can set a property of the object using the fact that the object is a hash reference (even though we didn't specify the *name* property in the class definition):

```
$object1->{name} = "Oscorb";
$object2->{name} = "Lotron";
```

And then, you can invoke a method:

```
$object1->print_name();
$object2->print_name();
```

This produces the following output, showing that we have two distinct instances on hand, each with different properties:

```
My name is: Oscorb
My name is: Lotron
```

We've barely scratched the surface of Perl's object-oriented capabilities, but you should now be able to recognize when these capabilities are used. For a more in-depth look at these capabilities, see the perltoot man page (run 'man perltoot' from the shell prompt), a tutorial for object-oriented Perl programming.

Tangram: Object-Relational Mapping in Perl

Tangram is a wonderful module for Perl that automatically maps your application objects to a relational database representation. It also happens to be free software. Tangram handles such features as aggregation, inheritance, polymorphism, and sophisticated retrieval facilities. You can get Tangram from CPAN (see the *CPAN* section in this chapter for instructions on installing a module from CPAN). Before you install Tangram, you may need to install the module Set::Object.

We discussed the problems of bridging objects and databases in Chapter 8, "Object-Oriented Design," in the section *Designing for a Three-Tier Architecture*. See the discussion of Figure 8.3 in Chapter 8 for an example of this problem. Also, see the section titled *Bridging Database and Objects* in Chapter 8 for more information. An object-relational mapping tool such as Tangram solves many of these problems by putting a sophisticated abstraction layer between the database and your objects.

In this section, we'll look at some of the functions you can do with Tangram, including an example that integrates Tangram and Tk. This discussion will only scratch the surface. However, Tangram includes some great documentation that explains this useful tool in more depth.

Defining a Schema and Classes

Tangram supports your efforts from start to finish. Before you can use Tangram you must tell it how your database is structured, and use the Tangram::Deploy module to create the tables and prepare the database. To define a schema, you must write a Perl module that creates a schema object. We suggest that you create this in a file that also contains class definitions, since this will keep your schema close to the classes it describes.

Let's look at the Objects.pm file, which contains a schema definition and class definitions for a simple contact database. It will support a company, employee, and job title. Objects.pm will handle the following:

Create a schema. A Tangram schema is encapsulated in the class Tangram::Schema. To define a class, you must create a nested hash that contains class definitions and pass it to Tangram::Schema's constructor. For example, this hash would define an object called Employee with a first name (fname), last name (lname), and two mysterious attributes, title and employer:

```
my $schema_def = {

    Employee => {
        fields => {
            string => [ qw(fname lname)    ],
            ref    => [ qw(title employer) ]
        }
    }
};
```

The mysterious attributes are actually references to other objects: the title is the job title, and the employer is the company the employee works for. These are defined as:

```
Company => {
    fields => {
        string => [ qw(name) ]
    }
},
Title => {
    fields => {
        string => [ qw(name) ]
    }
}
```

After we create a suitable schema definition, we feed it into the constructor for Tangram::Schema, as shown here:

```
$schema =
    Tangram::Schema->new(classes => $schema_def);
```

Export the schema. Every program that wants to work with this schema needs access to the schema object. In order to facilitate this, we add some curious matter to the Objects package declaration:

```
package Objects;
use Exporter;
@ISA = qw(Exporter);
@EXPORT_OK = qw($schema);
```

This strange code imports the Exporter module, and then inherits its capabilities by storing Exporter in the @ISA array, an array that is used internally by Perl. When you see @ISA being used this way, think Objects *is an* Exporter. Next, the @EXPORT_OK array contains all the symbols that are ok to export. Now, when we write a program that uses Objects, we need to specify an import list that includes $schema (this causes that program to pull in the $schema variable so it can use it):

```
use Objects qw($schema);
```

Define classes. So far, Tangram has taken care of creating the database side of your objects. It's up to you to create the class definitions. If your class definitions are simple enough, you can put them in the same module that contains the schema definition. Otherwise, you can organize them as you see fit. Before you start developing complicated classes in Perl, you should consult the online Perl documentation for stylistic suggestions and tips on advanced features. The Perl documentation is accessible using the perldoc command at the shell prompt.

In this example, our classes are simple enough that we can include them in the Objects.pm file. All of them will be based on a simple object called Generic, which contains nothing but a constructor (constructors are described in the earlier section *Classes*). Title and Company are both fairly dumb classes—they consist only of attributes. Employee, on the other hand, has a single method, to_string, which returns a description of the employee, including title and employer.

Here is the source code for Objects.pm. This is essentially the configuration data that our Tangram applications will use to do their job:

```perl
package Objects;
use Tangram;

# Export the Schema.
#
use Exporter;
@ISA = qw(Exporter);
@EXPORT_OK = qw($schema);

# Create the schema object. This encapsulates information
# about the tables.
#
my $schema_def = {

    Employee => {
        fields => {
            string => [ qw(fname lname)    ],
            ref    => [ qw(title employer) ]
        }
    },
    Company => {
        fields => {
            string => [ qw(name) ]
        }
    },
    Title => {
```

```
            fields => {
                string => [ qw(name) ]
            }
        }
};
$schema = Tangram::Schema->new(classes => $schema_def);

# Define Classes. All of them will be based on this
# simple class.
#
package Generic;

sub new
{
    my $class = shift;
    my $self = {};
    bless ($self, $class);
    return $self;
}

package Company;
@ISA = qw(Generic);

package Title;
@ISA = qw(Generic);

package Employee;
@ISA = qw(Generic);

# Return a description of the employee.
#
sub to_string {

    my $self = shift;

    # Get the company name, title, and employee
    # name.
    #
    my $company = $self->{employer}->{name};
    my $title   = $self->{title}->{name};
    my $name    = $self->{fname} . ' ' . $self->{lname};

    return "$name is a $title at $company.";
}

1; # modules must always return a true value, such as 1
```

Deploying the Schema

Before you can use the schema, you need to create the tables in the database. The Tangram::Deploy module does this for you, and also creates a number of other tables that tell Tangram about such things as the relationships between tables. This happens behind the scenes, so we don't need to be too concerned with how it works.

To deploy the schema:

1. Import the DBI and Tangram modules. Also, import modules that contain the schema definition and any class definitions (in our example, this is all stored in Objects.pm). Make sure you include an import list if you chose to export anything as we did with Objects.pm.
2. Connect to the database server using DBI.
3. Pass the database handle to $schema's *deploy* method.

The following example, deploy.pl, should be run once, to deploy the schema into the database:

```perl
#!/usr/bin/perl -w

use strict;

# Step One.
#
use DBI;
use Tangram;
use Tangram::Deploy;
use Objects qw($schema); # Local object definitions.

# Step Two.
#
my $dsn  = "dbi:mysql:database=contacts";
my $user = "bjepson";
my $pass = "open_sesame";
my $dbh = DBI->connect($dsn, $user, $pass);

# Step Three.
#
$schema->deploy($dbh);

$dbh->disconnect;
```

We recommend that you deploy the schema into an empty database. This avoids collisions with other database objects and minimizes overall clutter. Before you run it, make sure you change the $dsn, $user, and $pass variables accordingly. To run this example, type *perl deploy.pl* at the shell.

Creating Objects

You can create a new object and make it immediately persistent with Tangram. To accomplish this, follow these steps:

1. *Create a Tangram Storage Manager.* This object can take care of creating and retrieving objects. To create it, invoke Tangram::Storage's connect method. You don't need to create a database handle, since Tangram does this for you. Pass the schema object, connection string, user name, and password, as shown here (but change $dsn, $user, and $pass as appropriate for your system):

```
my $dsn  = "dbi:mysql:database=contacts";
my $user = "bjepson";
my $pass = "open_sesame";
my $storage =
    Tangram::Storage->connect($schema, $dsn, $user, $pass);
```

2. *Create an Instance of the Object.* Next, create an instance of the real object. This is the class you defined in Perl, and is (so far) independent of Tangram:

```
$company = new Company();
$company->{name} = "A Sample Company";
```

3. *Pass the Object to the Storage Manager's insert() Method.* The insert() method takes any kind of object as an argument. However, it looks for objects that are instances of classes that have the same name as the classes you defined in the schema object. The insert() method uses the information in the schema to figure out which attributes of the object to store in the database. It looks simple, but Tangram is really doing a lot of work for you:

```
$storage->insert($company);
```

Finding Objects

When it comes time to find objects, Tangram is very helpful. You can either retrieve all the objects (be warned, this can be memory intensive if you have a lot of objects), or retrieve a lightweight proxy object that stands in for the real objects until you retrieve them from the database.

To fetch all objects, use the storage manager's select() method, and pass in the class name. This code fetches all the employees:

```
@employees = $storage->select('Employee');
```

You can then invoke a method or fetch a property for one of these objects:

```
print $employees[0]->{lname}, "\n";
```

The storage manager's remote() method generates a stand-in for the real object that you can use to select a subset of the actual objects by using a filter. First, create a Tangram::Remote object:

```
$emp_remote = $storage->remote('Employee');
```

Next, create a filter object. The comparison operators are overloaded in such a way that the next statement puts a Tangram::Filter object in $filter. This filter will match only employees whose first name is Brian:

```
my $filter = $emp_remote->{fname} eq 'Brian';
```

Next, pass the remote object and the filter to the select() method to get the real objects:

```
my @employees = $storage->select($emp_remote, $filter);
```

Putting It All Together

The next listing, new_employee.pl, brings together all the techniques we described earlier. This is a Perl/Tk application that uses Tangram and the DBI to let the user create new employees. We use BrowseEntry components to let the user select existing titles and companies. Since the BrowseEntry also allows the user to freely type text into it, the user can specify companies and titles that don't exist yet. When this happens, the *insert()* method detects whether the specified company or title exists, and inserts it if it doesn't.

Here is the source code for new_employee.pl, which is shown in action in Figure 12.8:

```
#!/usr/bin/perl -w

use strict;
use DBI;
```

```perl
use Tangram;
use Tk;
use Objects qw($schema);
require Tk::BrowseEntry;

# Connect to the schema.
#
my $dsn  = "dbi:mysql:database=contacts";
my $user = "bjepson";
my $pass = "open_sesame";
my $storage =
    Tangram::Storage->connect($schema, $dsn, $user, $pass);

# Create a main window.
#
my $main = Tk::MainWindow->new(-title => "New Employee");

# Add a frame for the employee's first and last name.
#
my $name_frame = $main->Frame()->pack();

# Add fields for the first and last name.
#
my $fname = '';
my $lname = '';
$name_frame->Label( -text => 'Name:' )->pack(-side=>'left');
$name_frame->Entry( -width => 20,
                    -textvariable => \$fname
                  )->pack(-side => 'left');
$name_frame->Entry( -width => 20,
                    -textvariable => \$lname
                  )->pack(-side => 'left');

# Find all the company objects.
#
my @companies = $storage->select('Company');

# Use map() to extract the name from each company.
#
my @company_names = map { $_->{name} } @companies;

# Create a combo box for the companies.
#
my $company_name = '';
$main->BrowseEntry( -width => 30,
                    -variable => \$company_name,
                    -label => 'Choose Company:',
                    -choices => \@company_names
                  )->pack();
```

```perl
    # Find all the title objects.
    #
    my @titles = $storage->select('Title');

    # Use map() to extract the name from each title.
    #
    my @title_names = map { $_->{name} } @titles;

    # Create a combo box for the job titles.
    #
    my $title_name = '';
    $main->BrowseEntry( -width => 30,
                        -variable => \$title_name,
                        -label => 'Choose Title:',
                        -choices => \@title_names
                      )->pack();

    # Create a frame to hold an OK and Cancel button.
    #
    my $btn_frame = $main->Frame()->pack();

    # Create the OK and Cancel buttons.
    #
    $btn_frame->Button( -text => 'OK',
                        -command => sub { insert() }
                      )->pack( -side => 'left' );

    $btn_frame->Button( -text => 'Cancel',
                        -command => sub { $main->destroy }
                      )->pack( -side => 'right' );

    MainLoop(); # start the event loop.

    # Insert a new employee, and create the company and title
    # if they do not already exist.
    #
    # Refers to $fname, $lname, $company_name, and $title_name
    # that are defined above.
    #
    sub insert {

        my $company;  # the company object
        my $title;     # the title object

        # Use a filter to search for the selected company.
        #
        my $remote = $storage->remote('Company');
        my $filter = $remote->{name} eq $company_name;
        my @companies = $storage->select($remote, $filter);
```

```perl
        # If the company doesn't exist, create and insert it.
        #
        if (@companies == 0) {
            $company = new Company();
            $company->{name} = $company_name;
            $storage->insert($company);
            print "$company_name not found. Creating new company.\n";
        } else {

            # If it does exist, point $company at the object.
            #
            $company = $companies[0];
        }

        # Use a filter to search for the selected title.
        #
        $remote = $storage->remote('Title');
        $filter = $remote->{name} eq $title_name;
        my @titles = $storage->select($remote, $filter);

        # If the title doesn't exist, create and insert it.
        #
        if (@titles == 0) {
            $title = new Title();
            $title->{name} = $title_name;
            $storage->insert($title);
            print "$title_name not found. Creating new title.\n";
        } else {

            # If it does exist, point $title at the object.
            #
            $title = $titles[0];
        }

        # Finally, create the employee.
        #
        my $employee = new Employee();
        $employee->{fname} = $fname;
        $employee->{lname} = $lname;
        $employee->{title} = $title;
        $employee->{employer} = $company;
        $storage->insert($employee);

        $main->destroy; # close the main window.
    }
```

To run this example, simply change to the directory containing the Chapter 12 examples. Then, run the command *perl new_employee.pl*. You will need to change the $dsn, $user, and $pass variables for your system.

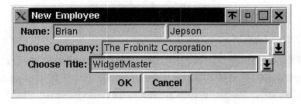

Figure 12.8 Adding a new employee.

Here is a short program (list.pl) that describes all the employees (you should run this after you've used new_employee.pl a few times):

```perl
#!/usr/bin/perl -w
use strict;
use DBI;
use Tangram;
use Objects qw($schema);

# Connect to the schema.
#
my $dsn  = "dbi:mysql:database=contacts";
my $user = "bjepson";
my $pass = "open_sesame";
my $storage =
    Tangram::Storage->connect($schema, $dsn, $user, $pass);

# Find all the employee objects.
#
my @employees = $storage->select('Employee');

# Identify each employee.
#
foreach my $emp (@employees) {
    print $emp->to_string(), "\n";
}
```

To run this example, simply change to the directory containing the Chapter 12 examples. Then, run the command *perl list.pl*. You will need to change the $dsn, $user, and $pass variables for your system.

Here is some sample output from list.pl:

```
Brian Jepson is a CEO at A Sample Company.
Raoul Frodus is a Director of Medical Research at FrodusCorp.
Oscar daCat is a Figurehead at Oscorb International.
Lotus daDog is a CEO at Oscorb International.
Lotron Megascorb is a Figurehead at FrodusCorp.
```

Summary

In this chapter, we looked at many different things you can do with Perl, from building user interfaces to working with object-relation mapping. Perl is a deep and rich language, and there is lots more you can do with it. In order to get the most out of it, you should take the time to learn it further. Explore the documentation that comes with Perl; the perldoc command can be run from the shell, and will get you started (try the command *perldoc perl* for an index of all the Perl documentation). As you learn more about Perl, you'll be able to build more interesting software.

GNOME

G NOME (the GNU Network Object Model Environment) is an ongoing project that aims to create a complete user environment for Unix and Unix-like systems. The term "user environment" is a little vague. To clarify, GNOME is not a windowing environment (instead, it uses the X Window System); it is not a window manager (GNOME cooperates with several window managers). Instead, the GNOME user environment consists of:

Applications. GNOME includes a variety of software applications, from complex applications such as personal information managers, spreadsheets and word processors, to simple applications such as address books, diversions, and multimedia utilities.

Application framework. This part of GNOME is of most interest to us. The application framework includes the libraries, documentation, and utilities that you'll use to build graphically rich applications that rely on features of the GNOME environment. Some of the GNOME libraries include Gnorba, a wrapper around CORBA; GTK+, a widget set and event-driven GUI application development kit; and GLIB, a library that includes support for data structures such as hashes and linked lists.

Session management. GNOME session management helps applications remember what state they were in when you log out. The next time you log in, the applications restores the desktop and applications. Web browsers can remember what document you were browsing, and your word processor can open the document you were editing and position the insertion point where you left off.

Desktop environment. The GNOME file manager resembles file managers found in other operating systems (such as the Macintosh Finder and Windows Explorer). It not only lets you browse files on your computer, but supports a variety of other file systems (including tar files and FTP sites). It also supports a document-centric user interface model by launching the corresponding application when you double-click on a document.

Figure 13.1 shows a screenshot of a GNOME desktop, with the Gnumeric spreadsheet and the GNOME calendar applications running.

Getting GNOME

Most current Linux distributions include a stable release of GNOME. The unstable (bleeding-edge) Debian distributions give you a good way of keeping up with the leading-edge GNOME releases. Also, Helix Code (www.helixcode.com) offers a GNOME distribution that works with many flavors of Linux.

Under RedHat (and RedHat-based systems, such as Mandrake Linux), you can select GNOME RPMs during initial installation, or install the gnome-*rpm files directly from the CD-ROM using the rpm utility. Under Debian, use the dselect program to install the GNOME packages you are interested in. RedHat Linux makes new releases available at ftp://updates.redhat.com, and new Debian packages appear when you run Update from within the dselect program.

For other distributions of Linux, consult the documentation that came with the distribution.

You can also get the latest version of GNOME by visiting www.gnome.org. At this site, you can find various binary releases of GNOME, as well as complete source code.

Keeping Up with the Developers

Although not for the faint of heart (or those wishing for a stable system), nothing is more exhilarating than tracking the development versions yourself. The best way to keep up with the latest developments is to learn about current developments, get the source, and compile it. To do this, you can follow these steps:

Subscribe to mailing lists. Before you download or compile the source code, monitor some of the core mailing lists for a while. There is a list of mailing lists at www.gnome.org. You can either subscribe to the lists or use the Web page to read recent postings. If you are planning to build GNOME from source, you probably want to read gnome-devel-list to figure out what the current trends in GNOME development are.

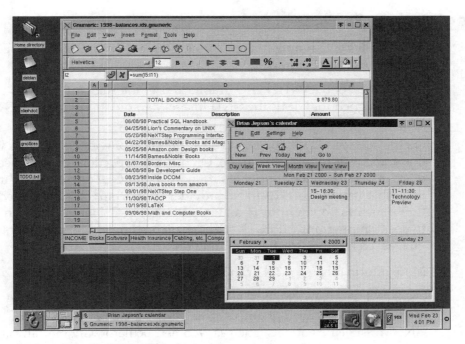

Figure 13.1   The GNOME desktop.

Read the Gnotices. Current news on GNOME can be found at http://news
.gnome.org/gnome-news/.

Use CVS. Like many open source projects, GNOME uses CVS to allow many
users to collaborate on the same source code. You can find instructions on
getting GNOME out of CVS in the GNOME FAQ (www.gnome.org/
gnomefaq/).

Compile, compile, compile. Follow the instructions in the GNOME FAQ to
keep your local copy of the CVS archive up to date, and recompile the
source code as often as you like.

The GNOME Application Framework

As someone who wants to develop an application for GNOME, you'll be
most interested in the application framework. Let's look at the parts of the
GNOME application framework that are most important to a database application developer. The assumption in this chapter is that a database application developer wants to develop a user interface, create application objects,
and have those objects interact with a database. While there are a variety of
other ways you can deal with the database, if you are interested in GNOME,
you are interested in developing a desktop application.

User Interface Services

GNOME relies on a number of libraries to support the user interface. Let's look at some of these libraries.

GTK+. Gimp Toolkit (GTK+) is a graphical user interface kit that was originally designed for GIMP, the GNU Image Manipulation Program. GTK+ is also the cornerstone of the GNOME user interface.

On the surface, GTK+ appears to be a collection of widgets (such as windows and user interface controls). On further inspection, you will see that it is a generalized object-oriented framework for GUI development in C and other languages. GTK+ also provides support for object-oriented features (such as polymorphism and inheritance) in C. Finally, you don't have to use C to program with GTK+. There are bindings for many other languages, including C++, Python, and Perl.

More information on GTK+ can be found at www.gtk.org.

libgnomeui. The core GNOME libraries (a package called gnome-libs) include a library called gnomeui. This library includes a number of GNOME-specific widgets (such as GnomeCalculator, GnomeCanvas, and GnomeEntry), utility functions for working with those widgets, and a top-level application container called GnomeApp.

libglade. This library works with the Glade user interface builder to separate the presentation of the user interface from the core application logic that backs it. libglade loads the user interface definitions at run-time, using an XML-based format to represent user interface elements. You can either edit these files by hand or use Glade to design the user interface. Since libglade loads the user interface definition at run-time, you can customize the user interface *without recompiling your application*.

Distributed Object Services

GNOME also has a number of CORBA-based features you can use to develop distributed objects or access objects that others have written.

ORBit. ORBit is the CORBA 2.2-compliant ORB that was developed for GNOME. A more complete description of ORBit (and CORBA in general) can be found in Chapter 15, "Introduction to CORBA."

GNORBA. This library is responsible for making CORBA easy to use from GNOME. It takes care of locating and activating the service that acts as a CORBA object directory (GOAD), integrating ORBit with the GTK+ event loop, and initializing GNOME applications that use CORBA.

GOAD. GOAD is the GNOME Object Activation Directory, a CORBA server that manages a master list of all CORBA services on your computer, and activates them on demand. With GOAD, you can get a list of services, activate a service by name, or register a newly created service with the GOAD server.

Data Access Services

GNOME-DB is a database application framework for GNOME. It takes care of managing connections to databases and offers a collection of widgets that are data-aware (you can, for instance, create a pop-up menu that gets its options from a database query). We'll look at GNOME-DB in detail later in this chapter.

GNOME Programming

While it is true that much of GNOME is written in C and most of the API is exposed through C bindings, you don't have to use C to write GNOME applications. Other languages, such as C++, Python, and Perl, enjoy a varying degree of support in GNOME. Perl may be the best-supported language (after C): Perl modules exist for GTK+, Glade, and much of the GNOME API (including ORBit and GOAD). C++ and Python can work with the GNOME and GTK+ API, but at the time of this writing, neither of them have specific support for GOAD (although there are Python bindings for ORBit, and GOAD support is probably not far off).

In this section, we're going to start with a simple introduction to GTK+, and then work our way to some of the more interesting and useful parts of GNOME. Although alternatives to C exist for GNOME developers, we're going to look exclusively at C in this chapter. You'll be surprised how GTK+ and GNOME conspire together to make the sometimes tedious C language a little easier to deal with!

Using GTK+

If you've used GUI toolkits such as Tk or Java's AWT, you will probably be comfortable with GTK+, at least once you get over the shock of an object-oriented framework for C. Even if you haven't worked with similar toolkits, you should find GTK+ easy to learn.

With GTK+, it's easy to put a window on the screen and fill it with widgets. It's a little trickier to define how your application should behave when someone does something to a widget (such as closing a window or clicking a button). These behaviors are defined through signal handlers, which are functions that you define in your program (you will also see these handlers referred to as *callbacks*). After you define a signal handler, you use a GTK+ function to connect the signal handler to a widget. The effect of this is to give the widget a pointer to the function. When the widget detects an action, such as a button press, it invokes the signal handler function.

There are some basic things you need to do to write a single-screen GTK+ application (the line numbers after some list items correspond to the listing that follows):

1. Sketch out the design of your screen on a napkin or the back of an envelope. After we look at the Glade user interface builder, the napkin will become unnecessary.

2. Write a C program that includes the gtk/gtk.h include file. This include file pulls in all the GTK+ include files you could possibly need—it's one-stop shopping. [line 1]

3. Decide how you want the screen's widgets to react to user input. Define signal handlers for certain types of actions (such as clicking a button, closing a window, or selecting something from a menu). For now, we'll just write the function prototype for a signal handler and write the body of the signal handler in a later step. [lines 3–6]

4. Initialize GTK+ by calling gtk_init with argc (the count of command-line arguments) and argv (an array containing all command-line arguments). This enables GTK+ to look for command-line options that affect its behavior. [line 14]

5. Create a top-level container, such as a window. In this example, we create a GtkWindow using gtk_window_new with the GTK_WINDOW _TOPLEVEL argument (this tells GTK+ to create a window that is the top-level window of its application). After we create the window, we set its title with gtk_window_set_title. [lines 17–18]

6. Add some widgets to the window. In this example, we use gtk_label_new to create a text label containing the string "Hello, World." Then, we use gtk _container_add to add the label to the window. The GTK_CONTAINER() macro casts the window to a GTK+ container object (this is one example of how GTK+ fakes polymorphism: one of GtkWindow's parent classes is GtkContainer). [lines 21–22]

7. Connect the widgets to the corresponding signal handlers. In this example, we connect the window to the window_closed function, which handles a user request to close the window (such an event can be initiated by clicking on the window close control). [lines 25–28]

8. Show the window and its widgets with gtk_widget_show_all(). [line 31]

9. Start the GTK+ event loop with gtk_main(). During this event loop, the execution of the program stops on this line. However, if an event is trig-

gered, the event's signal handler is invoked (after which control returns to the main loop). [line 34]

10. Next, we'll write the functions for the signal handler. In this example, when someone closes the window, it calls the gtk_main_quit() function, which shuts down the loop we started on line 34. Execution continues after the call to gtk_main(). The return FALSE statement is a signal to the GTK+ system that it's OK to remove the window (if we returned TRUE, the window would remain on-screen). [lines 42–52]

Here is the source code for gtk_hello.c:

```
1   #include <gtk/gtk.h>
2
3   /* Function prototype for signal handler */
4   static gint window_closed(GtkWidget*   w,
5                             GdkEventAny* e,
6                             gpointer     data);
7
8   int main(int argc, char* argv[]) {
9
10      GtkWidget* window;   /* a Window */
11      GtkWidget* label;    /* a label  */
12
13      /* Initialize GTK+ */
14      gtk_init(&argc, &argv);
15
16      /* Create the window  */
17      window = gtk_window_new(GTK_WINDOW_TOPLEVEL);
18      gtk_window_set_title(GTK_WINDOW(window), "Hello App");
19
20      /* Add some text */
21      label = gtk_label_new("Hello, World.");
22      gtk_container_add(GTK_CONTAINER(window), label);
23
24      /* Set up the event handler */
25      gtk_signal_connect(GTK_OBJECT(window),
26                          "delete_event",
27                          GTK_SIGNAL_FUNC(window_closed),
28                          NULL);
29
30      /* Show the window and its widget */
31      gtk_widget_show_all(window);
32
33      /* Initiate the event loop */
34      gtk_main();
35
36      /* exit the program */
37      return 0;
38
```

```
39  }
40
41  /* Event handler for window closed */
42  static gint window_closed(GtkWidget*   w,
43                            GdkEventAny* e,
44                            gpointer data)
45  {
46
47      /* Terminate the event loop, then tell
48       * GTK+ it's OK to delete the window
49       */
50      gtk_main_quit();
51      return FALSE;
52  }
```

Compiling and Running the GTK+ Example

It's very easy to compile the GTK+ example. The gtk-config utility can help you set the C and linker flags using the --cflags and --libs options. Here are the contents of a Makefile that can compile the example program:

```
gtk_hello: gtk_hello.c
    $(CC) $(CFLAGS) `gtk-config --cflags` \
    -o $@ $< `gtk-config --libs`
```

Use the cd command to change to the gtk_hello subdirectory under the ch13 example directory (you can get the example programs at this book's companion Web site at www.wiley.com/compbooks/jepson). Then, run the make utility and run the gtk_hello program that gets created:

```
bash-2.03$ cd ch13/gtk_hello/
bash-2.03$ make
cc `gtk-config --cflags` \
-o gtk_hello gtk_hello.c `gtk-config --libs`
bash-2.03$ ./gtk_hello
```

Figure 13.2 shows this example in action.

Figure 13.2   GTK+ says "Hello, world."

GTK+ versus OO Toolkits

Feature for feature, GTK+ compares very well with object-oriented graphical toolkits like Java's AWT. But how does it differ? Let's take a quick look:

Use macros for explicit casts. In an object-oriented language, such as Java, polymorphism is handled automatically. For example, the java.awt.Frame class (a top-level window class in Java's AWT) is a subclass of the java.awt.Container class (which can contain other objects). If you have a Frame called myFrame, you can invoke Container's add() method with:

```
myFrame.add(myWidget);
```

and Java traverses the inheritance tree to find the add() method in java.awt.Container. GTK+, on the other hand, can't do this, because C does not support OO constructs such as polymorphism. Instead, you need to convert a GtkWindow object to a GtkContainer object with the GTK _CONTAINER macro (this is essentially an *explicit cast*):

```
GTK_CONTAINER(window);
```

GTK+ supplies similar macros for all widgets and objects in the hierarchy.

No object methods. C does not support encapsulating behavior within objects, so you can't invoke a window.add() method. Instead, you need to call a function (gtk_container_add) that takes a container and a widget as an argument:

```
gtk_container_add(GTK_CONTAINER(window), label);
```

Namespaces. C does not support the notion of namespaces. For example, in a language like Perl, you might create a new Window with:

```
$window = new Gtk::Window();
```

In C, however, you must say:

```
window = gtk_window_new();
```

In Perl, the :: functioned as a qualifier that separates namespaces: the new() method resides in the Window namespace, which resides in the Gtk namespace. In C, the _ replaces the ::, and separates identifiers—there is no implication that a method called new() exists in a separate package. All identifiers live in the same namespace, and the gtk_window component of the name is an attempt to ensure that the function name is completely unique.

GTK+ Widgets

There are many widgets in GTK+ that you can choose from: buttons, text areas, and windows. Figure 13.3 shows just a few of these widgets, as well as their parent classes in the inheritance tree.

Developing User Interfaces with Glade

Glade is a user interface builder for GTK+ and GNOME. Glade is similar to commercial GUI builders in that you select a widget from a palette, and interactively draw the screen. Figure 13.4 shows Glade in action (the screen titled *window1* is a simple window I built with Glade).

You can find Glade in many Linux distributions, or you can visit the Glade home page at http://glade.pn.org for downloads and more information.

Glade uses a simple XML file format to specify the screen layout. It's so simple that you can edit these XML files directly (although the easiest way to deal with them is through the Glade program itself). Although Glade can generate code that uses the widget definitions, the libglade library makes it very easy to use these XML screen definitions directly in your own programs. We'll look at both approaches in this chapter, and you can decide what is best for your needs when it comes time to build your own programs.

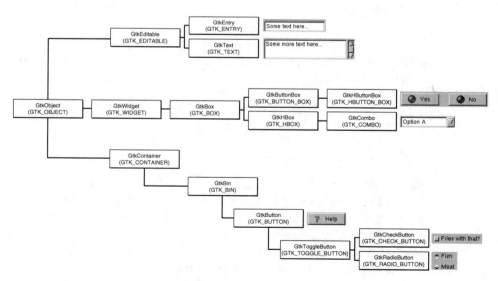

Figure 13.3   Some of the GTK+ widgets.

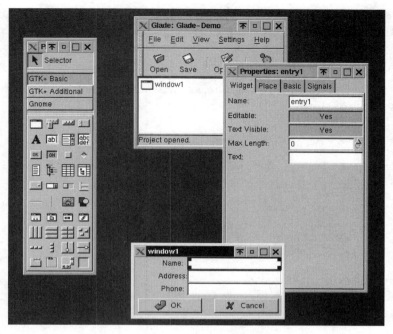

Figure 13.4 Using the Glade user interface builder.

Here are some characteristics of a .glade file:

Hierarchical organization. Every widget in a glade file is enclosed within a <widget> element. Widgets can contain other widgets, so we can have nested widgets, as in the following, which defines a label within a window:

```
<widget>
    <class>GtkWindow</class>
    <widget>
        <class>GtkLabel</class>
    </widget>
</widget>
```

Named signal handlers. You can specify signal handlers for your widgets:

```
<Signal>
    <name>delete_event</name>
    <handler>window_closed</handler>
</Signal>
```

Then, all you need to do is write the signal handlers and invoke the glade_xml_signal_autoconnect() method, as we'll see in the following example.

Exposes lots of the GTK+ API. The XML format that Glade uses supports a lot of the GTK+ API. For example, you can specify the name of an item, its label, type, and other properties. This eliminates the need for you to set these properties in your programs.

The following example, simple.glade, shows these characteristics. Here is the Glade source for simple.glade:

```
1   <?xml version="1.0"?>
2   <GTK-Interface>
3
4   <widget>
5
6     <class>GtkWindow</class>
7     <name>MainWindow</name>
8     <title>Hello App</title>
9     <type>GTK_WINDOW_TOPLEVEL</type>
10    <Signal>
11      <name>delete_event</name>
12      <handler>window_closed</handler>
13    </Signal>
14
15    <widget>
16      <class>GtkLabel</class>
17      <name>label</name>
18      <label>Hello, World</label>
19    </widget>
20
21  </widget>
22
23  </GTK-Interface>
```

Here is an explanation of what's going on in various places:

Line 1. We start out the .glade file with a directive that states the version of XML that's in use (you'll see something like this in every well-formed XML document).

Lines 2 and 23. The entire user interface is enclosed in a <GTK-Interface> element.

Lines 4, 6, and 21. The outermost widget is a GtkWindow.

Lines 7–9. That window is named MainWindow, its title is set to "Hello App," and its type is set to GTK_WINDOW_TOPLEVEL.

Lines 10–13. A signal handler is defined to react to someone closing the window.

Lines 15–19. A label is added to the window with the text "Hello, World."

As with the GTK+ application we saw earlier, there are some basic things you need to do to write an application that uses a Glade XML file (the line numbers in this list correspond to the file that follows):

1. Include the gtk/gtk.h and glade/glade.h include files. These files pull in all the other includes you'll need for the program. [lines 1–2]

2. As with the GTK+ example, define function prototypes for any signal handlers you have. [lines 4–9]

3. Define a GladeXML variable, xml, to hold the contents of the XML file. [line 13]

4. As with the GTK+ example, we call gtk_init() with argc and argv. [line 16]

5. Initialize the glade libraries by calling glade_init(). [line 19]

6. Use glade_xml_new() to read the contents of simple.glade, and store the contents in the variable xml. [line 22]

7. Next, we'll hook all the signal definitions in the simple.glade file up to the signal handlers in the program by calling glade_xml_signal_autoconnect(). In this example, it connects the window_closed signal handler to the MainWindow widget. [line 25]

8. As with the GTK+ example, we start the main loop. [line 28]

9. As with the GTK+ example, the code for the signal handlers appear at the end of the source listing. [lines 35–45]

Next, here is the source code for this example:

```
1   #include <gtk/gtk.h>
2   #include <glade/glade.h>
3
4   /* Signal handler for when the user closes
5    * the window.
6    */
7   gint window_closed(GtkWidget*   w,
8                       GdkEventAny* e,
9                       gpointer     data);
10
11  int main(int argc, char* argv[]) {
12
13      GladeXML *xml; /* an XML document */
14
15      /* Initialize GTK+ */
16      gtk_init(&argc, &argv);
17
18      /* Initialize Glade */
19      glade_init();
```

```
20
21      /* Load the UI definition from the file */
22      xml = glade_xml_new("simple.glade", NULL);
23
24      /* Connect the signals that are defined in the file */
25      glade_xml_signal_autoconnect(xml);
26
27      /* Enter the main GTK+ loop */
28      gtk_main();
29
30      /* Exit the application */
31      return 0;
32
33  }
34
35  /* Event handler for window closed */
36  gint window_closed(GtkWidget*   w,
37                     GdkEventAny* e,
38                     gpointer data)
39  {
40      /* Terminate the event loop, then tell
41       * GTK+ it's OK to delete the window
42       */
43      gtk_main_quit();
44      return FALSE;
45  }
```

This code produces a window that is identical to the one shown earlier in Figure 13.2. The code is different from the GTK+ example, but the application is more extensible. By separating the layout from the behavior, it's possible to customize this program without having to recompile.

Glade Tutorial

This tutorial introduces the use of the Glade user interface builder. There are three steps that we'll look at: Build the User Interface, Generate the Source Code, and Compile and Run the Application.

Stage One: Build the User Interface

First, let's build the interface with Glade. This will create an XML file that contains all the widgets we define. Here are the steps needed to build our sample user interface:

1. *Run Glade*. Start the X Window System, open a shell, and then execute the command *glade*. A blank project should appear as shown in Figure 13.5.

Figure 13.5 A blank project in the Glade user interface builder.

2. *Create a window.* Select the Palette window and click the Window widget (if you hover your mouse over each widget, a tooltip appears with the name of the widget). An empty window appears, as shown in Figure 13.6.

3. *Name and label the window.* Select the Window object and locate the Properties window. On the Widget tab, change the Name (the name of the widget for programming purposes) to read MainWindow, and the Title (the window title that the end user sees) to read "Glade Demo", as shown in Figure 13.7.

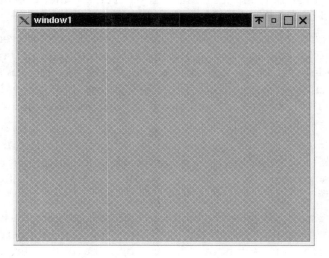

Figure 13.6 An empty window in Glade.

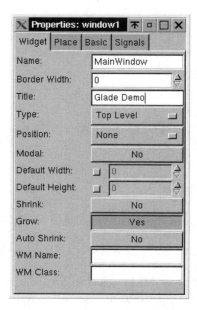

Figure 13.7 Setting the window's name and title.

4. *Add a signal handler to the window.* Select the Window object and locate the Properties window. On the tab labeled Signals, select the "..." button next to the Signal field. The Select Signal dialog appears. Scroll down to Gtk-Widget Signals and choose delete_event, then click OK. This creates a reference to a default signal handler name that we'll create later (see Figure 13.8). Click Add to add the signal handler.

5. *Partition the window into two regions.* We'll use a layout widget to create two regions: one for user input widgets, and another for buttons. From the Palette window, select the Vertical Box widget and then click in the window. Choose two rows and click OK. The window should now look as it did in Figure 13.6, except there will be a thin horizontal line in the center of the window.

6. *Add a row of buttons.* From the Palette window, select the Horizontal Button Box (not the Horizontal Box) widget and click in the lower box of the window. Choose two columns and click OK. The window should look similar to Figure 13.9.

7. *Pack the buttons snugly.* Click on the button box (the region surrounding the two buttons, not the buttons themselves) and then locate the Properties window. On the Properties window Widget tab, set Layout to "End," and Spacing to "5." On the Properties window Place tab, set Expand to "No". (See Figure 13.10.)

Figure 13.8 Adding a signal handler.

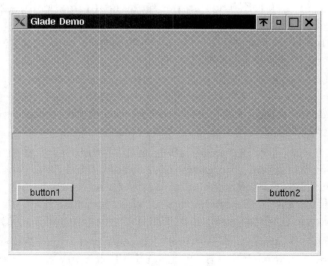

Figure 13.9 Adding a row of buttons.

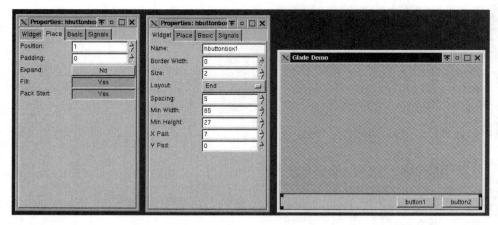

Figure 13.10   Customizing the buttons.

8. *Assign labels and names to the buttons.* Select the leftmost button, and then select the Properties window. On the Properties window Widget tab, select OK from the Stock Button pop-up menu. Then, change the Name field to ok_button. Select the rightmost button, and then select Cancel from the Stock Button pop-up menu. Change the Name field to cancel_button.

9. *Add signal handlers to each button.* Select the OK button, and then select the Signals tab of the Properties window. Click the button labeled "..." that is next to the field labeled Signal. Choose "clicked" from the GTK Button signals section and click OK. The handler name is automatically set to on_ok_button_clicked (or on_cancel_button_clicked). Click Add to add the signal handler (don't forget this step, or the signal handler won't be added). Do the same for the Cancel button.

10. *Add a table layout widget.* We'll add a table to the window so we can insert some evenly spaced fields and labels. Select the Table widget and click in the top region of the window. Choose three rows and two columns and click OK. (Figure 13.11 shows how the window is shaping up.)

11. *Add labels to each row.* Let's put some labels in the leftmost columns (these will be the prompts for some input fields). For each label, select the Label widget and then click the leftmost column of each row. Select each label and use the Widget tab of the Properties window to set each label's Label property to "Name:", "Address:", and "Phone:". (See Figure 13.12.)

12. *Add text entry fields to each row.* Next, we'll put some text entry fields in the rightmost columns. For each text field, select the Text Entry widget and click the rightmost column of each row. Select each field and use the Widget

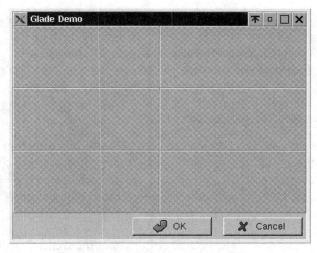

Figure 13.11 Our window, now with stock buttons and a table.

tab of the Properties window to set each text field's name property to entry-Name, entryAddress, and entryPhone. (See Figure 13.12.)

13. *Save the project.* We're almost done! Locate the main Glade window (it should be called Glade: <untitled>) and select Save from the File menu. Change the project name to GladeDemo. Before you click OK, make sure you take note of the Project Directory field; you can choose a different

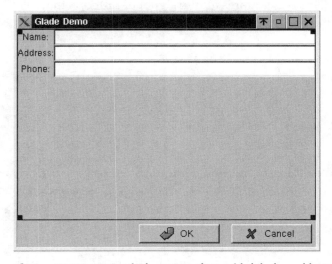

Figure 13.12 Our window, complete with labels and buttons!

directory if you'd like. On the General tab, make sure Language is set to C, then click OK to save the project.

Now we're done with the user interface, don't close Glade just yet, because we'll need it in the next stage.

Stage Two: Generate Source Code

Next, we'll generate the source code. This step creates a whole bunch of files, including files that automate the compilation of your application. After we generate the source code, we'll edit some of the source files to add the behavior we need for this application. Here are the steps you must take to generate and edit the source code:

1. *Build source code.* To generate the source code, select the main Glade window. At this point, it should be called Glade: GladeDemo. Select Build Source Code from the File menu. In a few seconds (or less), you should see a status message that states "Source code written." You may notice that there are a lot of files in the project directory. Table 13.1 lists some of the important ones.

2. *Change working directory.* Use the *cd* command to change to the src subdirectory of the project directory (see *Save the Project* in the previous section—you should have made a note of this directory).

3. *Write the delete_event signal handler.* Next, we need to write a signal handler for the main window's delete event. Open the src/callbacks.c file in your favorite editor. This file contains all the signal definitions that we'll write. Scroll down until you find the definition of the following function:

```
gboolean
on_MainWindow_delete_event (GtkWidget       *widget,
                            GdkEvent        *event,
                            gpointer         user_data)
{

  return FALSE;
}
```

This should look similar to the signal handlers we used in previous examples. We want to exit the application when a user clicks the close control, so change it to read:

```
gboolean
on_MainWindow_delete_event (GtkWidget       *widget,
                            GdkEvent        *event,
```

Table 13.1 Files Generated by Glade

FILENAME	DESCRIPTION
AUTHORS	Information about the authors of the program. You should put your contact information in here, at least.
ChangeLog	A log of changes made over time. It's up to you to put an entry in this file whenever you make a significant change.
NEWS	Use this file to put any major changes or news items you want your users to know about.
autogen.sh	Run this file to generate a configure script (see Stage Three, *Compile and Run the Application*).
gladedemo.glade	This is the Glade XML file.
src/callbacks.c, src/callbacks.h	This is where your signal handlers go.
src/interface.c, src/interface.h	Instead of reading the .glade file at run-time, your application will load the user interface that is defined in this file. Don't edit it, though, since it is automatically generated by Glade when you change or add a widget.
src/main.c	The main program. You can edit this if you need to.
src/support.c, src/support.h	Support functions that your application will use. This includes the lookup_widget() function.

```
                                  gpointer        user_data)
  {
    gtk_main_quit();
    return FALSE;
  }
```

Don't close callbacks.c yet—we need to make two more changes.

4. *Write Cancel signal handler.* Scroll down until you find the signal handler for the Cancel button:

```
  void
  on_cancel_button_clicked (GtkButton        *button,
                            gpointer         user_data)
  {

  }
```

We want the Cancel button to quit the application, so change this code to read:

```
void
on_cancel_button_clicked (GtkButton        *button,
                          gpointer          user_data)
{
  gtk_main_quit ();
}
```

5. *Write OK signal handler.* Here's where things get a little different from our previous examples. In this signal handler, we're going to look up the text entry fields and read their current contents. To do this, we use the lookup _widget function, which is only available in applications generated with Glade (it's in the generated file support.c), it is not part of libglade. Here is the default handler:

```
void
on_ok_button_clicked                      (GtkButton        *button,
                                           gpointer          user_data)
{

}
```

Here's what you should change this code to look like (line numbers begin at the top of the function here, not the top of the program source file):

```
1   void
2   on_ok_button_clicked (GtkButton        *button,
3                         gpointer          user_data)
4   {
5
6     /* Define each widget. */
7     GtkWidget *entryName, *entryAddress, *entryPhone;
8
9     /* Define strings to hold each widget's value */
10    gchar *name, *address, *phone;
11
12    /* Look up each widget */
13    entryName    = lookup_widget (GTK_WIDGET (button),
14                                  "entryName");
15    entryAddress = lookup_widget (GTK_WIDGET (button),
16                                  "entryAddress");
17    entryPhone   = lookup_widget (GTK_WIDGET (button),
18                                  "entryPhone");
19
20    /* Fetch the value of each widget */
21    name    = gtk_entry_get_text (GTK_ENTRY (entryName));
22    address = gtk_entry_get_text (GTK_ENTRY (entryAddress));
23    phone   = gtk_entry_get_text (GTK_ENTRY (entryPhone));
24
```

```
25    /* Print the name, address, and phone number */
26    g_print("Name: %s\n",    name);
27    g_print("Address: %s\n", address);
28    g_print("Phone: %s\n",   phone);
29
30    /* Exit the application */
31    gtk_main_quit();
32
33  }
```

Let's look at what this code does, step by step:

Line 7. Define local variables to hold references to the name, address, and phone number widgets.

Line 10. Define strings that we'll store the current text of those widgets in.

Lines 12–18. Because we don't have any global references to the name, address, or phone number widgets, we need some way of locating them. Glade provides a lookup_widget() method that is very useful. Simply pass it any widget on the form, and the name of the widget you are interested in, and it will find that widget for you. Because we're in the event handler for the OK button, we get a reference to that widget in the pointer *button*. So, to find entryName, entryAddress, or entryPhone, we just pass button and the name of each widget to lookup_widget(), and it returns the widget we want.

Lines 21–23. Next, we use the gtk_entry_get_text() method to get the current string that each widget holds. Note that we cast each widget using the GTK_ENTRY macro, because that method needs a GtkEntry object as an argument, and each widget is currently represented as a GtkWidget object. Again, this is one of the macros that helps GTK+ implement polymorphism.

Lines 26–28. Now, we simply use glib's g_print function to print out the current value of the name, address, and phone number. If this were a database application, we might store those values in a database table.

Line 31. We're all done here, so we call gtk_main_quit(), which terminates the GTK+ event loop.

6. *Review callback.c.* Here is a complete listing for callback.c, after all our changes:

```
#ifdef HAVE_CONFIG_H
#  include <config.h>
#endif

#include <gnome.h>

#include "callbacks.h"
```

```c
#include "interface.h"
#include "support.h"

void
on_ok_button_clicked (GtkButton       *button,
                      gpointer        user_data)
{

  /* Define each widget. */
  GtkWidget *entryName, *entryAddress, *entryPhone;

  /* Define strings to hold each widget's value */
  gchar *name, *address, *phone;

  /* Look up each widget */
  entryName    = lookup_widget(GTK_WIDGET(button),
                                "entryName");
  entryAddress = lookup_widget(GTK_WIDGET(button),
                                "entryAddress");
  entryPhone   = lookup_widget(GTK_WIDGET(button),
                                "entryPhone");

  /* Fetch the value of each widget */
  name    = gtk_entry_get_text(GTK_ENTRY(entryName));
  address = gtk_entry_get_text(GTK_ENTRY(entryAddress));
  phone   = gtk_entry_get_text(GTK_ENTRY(entryPhone));

  /* Print the name, address, and phone number */
  g_print("Name: %s\n",    name);
  g_print("Address: %s\n", address);
  g_print("Phone: %s\n",   phone);

  /* Exit the application */
  gtk_main_quit();

}

void
on_cancel_button_clicked (GtkButton       *button,
                          gpointer        user_data)
{
  gtk_main_quit();
}

gboolean
on_MainWindow_delete_event (GtkWidget       *widget,
                            GdkEvent        *event,
                            gpointer        user_data)
{
  gtk_main_quit();
  return FALSE;
}
```

Stage Three: Compile and Run the Application

Now that we've added some behavior to the program (that is, it does something when you click a button), let's compile and run it. One of the great things about Glade is that it builds a complete set of configuration files that will make it possible to compile and your application on practically any platform that GNOME and GTK run on!

1. *Change working directory.* Use the *cd* command to change to the project directory (see *Save the Project* in Stage One—you should have made a note of this directory).

2. *Run autogen.sh.* The autogen.sh program is a utility that generates and runs a script called configure. The configure script prepares the source directory and generates Makefiles for your source code.

NOTE

In order for autogen.sh to work, you will need the following packages, which should be available under any major Linux distribution: libtool, autoconf, gettext, and automake.

To run autogen, simply type the command:

```
./autogen.sh
```

It will build and run the configure script. When this is done, you will see this message:

```
Now type `make' to compile the package.
```

3. *Compile.* To compile the package, run the make command. This will start the compilation, which may take a few minutes. When it is finished, you will see something similar to:

```
gcc  -g -O2 -Wall -Wunused -Wmissing-prototypes -Wmissing-declarations
  -o gladedemo  main.o support.o interface.o callbacks.o -rdynamic
  -L/usr/lib -L/usr/X11R6/lib -rdynamic -lgnomeui -lart_lgpl -lgdk_imlib
  -lSM -lICE -lgtk -lgdk -lgmodule -lXext -lX11 -lgnome -lgnomesupport
  -lesd -laudiofile -lm -ldb1 -lglib -ldl
make[2]: Leaving directory `/home/bjepson/Projects/LinuxDB/eg/ch13
  /gladedemo/src'
make[2]: Entering directory `/home/bjepson/Projects/LinuxDB
  /eg/ch13/gladedemo'
make[2]: Leaving directory `/home/bjepson/Projects/LinuxDB/eg/ch13
  /gladedemo'
make[1]: Leaving directory `/home/bjepson/Projects/LinuxDB/eg/ch13
  /gladedemo'
```

4. *Run the program.* To run the program, cd to the src subdirectory and run ./gladedemo. Try typing in a name, address, and phone number, as shown in Figure 13.13.

If Something Goes Wrong

If you get an unusual error message at any stage, follow the instructions in any error message you receive. If that doesn't help, look at the INSTALL file that was automatically generated by Glade. If you are still stuck, run autogen.sh again, and note carefully any error messages you see.

You may also want to compare your generated project with the one that came with the Chapter 13 source code examples.

Finally, if nothing helps, pay a visit to the Glade home page at http://glade.pn.org. Look first for any troubleshooting documentation, such as a FAQ or mailing list archives. If that still doesn't help, you should consider subscribing to a relevant mailing list or newsgroup, and posting a question with a complete description of the problem you are having.

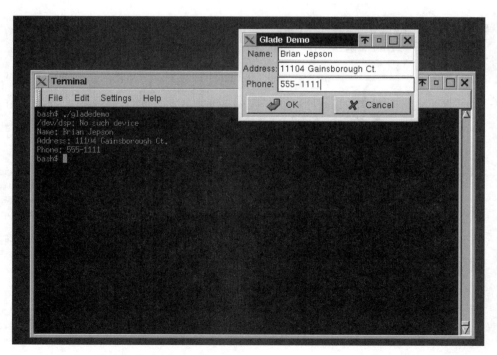

Figure 13.13 The GladeDemo application.

Overview of GNOME-DB

GNOME-DB is a data access architecture for GNOME that consists of three parts: the GDA (GNOME data access) UI library, the GDA client API, and GDA providers:

The *GDA UI Library* is a collection of widgets whose contents are dynamically bound to a data source. For example, you can define a list widget that is connected to a data source: Instead of storing each row, one by one, in the list widget, the GDA widget knows how to get its values from a result set. More importantly, when a user makes a selection in the list widget, you can find out other values from the corresponding row (such as the unique ID of the customer name someone selected in the widget).

The *GDA Client API* is a data access API that performs the same function as ODBC, DBI, or JDBC, but is modeled on Microsoft's ADO (ActiveX Data Objects), and has a strongly object-based object model.

Finally, a *GDA Provider* is a CORBA server that acts as a gateway to an underlying data source, such as an Oracle or PostgreSQL database server, or an ODBC driver that connects to a database server on your behalf. If you use the GNOME-DB ODBC provider, you are, in effect, using two data access APIs, GNOME-DB and ODBC: think of it as a GNOME-DB to ODBC bridge.

Providers and Data Sources

A GDA Provider is your gateway to a database. However, the GDA Provider only knows how to talk to a database server. If you've got several database servers, how do you tell the provider which database server to connect to? GNOME-DB uses a file called gdalib to configure data sources, which consist of the following information:

Data source name. This is a name that you choose, something to help you remember the purpose of the data source. It is the first line of a data source, and appears within [brackets].

Provider. This is the name of the GDA Provider, a CORBA server that gives the GDA client API access to the database.

DSN. This is provider-specific information, such as the name of the HOST on which the server can be found, or the DATABASE (one of many within the database server) you want to connect to.

Description. A description that explains the purposes of the data source.

Configurator. The name of a Bonobo component that is used to configure the data source. This is used by the front-end application, as described in the section *Configuring Data Sources*, later in the chapter. As of this writing, the Configurator was not yet implemented.

The data sources are stored in a file called *gdalib*, which resides in the user's private .gnome directory. Let's look at an excerpt from a gdalib file. The name of the data source is MyDatabase, and it uses the gda-postgres Provider to connect to the database named *bjepson* on the local PostgreSQL server, as the user bjepson (under PostgreSQL, each user's private database is named after his or her user name):

```
[MyDatabase]
Provider=gda-postgres
DSN=DATABASE=bjepson;HOST=localhost
Description=My Personal Database
Configurator=None
Username=bjepson
```

Don't worry about setting up this file right now. We'll talk more about it in the section *Configuring Data Sources*.

How does GNOME-DB use these data source descriptions? When you run a GNOME-DB application, one of the first things you'll see is the login screen (refer Figure 13.17 later in this chapter), which prompts you to select a data source and supply your user name and password. The user name you supply at login overrides (and replaces) whatever setting you have in your gdalib file.

GNOME-DB in Action

Let's illustrate how these components work together in two informal scenarios, illustrated with sequence diagrams. As you read these, keep the following in mind:

- While the scenarios are very close to how GNOME-DB works, they are intended as a conceptual description to help you understand how the pieces go together, not an exact description.
- When you write your own GNOME-DB programs, you don't need to worry about all these details!

Scenario: User connects to database (see Figure 13.14).

Participants: User, Application, GDA Client library, GDA Provider, and Database.

Scenario: Fill a grid with the results of a query (see Figure 13.15).

Participants: Application, GDA Client Library, GDA Provider, Database, GnomeDbGrid.

Prerequisites: User connects to database.

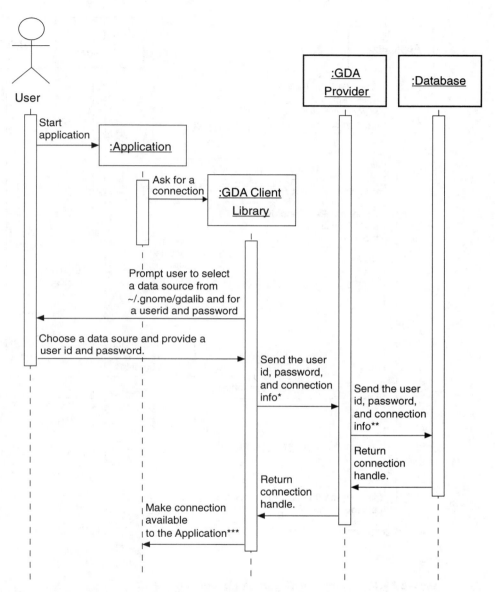

Figure 13.14 Sequence diagram for connecting to a database.

* The GDA client library finds the provider by looking up the data source in ~/.gnome/gdalib.

** The GDA Provider connects to database using linked-in client library, such as ODBC, libpq, or libmysqlclient.

*** All further conversation between the GDA client library and the database will be done through the GDA Provider (an Adapter pattern).

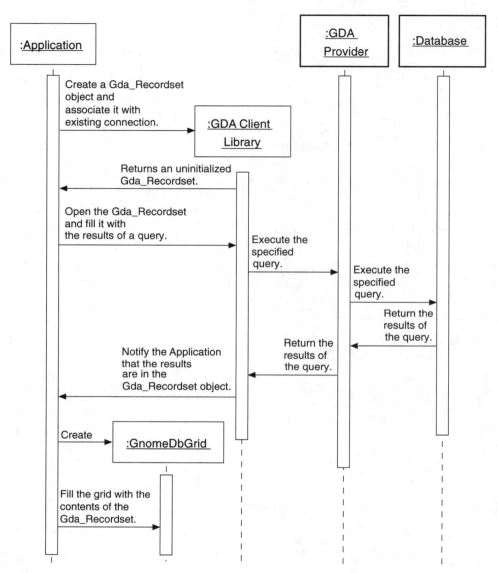

Figure 13.15 Sequence diagram for populating a grid.

Getting GNOME-DB

The GNOME-DB home page is at www.gnome.org/gnome-db. At this page, you can obtain source code snapshots or prepackaged binary releases of GNOME-DB. You can also access GNOME-DB source code using GNOME's CVS server.

Binary Packages

See the GNOME-DB home page for binary packages and installation instructions.

Source Code Snapshots

Although GNOME-DB was in prerelease form when this chapter was written, the source code snapshots are relatively stable, since the source code snapshots are released when various milestones are reached in development. The source code archives should be available on the www.gnome.org/gnome-db/download.html page, but check the GNOME-DB home page for links.

GNOME-DB CVS Archive

If you want to be on the cutting edge, you might want to get the latest version of GNOME-DB out of the CVS archive. If you do so, you should subscribe to the GNOME-DB mailing list, and try to keep your CVS archive up to date. During the preparation of this book, we kept our local copy of the repository up to date on a daily basis, but we only did complete builds of GNOME-DB once a week, or when a major feature was added. We knew about new features because we kept an eye on the GNOME-DB mailing list.

Instructions on subscribing to the mailing list can be found at www.gnome.org/gnome-db/mailing_lists.html or www.gnome.org/mailing-lists/index.shtml.

To get GNOME-DB out of CVS (this procedure may change, so visit the GNOME-DB home page for complete details):

1. Start up a shell by logging in, or starting a terminal (such as xterm) under the X Window System.
2. Set the CVSROOT environment variable to :pserver:anonymous@anoncvs.gnome.org:/cvs/gnome.
3. Log in to the repository with the command 'cvs login' when prompted for the password, press the Enter key, since the password is blank.
4. Use cd to change to the directory you want to copy the repository to.
5. Issue the command 'cvs -z3 checkout gnome-db' This copies the repository to your machine, using compression to save bandwidth (don't use an argument greater than 3 to -z, since it puts stress on the server's CPU).
6. The GNOME-DB repository will be created in a directory called gnome-db.

Here is an example session (commands I typed are shown in **bold**, my comments in *italic*):

```
bash-2.03$ cd /home/bjepson/src
bash-2.03$ export \
           CVSROOT=:pserver:anonymous@anoncvs.gnome.org:/cvs/gnome
bash-2.03$ cvs login
(Logging in to anonymous@anoncvs.gnome.org)
CVS password: [press the enter key]
bash-2.03$ cvs -z3 checkout gnome-db
cvs server: Updating gnome-db
U gnome-db/.cvsignore
U gnome-db/ABOUT-NLS
[...] lots of the file listing omitted [...]
U macros/gperf-check.m4
U macros/linger.m4
U macros/need-declaration.m4
bash-2.03$ ls gnome-db
ABOUT-NLS    TODO       gda-clnt-ui      gda-sybase-server
AUTHORS      acconfig.h  gda-dev          gdalib.sample
[...] some of the file listing omitted [...]
```

To update your local copy of the CVS repository:

1. Start up a shell by logging in, or starting a terminal (such as xterm) under the X Window System.

2. Use cd to change to the top-level directory of the repository. This is the gnome-db subdirectory you created when you checked out the archive, not the directory that contains gnome-db.

3. Issue the command 'cvs -z3 update -P' This checks the repository to see what's new, and updates your copy. There are some codes that are displayed at the left of the output, as described in Table 13.2.

Table 13.2   CVS Status Codes

CODE	MEANING
P	Indicates that *patch(1)* was used to update your copy.
U	A new copy of the file was transferred.
A	A new file has been added since your last update.
R	Indicates that a file is obsolete and was removed.
M	You changed your local copy of the file, but CVS merged the official changes with your copy.
?	Means you have a file that the repository doesn't recognize (this is common, because compilation often creates transitory files).
C	You've modified the file but CVS couldn't merge it. See the man page for cvs(1) for details on resolving this.

4. Your repository is now up to date.

Here is an excerpt from an update session:

```
bash-2.03$ cd /home/bjepson/src/gnome-db
bash-2.03$ cvs -z3 update -P
? gnome-db.spec
cvs server: Updating .
U ChangeLog
U README
U configure.in
U gnome-db.spec.in
cvs server: Updating doc
cvs server: Updating doc/C
cvs server: Updating doc/clientlib
cvs server: Updating fe
cvs server: fe/fe_import.c is no longer in the repository
[...] some stuff omitted [...]
```

Compiling and Installing GNOME-DB

The compilation and installation instructions are slightly different, depending on whether you are using a binary release, snapshot, or if you have gotten gnome-db out of CVS.

Binary Release

With a binary release, the compilation step is completely skipped. However, you may find that there are additional configuration steps needed. See the instructions that accompany the binary release for more details.

Source Code Snapshot

If you have downloaded a snapshot of GNOME-DB, you should extract the archive, configure the source, compile it, and install it. To do this, follow these steps:

1. *Get the archive.* Download the archive from www.gnome.org/gnome-db and save it to the directory you want to compile GNOME-DB in (this is different from where it will be installed).

2. *Extract it.* Extract the archive with the tar utility, as shown here:

```
bash-2.03$ tar xvfz gnome-db-0.0.90.tar.gz
gnome-db-0.0.90/
gnome-db-0.0.90/Makefile.in
gnome-db-0.0.90/README
```

```
gnome-db-0.0.90/stamp-h.in
[...] much of listing omitted [...]
```

3. *Change directory.* Once you have extracted the archive, use cd to change to the directory (the name of which will be dependent on the version of the snapshot):

```
bash-2.03$ cd gnome-db-0.0.90
```

4. *Study.* Examine the files named INSTALL and README. If anything in those files supersedes or overrides the remaining steps, defer to those files, since some steps may have changed.

5. *Configure the source tree.* Use the configure utility to configure the source code. At the time of this writing, the GNOME-DB configure utility supports some of the switches shown in Table 13.3. Another important switch is --prefix. This controls the top-level directory where gnome-db will be installed.

   Here is an example invocation of GNOME-DB's configure:

```
bash-2.03$ ./configure --prefix=/usr --with-mysql=/usr/local \
           --with-postgres=/usr
creating cache ./config.cache
checking for a BSD compatible install... /usr/bin/install -c
[...] most of the output deleted [...]
creating testing/Makefile
creating stamp.h
creating config.h
```

6. *Compile the source.* Once you've configured the source, you can run 'make' to compile it. This will take a while:

```
bash-2.03$ make
make  all-recursive
make[1]: Entering directory `/usr/src/bjepson/gnome/gnome-db'
Making all in macros
[...] most of the output deleted [...]
cat-id-tbl.c changed
cd . && rm -f stamp-cat-id && echo timestamp > stamp-cat-id
make[2]: Leaving directory `/usr/src/bjepson/gnome/gnome-db/po'
make[2]: Entering directory `/usr/src/bjepson/gnome/gnome-db'
make[2]: Leaving directory `/usr/src/bjepson/gnome/gnome-db'
make[1]: Leaving directory `/usr/src/bjepson/gnome/gnome-db'
```

7. *Install the binary.* To install the libraries, binary programs, and header files, become root via the su command, and run the command 'make install':

```
[root@oscar gnome-db]# make install
Making install in macros
make[1]: Entering directory `/usr/src/bjepson/gnome/gnome-db/macros'
```

Table 13.3 Some Command-Line Switches Recognized by GNOME-DB's Configure

SWITCH	TOP-LEVEL DIRECTORY OF...	EXAMPLE
--with-mysql=DIR	...your MySQL installation.	--with-mysql=/usr/local
--with-postgres=DIR	...your PostgreSQL installation.	--with-postgres=/usr
--with-sybase=DIR	...your Sybase installation	--with-sybase=/opt/ sybase-11.9.2/bin
--with-oracle=DIR	...your Oracle installation	--with-oracle=$ORACLE _HOME7
--with-sybase=DIR	...your Sybase installation	--with-sybase=~sybase

```
make[2]: Entering directory `/usr/src/bjepson/gnome/gnome-db/macros'
make[2]: Nothing to be done for `install-exec-am'.
[...] most of the output deleted [...]
        /usr/bin/install     -c     -m     644     ./gnome_db.gnorba
/etc/CORBA/servers/gnome_db.gnorba
make[2]: Leaving directory `/usr/src/bjepson/gnome/gnome-db'
make[1]: Leaving directory `/usr/src/bjepson/gnome/gnome-db'
```

8. *Test it.* GNOME-DB comes with a few programs, including gdafe, the front-end program. You can use this program to work with databases and tables. Test it out now by starting a shell terminal (such as xterm) under the X Window System, and run the command 'gdafe'. If GNOME-DB was compiled and installed correctly, the gdafe program should appear, as shown in Figure 13.16.

Configuring Data Sources

Before you can connect to a data source, you'll need to configure your gdalib file. You can do this by copying and modifying the gdalib.sample file, which is included with the gnome-db distribution, or you can use one of the tools designed for this purpose.

The GDA Manager (gda-mgr or gda-manager) is the GNOME-DB configuration utility, and will be used to create or modify system-wide and personal data sources. A personal data source is a data source that's available to a particular user, while a system data source is available to all users. Availability does not determine access; you still need to supply a user name and password when you log in, and it's possible that two users may have different data sources that ultimately point to the same database and server. You should think of a data source as a convenient tool for grouping information about a connection so you don't have to remember it every time you want to log in.

At the time of this writing, gda-mgr was still a work in progress. In the examples that follow, we will go over the steps needed to copy and modify the gdalib.sample file. Before you proceed, please check the GNOME-DB documentation, since gda-mgr may be in a usable state by the time this book is published.

To configure a data source:

1. If you don't already have it, obtain the source code distribution of GNOME-DB.

2. Copy the file gdalib.sample to ~/.gnome/gdalib (the file named gdalib that is contained in the .gnome subdirectory of your home directory). The gdalib.sample file can be found in the top-level directory of the GNOME-DB source distribution:

```
bash-2.03$ cd /usr/src/bjepson/gnome/gnome-db
bash-2.03$ cp gdalib.sample ~/.gnome/gdalib
```

3. Open your copy of the gdalib file in a text editor, such as vi or emacs. Add a data source description to the file. A sample data source description is shown here, and explained in Table 13.4.

```
[MySQL]
provider=gda-mysql
dsn=DATABASE=bjepson_db;UNIX_SOCKET=/tmp/mysql.sock
Description=Brian Jepson's MySQL database
Configurator=None
```

Table 13.4 Data Source Breakdown

LINE	DESCRIPTION
[MySQL]	The name of the data source.
provider=	The name of the GDA provider.
dsn=	Information used by the provider to connect to a database server. For the gda-odbc provider, this is an ODBC data source. For all other providers, it is a semicolon-delimited list of keyword/value pairs (KEYWORD1=VALUE1;KEYWORD2=VALUE2). See Table 13.5 for an explanation of the various keywords that can be used.
	With Oracle, you can leave the dsn blank, because the client library will make use of the environment variable $ORACLE_SID (this should contain the name of your Oracle system identifier).
Description=	A verbose description of the data source.
Configurator=	Reserved for future use.

Table 13.5 DSN Keywords for Various Providers

DSN KEYWORD	DESCRIPTION	SUPPORTED BY
DATABASE	The database to connect to. This must be a database on the server (see HOST) that you have access to.	gda-mysql, gda-postgres
HOST	The name of the host that the database server resides on.	gda-mysql, gda-postgres
LOGIN	The user id to use when connecting.	gda-postgres
PASSWORD	The password to use when connecting.	gda-postgres
PORT	The TCP port that the database server listens on.	gda-mysql, gda-postgres
UNIX_SOCKET	A Unix socket to use instead of a TCP port. This is generally faster, but only available on the local host.	gda-mysql

4. Add a reference to the data source in the [Datasources] section of your gdalib file. You should put the name of the data source on the left of the equals sign, followed by a more verbose description (or you can just use the name of the data source, which I used):

```
[Datasources]
MySQL=MySQL
```

Using GNOME-DB

Before we get into the details of programming with GNOME-DB, let's take a quick look at some of the tools that come with it. These tools will let you test out whether you can connect to the database with GNOME-DB, and will also introduce you to some of the widgets, such as the login and grid widgets.

The Front-End (gdafe)

The GNOME-DB front-end program, gdafe, is a lot like some of the front-end applications we saw in Chapter 9, "Databases." The main difference is that gdafe is built with the components that make up GNOME-DB. Let's look at some brief instructions for using gdafe.

To start gdafe, select *SQL Front End* from the GNOME-DB submenu of the GNOME Applications menu. The GNOME Applications menu usually appears at the top of the main GNOME panel menu (the footprint menu on the GNOME panel). You can also start gdafe by running the command *gdafe* from within an xterm or gnome-terminal (or other X Window shell).

Connect to a database. When you start up gdafe, the main window appears as shown in Figure 13.16. At this point, you must connect to a data source. To connect to a data source:

1. Click Connect or select Open Connection from the File menu. The Open Connection dialog appears, as shown in Figure 13.17. This dialog uses the GnomeDbLogin widget, which we'll look at in the next section, *Programming GNOME-DB*.

2. Select the data source from the GDA Datasource menu. Only data sources defined in gdalib appear here.

3. Supply a user name and password.

4. Click OK to connect.

If all went well, you didn't get any error messages, and the gdafe window expanded to include a tab labeled SQL. If you did receive error messages, it may indicate that your gdalib file is not configured correctly. If you re-read the preceding section on setting up data source, double-check the contents of the file, and you still cannot log in, you should consult the GNOME-DB documentation, since it is possible that 1) something changed since the writing of this book, or 2) the gda-mgr application is fully functional, and should be used to configure your data sources.

Issue a query. After you make a connection, the SQL tab appears with a top section and bottom section, as shown in Figure 13.18. To execute a query, type some SQL into the top part, and click the leftmost icon. The query should be executed, and the results appear in a grid in the lower region, as shown in Figure 13.18. This grid is a GnomeDbGrid object, which we'll learn more about in the next section.

The gdafe application offers more, such as the ability to define tables, peruse the objects in a database, and view or create various trace files and logs. You should consult the GNOME-DB documentation for more details.

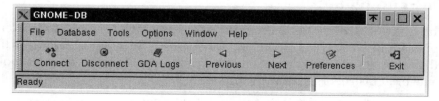

Figure 13.16 The GNOME-DB front-end.

Figure 13.17 The GNOME-DB login dialog.

Programming GNOME-DB

Now, we get to the meat of the chapter: writing your own GNOME-DB applications. To develop with GNOME-DB, you'll need to be comfortable with C programming and GTK+. GNOME and GNOME-DB conspire to shield the developer from a lot of details involved with CORBA, so you don't have to worry about the CORBA parts that are working under the hood. Also, the use of libglade simplifies a lot of the complexity of building applications.

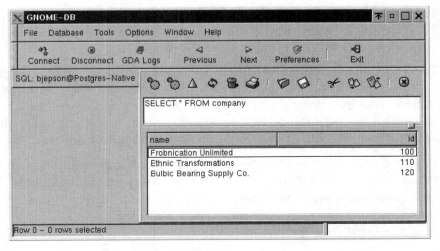

Figure 13.18 The GNOME-DB front-end in action.

Make a Connection

When we used gdafe, remember that we needed to open a connection to a data source before we could do anything. In your programs, you'll need to do the same thing. To make this easy, two widgets are available: Gnome-DbLogin and GnomeDbLoginDlg. If you want to write your own dialog, you can put GnomeDbLogin in it (as is done in gdafe). Otherwise, you can use GnomeDbLoginDlg, which gives you a nice dialog you can use.

We've written a small program, login.c, that we'll reuse in other examples here. This program is responsible for:

Creating and activating a login dialog. This is handled by a function called login_db(), which takes a single argument: an uninitialized Gda_Connection object. Here is an example invocation of login_db():

```
/* Create a new connection object. */
Gda_Connection* cnc;
cnc = gda_connection_new(orb);

/* Try to log in. If the login fails, exit the program
 * with a message.
 */
if ( !login_db(cnc) ) {
    fprintf(stderr, "Login failed.\n");
    return(-1);
}
```

As you can imagine, login_db is the function that is of most interest to external objects. All the remaining functions are used internally.

Providing an event handler to close the dialog. When the user clicks the dialog's Cancel button, or when a connection is successfully made, we want to close the dialog. This is handled by the close_dialog() function.

Providing an event handler to close the dialog window. Although this may appear to be a special case, it's really quite different. When a user selects close from the window's control menu, it triggers a delete event. This event handler, on_logindlg_delete_event(), only needs to call gtk_main_quit() and return FALSE to allow GTK+ to close the window down.

Here is the source code for login.c (the source code can be found on the companion Web site [www.wiley.com/compbooks/jepson] in the Chapter 13 examples, under the subdirectory db_login):

```
1   #include "login.h"
2
3   /* FUNCTION: close_dialog()
4    *
```

```
 5     * Event handler invoked when the user clicks the cancel
 6     * button or after a successful connection is made.
 7     */
 8    gint close_dialog(GtkObject* dialog) {
 9
10      /* Close the dialog */
11      gnome_dialog_close(GNOME_DIALOG(dialog));
12
13      dialog = NULL;      /* destroy the dialog */
14
15      gtk_main_quit();  /* terminate the main loop */
16    }
17
18    /* FUNCTION: on_logindlg_delete_event()
19     *
20     * Event handler invoked when the user clicks the close
21     * button on the dialog window.
22     */
23    gint on_logindlg_delete_event(GtkWidget*   w,
24                                  GdkEventAny* e,
25                                  gpointer data)
26    {
27      gtk_main_quit(); /* Quit the main loop */
28      return FALSE;      /* Delete event must return FALSE */
29    }
30
31    /* FUNCTION: login_db()
32     *
33     * Display a login dialog and return true if the
34     * connection succeeded.
35     */
36    gboolean login_db(Gda_Connection* cnc) {
37
38      GtkWidget* login;    /* A login widget */
39      GtkWidget* logindlg; /* A login dialog widget */
40
41      /* Create a login widget */
42      login    = gnome_db_login_new(cnc, NULL, NULL);
43
44      /* Create a login dialog that uses that widget */
45      logindlg = gnome_db_logindlg_new(GNOME_DB_LOGIN(login),
46                                      "Please Log In");
47
48      /* Connect the dialog window's delete_event to the
49       * on_logindlg_delete_event() handler.
50       */
51      gtk_signal_connect(GTK_OBJECT(logindlg),
52                        "delete_event",
53                        GTK_SIGNAL_FUNC(on_logindlg_delete_event),
54                        NULL);
55
```

```
56    /*
57     * Connect the connection's open event to the close_dialog()
58     * handler.
59     */
60    gtk_signal_connect_object_after(GTK_OBJECT(cnc),
61                                    "open",
62                                    GTK_SIGNAL_FUNC(close_dialog),
63                                    GTK_OBJECT(logindlg));
64
65    /* Connect the cancel button to the close_dialog() handler()
66     */
67    gtk_signal_connect(GTK_OBJECT(logindlg),
68                       "cancel",
69                       GTK_SIGNAL_FUNC(close_dialog),
70                       NULL);
71
72    /* Hide the dialog when it is closed */
73    gnome_dialog_close_hides(GNOME_DIALOG(logindlg), TRUE);
74
75    /* Display the dialog */
76    gnome_db_logindlg_popup(GNOME_DB_LOGINDLG(logindlg));
77
78    /* Start a GTK loop */
79    gtk_main();
80
81    /* Return true if the connection is open */
82    return gda_connection_is_open(cnc);
83
84  }
```

And here is the accompanying header file (login.h):

```
#include <gda.h>
#include <gda-connection.h>
#include <gda-ui.h>

gboolean login_db(Gda_Connection* cnc);
```

Now, let's look at what various blocks of code do in login.c:

Line 1. This line brings in the login.h header file, which contains #include directives for the header files required for GNOME-DB applications, and also defines the functions that we want other programs to know about (in this case, just login_db).

Lines 8–16. The close_dialog() function appears here, which is similar to event handlers we looked at earlier in this chapter.

Lines 23–29. This is the on_logindlg_delete_event() function, which handles requests to delete the window.

Lines 38–39. Declare variables for the login widget (login) and the login dialog (logindlg), which will contain the login widget. The login widget takes care of presenting a list of available data sources, as well as recently used data sources. The login dialog takes care of presenting a dialog window and some buttons.

Lines 42 and 45. Create the login widget and login dialog. To create the login widget, we pass it the connection object, cnc. To create the login dialog, we pass it the login widget (since that widget is contained within the dialog, it needs to have access to it).

Lines 51–54. This connects the on_logindlg_delete_event() handler to the dialog, so that when a user closes the dialog's main window, that event handler is called.

Lines 60–63. So far, we've only seen signal handlers that were connected to widgets. This one's a little different; we're connecting the close_dialog signal handler to the connection object's *open* event. So, when the connection to the data source is successfully established, the dialog automatically goes away.

Lines 67–70. Here, we connect the close_dialog signal handler to the Cancel button, so if the user presses Cancel, the dialog will go away.

Line 73. This tells the dialog to hide itself when it's closed. The signal handlers take care of deleting or destroying it.

Line 76. This line displays the dialog on the user's screen.

Line 79. As with other programs, this line starts the GTK+ main loop, which continues until one of the event handlers shuts it down.

Line 82. Finally, we check to see if the connection is open and return true (is open) or false (is *not* open) to the calling program. That way, the caller can check to see if db_login() managed to successfully open the connection.

The login.c program is driven by another program, db_login.c, which contains the main() function. Here is the source code for db_login.c:

```
1   #include "db_login.h"
2
3   Gda_Connection* cnc;   /* Database connection */
4
5   /*
6    * The main function.
7    */
8   int main(int argc, char* argv[]) {
9
10    CORBA_ORB orb;
11    CORBA_Environment ev;
12
13    CORBA_exception_init(&ev);
```

```
14    orb = gnome_CORBA_init("db_login", /* app_id */
15                      "1.0",       /* app_version */
16                      &argc,
17                      argv,
18                      0,           /* gnorba_flags */
19                      &ev);        /* CORBA environment */
20
21    /* Use the ORB to create a new connection object. */
22    cnc = gda_connection_new(orb);
23
24    /* Try to log in. If the login fails, exit the program
25     * with a message.
26     */
27    if ( !login_db(cnc) ) {
28        fprintf(stderr, "Login failed.\n");
29        return(-1);
30    }
31
32    /* Close the connection */
33    gda_connection_close(cnc);
34
35    return (0);
36  }
```

And here is the accompanying header file (db_login.h):

```
#include "login.h"
#include <stdio.h>
#include <libgnorba/gnorba.h>
#include <gda.h>
#include <gda-connection.h>
```

Let's look at what the db_login.c program does:

Line 1. First, we include db_login.h, which brings in some other header files.

Line 3. Declare the Gda_Connection object. In this example program, we only use this connection in one function. However, in future examples, we'll use it in more places.

Line 10. Declares the CORBA ORB. For more information, see *A Simple ORBit Example* in Chapter 15.

Line 11. Declares the CORBA environment.

Line 13. Initializes the CORBA environment.

Lines 14–19. These lines use the gnome_CORBA_init() function to create the CORBA ORB object, passing in some information about the application, argc and argv, and the CORBA environment. The gnome_CORBA_init() function also takes the place of gnome_init, which initializes the GNOME libraries.

The next to the last argument to gnome_CORBA_init() are flags to GNORBA, the GNOME interface to CORBA. In this example, we don't use any flags.

Line 22. Creates a new connection object. Notice that you have to pass in the orb variable, since GNOME-DB uses CORBA extensively under the hood. In most GNOME-DB applications, this is the last you'll see of CORBA—everything else is handled behind the scenes.

Line 27–30. Call the login_db() function, and report an error if the connection fails.

Lines 33–35. Because this example just tries to make a connection, it's not going to do anything else that's interesting. So, we close the connection right away and return from main().

To compile this example, change to the db_login subdirectory and run the *make* command. Here is the Makefile:

```
 1   CFLAGS = -c `gda-config --cflags gdaui gnome`
 2   LIBS = `gda-config --libs gdaui gnome`
 3
 4   OBJS = db_login.o login.o
 5
 6   all: db_login
 7
 8   login.o: login.c login.h
 9           $(CC) $(CFLAGS) -o $@ $<
10
11   db_login.o: db_login.c db_login.h login.h
12           $(CC) $(CFLAGS) -o $@ $<
13
14   db_login: $(OBJS)
15           $(CC) -o $@ $(OBJS) $(LIBS)
16
17   clean:
18           rm -f $(OBJS) db_login
```

In the remaining examples in this chapter, the Makefiles will be very similar. Let's take a look at what each line does. As you read through this, keep in mind that make does not execute the Makefile in sequence; instead, it examines the dependencies between components, looks to see which have been modified since the last compilation, and only builds those parts that need to be built.

Line 1. When you want to compile a program that uses an optional library, such as those that come with GNOME-DB, you need to tell the C compiler where to find the header files (such as gda.h). The gda-config utility is part of GNOME-DB, and takes care of setting these values. In this line, we tell gda-config to tell us the CFLAGS, and pass the options *gdaui* and *gnome*, which tell it that we want to compile a GNOME application that uses the GDA user interface library.

The -c option tells the compiler not to worry about external dependencies (such as functions from the GNOME-DB or GNORBA libraries) until we link (in lines 14–15).

Line 2. Again, the gda-config utility is used, this time to get the linking flags for our application (this handles linking in all the GNOME and GDA libraries).

Line 4. These are the two object files that we'll link to create the final executable.

Line 6. This is a target that specifies the ultimate goal of this Makefile: creating the executable file db_login.

Lines 8 and 9. These lines tell make that login.o is dependent on login.c and login.h, and that it should use the C compiler ($CC) and the CFLAGS we set in lines 1 and 2 to compile these files. The $@ refers to the target (login.o) and the $< refers to the first dependency, login.c.

Lines 11 and 12. These lines function identically to lines 8 and 9, but they compile db_login.c to db_login.o.

Lines 14 and 15. These lines contain instructions to link the object files (see line 4) into a final executable. The GNU C compiler is capable of linking, so it is used here instead of ld (which is the name of the standard Unix linker).

Lines 17 and 18. This target cleans up the executable (db_login) and the object files. It is useful if you want to package up the file before shipping it out.

When you run the compilation, the following things happen:

1. db_login.o is created.
2. login.o is created.
3. db_login.o and login.o are linked to the GDA client and UI libraries, as well as a bunch of other libraries, producing the final executable: db_login (to see a list of the libraries, run the command gda-config—libs gdaui gnome at the shell).

To run the program, simply run the command *db_login* from the shell. In most cases, the current directory (which contains the program db_login) won't be in your PATH, so you should try ./db_login instead (don't add . to your path, since it can be a security hole). When you run the program, the login dialog appear as shown earlier in Figure 13.17. Select a valid data source, supply your user id and password, and click OK to log in. Remember that this program doesn't do anything after logging on to the datasource, so it will exit immediately after you log on.

If you can't log in with this program, don't try to debug it yet. Next, we'll see how you can use GNOME-DB's error handling to get verbose descriptions of errors. Hopefully, this will help you out if you had any trouble logging in to the database. In all the programs that follow, login.c and login.h will be reused as is—no changes will be made to the listings for those files you saw previously.

Trap Errors

In the previous example, there was no explicit error handling. So, if you tried to connect to a bogus data source, or if you supplied the wrong user id or password, it would simply keep the dialog on the screen as if nothing had happened. As it turns out, we can make some simple modifications to support error handling.

First, we'll encapsulate all the error handling behavior in an error.c program file (which has an accompanying head, error.h). This program has the duty of defining an error handler and hooking up a Gda_Connection object's error handler to that function. In the error handler, on_error(), we create an error dialog that is connected to the connection that had the error, and display it. Figure 13.19 shows the result of logging in to a data source with the wrong user id and password.

Here is the listing for error.c:

```
#include "error.h"

/*
 * When an error occurs, display a dialog with
 * the list of errors.
 */
void on_error(GtkObject* cnc) {

  GtkWidget *error_dialog;

  /* Create an error dialog */
  error_dialog = gnome_db_errordlg_new(GDA_CONNECTION(cnc),
                                       "Database Error");

  /* Display the dialog */
  gtk_window_set_modal(GTK_WINDOW(error_dialog), TRUE);
  gnome_db_errordlg_show_errors(GNOME_DB_ERRORDLG(error_dialog));

}

/*
 * Connect the on_error routine to the connection's error signal.
 */
```

```
void register_error_handler(Gda_Connection* cnc) {

  /* If we have a connection error, invoke the
   * error handler.
   */
  gtk_signal_connect(GTK_OBJECT(cnc),
                     "error",
                     GTK_SIGNAL_FUNC(on_error),
                     NULL);
}
```

And here is the listing for error.h:

```
#include <gda.h>
#include <gda-connection.h>
#include <gda-ui.h>

void register_error_handler(Gda_Connection* cnc);
```

We didn't have to make too many modifications to the db_login program to make this work. All that we did was to add these two lines before line 24 (see the earlier listing for db_login.c):

```
/* Set up an error handler for the connection */
register_error_handler(cnc);
```

And, we added this line to the top of db_login.h:

```
#include "error.h"
```

Next, let's move on to a full example program, which will prove to be more interesting than logging in and handling errors (although it will handle these functions using the programs we just looked at).

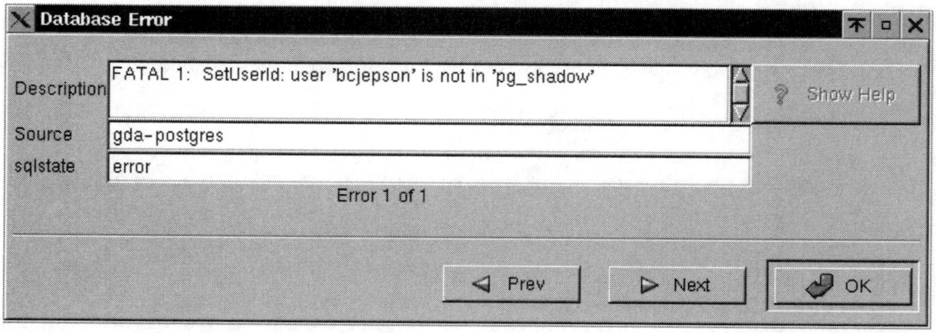

Figure 13.19 The GNOME-DB error dialog.

Glade Meets GNOME-DB

Let's take a look at an example program that combines Glade with GNOME-DB. In this example, we'll use the Glade custom object to display a GDA combo (pop-up, editable menu) and a GDA grid. This example was developed using the Glade GUI builder, but instead of generating the application from within Glade, we're going to use libglade to load the user interface at runtime.

The Glade UI Definition

This application uses the db_gui.glade file, which describes the user interface shown in Figure 13.20. Let's look at each important widget in the file.

The app GnomeApp widget. This is the top-level window. It is similar to the GtkWindow objects we saw in earlier examples, but it is an instance of GnomeApp, which is a top-level container for GNOME applications. Here is some of the relevant XML from the Glade file (as you can see, it has one signal handler associated with it, which handles the deletion of the window):

```
<widget>
  <class>GnomeApp</class>
  <name>app</name>
  <signal>
    <name>delete_event</name>
    <handler>on_app_delete_event</handler>
  </signal>
  <title>GNOME-DB Example</title>
  <type>GTK_WINDOW_TOPLEVEL</type>
  <position>GTK_WIN_POS_NONE</position>
  <!-- ... all the child widgets not shown ... -->
</widget>
```

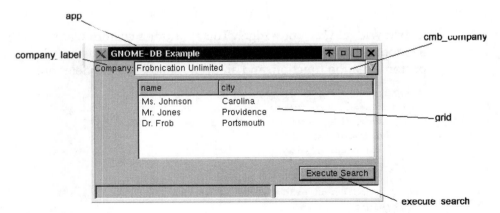

Figure 13.20 Our GNOME-DB application window, with important widgets labeled.

The company_label GtkLabel widget. This widget is a plain text label that acts as a prompt for the cmb_company widget:

```
<widget>
  <class>GtkLabel</class>
  <name>company_label</name>
  <label>Company:</label>
  <justify>GTK_JUSTIFY_LEFT</justify>
</widget>
```

The cmb_company Custom widget. This custom widget is created by a function called get_company_combo that we wrote for this example (we'll see it shortly). Here is how a custom widget works: libglade doesn't need to know what type of widget it is, because GTK's polymorphism allows everything to be treated as a GtkWidget object. So, all we need to do is write the *get_company_combo* function, create whatever kind of widget we feel like creating (in this case, it's a GnomeDbCombo object), and cast it to a GtkWidget when we return it from the function.

This combo also has a *delete_event* event handler. The purpose of this event handler is (in the spirit of cleaning up after ourselves) to release the underlying Gda_Recordset object that powers the combo.

Here is the definition of the custom widget:

```
<widget>
  <class>Custom</class>
  <name>cmb_company</name>
  <signal>
    <name>delete_event</name>
    <handler>on_combo_delete_event</handler>
  </signal>
  <creation_function>get_company_combo</creation_function>
</widget>
```

The grid widget Custom widget. This is another custom widget; in this case, a GnomeDbGrid object. As with the cmb_company Custom object, it has a custom creation function, and an event handler for its deletion:

```
<widget>
  <class>Custom</class>
  <name>grid</name>
  <width>350</width>
  <height>128</height>
  <signal>
    <name>delete_event</name>
    <handler>on_grid_delete_event</handler>
  </signal>
  <creation_function>get_grid</creation_function>
</widget>
```

The execute_search GtkButton widget. As its name implies, this button executes the search. Once the search is completed, it fills the grid with the results. We'll see the mechanics behind this when we look at execute _search's event handler, *on_execute_search_clicked*. Here is the XML definition of this widget:

```
<widget>
  <class>GtkButton</class>
  <name>execute_search</name>
  <signal>
    <name>clicked</name>
    <handler>on_execute_search_clicked</handler>
  </signal>
  <label>Execute Search</label>
</widget>
```

The Application Source Code

The application is made up of the following source files:

SAMPLE_DATA.SQL. This includes all of the data needed by the sample program. It has definitions and data for the company and contact tables. Here is the source to SAMPLE_DATA.SQL:

```
DROP TABLE company;
CREATE TABLE company
     (name CHAR(35),
      id   INT);
INSERT INTO company VALUES('Frobnication Unlimited',   100);
INSERT INTO company VALUES('Ethnic Transformations',   110);
INSERT INTO company VALUES('Bulbic Bearing Supply Co.', 120);

DROP TABLE contact;
CREATE TABLE contact
     (name     CHAR(20),
      company  INT,
      city     CHAR(20));
INSERT INTO contact VALUES('Ms. Johnson', 100, 'Carolina');
INSERT INTO contact VALUES('Mr. Jones',   100, 'Providence');
INSERT INTO contact VALUES('Dr. Frob',    100, 'Portsmouth');
INSERT INTO contact VALUES('Ellis Danforth', 110, 'Wakefield');
INSERT INTO contact VALUES('Fr. Benway',     110, 'Interzone');
INSERT INTO contact VALUES('Bear Bearing', 120, 'Warwick');
INSERT INTO contact VALUES('Bull Bulbic',  120, 'Arctic');
```

db_gui.c and db_gui.h. This is the main program.

table_combo.c and table_combo.h. This includes support functions for a specialized implementation of the GnomeDbCombo object that is tied to a table (the GnomeDbCombo object is usually associated with a record set, and table_combo.c takes some of the manual steps out of working with it).

error.c and error.h. These include the error handling functions we looked at in the *Trap Errors* section of this chapter. We won't be repeating the source listings here, since they are included in that section.

login.c and login.h. These include the login automation functions we looked at in the *Make a Connection* section of this chapter. We won't be repeating the source listings here, since they are included in that section.

Let's take a close look at the new programs, table_combo.c and db_gui.c.

The table_combo.c Program

In the discussion that follows, I make the distinction between public and private functions. Although C doesn't enforce this, we are following the convention that public functions (that you want other programs to use) appear in the header file (table_combo.h), while private functions (those used internally) do not appear in the header file.

The create_gda_combo() public function. This function creates a new GnomeDbCombo object, issues a database query, and fills the combo with the results of the query. Because this is the first time we've executed a query, let's look at some of the steps it takes (this is a stripped-down version of the complete listing):

```
 1  GtkObject* grs;           /* A recordset */
 2  gchar sql_buffer[1024];   /* The SQL command */
 3  gint rc;                  /* Result code */
 4
 5  /* Execute the query */
 6  grs = gda_recordset_new();
 7  gda_recordset_set_connection(GDA_RECORDSET(grs), cnc);
 8  sprintf(sql_buffer, "SELECT %s, %s FROM %s",
 9                      label_col,
10                      id_col,
11                      table);
12  rc = gda_recordset_open_txt(GDA_RECORDSET(grs),
13                              sql_buffer,
14                              GDA_OPEN_FWDONLY,
15                              GDA_LOCK_READONLY,
16                              0);
17  if (rc < 0) {
18    fprintf(stderr, "Could not execute query.\n");
19    gtk_main_quit();
20  }
```

Line 1. Define a variable for the recordset object. The recordset is an object that holds the results of an SQL query.

Line 2. Define a character buffer to hold the contents of the query.

Line 3. Define an integer variable to hold the result code of the query.

Line 6. Create a new result set.

Line 7. Associate that result set with an existing connection object (assume that this was initialized as discussed in the section titled Make a Connection).

Lines 8–11. Store the text of the SQL query into the sql_buffer variable. This takes the form of SELECT *column, another-column* FROM *table-name*.

Lines 12–16. Open the recordset. This has the effect of executing the SQL query and putting the results into the recordset object.

Lines 17–20. If the query failed, print an error message and quit.

After this function creates a recordset, it creates a new GnomeDbCombo object with that recordset as the combo's source for its data.

To use this function, you must pass in a connection object, the name of a table, and the names of two columns in that table: the id column (the table's primary key) and the label column (this is the column that's used as the text of the combo menu).

The get_selected_value() private function. This function takes the Gnome-DbCombo object's underlying recordset, repositions it to be in sync with the current selection, and returns one of the column values from the recordset. So, you can use this to get the currently selected item, by specifying the column that corresponds to the label, or to get the id value of the currently selected item, by specifying the column that corresponds to the id.

The get_selected_label() public function. This is just a simple wrapper around the get_selected_value function that fetches the label of the currently selected item.

The get_selected_id() public function. This is another wrapper around get_selected_value, but it gets the id of the currently selected item. Here is the power of table_combo.c: When a user makes a selection of a company name, it is not always meaningful to use that name in any subsequent queries. If you've designed a normalized database design, you will be more interested in the id, so you can do a query like "SELECT * FROM contacts WHERE company = selected_id." This function lets the user select a company name, such as Bulbic Bearing Supply Co., and lets the application find out that the id of that selection is 120 (see SAMPLE _DATA.SQL).

The on_combo_delete_event() private function. This function takes care of closing the underlying result set when the application is closed (each widget's delete event will be fired eventually).

Here is the source code for table_combo.h:

```
#include <gda.h>
#include <gda-connection.h>
#include <gda-ui.h>

/* Define constants that relate to the position
    of the label and id column in the initial query
*/
#define LABEL_COLUMN 0
#define ID_COLUMN 1

gchar* get_selected_label(GtkWidget* combo);
gchar* get_selected_id(GtkWidget* combo);
GtkWidget* create_gda_combo(Gda_Connection* cnc,
                            gchar* table,
                            gchar* label_col,
                            gchar* id_col);
```

Here is the source code for table_combo.c:

```
#include "table_combo.h"

/*
 * Get a value from the currently selected row.
 */
gchar* get_selected_value(GtkWidget* combo, gint column_index) {

  Gda_Recordset* grs; /* The underlying record set */
  Gda_Field* field;   /* The field whose value we need */
  gchar buffer[64];   /* A buffer to hold the return value */

  /* Reposition the record set on the selected row */
  grs = gnome_db_combo_get_recordset(GNOME_DB_COMBO(combo));
  gnome_db_combo_sync(GNOME_DB_COMBO(combo));

  /* retrieve the field we're interested in and return it */
  field = gda_recordset_field_idx(grs, column_index);
  gda_stringify_value(buffer, sizeof(buffer), field);
  return g_strdup(buffer);

}

/*
 * Return the label of the currently selected item.
 */
```

```
gchar* get_selected_label(GtkWidget* combo) {
  return get_selected_value(combo, LABEL_COLUMN);
}

/*
 * Return the id of the currently selected item.
 */
gchar* get_selected_id(GtkWidget* combo) {
  return get_selected_value(combo, ID_COLUMN);
}

/* Close the recordset when the Combo is deleted */
gint on_combo_delete_event(GtkWidget* combo, gpointer data) {
  Gda_Recordset* grs;
  grs = gnome_db_combo_get_recordset(GNOME_DB_COMBO(combo));
  gda_recordset_close(grs);
  return FALSE;
}

/* Create and return a GDA Combo object */
GtkWidget* create_gda_combo(Gda_Connection* cnc,
                            gchar* table,
                            gchar* label_col,
                            gchar* id_col)
{

  GtkObject* grs;           /* A recordset */
  gchar sql_buffer[1024]; /* The SQL command */
  gint rc;                  /* Result code */
  GtkWidget* combo;         /* The combo object */

  /* Execute the query */
  grs = gda_recordset_new();
  gda_recordset_set_connection(GDA_RECORDSET(grs), cnc);
  sprintf(sql_buffer, "SELECT %s, %s FROM %s",
                      label_col,
                      id_col,
                      table);
  rc = gda_recordset_open_txt(GDA_RECORDSET(grs),
                              sql_buffer,
                              GDA_OPEN_FWDONLY,
                              GDA_LOCK_READONLY,
                              0);
  if (rc < 0) {
    fprintf(stderr, "Could not execute query.\n");
    gtk_main_quit();
  }

  return gnome_db_combo_new(GDA_RECORDSET(grs), LABEL_COLUMN);

}
```

The db_gui.c Program

This is the main program that runs the whole show—it's similar to earlier main programs in that it takes care of invoking the login functions, setting up error handling, and other similar duties.

The on_app_delete_event() function. This is the event handler that manages the closing of the main application window.

The on_execute_search_clicked() function. This function takes care of filling the grid with data when the user clicks the Execute Search button. It does so by first looking at the currently selected company id (using get_selected _id) and constructing an SQL query similar to SELECT name, city FROM contact WHERE company = *selected-id*. Then, it puts the results into a recordset, and associates that recordset with the grid. Finally, it calls gtk _widget_show, which refreshes the display of the grid.

The get_company_combo() function. This is a little wrapper function to invoke the create_gda_combo function in table_combo.c. It's here for libglade's benefit, so that we can just put the name of this function into the creation function portion of the glade XML file. See *the cmb_company Custom widget* in the *Glade UI Definition* section, earlier in this chapter.

The get_grid() function. This is another convenience method for libglade's sake (see *the grid widget Custom widget* in the Glade UI Definition section, earlier in this chapter). This function creates an empty recordset using an impossible condition, WHERE 6 = 9 (in tribute to the Jimi Hendrix song of a similar name). Then, it uses that recordset to create a new GnomeDbGrid object and returns it.

The main() function. This function is similar to other main functions we have seen. It sets up the CORBA and GNOME environments, configures an error handler, and initiates a login sequence. If all goes well, it then uses libglade441s glade_xml_new and glade_xml_signal_autoconnect to set up the user interface. The gtk_main function kicks everything off, and continues running until the user exits the application.

Here is the source code for db_gui.h:

```
#include "login.h"
#include "error.h"
#include "table_combo.h"
#include <stdio.h>
#include <libgnorba/gnorba.h>
#include <glade/glade.h>
#include <gda.h>
#include <gda-connection.h>
```

Here is the source code for db_gui.c:

```c
#include "db_gui.h"

Gda_Connection* cnc;  /* Database connection */
GladeXML *xml;        /* Glade XML document */

/*
 * Event handler for closing
 * the main application window
 */
gint on_app_delete_event(GtkWidget*  w,
                         GdkEventAny* e,
                         gpointer data)
{
  gtk_main_quit();
  return FALSE;
}

/*
 * Event handler for clicking the Execute Search
 * button.  This requeries the database and refreshes
 * the data in the grid.
 */
gint on_execute_search_clicked(GtkWidget* execute_search) {

  GtkWidget* cmb_company; /* The company combo */
  GtkWidget* grid;        /* The grid */
  GtkObject* grs;         /* A recordset */

  gchar *company_id;      /* selected company */
  gchar sql_buffer[1024]; /* Buffer for SQL statement */
  gint rc;                /* Return value of issuing SQL */

  /* Get the grid object and the combo object */
  grid        = glade_xml_get_widget(xml, "grid");
  cmb_company = glade_xml_get_widget(xml, "cmb_company");

  /* Get the selected ID value from the combo */
  company_id = get_selected_id(cmb_company);

  /*
   * Create an SQL statement that fetches all rows
   * from the contact table for the selected company.
   */
  sprintf(sql_buffer,
          "SELECT name, city FROM contact WHERE company = %s",
          company_id);

  /* Create a new recordset and query the database. */
```

```c
    grs = gda_recordset_new();
    gda_recordset_set_connection(GDA_RECORDSET(grs), cnc);
    rc = gda_recordset_open_txt(GDA_RECORDSET(grs),
                                sql_buffer,
                                GDA_OPEN_STATIC,
                                GDA_LOCK_PESSIMISTIC,
                                0);
  if (rc < 0) {
    fprintf(stderr, "Could not issue query.\n");
    gtk_main_quit();
  }

  /* Update the grid with the new recordset */
  gnome_db_grid_set_recordset(GNOME_DB_GRID(grid),
                              GDA_RECORDSET(grs));
  gtk_widget_show(grid);

}


/*
 * Create a combo dialog for the company table
 */
GtkWidget* get_company_combo() {
  return create_gda_combo(cnc, "company", "name", "id");
}

/*
 * Create a grid object with an empty result set.
 */
GtkWidget* get_grid() {

  GtkObject* grs;
  gint rc;

  /* Create an empty recordset (where 6 = 9) */
  grs = gda_recordset_new();
  gda_recordset_set_connection(GDA_RECORDSET(grs), cnc);
  rc = gda_recordset_open_txt(GDA_RECORDSET(grs),
                              "SELECT * FROM contact "
                              "WHERE 1 = 0",
                              GDA_OPEN_STATIC,
                              GDA_LOCK_PESSIMISTIC,
                              0);
  if (rc < 0) {
    fprintf(stderr, "Could not issue query.\n");
    gtk_main_quit();
  }

  /* Create a grid object with the recordset */
```

```
  return gnome_db_grid_new(GDA_RECORDSET(grs));
}

/* Close the recordset when the Grid is deleted */
gint on_grid_delete_event(GtkWidget* grid, gpointer data) {
  Gda_Recordset* grs;
  grs = gnome_db_grid_get_recordset(GNOME_DB_GRID(grid));
  gda_recordset_close(grs);
  return FALSE;
}

/*
 * The main function.
 */
int main(int argc, char* argv[]) {

  CORBA_ORB orb;
  CORBA_Environment ev;

  CORBA_exception_init(&ev);
  orb = gnome_CORBA_init("db_gui", /* app_id */
                         "1.0",       /* app_version */
                         &argc,
                         argv,
                         0,           /* gnorba_flags */
                         &ev);        /* CORBA environment */

  /* Use the ORB to create a new connection object. */
  cnc = gda_connection_new(orb);

  /* Set up an error handler for the connection */
  register_error_handler(cnc);

  /* Try to log in. If the login fails, exit the program
   * with a message.
   */
  if ( !login_db(cnc) ) {
      fprintf(stderr, "Login failed.\n");
      return(-1);
  }

  /* Initialize Glade */
  glade_gnome_init();

  /* Load the UI definition from the file */
  xml = glade_xml_new("db_gui.glade", NULL);

  /* Connect the signals that are defined in the file */
  glade_xml_signal_autoconnect(xml);
```

```
gtk_main(); /* main loop */

/* Close the connection */
gda_connection_close(cnc);

return (0);
}
```

Compile and Run db_gui

The following Makefile takes care of compiling db_gui (it should look similar to earlier Makefiles we saw):

```
CFLAGS  = -c `gda-config --cflags gdaui gnome`
CFLAGS += `gnome-config --cflags libglade`

LIBS = `gda-config --libs gdaui gnome`
LIBS += `gnome-config --libs libglade`

OBJS = db_gui.o login.o error.o table_combo.o

all: db_gui

login.o: login.c login.h
$(CC) $(CFLAGS) -o $@ $<

table_combo.o: table_combo.c table_combo.h
$(CC) $(CFLAGS) -o $@ $<

error.o: error.c error.h
$(CC) $(CFLAGS) -o $@ $<

db_gui.o: db_gui.c db_gui.h login.h
$(CC) $(CFLAGS) -o $@ $<

db_gui: $(OBJS)
$(CC) -o $@ $(OBJS) $(LIBS)

clean:
rm -f $(OBJS) db_gui
```

As with earlier examples, compile this program by running *make*. After make is finished, you can run it with the command ./db_gui. When you run it, log in to a data source, and the main window should appear as shown in Figure 13.20.

Summary

In this chapter, we took a whirlwind tour of the various options available to database developers who want to work with GNOME. Although GNOME is not the only application framework for Linux, it offers an advanced database architecture that can make it very easy to develop complicated database applications. As other alternatives emerge and/or evolve for other application frameworks (such as KDE and GNUstep), they will merit as much attention as we have given to GNOME-DB.

Software Architecture

I n Chapters 5 through 8, we discussed the process of developing software, and specifically, object-oriented programming. Object-oriented programming is a set of constructs that enable modularity in the software development process. In this chapter, we are going to discuss the process of deploying software, and examine how this process impacts the software development process, and particularly object-oriented design.

When you deploy software, you want the program to run correctly from start to finish. The fact that there are no defects in the development system does not mean that there will not be defects in the production system. You want your program to run as quickly and efficiently as possible. You want your program to be able to recover from any unforeseen conditions. You want to be able to upgrade your program. You only want people using your program who are authorized to use it. You want as many people as possible to be able to use your software. Bottom line: Getting people to use new software tools is difficult enough, so you don't need any more problems, especially problems that are external to the software itself.

Modularity and Troubleshooting

A modular design is key to effective troubleshooting. If the system is broken, you need to be able to isolate the cause, or be able to replace the whole system, and if your job is to troubleshoot, chances are that replacing the whole system is not an option. So, you need to be able to isolate the cause. How do you do that? You take the largest testable chunk of the system and you see if that chunk is working. If that chunk works, put it back in and move on to the next largest chunk. If the first chunk doesn't work, you take the largest testable chunk of the first chunk and repeat the process. When you find the broken part, you replace it with a working part. But if it is not a modular design, you can't start by isolating the faulty component, and you need to take the whole thing apart, starting at the beginning.

The most depressing aspect of troubleshooting is that the goal of the whole activity is to get the application back to where it was before someone started messing with it. Instead of replacing the timing belt whenever it breaks, get a tune-up every six months. A tune-up is a different activity than trouble-shooting. In troubleshooting, either the system works or it doesn't. In tuning, results come as a function (points on the curve, which is the range of possible performance), and your job is to find the sweet spot in the function (getting the most efficiency from what you put in). But again, modular design is the key to effective tuning. If you cannot isolate portions of the system from the effects of the system as a whole, it is very difficult to find out if the system as a whole is running as efficiently as it could.

Tuning doesn't necessarily need to be about halting (or slowing) the decline of a system. Suppose your problem is that you keep getting killed in Quake because by the time your screen redraws, you are already dead. You run a series of tests and you figure out that the problem is that your video subsystem is too slow. If your video subsystem is a separate, removable component, all you have to do is replace the old, slow video card with a new, fast, video card, and presto, Quake is a whole new game.

To summarize, a modular design allows your system to be flexible, reliable, and scaleable, and these are all good things. In addition, a modular design gives you the freedom to make implementation choices.

Architectural Choices

Suppose you were building single-family homes. If you were working with a shell that required a full basement, rather than just a slab, that would limit the possible sites where you could construct this house. So ok, you could change the shell you were working with. But what if the blueprints specify a wall size that can only be accomplished with the basement-loving shell? Then you really have no choice, because even if you weren't locked in to buying that particular shell, and even if your carpenters were trained to work with a variety of different shells, your architect made it impossible for you to deal with the situation (if the architect explains his design choice by saying "That's why there is a basement," you have my permission to throttle him).

As a software architect, the major implementation choices you can make are: where the program is going to be stored, where the program is going to execute, and where the data is going to be stored. In making these choices, there are three facts to consider:

Network speed. Accessing information across a network is an order of magnitude slower than accessing information from local disk, which is an order of magnitude slower that accessing information from main memory, which is an order of magnitude slower that accessing information from process memory.

Complexity. The management complexity of a piece of software rises linearly with the number of sites where it stores data.

Price versus performance. The price-performance curve of computer hardware is sublinear; that is, a system that costs twice as much will be less than twice as good, and a system that costs four times as much will be much less than four times as good.

Another thing to remember is that it is quite possible to implement solutions to architectural problems using both hardware and software. Suppose you need to scale the processing power in a linear fashion? A hardware solution would use Symmetric Multi-Processing (SMP), and would place additional processors in a single machine. A software solution would use load-balancing algorithms to spread the processing burden across multiple machines, each of which has a single processor (Linux supports both approaches). Suppose you need to scale storage capacity in a linear fashion? A hardware solution would use a Storage Area Network (SAN) to link additional storage devices to a single machine. A software solution would use the Network File System (NFS) to link the storage devices of multiple machines. Suppose you need to encrypt data sent across the network? A hardware solution would use a network card that encrypts data using a Virtual Private Network. A software solution would use Secure Sockets Layer (SSL) to encrypt data using a public key encryption algorithm.

Within these parameters, you can make a lot of different choices, but as a rule of thumb you should have *centralized storage* (such as linking additional storage devices to a single machine) and *distributed execution* (such as the load-balancing described earlier).

Message Passing Facilities

To me, the three greatest triumphs of programming are C, Unix-like operating systems, and TCP/IP. I say that not only because they are wonderful, capable programs, but because these three programs provide the foundation for almost *every other program in existence*. GNU C makes it possible to control a single process and address space. Unix (operating systems in general, if you want to be charitable) makes it possible to control multiple processes and devices. TCP/IP makes it possible to control multiple machines. With these three programs, programmers have almost unlimited possibilities for developing software.

Modern compilers are wonderful things, and if you have ever programmed in assembler, you know what I am talking about. If you have never programmed in assembler, please don't put this book down and start trying now. I am not a sadist, and the prose explanation should be quite enough to disabuse you of that notion.

Let's take two, very straightforward lines of code from the Book example (see Chapter 5, "Object-Oriented Programming"), and then talk about what they look like in assembler.

Here is the code in C++:

```
Book bk = new Book();
int x = bk.setCheckOutDate("01-01-2000");
```

Through compiler magic, we don't have to do all the messy stuff that happens in assembler, such as:

- Repeating the definition of the Book object
- Allocating contiguous register addresses to hold this instance of the Book object
- Remembering which addresses we allocated or checking that these registers still have the data we placed in them
- Figuring out the offset of the setCheckOutDate code segment
- Storing the current state of the executing program segment on the stack while we move into the subroutine
- Allocating memory for the parameter data or the return data
- Assigning the register value of the parameter address into the subroutine
- Assigning the register of the result address into the executing program

- Popping the subroutine off of the stack when it returns
- Reloading the main program and restoring its execution state with the new return value

The point of bringing up all these things we don't have to worry about is not to make you hate and fear assembler (although that is a natural human reaction), but to point out that these system-level functions need to exist for any type of message passing program to work. The fact that the compiler will provide all of these functions for message passing inside a single process/flat memory architecture is a great help. What we are now going to examine are the tools that will implement these system-level functions in alternate architectures, outside of the process space, passing messages between multiple programs.

As an example, let's look at another simple book example. In this example, we are assuming that a book component (Wiley.Book) has been shipped to us in binary format by the publisher. The book component is loaded on demand by our application, though it runs in another process. In this case, we talk to the book through a local placeholder, or stub, which forwards requests to the real book object. If the book was running in-process, we would just make method calls directly on the object.

Here is the code:

```
Book bk = (Book) CreateObject("Wiley.Book");
int x = bk.setCheckOutDate("01-01-2000");
```

Now, let's start looking at the things we don't have to worry about. By using a component object model, we don't have to:

- Find the program identified by "Wiley.Book"
- Load the "Wiley.Book" program into memory or find an already running version of the program
- Manage the execution state, offsets, or concurrency between the local "Wiley.Book" placeholder and the remote "Wiley.Book" instance
- Find some piece of shared memory to place the argument
- Do any data type translations to turn data types supported by the local Book program into data types supported by the remote "Wiley.Book" program

All of these functions are provided by the component object model's infrastructure, and that makes things a whole lot easier when attempting to pass messages between processes. This is similar to CORBA, except that the two processes run on the same machine. In CORBA, which we explore in the next chapter, objects can be distributed across various machines.

Networking

Data Networking is a very interesting subject. Signal processing, copper and fiber optic cabling, Ethernet, Packet framing and switching, and Routing are all complex and diverse subjects: What makes TCP/IP one of the great achievements in computing is that it provides a standardized interface to every possible engineering solution from all of the preceding disciplines. The way that TCP/IP accomplishes this is to break the networking infrastructure into a series of layers, in which each layer only has to be aware of the layer directly below it, and the layer directly above it. The top layer of the TCP/IP stack (also referred to as the OSI model) is called the Application layer. This is the layer that software programs use to put data onto the network, and since BSD 4.3, the operating system interface that programmers use to access the Application layer has been called a socket. Sockets, like most good things in Unix, act something like a file; you can open them, read from them, write to them, and close them.

Communication requires two participants: one who is talking, and one who is listening. Dialog requires that there be some way for the person who was listening to talk once in a while. And if you've ever been party to a meta-discussion about interpersonal communication, you know that there needs to be some way to start a conversation in a silent room. TCP/IP protocols are the mechanisms that network programs use to keep from going to bed angry, and Client/Server is a framework that uses TCP/IP protocols to create useful application programs.

Client/Server defines two participants, a client and a server. The server's job is to listen until spoken to. The client's job is to start up a conversation. Client and server punctuate and signify their conversation using a pre-agreed protocol, which governs when the client may speak, when the server may reply, and what the possible topics of conversation are. SMTP is an example of a client-server TCP/IP protocol. In SMTP:

- The client says hello to the server.
- The server says hello to the client.
- The only possible topic of conversation is about sending e-mail.
- The client and server agree that the end of one line means that the other party can begin speaking.

Telnet is another example of a TCP/IP protocol; in Telnet the client sends a user name and password to the server, the server authenticates the client and then passes the client off to an instance of the client's default shell, after which the client and the shell can converse about anything under the sun.

Let's look at how sockets make it possible to pass messages between programs on different machines (this example is pseudocode—it won't really run, but it's meant to give you an idea of what happens):

```
Socket s = new Socket(getHostByName("www.wiley.com"),
                      getProtocolByName("BookServer"));
s.open();
s.write("setCheckOutDate");
if (s.read()) {
    s.write("01-01-2000");
    int x = s.read();
}
s.close();
```

Through the magic of TCP/IP, we don't have to:

- Figure out where the machine that calls itself www.wiley.com is on the Internet
- Figure out how to find the BookService process on that machine
- Make sure that the checkOutDate argument arrives at its intended destination
- Figure out how to translate between the way data is represented on the network and the way data is represented in our program

Whenever anyone tells me that I don't need to know something, the first thing I do is try and figure it out, so let's go a little deeper into the BookService example. The first thing we need to do is find the IP address that identifies www.wiley.com. The socket function that does this is getHostByName. Having gotten the true address of the server, we need to tell the server that we want to use the BookServer protocol to communicate. For the purpose of the example, let's assume that a protocol called BookService actually exists (as far as we know, it doesn't), and consists of a method name, an acknowledgment, an argument, and a response.

So, given that the protocol contains all the information the server will need to manage the execution issues on the remote machine, the only remaining issue is to make sure that the arguments are passed in an intelligible way. There is no guarantee that the remote program supports the same endian-ness, let alone higher-level data types, so, in a real-world example, we would use a construct called eXternal Data Representation (xdr), and a set of library functions that handle converting native data types to xdr and back again.

The Wonder of Relational Databases

While component object models and client server offer a great deal of flexibility in how and where your program executes, they don't say anything at all about where your program's data is stored. Relational Databases are another programming wonder, but before we get into the mechanics of how relational databases work in a message passing environment, let's look why relational databases are useful.

In addition to providing access to processor cycles and register areas, operating systems also provide a standardized interface to disk drives and permanent storage. The operating system interface to permanent storage generally is implemented in the form of file systems, directories, and files. File systems allow access to multiple physical devices, directories break file systems into groupings of files and other directories, and files are a series of bytes of arbitrary length. Since file systems and directories are merely organizing constructs, we will concentrate on files.

Files as Databases

The file interface is small. You can create files, open files, read from files, write to files, close files, and delete files. The file system is also powerful, because, although there a limited number of functions you can use, there is no limit on how you do use the available functions. Let's look at how we would use a file in our book example.

Being able to figure out the return date for a book at checkout is all well and good, but if you don't write this information down somewhere (and hopefully somewhere where you can find it again), the point is moot. In addition to calling the Book.setCheckOutDate(), we also need to be able to record which book is being checked out, when it is due back, and who is checking it out.

Here is some code:

```
File f = new File("/data/Library/Checkout.dat");
f.open();
f.write(Book.getID());
f.write("\t");
f.write(Book.getCheckOutDate());
f.write("\t");
f.write(Patron.getID());
f.close();
```

The code is pretty straightforward: Find the data file, open it, record the checkout data as a tab-separated series of strings, and close the file. From the point of view of our checkout program, we've done our job; the program has adequately recorded which book is being checked out, when it is due back, and who is checking it out. However, from the point of view of programs that might call the checkout function, the implementation is horribly flawed in that it doesn't take into account two special properties of files: that the same file may be used by consecutive executions of the program, and that the same file may be used by concurrent executions of the program.

The problem with consecutive execution is fairly clear: While the checkout data will be persistent after the program runs, the next book that gets checked out will overwrite the data for the previous book!

The way in which the operating system deals with this is called a file pointer. What the file pointer does is record the current offset of read and write operations from the beginning of the file, and allow programs to reset the pointer to the beginning of the file or to advance the file pointer an arbitrary number of bytes into the file. Most file interfaces extend this functionality by offering two versions of the open function; one opens the file and sets the file pointer to the beginning of the file, the other opens the file and advances the file pointer to the end of the file. The second version of the open function is generally referred to as *append mode*. So to fix the consecutive execution problem, the second line of code should read something like this:

```
f.open(FILE_APPEND);
```

For operating systems that don't support preemptive multitasking, the problem with concurrent execution is moot (since two programs can't write to the file at the same time). However, since this book is about a real operating system, we need to worry about what happens if two programs try to access the same file at the same time.

The root cause of the problem is that to ensure that we have the correct book, due on the correct date, from the correct patron, all three calls to write() need to occur exactly as written. If the calls to write() from one instance of the checkout program are interleaved with calls to write() from another instance of the checkout program, we are no longer recording correct data (because, milliseconds after process one opens the file, process two writes to the sample place process one wants to write to, before process one has a chance to write anything at all). The way in which the operating system deals with this is called a *file lock*. What the file lock does is keep any other program from opening the file until the first program has closed it.

So, to fix the concurrent execution problem, the second line of code should read something like this:

```
f.open(ACQUIRE_LOCK, FILE_APPEND);
```

Now the checkout program does what it is supposed to do from a programming standpoint, and can be called with some degree of confidence by other programs. But, let's look at this implementation in terms of the functional specification of the larger system. If you can check books out of the system, you should also be able to check books into the system, you should be able to renew loans, you should be able to find out all the books that a single patron has checked out, you should be able to find out if all copies of the same book have been checked out. If we use a file-based approach, all of this functionality must be implemented based on this file format:

1111	12-31-99	5555
1234	01-01-00	1234
5555	01-05-00	1234
1234	01-15-2000	5555
5555	01-19-2000	1234

The first problem is trying to figure out what data is getting stored in which column, and what data type should we be using to make sense out of the information in that column. Even if we have documented the file format, how do we determine which patron corresponds with number 1234, or whether books 1234 and 5555 are different copies of the same volumes? Checking books in to the system requires that we be able to find the correct checkout information for a particular book. As the file gets larger, this will become a time-consuming operation, and because we have to lock the entire file whenever a book is being checked out, we may have to disable all checkout activity while we perform check-in activity. And, even if our program deals with all of these scenarios appropriately, what happens if a system external to the program (such as the disk itself) fails in the middle of a checkout operation?

Client-Server Relational Databases to the Rescue

Seeing the ridiculous amount of effort required to develop file-based applications, you can understand how a little thing like the fact that the checkout date has eight characters in the first three records and 10 characters in the rest of the records could slip through the cracks. Thankfully, relational databases address all of these concerns extremely well, bringing robust, standardized, programmable implementations of meta-data, referential integrity, table indexing, record-level locking, and transaction processing to the rescue of programmers everywhere.

While relational databases came to prominence by fixing the nightmarish problems of file-based applications, they rose to fame by supporting message passing applications with two essential capabilities: stored procedures, which allowed programmers to write code that would execute inside the database; and database drivers, which allowed programmers to write network client programs that communicate with a remote database server without programmers having to write network servers, custom protocols, or make direct calls to the socket interface.

So, without further background ado, let's return to the checkout example, using pseudocode and an SQL database:

```
Connection conn = getConnection(DATABASE_URL, USERNAME, PASSWORD);
CallableStatement cstmt = conn.prepareCall(
    "UPDATE book SET checkout_date = ? WHERE id = ?");

cstmt.setString(1, "01-01-2000");
cstmt.setInt(2, bookid);
cstmt.execute();
```

In addition to handling all the pesky problems of storing, relating, retrieving, and managing persistent data, this client-server code retains most of the syntactic elegance of a component object model, while adding the distributed execution capabilities of a socket program.

Summary

Using either of the message passing frameworks we have looked at will still leave you with architectural problems. Component object models have an elegant syntax for crossing process boundaries, but do not provide much as far as distributed execution, and don't address the issue of centralized storage at all. Client-server is a very powerful interface for networking, but the code is ugly, protocols are not easily extensible, and while it can get you to your centralized storage, it doesn't help you actually store anything. In the next chapter, "Introduction to CORBA," we'll look at an architecture for distributing components across different machines and/or operating systems.

Introduction to CORBA

The Common Object Request Broker Architecture (CORBA) is a technology that lets objects communicate with each other across networks, between operating systems, and in different programming languages. For example, you can create an object in C++, run it on a Linux-based system, and connect to it from an object written in Java that's running on another machine running a different operating system (such as Windows, Solaris, or MacOS).

CORBA can also be used to connect objects running on the same system, or even within the same process. This feature makes CORBA suitable for building a general-purpose component model, as with GNOME's Bonobo, which uses CORBA for creating compound documents (such as embedding a drawing in a spreadsheet).

CORBA was introduced in 1991 by the Object Management Group (OMG), which continues to revise and maintain the CORBA specification, and act as a clearinghouse for information (www.omg.org/corba/).

Why should CORBA be of interest to Linux database developers? Here are some reasons:

- CORBA is the foundation of GNOME's component model, Bonobo, which supports component reuse, embedded objects, and compound documents (in these respects, it is similar to Microsoft's COM/ActiveX). GNOME's database API, gnome-db, is implemented as a collection of CORBA servers.

- CORBA is an industry-accepted standard for interoperability between objects running on different systems, different operating systems, and in different programming languages. At least two CORBA implementations ship with Linux distributions, and one of them (MICO) has even been ported to the PalmOS platform. Despite competing technologies (such as Microsoft's DCOM and Java's RMI), CORBA is the most pervasive solution for connecting objects together.

CORBA Terminology

CORBA is heavily tied to the object-oriented concepts described in Chapter 5, "Object-Oriented Programming," but expands on many of those concepts (by extending the object-oriented paradigm to distributed computing). Here are some CORBA terms that will make it easier to understand the examples that follow:

Interface. A language-neutral definition of the functions and data that a CORBA object exposes. The interface is a promise that a component will support certain functions, and expose certain data attributes.

Implementation. An application that implements all of the features defined in an interface.

Server. A process that allows remote and local applications (clients) to access an instance of the implementation.

Client. An application that can connect to a server and invoke its methods.

Skeleton. The raw, prototypical definition of the implementation. The implementation fleshes out the skeleton.

Stub. The definition of the object that the client actually talks to. The client invokes methods defined in the stub; the stub forwards the requests to the implementation by connecting to the server.

ORB. The Object Request Broker, software that is capable of acting as a server for objects or as a client. As a client, the ORB lets you locate objects and invoke their methods. As a server, the ORB allows clients to connect to the object. This software is implemented as a shared library in MICO and ORBit. When you execute a client or server, the ORB is started along with the client or server.

IDL. Interface Definition Language, a C++-like programming language you use to write interfaces.

IDL Compiler. This tool converts IDL into source code for you, including stubs, skeletons, and header files. Some IDL compilers will also generate skeleton implementations that you can fill in with your own code to create full implementations.

IOR. Interoperable Object Reference, a string representation of an object that a client uses to connect to the object's ORB. Here is a rough analogy: An IOR is to an ORB as a host name is to a server.

Object Adapter. Software that acts as an interface between the object and the ORB.

BOA. The Basic Object Adapter. This is the first object adapter in the CORBA specification. Over time, it has been mutated by various vendor extensions to the point where implementations are not compatible at the source level.

POA. The Portable Object Adapter. This is an object adapter from more recent CORBA specifications. It addresses many of the limitations that led to the incompatible extensions to BOA, and should be source-code compatible across implementations. Using POA, a server written in C++ should be portable across CORBA implementations that support C++.

Language Binding. A connection between a particular language and an ORB. This includes libraries, header files, and IDL compilers that support the language in question. For example, ORBit's C binding lets you write clients and servers in C.

IIOP. This is the Internet Inter-ORB Protocol. It allows ORBs, including those from different CORBA implementations, to talk to each other. For example, ORBit and MICO can talk to each other using IIOP.

Figure 15.1 shows the relationship of some of these items.

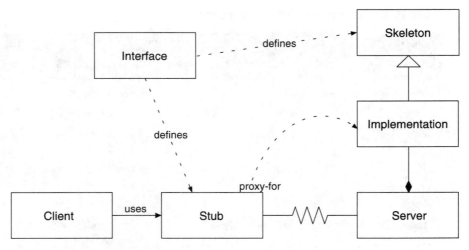

Figure 15.1   Some relationships in CORBA.

CORBA Implementations for Linux

What is a CORBA implementation? Is it a daemon? An API? A collection of tools? In reality, it's a little bit of each. At a minimum, each implementation includes an ORB, an IDL compiler, and headers and libraries that you can use to compile your own applications.

Table 15.1 lists some free CORBA implementations that run under Linux. Of these, we will only look at MICO and ORBit in this chapter.

MICO

MICO aims for full CORBA compliance. MICO is implemented in C++, has a binding for C++, and has been branded as CORBA compliant by the Open-Group. Bindings are available for other languages, such as Perl, Eiffel, and Tcl.

MICO can be installed under Debian systems using dselect. Under RedHat, use the gnorpm or rpmfind utility to locate the mico and mico-devel packages. If you have trouble finding MICO for your system, visit the MICO home page (see Table 15.1).

ORBit

ORBit is a standards-compliant CORBA implementation that aims for high performance. It is implemented in C, and the default bindings support C. Bindings are available for other languages, such as C++, Perl, and Python.

Table 15.1   Some Free CORBA Implementations

IMPLEMENTATION	IDL COMPILER	DEFAULT LANGUAGE BINDING	HOME PAGE
MICO	idl	C++	www.mico.org/
ORBit	orbit-idl	ANSI C	www.labs.redhat.com/orbit/
OmniORB	omniidl2	C++	www.uk.research.att.com/omniORB/
JacORB	idl	Java	www.inf.fu-berlin.de/~brose/jacorb/
Fnorb	fnidl	Python	www.fnorb.org
JavaORB	idl2java	Java	www.multimania.com/dogweb/
TAO (The ACE ORB)	idl	C++	http://theaceorb.com/

ORBit is the ORB used by GNOME, the GNU Network Object Model Environment. Because GNOME is a core part of most Linux distributions, ORBit is often installed by default on many Linux systems, including Debian and RedHat.

Using CORBA

Let's take a look at some CORBA examples, each of which is composed of a client and a server.

If you would like to run some example programs as you read through this section, you can find the example programs on the companion Web site at www.wiley.com/compbooks/jepson. Each of the examples are in their own directory, and include a Makefile and shell script to run the programs. You can change to the directory that contains the example, run the *make* command, and then run the ./RunDemo script to execute the example.

NOTE

We tested the MICO example on a RedHat 6.1 system. As of this writing, there is an unstated dependency between the mico-devel package and the libelf package. If you do not install the libelf package from your RedHat distribution media, the mico-ld command will not work, and you will not be able to compile the example programs.

All of these directories are contained in the ch15 subdirectory of the example code. Table 15.2 lists the subdirectory names for each example.

A Simple MICO Example

Let's take a look at a simple server using MICO—this server will represent a single employee object, as defined by the following IDL (Employee.idl). This IDL defines an Employee object with a name and a salary, and a method to give the employee a raise:

```
interface Employee {

    readonly attribute string name;
    readonly attribute unsigned long salary;
```

Table 15.2   Location of Example Programs

SECTION NAME	SUBDIRECTORY NAME
A Simple MICO Example	MICO-Simple/
A Simple ORBit Example	ORBit-Simple/

```
    // Raise employee's salary.
    //
    void raise(in unsigned long amount);

};
```

Before We Write Some Code

To generate stubs and skeletons, run the idl utility on the Employee.idl file:

```
idl Employee.idl
```

This creates two files:

Employee.cc. This file contains the stub (an object called Employee) and the skeleton (an object called Employee_skel) for the implementation of Employee.

Employee.h. This is the header file for the classes in Employee.cc.

Once you have these files, you can write your own implementation, server, and client.

The Implementation

To write the implementation:

1. *Figure out what you want to call the implementation class.* You can give it any legal name, but it needs to be different from the stub and skeleton class, such as Employee_impl.
2. *Create a header file with the class definition, such as Employee_impl.h.* The class must:
   a. Inherit from the skeleton class.
   b. Define any private data members you need (at a minimum, you need data members that correspond to each attribute you defined in the interface).
   c. Define a constructor.
   d. Define methods for each operation in the interface definition.
   e. Have accessor methods for each attribute in the interface.
3. *Create a C++ source file with the implementation of the class, such as Employee_impl.cc.* This implementation follows the definition you put in the header file.
4. *Compile the C++ source file to an object file, such as Employee_impl.o.*

Let's perform each of these steps:

Step 1. We'll call the implementation Employee_impl.

Step 2. Here is the Employee_impl.h file. We have defined two private data members (_name and _salary) to hold the attributes, and four methods. The first method is the constructor, which needs the name of the employee as an argument. The second method raises the employee's salary by the amount specified in the argument, and the remaining two methods return the values of the name and salary.

```
#include "Employee.h"

// Step 2A. Inherit from Employee_skel.
//
class Employee_impl : virtual public Employee_skel {

    // Step 2B. Define private data members.
    //
    char *_name;              // Name.
    CORBA::ULong _salary;  // Salary.

  public:

    // Step 2C. The constructor.
    //
    Employee_impl(const char *thename);

    // Step 2D. Define methods for each operation in
    // the interface.
    //
    virtual void raise(CORBA::ULong amount);

    // Step 2E. Define accessor methods for each
    // attribute.
    //
    virtual char *name();
    virtual CORBA::ULong salary();

};
```

Step 3. Here is the implementation itself, Employee_impl.cc. All of the methods defined in Employee_impl.h are implemented here. Notice that before we assign or return a string, we duplicate it first using CORBA::string_dup(). This avoids returning a reference to a locally-allocated block of memory (which would probably cause your application to segfault).

```
#include "Employee_impl.h"

// The constructor.
//
Employee_impl::Employee_impl(const char *thename) {
    _salary = 0;
    _name = CORBA::string_dup(thename);
}

// Give the employee a raise.
//
void Employee_impl::raise(CORBA::ULong amount) {
    _salary += amount;
}

// Define methods for the two attributes.
//
CORBA::ULong Employee_impl::salary() {
    return _salary;
}

char *Employee_impl::name() {
    return CORBA::string_dup(_name);
}
```

Step 4. Compile the implementation with mico-c++ (a wrapper around your C compiler). For now, compile it to an object file. When we develop the server, we'll link the server to this object file. You can compile it with this command (the -I. tells it to look for include files in the current directory):

```
mico-c++ -I.    -c Employee_impl.cc -o Employee_impl.o
```

The Server

To develop the server:

1. Write a program, such as Server.cc, that:
   a. Includes the header file from the implementation.
   b. Initializes an ORB and Basic Object Adaptor (BOA).
   c. Creates an instance of the implementation.
   d. Communicates the IOR for this server, perhaps by writing it to standard output or to a file. (If you write it to standard output, make sure you set stdout to unbuffered mode with setvbuf, or it may not get written until the program exits!)

e. Tells the BOA that the implementation is ready, and run the ORB with the run() method. When the ORB is finished, the next lines of code are executed.

f. Cleans up by releasing the server and returning from the application.

2. Compile the skeleton to an object file.

3. Compile and link the server against the skeleton and implementation object files.

Step 1. Here is the source code to Server.cc:

```cpp
#include "Employee_impl.h"  // 1A. Include the implementation

// The server.
//
int main( int argc, char *argv[] ) {

    // 1B. Initialize an ORB and BOA.
    //
    CORBA::ORB_var orb =
        CORBA::ORB_init(argc, argv, "mico-local-orb");
    CORBA::BOA_var boa =
        orb->BOA_init( argc, argv, "mico-local-boa" );

    // 1C. Create an instance of the implementation.
    //
    Employee_impl* server = new Employee_impl("Brian");

    // 1D. Communicate the IOR for this server.
    //
    CORBA::String_var ref = orb->object_to_string( server );
    setvbuf(stdout, (char *)NULL, _IONBF, 0); /* unbuffer stdout */
    cout << ref;

    // 1E. Tell the BOA that the object is ready, and run
    // the ORB.
    //
    boa->impl_is_ready( CORBA::ImplementationDef::_nil() );
    orb->run();

    // 1F. Release the server and return.
    //
    CORBA::release( server );
    return 0;

}
```

Step 2. Compile the skeleton with mico-c++ (remember, the skeleton and stub code are both contained in Employee.cc, which was created when you ran the idl utility):

```
mico-c++ -I.    -c Employee.cc -o Employee.o
```

Step 3. Compile the server to an object file, and use mico-ld to link the object file, the skeleton object file, and the implementation object file against the mico shared library to produce the final server executable (*-lmico2.3.0* tells mico-ld to link against libmico2.3.0.so, which may reside in /usr/lib or /usr/local/lib):

```
mico-c++ -I.    -c Server.cc -o Server.o
mico-ld -I. Employee.o Employee_impl.o Server.o -lmico2.2.7 -o Server
```

NOTE
The actual name of the mico library (-lmico2.2.7) may vary, depending on what version of MICO you have.

Figure 15.2 shows how the source code files go together for the server.

The Client

To create the client:

1. Write a program, such as Client.cc, that:
   a. Includes the header file from the implementation.
   b. Creates an ORB.
   c. Obtains the IOR somehow, such as reading from standard input or a file.
   d. Converts the IOR into a CORBA object, and casts it to the appropriate class.

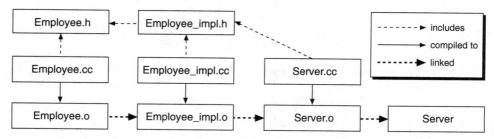

Figure 15.2 Source code organization for simple MICO server.

e. Invokes some methods on the object.

f. Returns from the application.

2. Compile and link the client against the skeleton object files.

Step 1. Here is the source code to Client.cc:

```cpp
#include <iostream.h>
#include <fstream.h>
#include "Employee.h"  // 1A. Include the implementation.

int main( int argc, char *argv[] )
{

  // 1B. Create the ORB.
  //
  CORBA::ORB_var orb =
      CORBA::ORB_init( argc, argv, "mico-local-orb" );

  // 1C. Read the IOR from standard input.
  //
  char ref[1000];
  cin >> ref;

  // 1D. Convert the IOR into a CORBA::Object, and cast
  //      it to an Employee object.
  //
  CORBA::Object_var obj = orb->string_to_object ( ref );
  Employee_var server = Employee::_narrow( obj );

  // 1E. Invoke some methods on the object.
  //
  server->raise( 25000 );
  cout << server->name() << "'s salary is "
       << server->salary() << endl;

  // 1F. Return from the application.
  //
  return 0;

}
```

Step 2. Compile the client to an object file, and use mico-ld to link the object file and the skeleton object file against the mico shared library to produce the final server executable:

```
mico-c++ -I. -c Client.cc -o Client.o
mico-ld -I. Employee.o Client.o -lmico2.2.7 -o Client
```

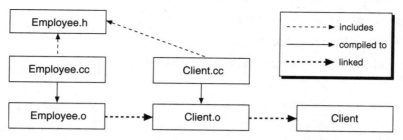

Figure 15.3 Source code organization for simple MICO client.

NOTE
Again, the actual name of the mico library (-lmico2.2.7) may vary, depending on what version of MICO you have.

Figure 15.3 shows how the source code files go together for the client. Unlike the server, we don't link to the implementation. As the CORBA architecture would suggest, this is because the client *never connects directly* to the implementation; it always connects to it through a server.

Running the Example

After following these steps, you should have two executables: Server and Client. The server creates an instance of an employee named Brian, and lets clients connect. The client program connects, raises the employee's salary by $25,000, and then finds out the employee's name and current salary.

NOTE
All of the steps we just went through are handled by the Makefile—if you want to, you can just type *make* in the example directory to compile the example.

To run this example, you must first run Server. This starts the server and displays its IOR (the ./ makes sure you are running the executable name Server in the current directory, and not some other program named Server):

```
bash2-2.03$ ./Server
IOR:010000001100000049444c3a456d706c6f7965653a312e30000000000020000000000
0000340000000010100001a0000006f73636f72622e736b696e67312e72692e686f6d652e
636f6d003f070c000000424f41c0a8fe6600000e3e0301000000240000000100000001000
0000010000001400000000100000001000100000000000901010000000000
```

This IOR isn't much good unless you can pass it to the client, so, instead of starting it as just shown, redirect the output to a file and use & to put the server in the background:

```
bash2-2.03$ ./Server > ior.txt &
[1] 3648
```

The client will read the IOR from standard input, so feed the ior.txt file into the client using redirection. Every time you run it, it will raise and display Brian's salary:

```
bash2-2.03$ ./Client < ior.txt
Brian's salary is 25000
bash2-2.03$ ./Client < ior.txt
Brian's salary is 50000
bash2-2.03$ ./Client < ior.txt
Brian's salary is 75000
```

When you are done testing, you should kill the server (this kills the job started by the ./Server command):

```
bash2-2.03$ kill %./Server
```

or, use the process ID it displayed when you ran it (make sure you use the right process ID, or you might shut down something important!):

```
bash2-2.03$ kill 3648
```

Summary of Developing the MICO Example

In this example, we developed a CORBA client and server. The client found the server by using its IOR, and then invoked some of its methods. Here is a summary of the steps we took:

1. Write the interface definition.
2. Generate stubs and skeletons with the idl utility.
3. Develop and compile the implementation.
4. Develop and compile the server.
5. Develop and compile the client.
6. Execute the server and client.

Here is a Makefile that automates the compilation:

```
# Set the C++ compiler to mico-c++, and the linker
# to mico-ld.
#
CXX     = mico-c++
```

```
LD          = mico-ld

# Add the current directory to the include list.
#
CXXFLAGS = -I.

# Add the mico shared library.  You might need to look
# around in /usr/lib or /usr/local/lib if your mico
# shared library has a different name.
#
LDLIBS = -lmico2.2.7

# Object files for Server and Client
#
SERVEROBJS = Employee.o Employee_impl.o Server.o
CLIENTOBJS = Employee.o Client.o

# Makefile rules.
#
all: Server Client

Employee_impl.o: Employee_impl.h

Server: Employee.h Employee_impl.h $(SERVEROBJS)
      $(LD) $(CXXFLAGS) $(LDFLAGS) $(SERVEROBJS) $(LDLIBS) -o $@

Client: Employee.h $(CLIENTOBJS)
      $(LD) $(CXXFLAGS) $(LDFLAGS) $(CLIENTOBJS) $(LDLIBS) -o $@

Employee.h Employee.cc : Employee.idl
      idl Employee.idl

clean:
      rm -f Employee.cc Employee.h *.o Server Client
```

Here is a shell script, RunDemo, that automates the testing of this example:

```
#!/bin/sh

# Start the server.
#
./Server > ior.txt &
server_pid=$!
sleep 1

# Kill the server when we exit the shell.
#
trap "kill $server_pid" 0
```

```
# Run the client a few times.
#
./Client < ior.txt
./Client < ior.txt
./Client < ior.txt
```

A Simple ORBit Example

Now, we'll look at how we can implement the Employee interface in ORBit. We'll use the same IDL as in the previous example, but things will be significantly different; because we are using C instead of C++, there is something of a mismatch between CORBA's object-oriented nature and C's procedural nature. Fortunately, ORBit makes it easy to bridge this gap.

Let's take a look at the IDL file for Employee (Employee.idl):

```
interface Employee {

    readonly attribute string name;
    readonly attribute unsigned long salary;

    // Raise employee's salary.
    //
    void raise(in unsigned long amount);

};
```

Before We Write Any Code

First, let's run the IDL compiler on the IDL file.

You can use the orbit-idl utility to generate the stubs and skeleton. If you use the --skeleton-impl flag to orbit-idl, it will also generate a skeleton implementation that you can fill in. Because ORBit implementations are more complex than C++-based ORBs, we strongly urge you to take advantage of this feature. We also suggest that you use the --c-output-formatter to format the files that orbit-idl generates. In this example, we're using indent to format the code, and keep maximum line length down to 65 characters:

```
orbit-idl --c-output-formatter='indent -l65 -lc65' \
          --skeleton-impl Employee.idl
```

This generates the following files:

Employee-stubs.c. The Employee stub.

Employee-skels.c. The Employee skeleton.

Employee-common.c. Common code shared by various files.

Employee.h. Definitions and function prototypes used by the stub and skeleton.

Employee-skelimpl.c. A skeletal implementation that you can use as the basis of your program. How is this different from the skeleton? Employee-skels.c is the skeleton as described in the glossary at the beginning of this chapter. Employee-skelimpl.c is the implementation, but it's called skeletal because the code hasn't been written yet (we're going to write it now).

The Implementation

To develop your implementation:

1. Rename the skeleton implementation you created in the earlier step to something that won't get overwritten if you run orbit-idl again, such as Employee-impl.c.

2. Write your code into Employee-impl.c:

   a. Define any private data members in the impl_POA_Employee struct near the comment titled "App-specific servant structures." When you need to refer to a data member, refer to it through the newservant object in the impl_Employee__create method, and through the servant object in the implementation methods. Also, be aware that the names of these attributes are prefixed with attr_, as in attr_name or attr_salary.

   b. Put any initialization code into the impl_Employee__create function (this function name is based on the interface name, so other objects you write will have a different name).

   c. Write accessor functions for any attributes in the interface definition. These accessor functions are different from MICO's—instead of being the same name as the attribute, they are prefixed with impl_Employee __get_, as in impl_Employee__get_salary() and impl_Employee__get _name(). You can find these in the *Stub Implementations* section of the skeletal implementation.

   d. Finally, write functions for all operations in the interface definition. All of the functions are already defined for you—all you need to do is write the code. The functions appear after the comment titled "Stub Implementations."

Step 1. This step is straightforward: simply rename the generated file, with a command such as:

```
mv Employee-skelimpl.c Employee-impl.c
```

Step 2. Because the file that orbit-idl generates is very large, we won't look at it in its entirety. However, we will look at the code that pertains to each of the steps.

Step 2a. This implementation doesn't need any member variables beyond the publicly accessible attributes. The orbit-idl utility defines these for you, so you don't need to change this structure:

```
/*** App-specific servant structures ***/
typedef struct
{
  POA_Employee servant;
  PortableServer_POA poa;
  CORBA_char *attr_name;

  CORBA_unsigned_long attr_salary;


}
impl_POA_Employee;
```

Step 2b. We're going to mess with things a little bit here. First of all, we're going to change the constructor so that it takes the name of the Employee as an argument. Then, we're going to initialize the name and salary when the object is created. Our changes are shown in **bold**, and the original constructor is commented out (and shown in *italics*):

```
/*** Stub implementations ***/

/*
 * Original prototype:
 * static Employee
 *   impl_Employee__create (PortableServer_POA poa,
 *                          CORBA_Environment * ev)
 */

static Employee
impl_Employee__create (PortableServer_POA poa,
                       char *thename,
                       CORBA_Environment * ev)
{
  Employee retval;
  impl_POA_Employee *newservant;
  PortableServer_ObjectId *objid;

  newservant = g_new0 (impl_POA_Employee, 1);
  newservant->servant.vepv = &impl_Employee_vepv;
  newservant->poa = poa;

  /* Initialize instance variables */
```

```
newservant->attr_name    = CORBA_string_dup(thename);
newservant->attr_salary = 0;

POA_Employee__init ((PortableServer_Servant) newservant, ev);
objid =
  PortableServer_POA_activate_object (poa, newservant, ev);
CORBA_free (objid);
retval =
  PortableServer_POA_servant_to_reference (poa, newservant,
                                           ev);

return retval;
}
```

Step 2c. Next, define the accessor methods. In the generated file, each of these functions have a default body that declares a return value, and returns it. Since we just want these to return the values of the attributes they correspond to, we delete those lines (shown struck out in the listing) and add in a return statement that returns the current value of the attribute (shown in **bold**):

```
static CORBA_char *
impl_Employee__get_name (impl_POA_Employee * servant,
                         CORBA_Environment * ev)
{
    CORBA_char *retval;
    return retval;
    return CORBA_string_dup(servant->attr_name);
}


static CORBA_unsigned_long
impl_Employee__get_salary (impl_POA_Employee * servant,
                           CORBA_Environment * ev)
{
    CORBA_unsigned_long retval;
    return retval;
    return servant->attr_salary;
}
```

Step 2d. Next, fill in the definitions of any functions that correspond to operations in the interface definition. If these functions have return values, they will have default return value declarations, as did the functions for the attributes in the previous step:

```
static void
impl_Employee_raise (impl_POA_Employee * servant,
                     CORBA_unsigned_long amount,
                     CORBA_Environment * ev)
{
    servant->attr_salary += amount;
}
```

The Server

To develop the server:

1. Write a program, such as Server.c, that:
   a. #includes the implementation source code. The orbit-idl utility does not emit a header file for the implementation, which makes it more complicated to include the header file for the implementation, compile the implementation to an object file, and link it to the server. So, instead, we just include the whole implementation in the server with the #include directive.
   b. Declares variables for various CORBA and POA data structures.
   c. Declares a variable for an instance of the implementation.
   d. Initializes the CORBA and POA objects.
   e. Creates an instance of the implementation.
   f. Communicates the server's IOR, perhaps by writing it to a file or standard output (if you write it to standard output, make sure you set stdout to unbuffered mode with setvbuf, or it may not get written until the program exits!).
   g. Activates the POA manager.
   h. Runs the ORB, so clients can connect to it.
   i. Returns from the application.
2. Compile the Employee-common.c file to an object file.
3. Compile the Employee-skels.c file to an object file.
4. Compile and link the server against the Employee-common.o and Employee-skels.o files, as well as the ORBit shared libraries (libORBit.so, libIIOP.so, libORBitutil).

Step 1. The following listing contains the source code for the server. Of the steps listed, the only ones you should need to customize for implementations of other objects are 1C and 1E. If you use an alternate method to deliver the IOR, you will also change step 1F. The code for the rest of the steps should work fine for other servers you choose to write. However, we don't want to encourage you to blindly trust us—as you explore more of CORBA, you should take advantage of the documentation that comes with the various CORBA implementations, as well as other books on the topic.

```
#include <stdio.h>

/*
 * 1A. Include the implementation.
```

```
 *
 */
#include "Employee-impl.c"

int main(int argc, char* argv[]) {

  /*
   * 1B. Declare all variables for CORBA and POA.
   *
   */
  CORBA_ORB           orb;
  CORBA_Environment*  ev;
  CORBA_char*         ior;
  PortableServer_POA         root_poa;
  PortableServer_POAManager pm;

  /*
   * 1C. Declare a variable for the
   * implementation instance.
   *
   */
  Employee instance;

  /*
   * 1D. Initialize the CORBA environment and POA
   * objects.
   *
   */
  ev = g_new0(CORBA_Environment,1);
  CORBA_exception_init(ev);
  orb = CORBA_ORB_init(&argc, argv, "orbit-local-orb", ev);
  root_poa = (PortableServer_POA)
      CORBA_ORB_resolve_initial_references(orb, "RootPOA", ev);

  /*
   * 1E. Create an instance of the implementation - we're
   * passing the employee's name (Brian) to the constructor.
   *
   */
  instance = impl_Employee__create(root_poa, "Brian", ev);

  /*
   * 1F. Get an IOR for this instance, and display it to
   * standard output.
   *
   */
  ior = CORBA_ORB_object_to_string(orb, instance, ev);
  setvbuf(stdout, (char *)NULL, _IONBF, 0); /* unbuffer stdout */
  printf("%s", ior);
  CORBA_free(ior);
```

```
/*
 * 1G. Activate a POA manager to manage access
 * to this server.
 *
 */
pm = PortableServer_POA__get_the_POAManager(root_poa, ev);
PortableServer_POAManager_activate(pm, ev);

/*
 * 1H. Run the object, which lets remote clients
 * connect to it.
 *
 */
CORBA_ORB_run(orb, ev);

/*
 * 1I. Return from the application.
 *
 */
return 0;

}
```

Step 2. You can compile the Employee-common.c file with this command:

```
gcc -I/usr/lib/glib/include -c Employee-common.c -o Employee-common.o
```

Step 3. You can compile the Employee-skels.c file with this command:

```
gcc -I/usr/lib/glib/include   -c Employee-skels.c -o Employee-skels.o
```

Step 4. Compile and link the server with the following commands (because the server includes the implementation, there is no need to compile the implementation or to link the server to it):

```
gcc -I/usr/lib/glib/include -c Server.c -o Server.o
gcc -o Server Server.o Employee-common.o Employee-skels.o \
            -lORBit -lIIOP -lORBitutil
```

Figure 15.4 shows how the source code files go together for the ORBit server.

The Client

To create the client:

1. Write a program, such as Client.c, that:
   a. Declares all the variables needed for the ORB and CORBA environment.

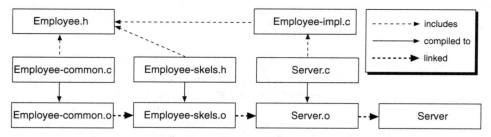

Figure 15.4 Source code organization for the simple ORBit server.

b. Initializes the ORB.

c. Obtains the IOR somehow, such as reading from standard input or a file.

d. Converts the IOR into a CORBA object.

e. Invokes some methods on the object. Things look a little different here than they do in the C++ example we saw earlier. Instead of invoking a method with syntax like server->raise(25000), we'll use the slightly longer Employee_raise(server, 25000, &ev). The Employee_ prefix is a workaround for the fact that we aren't using C++, which manages namespaces for us (C++ knows how to distinguish Employee's raise() method from other methods of the same name, but C doesn't have an easy way to do this). In addition, since we're not invoking the method of an object, we need to pass in a reference to the CORBA server (server) and the CORBA environment (&ev).

Note that with the _get_salary() and _get_name() methods, an extra underscore is inserted by prefixing it with Employee_. For example, Employee__get_name() has two underscores between Employee and get.

f. Releases any objects it created and returns.

2. Compile and link the client against the skeleton object files.

Step 1. Here is the source code to Client.c:

```c
#include "orb/orbit.h"
#include "Employee.h"
#include <stdio.h>

int main(int argc, char* argv[]) {

  /*
   * 1A. Declare all variables for CORBA.
   *
   */
```

```
        CORBA_Environment ev;
        CORBA_ORB        orb;
        CORBA_Object     server;
        CORBA_char       ior[1000];
        CORBA_exception_init(&ev);

        /*
         * 1B. Initialize the ORB.
         *
         */
        orb = CORBA_ORB_init(&argc, argv, "orbit-local-orb", &ev);

        /*
         * 1C. Read the IOR from standard input.
         *
         */
        fgets(ior, 1000, stdin);

        /*
         * 1D. Turn the IOR into a CORBA object. server
         * corresponds to an instance of the Employee
         * object.
         *
         */
        server = CORBA_ORB_string_to_object(orb, ior, &ev);

        /*
         * 1E. Invoke some methods on the object.
         *
         */
        Employee_raise(server, 25000, &ev);
        printf("%s's salary is %ld.\n",
                Employee__get_name(server, &ev),
                Employee__get_salary(server, &ev));

        /*
         * 1F. Clean up and return from the application.
         *
         */
        CORBA_Object_release(server, &ev);
        CORBA_Object_release( (CORBA_Object) orb, &ev);
        return 0;

}
```

Step 2. Compile and link the client with the following commands:

```
gcc -I/usr/lib/glib/include -c Client.c -o Client.o
gcc -I/usr/lib/glib/include   -c Employee-stubs.c -o Employee-stubs.o
gcc -o Client Client.o Employee-common.o Employee-stubs.o \
            -lORBit -lIIOP -lORBitutil
```

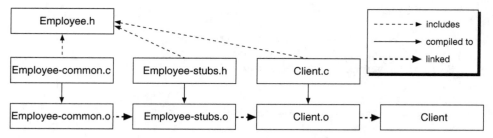

Figure 15.5 Source code organization for the simple ORBit client.

Figure 15.5 shows how the source code files go together for the ORBit client.

Running the Example

After following these steps, you should have two executables: Server and Client. The instructions in the section titled *Running the Example*, under *A Simple MICO Example*, apply to this example, as well.

Summary of Developing ORBit Example

In this example, we implemented a CORBA client and server in C. As with the C++/MICO example, the client finds the server by using its IOR. Here is a summary of the steps we took:

1. Write the interface definition.
2. Generate stubs, skeletons, and a skeletal implementation using orbit-idl.
3. Develop the implementation.
4. Develop and compile the server.
5. Develop and compile the client.
6. Execute the server and client.

Here is a Makefile that automates the compilation:

```
# C compiler and linking flags.
#
CFLAGS = -I/usr/lib/glib/include
LFLAGS = -lORBit -lIIOP -lORBitutil

# Object files for client and server.
#
CLIENTOBJS = Employee-common.o Employee-stubs.o
```

```
SERVEROBJS = Employee-common.o Employee-skels.o

# Build targets.
#
all : idltargets Client Server

Client.o : Employee.h

Employee-impl.o : Employee.h

Employee-skels.o : Employee.h

Employee-stubs.o : Employee.h

Server.o : Employee-impl.c

Client : Client.o $(CLIENTOBJS)
    $(CC) -o $@ Client.o $(CLIENTOBJS)  $(LFLAGS)

Server : Server.o $(SERVEROBJS)
   $(CC) -o $@ Server.o $(SERVEROBJS) $(LFLAGS)

clean :
    rm Employee-stubs.[oc] Employee-skels.[oc] \
    Employee.h Employee-common.[oc] Server.o Client.o \
    Server Client

#
# IDL compiler rules
#
idltargets : Employee-stubs.c Employee-common.c Employee-skels.c
Employee.h

Employee-stubs.c : Employee.idl
    orbit-idl Employee.idl

Employee-common.c : Employee.idl
    orbit-idl Employee.idl

Employee-skels.c : Employee.idl
    orbit-idl Employee.idl

Employee.h : Employee.idl
    orbit-idl Employee.idl
```

You can use the same program shown in the MICO example Summary to automate the testing of this example.

CORBA Goodies

Let's take a look at some utilities and services that can help you in working with CORBA applications.

Naming Services

In the examples we saw in this chapter, we had to get the IOR from the server to the client somehow; otherwise, there was no way the client could have found the server. CORBA also supports a naming service that allows clients to find an object based on its name.

Each CORBA implementation discussed supports some kind of naming service. The biggest trick in using a naming service is telling the client application how to find the naming service. Each implementation solves this problem in its own way.

ORBit uses GOAD, the GNOME Object Activation Directory. GOAD is coupled to a user's GNOME session: GNOME applications use a feature of the X server to find the IOR of the naming server.

MICO ships with a daemon called *nsd*, the name service daemon. MICO uses its own addressing scheme to help clients locate this service.

Java 2

JDK 1.2 (also known as Java 2) includes a CORBA-compliant ORB, and a CORBA API. As a result, you can develop CORBA clients and server using Java 2. The IDL compiler, idltojava, does not come with the JDK distribution. The idltojava compiler is available as a separate download, but as of this writing, only Solaris and Windows versions were available. Until an idltojava compiler is available for Linux, the only way you can take advantage of Java 2's new CORBA features is to compile your IDL on one of the supported platforms. There have been reports that idltojava runs under WINE (www.winehq.com), a Win32 implementation for Linux, but we were unable to confirm these reports.

More information on idltojava can be found at www.javasoft.com/products/jdk/idl/.

Mod_Corba

Mod_Corba is a plug-in module for Apache (www.apache.org) that exposes all the functionality of the Apache module API as a CORBA object. As a result, you can extend Apache using CORBA objects you develop yourself. The Mod_Corba home page is at www.netrinsics.com/Mod_Corba.html.

Summary

In this chapter, we took a brief look at using CORBA on Linux. This chapter did not provide a comprehensive overview of CORBA (it would take an entire book!). For further studies in CORBA, we suggest that you consult the beginner's documentation and reading list on the OMG's CORBA for Beginner's Page at www.omg.org/corba/beginners.html. Also, you should spend some time looking at the CORBA on Linux pages at http://linas.org/linux/corba.html.

Reference

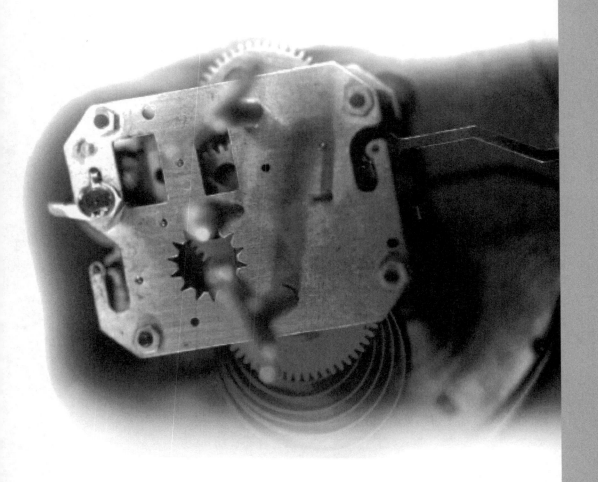

SQL Reference

SQL is the accepted standard for database definition and manipulation. Here, we give some examples of standard syntax that will assist you in setting up, populating, manipulating, and accessing your databases. Most major and minor database management systems (DBMSs) implement one of the SQL standards at least partially. You should check the documentation for your own DBMS to determine its specific syntax. However, the syntax given here should work in most environments. This short appendix will help you with SQL, and builds on the syntax shown in Chapter 2, "Database Design"; you can find more extensive examples in books devoted to SQL or relational databases. A book that has extensive chapters on SQL with many examples of syntax supporting a well-developed schema example is Elmasri and Navathe's, *Fundamentals of Database Systems*, Third Edition (Addison-Wesley, 1999).

NOTE

The examples in this appendix use a semicolon as the command delimiter. See *SQL Monitors* in Chapter 9, "Databases," for a description of how to send these commands to the database, and which delimiter you must use.

CREATE TABLE

Use the CREATE TABLE statement to create a new table. We introduced the CREATE TABLE statement in Chapter 2. Let's look at some special clauses supported by this statement.

The CONSTRAINT Clause

On database servers that support it, use the CONSTRAINT clause to restrict the range or types of acceptable values in a column. For example, values that are not permitted to be null are labeled as NOT NULL. Also, the primary keys can be specified using the keyword PRIMARY KEY. The CHECK constraints can be used to define the acceptable range of values for a column.

Be aware that some DBMSs differ on the defaults for some of these constraints. For example, most assume that a column can be NULL unless specified with NOT NULL, while a few such as Sybase assume the opposite—that a column is NOT NULL unless designated with NULL.

For a complete discussion of this clause, see the section *Invalid Values* in Chapter 9.

Enforcing Relationships

On some database systems, you can use special clauses of the CREATE TABLE command to specify the types of relationships between tables. These relationships are enforced in such a way that, for example, you can't delete an author who still has books listed under her name. For a complete discussion of this topic, see the section *Declarative Referential Integrity* in Chapter 9.

Data Types

There are a variety of data types available in SQL. The types char , int, smallint, float, real, and double are usually available. In addition, there is a date type, which (usually) requires data in the form YYYY-MM-DD, to represent year, month, and day. There is also a timestamp type that permits the specification of time using HH:MM:SS for hours, minutes, and seconds. For a discussion of dates and data types, see the section *Data Types* in Chapter 9.

Autoincrement Columns

In some cases, you will want to define columns that are incremented in sequence each time a row is inserted. This is useful for defining primary keys, and guaranteeing that each row has a unique value for its primary keys. There is a discussion of this topic in Chapter 9, in the section *Generating Unique Values*.

CREATE/DROP Index

To assure that your database performs well, you will want to place indexes on columns used frequently for searches and joins. However, indexes were dropped from the last SQL standard as they were viewed as low-level constructs, not to appear in the formal definition of the query language. Thus, you should look at the specific instructions for your database regarding indexing. See Chapter 2 for a few generic commands that work with most systems.

Putting Data into the Database

Once you have created your database tables, you will want to populate (put some data into) the database. This is done with the SQL INSERT command.

For example:

```
INSERT INTO publisher
    VALUES  ('John Wiley & Sons, Incorporated',  'New York',
             '1000 Brick Street, New York, NY 033416', 100);
```

To insert a subset of column values into a given row:

```
INSERT INTO publisher (name, id)
    VALUES  ('John Wiley & Sons, Incorporated',  100);
```

If you try to insert a row that is missing a key or NOT NULL column value, you will get an error message. Many systems will also generate errors if you violate other specified constraints, but this is not always guaranteed. Read your documentation to see which constraint types will generate such errors and, if so, how it is done.

For more information, see the section *Putting Data into the Database* in Chapter 2.

UPDATE

To update a row in your database, use the following syntax:

```
UPDATE publisher
    SET name = 'Wiley Computer Publishing'
    WHERE id = 100;
```

As with the INSERT command above, upon execution, the UPDATE command may trigger pre-defined constraints, generating errors where such constraints are violated. Again, please read your documentation to see which constraint types will generate such errors and, if so, how it is done.

For more information, see the section *Updating Data in the Database* in Chapter 2.

ALTER TABLE (Changing the Structure of a Table)

To add a column to a table, use the ALTER TABLE statement:

```
ALTER TABLE publisher ADD phone CHAR(14);
```

The ALTER TABLE statement uses the same column definitions as the CREATE TABLE statement (see *Creating Tables* in Chapter 2).

Under Sybase, when you add a column with ALTER TABLE, the new column must accept NULLs. This is because when Sybase's ALTER TABLE statement adds the column to any existing rows, their values are automatically set to NULL. Under some other database systems, you can specify NOT NULL in ALTER TABLE statement (however, for this to succeed under Oracle, the table must not have any rows):

```
ALTER TABLE publisher ADD phone CHAR(14) NOT NULL;
```

Consult your database server's documentation for details on the ALTER TABLE statement.

To drop a column with ALTER TABLE, use the DROP clause:

```
ALTER TABLE publisher DROP phone;
```

DROP TABLE

To drop a table, use the following syntax:

```
DROP TABLE publisher;
```

SQL Query Fundamentals

Please refer to Chapter 2 for more information about basic query operations on a database. Here is some specific SQL syntax with a few tips to prevent errors in constructing your queries.

First things first. Here are the definitions of tables we'll look at in this section:

```
CREATE TABLE publisher
    (name CHAR(32),
     code CHAR(32));

CREATE TABLE book
    (title           CHAR(50) NOT NULL,
     isbn            CHAR(25),
     publisher_code CHAR(25));

CREATE TABLE banned_book (isbn CHAR(25));

CREATE TABLE borrowed_book
    (isbn CHAR(25), borrowed_date DATE);
```

The following command shows a basic SELECT statement. The SELECT statement allows you to extract (or "project") any subset of specific rows and columns from any combination of tables in your database, based on logical conditions applied to the source tables. The process of combining multiple tables within a single statement is known as a "join." Joins are discussed in Chapter 2, in the section called *Joins*.

```
SELECT title, name
    FROM publisher, book
    WHERE publisher_code = code;
```

Here we are joining two tables from book's foreign key *publisher_code* to publisher's primary key *code*, and projecting only the title and name of the publisher. While we joined only two tables here, it is common and often necessary to join many at a time as long as you remember to provide the correct join conditions for all tables involved (often, where there are n tables, there are $n - 1$ joins).

Common errors that occur with simple queries include:

Forgetting to provide the join condition (such as WHERE publisher_code = code). This error will result in a table containing all possible combinations (also known as the Cartesian product) of book titles and first authors with the publisher's address. This can get pretty big if you have a lot of rows in each table.

Forgetting to specify the table with which a column is associated. You are not required to specify that *name* comes from the *publisher* table. However, if more than one table being joined has a column called *name*, you would then be required to specify the table (as in *publisher.name*).

Trying to join two tables on nonkey or foreign key columns. Foreign keys are meant as the vehicle for joining two tables. If you use arbitrary columns (such as *publisher_code = publisher.name*), you might get unexpected results due to the fact that nonkey columns may not uniquely identify columns. For example, if you have a table that contains people's names and you try to join this table with another based upon last name only, you will associate each Smith patron with all the rows in another table that match that last name. This results in a smaller Cartesian product than would occur if you specified no join condition, but you still get bogus data, as shown in Table A.1.

Only a unique identifier such as a user ID will give you correct results. If your database is well-normalized (because there won't be a last name in the *borrows* or *loan* table), then it will be harder to make such mistakes, but you should be aware of these kinds of errors.

Retrieving All Columns

Here is a tip to simplify your queries. If you are retrieving all columns of a table, or a set of joined tables, you can make use of the "*" notation.

```
SELECT *
FROM book;
```

The asterisk indicates that all columns from the book table will be included in the result.

Aliases

Sometimes we wish to rename the columns in a result set. Here is an example of the use of an alias to accomplish this:

```
SELECT name AS PublisherName
FROM publisher;
```

Table A.1   John Smith Borrowed *Now Wait for Last Year*, But All the Smiths Are Held Accountable

FIRSTNAME	LASTNAME	BOOKBORROWED
John	Smith	Now Wait for Last Year
Joe	Smith	Now Wait for Last Year
Bob	Smith	Now Wait for Last Year

This can be used to make the results more meaningful to people who have to read the output, as shown here:

```
mysql> SELECT name AS PublisherName
    -> FROM publisher;
+---------------------------+
| PublisherName             |
+---------------------------+
| Grove                     |
| Vintage Books             |
| Wiley Computer Publishing |
+---------------------------+
3 rows in set (0.00 sec)
```

Querying with NULLs and Sets

Sometimes a null value has meaning in the context of your application logic; thus, you might wish to execute a query that selects all records with NULL in a particular column. For example, this statement gets all the books that have an unknown publisher:

```
SELECT title
    FROM book
    WHERE publisher_code IS NULL;
```

You might also wish to query based upon a set of values for a particular column. The next query selects all books where the publisher code is in the list '0-679', '0-802':

```
SELECT title
    FROM book
    WHERE publisher_code IN ('0-679', '0-802');
```

You can also use IN to compare rows to the results of a query. This command fetches all the books that are listed in the banned_books table:

```
SELECT title
    FROM book
    WHERE isbn IN (SELECT isbn FROM banned_book);
```

As of this writing, Mini SQL and MySQL do not support the IN keyword.

DISTINCT

Some queries will give you repetition in your result rows unless you specify with the keyword DISTINCT. In this example, we can see the names of books that were checked out without having to see multiple rows for all the dates on which they were checked out:

```
SELECT DISTINCT title
    FROM book, borrowed_book
    WHERE book.isbn = borrowed_book.isbn;
```

Aggregate Queries

SQL has aggregate features to assist you in finding maximum, minimum, count, sum, and average values. For example, let's get a count of all the loans the library ever made:

```
SELECT COUNT(*)
    FROM borrowed_book;
```

We can also group this by each book title, as in:

```
SELECT title, COUNT(*)
    FROM book, borrowed_book
    WHERE book.isbn = borrowed_book.isbn
    GROUP BY title;
```

Consult your database documentation for which aggregate functions are supported.

Views

SQL permits the definition of named views or virtual tables. Since the result of any SQL query is a table, this table can itself be used as a virtual table within the database. Views are simply the named results of given queries. For example, to define a *banned books* view, we can execute the following SQL statement:

```
CREATE VIEW banned_book_info
AS SELECT title, isbn
    FROM book
    WHERE isbn IN (SELECT isbn FROM banned_book);
```

Then, you can use SELECT to get data out of this view as though it were a regular table:

```
SELECT * FROM banned_book_info;
```

A word of caution: The modification of views poses a special problem with regard to database consistency. The problem is that if you modify a view, you will want the base tables from which it is derived to remain consistent. However, if you modify a view, the changes that should be made to the base tables will not necessarily be uniquely determinable. This is especially true when using aggregate functions and joined tables. Read the documentation of your system to determine if you are able to update views, and pay special attention to how this is done to avoid surprising results. Also do a little reading in a database text to be aware of the problems that can arise if this is not done with caution.

As an example, most systems do not permit the update of views that are derived from joins. Consider a view based on some of the tables defined in Chapter 2:

```
CREATE VIEW borrowed_books
    AS SELECT last_name, title
        FROM patron, borrows, book
        WHERE borrows.patron_id = patron.patron_id
        AND    borrows.isbn     = book.isbn;
```

Now suppose that you wish to alter the view by changing the spelling of the last name Smith to Smyth in the row, *Smith, The Tragic Empress.* However, there are two ways to effect this change in the view from the perspective of the base tables. One way is to change every last name spelled Smith to Smyth. Another is to change this spelling only for the rows in *borrow* involving Smith and *The Tragic Empress.* Now if for some reason, there is no patron named Smith, the database will have problems. As you can see, the solution is not straightforward. In general you should be careful with updates over views.

DELETE

The format of a basic DELETE command is simple. To delete a row from a table:

```
DELETE FROM publisher
    WHERE name = 'Old Foggy Bottom';
```

Beyond this basic use, the DELETE command can also be used in combination with many of the joining and nested querying techniques described above in order to target exactly the rows that should be deleted. Of course, deletion can be a risky operation, so exercise this command with caution and make frequent backups!

UML Reference

I n this appendix, we'll take a look at various bits of UML notation.

Class Diagram

The class diagram shows the attributes and methods of classes, as well as their relationships between each other. Let's look at some examples:

Class. A class definition is shown as a box with the name of the class. Within that box, the attributes of the class appear, followed by the methods. Figure B.1 shows a class that represents a motorized vehicle. It can start and stop its engine (methods) and has a weight and maximum speed (attributes).

MotorizedVehicle
+maximum_speed: +weight:
+start_engine( ) +stop_engine( )

Figure B.1 A class definition.

Generalization. Generalization shows that one class is the generalization of another. This is closely related to the concept of class inheritance. Figure B.2 shows automobile and riding lawnmower class definitions, both of which are specializations of the motorized vehicle class. The motorized vehicle class can be said to be a generalization of the other two classes.

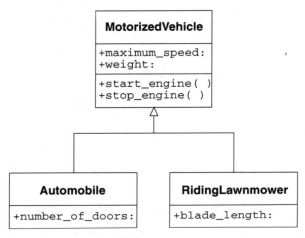

Figure B.2 Generalization.

Association. Associations show the relationships between classes. Figure B.3 shows a person and an automobile. The relationship is known as *drives*, and each role is qualified as *driver* and *vehicle*.

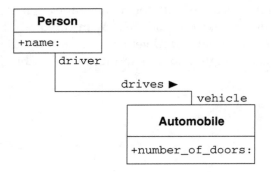

Figure B.3 Two associated classes.

Part-of relationships. There are two ways that we can model the relationships between parts and whole. The first is aggregation, which is the simplest form: It says that one thing is the part of another. If the whole were to go away, the part would still exist. Figure B.4 shows an example of aggregation: A Person is a member of a Club. If the club were dissolved tomorrow, the Person would still exist. The hollow diamond indicates that a club aggregates its members.

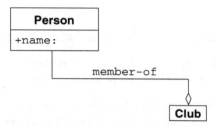

Figure B.4   Aggregation.

Composition, on the other hand, signifies a stronger relationship. In composition, if the whole is deleted, the part goes with it. Figure B.5 shows the relationship of a book to its chapter. The chapter is an intrinsic part of the book, and if the book is destroyed, the chapter goes with it. The filled diamond indicates the composite nature of the relationship.

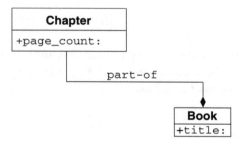

Figure B.5   Composition.

Multiplicity. In some cases, you may want to show how many of one thing is associated with another. Consider Figure B.6, in which exactly one (signified by 1) book is associated with many (signified by *) chapters.

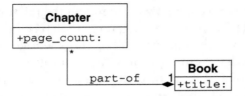

Figure B.6   Exactly one Book is associated with many Chapters.

Sequence Diagram

The sequence diagram shows a number of events that occur in sequence, with time starting at the top and ending at the bottom. Here are some examples:

Sending a creation message. To create an instance of a class, you need to send a create() message. Figure B.7 shows a Web browser creating a socket object.

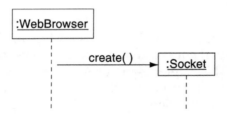

Figure B.7   A creation message.

Sending a message. Once you have created an object, you'll want to send messages to it. Figure B.8 shows the Web browser sending a message that asks a newly created socket to connect to a host.

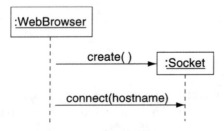

Figure B.8   Sending a message.

Collaboration Diagram

A collaboration diagram shows how objects cooperate. Let's look at some examples:

An object (an instance of a class). An instance of a class is shown as a box. The name is underlined, and preceded by a colon, as shown in Figure B.9.

:SpreadSheet

Figure B.9 An instance of a spreadsheet object.

A named object. You can give names to instances by putting the name of the object before the colon. Figure B.10 shows sheet1, a spreadsheet with a name.

sheet1:SpreadSheet

Figure B.10 A named instance of a spreadsheet.

Sending a message. Figure B.11 shows how to send a message. In this example, we're passing sheet1 to the Printer, telling it to print the spreadsheet.

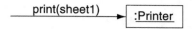 print(sheet1) :Printer

Figure B.11 Sending a message to the printer.

Figure B.12 shows a conditional message, in which case the spreadsheet is only printed if a cell A1's contents say it's OK to print.

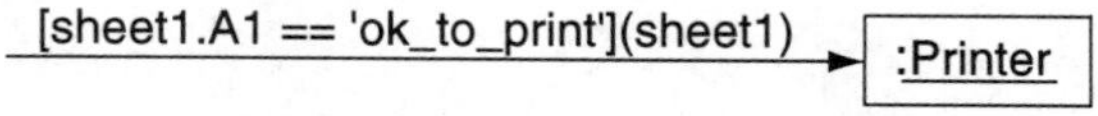

[sheet1.A1 == 'ok_to_print'](sheet1) :Printer

Figure B.12 Sending a conditional message to the printer.

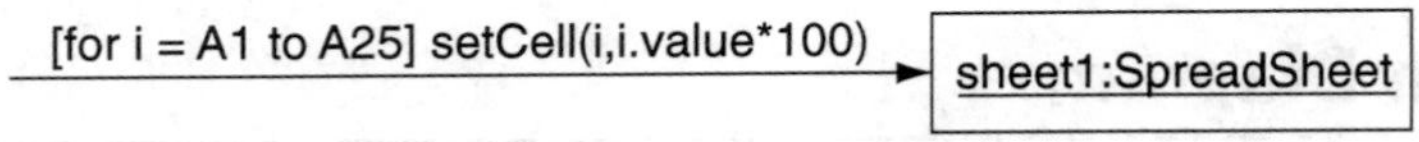

[for i = A1 to A25] setCell(i,i.value*100) → sheet1:SpreadSheet

Figure B.13   Sending a message to the spreadsheet in a loop.

You can also send messages in a loop. Figure B.13 shows how you could set the values in a range of cells.